THE STEPS TO THE SUPREME COURT

Also by Peter Irons

THE STEPS TO THE SUPREME COURT

A Guided Tour of the American Legal System

PETER IRONS

WILEY

John Wiley & Sons, Inc.

Published by John Wiley & Sons, Inc., Hoboken, New Jersey
Published simultaneously in Canada

For general information about our other products and services, please contact our Customer Care Department within the United States at (800) 762-2974, outside the United States at (317) 572-3993 or fax (317) 572-4002.

Wiley also publishes its books in a variety of electronic formats and by print-on-demand. Some content that appears in standard print versions of this book may not be available in other formats. For more information about Wiley products, visit us at www.wiley.com.

ISBN 978-1-118-11499-5 (paper); ISBN 978-1-118-13804-5 (ebk);
ISBN 978-1-118-13805-2 (ebk); ISBN 978-1-118-13806-9 (ebk)

Printed in the United States of America

10 9 8 7 6 5 4 3 2 1

Contents

Preface

"How Did You Get Here?"

There's an old story, perhaps apocryphal, about an exchange between former Justice Felix Frankfurter and a lawyer from Texas, making his first argument in the Supreme Court. Frankfurter asked, "How did you get here?" The puzzled lawyer paused and then replied, "I took a train from Houston to Washington, and a cab from Union Station to the Court." After the courtroom laughter subsided, the red-faced lawyer realized that Frankfurter was asking how his case got to the Court, not about his own travel. Frankfurter, a stickler for procedural regularity, may have spotted a problem in the case record and wanted it clarified.

I've tried to track this story down, with no success yet, but it does make a point that I'll develop in this book, whether it's true or not. Most people have no idea how the cases the justices decide each year—fewer than 2 percent of those they are asked to review—get to the Supreme Court for argument, a process that often takes four or five years between their initial filing in a state or federal court and their final decision.

Justice Frankfurter's question to the neophyte lawyer—if he really did ask it—was not meant to be facetious or badgering. Frankfurter was the acknowledged expert on Supreme Court procedure; as a Harvard

Law School professor before he was named to the Court in 1939 by President Franklin D. Roosevelt, he had cowritten a classic book, *The Business of the Supreme Court*, and was a leading force behind congressional passage of the Judiciary Act of 1925. This law gave the justices "discretionary jurisdiction" over which cases they would hear and decide and freed them from a deluge of what Frankfurter called "peewee" cases that wasted the Court's time. As we will see throughout this book, the concept and exercise of "discretion" are essential at every stage of the legal process, allowing judges to focus on cases that raise important questions. There are still "peewee" cases, but few of them reach the Supreme Court or even come to trial.

By the end of our tour, we will have visited twenty courtrooms in thirteen states and the District of Columbia, in cases that were heard and decided by more than a hundred judges and argued by more than thirty lawyers on both sides. My role as your tour guide is to explain each step in the legal process and to leave you with a better understanding of both the strengths and the weaknesses of a system that affects the lives of every American. I have tried to explain legal terms and concepts in plain English, in case they may not be familiar to all readers, and I have placed many words and phrases in boldface type, both for emphasis and to assist readers, especially students, in taking notes (because certain words and phrases might appear in legal documents or on exams).

The aim of this book is to discuss a few cases, both civil and criminal, in enough depth so that readers can follow each step in the legal process and understand what lawyers and judges were doing and also to meet the people involved on both sides of these cases. I chose the Paul House murder case from Tennessee for several reasons. First, there is no more serious criminal offense than murder, and the charge against House, once I read the Supreme Court opinion on his case, seemed to me such a travesty of justice that it deserved a full autopsy, so to speak.

Given my personal interest in law and religion, I chose the Ten Commandments cases from Kentucky and Texas, in part because their differing outcomes showed the difficulties imposed on lower-court judges in pending Decalogue cases by the Court's conflicting opinions. I have also included accounts of two cases that involved challenges to the display of Latin crosses on public property, one on Mt. Soledad, the highest point in San Diego, California, the other in a remote area of the Mojave Natural Preserve, a national park in southern California, both of which illustrate the influence of local and national politics on conflicts over religion in the public sphere.

Another reason I chose these cases is that most Americans have strong opinions about the issues they raise, on both sides of the political spectrum. Public opinion polls have consistently shown majorities supporting capital punishment, although by diminishing margins in recent years, and favoring the display of religious symbols in public places, but with outspoken opposition to both practices. It's easy to provoke debate, mostly civil but sometimes heated, on these issues, with partisans on both sides often impervious to countering opinions and arguments. Those factors make these cases and their underlying issues ideal, in my view, for a book whose goal is not to change opinions, but to educate readers and to stimulate thought about the legal (and moral) issues these cases raise. When you finish this book, I hope you'll agree that I've succeeded in my goal. So let's begin our tour of the American legal system.

Introduction

"The Judicial Power of the United States": How Our Courts Were Framed and How They Function

We begin our tour of the American legal system with a brief excursion into history, back to Philadelphia, Pennsylvania, during the hot and muggy summer of 1787. On May 25, twenty-nine men from seven states gathered to draft a constitution for the United States. The Constitutional Convention ended on September 17, with approval of the draft that was submitted to the thirteen states for ratification by special conventions. By that time, fifty-five delegates from every state but Rhode Island (which refused to participate) had attended the convention's sessions. The meetings were conducted behind closed doors and windows, to protect the secret deliberations from eavesdroppers, which left the delegates sweltering in their chamber.

We all know from history classes about the revolution that freed the British colonies in North America from rule by the English monarchy and its colonial officers. Fewer of us know about the failed effort

1

to create a "firm league of friendship" among the newly independent states through adoption of the Articles of Confederation in 1781. Jealous of their sovereignty, the states began to squabble over such issues as trade, taxation, and rights to waterways. The Confederation Congress, in which each state had veto power over any legislation, proved incapable of resolving these disputes. Several members of the impotent Congress became frustrated by this paralysis and fearful that conflicts between states might lead to violence. They decided that it was time to replace the articles with a constitution that would establish a strong federal government with powers to enact and execute laws that would bind the fractious states to their provisions.

Among the things these men would create and adopt were the primary principles of our justice system: an independent judiciary, bound by existing laws, answerable in the end only to higher courts, and ultimately the Constitution, whose provisions are "the supreme law of the land." Like so many other advances made by the Founding Fathers, nothing quite like this judicial system had existed before.

The guiding force behind the Constitutional Convention was a remarkable man, James Madison, justly known as the "father" of the Constitution and the Bill of Rights. Born in 1751, the eldest of ten children of a prosperous Virginia plantation owner and slaveholder, Madison attended the College of New Jersey (now Princeton University), where he absorbed the antislavery views of his tutors and their advocacy of popular government. Returning to Virginia, Madison plunged into politics, serving in the Virginia House of Delegates and winning election to the Confederation Congress.

Convinced that the Articles of Confederation had failed, Madison decided to bring the quarreling states together in meetings to resolve their differences. Backed by his state's legislature, Madison enlisted an influential and wealthy New York lawyer, Alexander Hamilton, in convening the Philadelphia convention, at which Madison proposed what was called the "Virginia Plan." Its thirteen provisions were based on a tripartite system of national government, with a Congress of two bodies, one of representatives elected by popular vote in state districts and the other of senators, although Madison did not specify their method of election. Madison also did not propose a method of selecting a "national executive," whose duties would be limited to administering the laws passed by Congress. Finally, the Virginia Plan proposed a "national judiciary," with jurisdiction to resolve disputes between the state and federal governments. Sparse on details, Madison's plan nonetheless laid out a structure for a national government with a separation of powers between its three branches and "checks and balances" to prevent any one branch from dominating the others.

Looking back from the perspective of two centuries, it seems astounding that the delegates to the Philadelphia convention of 1787 spent so little time—and so few words—debating the structure and powers of the "national judiciary" that Madison proposed in the Virginia Plan. Since its creation by Article III of the Constitution, the Supreme Court has exercised "the judicial power of the United States" in thousands of cases that have decided whether state and federal laws conform to the Constitution, a power that is sanctified in Article VI as the "supreme law of the land." This awesome power—limited only by the equally awesome power of Congress and the states to amend the Constitution—appears at first glance to have been created without much debate by the Philadelphia delegates and without a full understanding of its future implications.

On closer inspection, however, it seems clear that the delegates who drafted the final version of the Constitution's judicial provisions were united in supporting a "national judiciary" with expansive powers over state and federal legislation. They arrived at this destination by varied routes, but the notion of "judicial review" of legislation—meaning that a court could invalidate laws that violate constitutional provisions and principles—was not foreign to them. Once the concept of an independent federal judiciary gained majority support, the delegates did not shrink from vesting the Supreme Court with the powers needed for its later role as the dominant branch of the national government.

The vague outlines of the James Madison's Virginia Plan for the Constitution provided for "one or more supreme tribunals" and for "inferior tribunals" with jurisdiction over "questions which may involve the national peace and harmony." Madison proposed that judges for these courts be chosen by the "national legislature," but the initial debate on this proposal showed that other delegates supported a selection by the "national executive." Speaking on June 5, James Wilson of Pennsylvania "opposed the appointment of judges by the national legislature,"

Madison reported. "Intrigue, partiality, and concealment were the necessary consequences" of allowing lawmakers to choose judges, Wilson argued. A signer of the Declaration of Independence, Wilson spoke now as a prosperous Philadelphia lawyer and a member of the Confederation Congress. Although he supported the popular election of federal officials, Wilson recognized that politicians were tempted to reward their backers with such prizes as judicial office. Wilson later won such a prize when George Washington rewarded him with a Supreme Court seat for supporting ratification of the Constitution.

John Rutledge of South Carolina spoke for other delegates who opposed the appointment of judges by the "national executive." He was "by no means disposed to grant so great a power to any single person," Madison recorded. "The people will think we are leaning too much towards monarchy." Although he differed with Wilson on this issue, Rutledge also won appointment from Washington to the Supreme Court, not once but twice, although, when Washington nominated him for Chief Justice in 1795, he was rejected by the Senate for political reasons.

While his fellow delegates argued over the legislative and executive branches for more than a month, Madison devoted some of his spare time to pondering the question of judicial appointments. After listening on July 18 to half a dozen familiar speeches by advocates of legislative or executive appointment, Madison tried to break the impasse. He proposed that federal judges "be appointed by the executive with the concurrence of one-third at least" of the Senate. Madison argued that his proposal "would unite the advantage of responsibility in the executive with the security afforded in the second branch against any incautious or corrupt nomination by the executive." After listening to half a dozen more speeches on the issue, Madison realized that his proposal had no chance of gaining approval. Without a recorded vote, the delegates agreed once again to defer the question for a later decision.

Weeks later, after heated debate and threats of walk-outs that would end the convention, the delegates adopted the Great Compromise that legitimated slavery and gave the smaller states equal votes in the Senate. Between July 21 and September 12, when the convention neared its end, not a single delegate rose to speak on the issue of judicial appointments. On August 6, however, the Committee on Detail, which had worked diligently for weeks to prepare a draft of the Constitution, based on the tentative votes of the Committee of the Whole, reported its efforts to the delegates. This draft included language that became, with little change, the wording of Article III of the Constitution, establishing the Supreme Court and providing for its jurisdiction. On the issue that had most divided the delegates—whether members of the Supreme Court should be chosen by the president or the Senate—the committee placed this power in the Senate. Madison was a member of the Committee on Detail, but he obviously failed to persuade his fellow members that judicial appointments should be shared by the president and the Senate.

After weeks of debate on the draft Constitution by the Committee on Detail, the delegates finally reached Article III on August 27 and almost hurried their way through it, with little discussion or debate. They agreed to vesting "the judicial power of the United States" in a Supreme Court "and in such inferior courts" as Congress might create. They also agreed to give the Supreme Court jurisdiction over "all cases under laws passed by the legislature of the United States" and to "controversies" between states, "between a state and citizens of another state," and "between citizens of different states." Through this jurisdictional scheme, the delegates intended to place all cases that did not arise solely within a single state into a federal judicial forum. Although only a few delegates voiced their concerns on this issue, these jurisdictional provisions obviously reflected fears that state judges might be biased against out-of-state litigants or against the federal government itself. The delegates also voted to vest the power of judicial appointment in the president, subject to confirmation by a majority of the Senate, a sharing of power that has led to many bruising and closely divided confirmation battles during the last two centuries, with no end in sight.

With hardly any debate, the delegates approved the creation of a branch of the national government with sweeping jurisdiction and awesome—if still untested—power to strike down laws of both the states and Congress. Many delegates, in fact, seemed unaware that they had granted these powers to the national judiciary. In designing the judicial branch of government, the delegates also added to its broad jurisdiction in Article III the additional power in Article VI (known as the Supremacy Clause) to make the Constitution and federal laws "the supreme law of the land, and the judges in every State shall be bound thereby, any Thing in the Constitution or Laws of any State to the Contrary notwithstanding."

Between them, the provision in Article III that gave the Supreme Court jurisdiction to decide all "cases and controversies" arising under the Constitution and the Supremacy Clause of Article VI established in that body what we now call the power of "judicial review" over both federal and state laws. With hardly another word on the convention floor, the delegates approved the draft Constitution, including Articles III and VI, in their final vote on September 12, 1787. They submitted the document for ratification by state conventions, with the votes of nine of the thirteen states required for its adoption. The weary delegates then returned to their home states, where most joined the fierce battles over ratification. The "Federalists," who supported a strong national government, as outlined in the Constitution, were pitted against the "Anti-Federalists," who denounced its incursions on state powers and failure to provide a Bill of Rights to protect citizens against overreaching federal power. These battles finally ended on June 21, 1789, when New Hampshire, by the narrow margin of 57–47, became the ninth and final state needed to ratify the Constitution.

The Structure of the Federal and State Legal Systems

Now that we have looked, however briefly, at the debates in the Constitutional Convention that produced Articles III and VI of the Constitution, it seems useful to provide a basic overview of the structure and functions of the American legal system, on both the federal and the state levels. As we saw, the apex of this system lies in the United States Supreme Court. In fuller detail, Article III provides that "The judicial power of the United States, shall be vested in one supreme court, and in such inferior courts as the Congress may from time to time ordain and establish. The judges, both of the supreme and inferior courts, shall hold their offices during good behavior," this latter term left undefined by the Framers. In practical terms, it means that federal judges have life tenure in their posts and can be removed only through impeachment; this provides a guarantee of judicial independence. Impeachment of federal officials, including judges, "civil officers of the United States" such as cabinet members, and the vice president and the president, is governed by Article II of the Constitution, which lists the impeachable offenses as "treason, bribery, or other high crimes and misdemeanors," this latter term also left undefined by the Framers. We shall return to impeachment later in this introduction, when I discuss judicial independence in both the state and the federal courts.

The Constitution's Framers left to Congress the job of setting the number of Supreme Court justices and of judges on the "inferior courts" in the federal system. The first Congress provided for six justices and established three judicial districts, dividing the states into northern, central, and southern districts, with varying numbers of judges in each. In choosing his first six justices, President George Washington broke with geographical lines, picking one from New England, two (including Chief Justice John Jay) from New York and Pennsylvania, and three from southern states. Washington's home and political base in Virginia perhaps influenced his choices, all of whom were staunch supporters of his Federalist cause and of political and judicial "nationalism," as opposed to the "states' rights" and the limited government credos of Thomas Jefferson and his allies.

One point worth noting is that service on the Supreme Court, during its first decades, was not considered a plum or an honor, partly because the salary was well below what most prominent lawyers could earn in private practice, and because the Court had few cases to decide. During its first decade, in fact, the Supreme Court had a sparse docket, with few cases rising on appeals from district courts. In fact, its first session in 1790 was adjourned for lack of a quorum and because there was no "business" on its docket. The Court even skipped several "terms" of court in its early years for lack of business.

A more significant reason that several prospective nominees, including Patrick Henry, turned down Washington's offers of Supreme Court seats, was that justices were required to spend several months of each year in **circuit-riding** duties, sitting with district judges to hear and decide cases in the states. Given the deplorable state of roads and inns at the time, most justices resented their circuit-riding to remote locations. Justice Thomas Johnson, who joined the Court in 1792, resigned the following year because, as he wrote to Washington, "I cannot resolve to spend six months in the year of the few I have left from my family on roads at taverns chiefly and often in situations where the most moderate desires are disappointed; my time of life, temper and other circumstances forbid it." Chief Justice John Jay also complained that his circuit-riding duty "takes me from my family half the year, and obliges me to pass too considerable a part of my time on the road, in lodging houses, & inns." Several of the early justices, including Jay, resigned from the Supreme Court to return to more lucrative private practices or to seek political office in their home states. Jay left the Court in 1796 and won election as New York's governor, the job he had always wanted.

Not only did the low salary and the circuit-riding duties make a Supreme Court seat an insufficient attraction for most eminent lawyers, the Court's first major decision, *Chisholm v. Georgia* in 1793, provoked a political uproar that threatened to destroy the Court's credibility. In this case, a citizen of South Carolina, Alexander Chisholm, sued the state of Georgia to recover money owed to an estate for which he served as executor, alleging that Georgia had not paid for military uniforms and cloth during the Revolution. This was an "easy" case for the justices, because Article III of the Constitution gave the Supreme Court jurisdiction over suits "between a State and Citizens of another State," which the *Chisholm* case clearly satisfied.

The Court's decision, however, provoked a swift and ferocious reaction from state lawmakers, who feared a flood of similar Revolution-era suits from disgruntled creditors. State legislatures besieged Congress with resolutions demanding a constitutional amendment to overturn the Court's ruling. The Georgia house even passed a bill providing that any federal official who attempted to enforce Chisholm's judgment would be "guilty of felony and shall suffer death, without benefit of clergy, by being hanged." The bill never became law, and no officials were hanged, but Congress responded by adopting the Eleventh Amendment in 1794, providing that the "judicial power of the United States" did not extend to suits "against one of the United States by citizens of another state" or by subjects of foreign nations. I mention this case and the furor it provoked to underscore the low esteem in which the Supreme Court was held during its early years, far overshadowing more recent campaigns to "Impeach Earl Warren" and other political attacks on federal judges and efforts to amend the Constitution to overturn decisions on such controversial issues as abortion and school prayer.

Not until 1801, when President John Adams named John Marshall as chief justice, did the Supreme Court begin to repair its damaged influence and esteem. Marshall, a prominent Virginia lawyer, headed the Court for thirty-five years, until his death in 1836. Unlike his hapless predecessors (one of whom the Senate rejected on political grounds), Marshall possessed both an iron will and a personal charm that turned the Court into a bulwark of judicial "nationalism" that "states' rights" presidents such as Thomas Jefferson and Andrew Jackson could not dislodge, even as they denounced many of the Court's decisions. Marshall's successor as chief justice, Roger Taney of Maryland, a die-hard defender of slavery, came close to fatally damaging the Court's prestige with his infamous decision in 1857 in the *Dred Scott* case. He held that no black person, whether slave or free, was a citizen of any state, which provoked a political uproar that paved the way for the "secession" of southern states and the bloody Civil War. However, with his choices for the Supreme Court before and after Taney's death in 1864, President Abraham Lincoln restored the Court to the esteem it had enjoyed under John Marshall, even in the face of political opposition to its rulings.

As the nation grew in area and population, and with the admission of new states to the Union, Congress periodically expanded the number of federal district courts, as well as judges to serve on them. Not until 1891, however, did Congress create an intermediate level of federal courts, setting up nine (now twelve) circuit courts of appeals, to reduce the huge number of appeals from district court rulings that clogged the Supreme Court's docket. Each circuit court (with the exception of that for the District of Columbia) has jurisdiction over cases from the district courts in several states and territories. There are currently ninety-four federal district courts; each state and territory has at least one, and several states with large populations have three or four districts. Each district court funnels appeals from its rulings into the circuit courts. Congress sets the number of judges on each court; the district courts currently are staffed by 987 judges, with 260 on the courts of appeals.

With their jurisdiction limited to cases brought under federal statutes and to so-called **diversity** cases, in which the parties reside in different states and which are decided under applications of state law, the caseloads of the federal courts are far lower than those of state courts. In 2009, the 94 district courts handled 326,112 cases; of these, 250,565 were **civil cases** and 75,547 were **criminal prosecutions** under federal laws, the bulk of these being immigration and drug cases. The courts of appeals in 2009 handled 60,358 cases; 31,388 were civil and 14,676 were criminal. In other words, about one-fifth of the cases decided in the district courts were appealed to the circuit courts. As I noted in the preface, however, the Supreme Court has had "discretionary jurisdiction" over appeals from lower state and federal courts since 1925 and exercises it sparingly. Most appeals to the Supreme Court come through "petitions for a writ of certiorari." A **writ of certiorari** basically instructs the lower court to "send the record to us." During the Supreme Court "term" that began in October 2009 and ended in June 2010, the justices received 7,738 **cert petitions** (as they are generally called) from state and federal courts; about half were filed by state and federal prisoners, and only a handful of these "jailhouse" petitions are ever granted. During its 2009–2010 term, the Court **granted cert** and issued decisions and opinions in just 85 cases that were decided on the merits. As we can see, the chances of getting full review by the Supreme Court are less than 2 percent of all of the cert petitions.

It's important to note that the vast majority of cases in the American legal system, both civil and criminal, begin in state courts: more than 98 percent of the total. State courts have jurisdiction over most legal matters, from traffic offenses to murders, and from landlord–tenant disputes to multibillion-dollar conflicts between giant corporations. There are roughly 34 million cases filed each year in state courts, about evenly divided between civil and criminal cases. Fewer than one out of twenty of these cases ever reaches trial; the remainder are settled between the parties, sparing state judges an enormous workload if each case (or even a significant fraction) went to trial. The legal system, in fact, encourages and facilitates pretrial settlement, most often through agreements between civil parties and dismissals or plea bargains in criminal cases. If we look at the court system as a pyramid (or, really, two overlapping pyramids of state and federal courts, joined at the top by the Supreme Court), more than 90 percent of all cases that enter the system each year drop out before they reach the appellate stage, and more than 99 percent of the remainder drop out before any appeal to the Supreme

Court. In short, the chance of any case in the federal and state courts being decided by the Supreme Court is roughly one in every half million.

The Influence of Politics (and Money) on the Legal System

The factor of politics is one that most judges and lawyers don't like to admit or discuss, but it's an ever-present feature of the legal system. There's an old saying that "a judge is a lawyer who knows a governor (or a senator)." Election or appointment to a judicial position is clearly dependent on political factors, however much we may hope that merit alone decides who becomes a judge. Some governors and senators do set up "merit panels" to recommend candidates for appointive positions. But it stands to reason, for example, that in nominating candidates for federal judgeships, presidents will prefer those who have supported their party. Figures bear this out. Of all presidents since Lyndon Johnson, only Gerald Ford nominated even one out of five candidates (21 percent) who belonged to the other party. Johnson was the most partisan president, naming 94 percent of fellow Democrats to the federal bench; Richard Nixon was the most partisan on the other side, with 93 percent Republican nominees.

The federal bench is currently dominated by Republicans; of 987 district court judges, 59 percent were named by Republican presidents, with 63 percent of the 260 court of appeals judges owing their positions to GOP presidents. These figures will change as judges nominated by President Obama join these courts, even more so if he wins reelection in 2012. But Republican dominance of the federal bench will continue for at least several more years.

Although current chief justice John Roberts has referred to judges as being like umpires in sporting events, calling them as they see them, impartially and according to the dictates of the rule book, the truth is that judicial umpires from both sides still make decisions with political consequences out of personal political beliefs.

We can see the effect of the partisan makeup in voting on controversial issues in the courts of appeals. A recent study showed that in affirmative-action cases, Democratic judges voted for plaintiffs 74 percent of the time; Republicans only 48 percent. In sex discrimination cases, Democrats voted for plaintiffs 51 percent of the time; Republicans only 35 percent. In abortion cases, Democrats sided with plaintiffs in 70 percent of the cases; Republicans in 49 percent. In capital punishment cases, Democrats sided with defendants 42 percent of the time; Republicans only 20 percent.

Although these differences are significant, one might expect greater disparity between judges of different parties; however, most cases are decided on the basis of precedent, which judges from both parties generally follow. And, contrary to popular belief, with the media and politicians largely to blame, few appellate judges are hard-core ideologues on either side. Most fit within the broad legal "mainstream" and generally stick to established precedent, if only to avoid being overruled by the Supreme Court.

These voting differences are most evident on the Supreme Court, which decides the "hard cases." It is less bound to precedent, which it can (and often does) overrule. The Court currently (as of 2011) has two identifiable blocs, with four liberals and four conservatives, a loosely defined (and often misleading) distinction, but widely used by politicians and pundits on both ends of the political spectrum. Most often, judicial liberals side with plaintiffs in cases that involve race and gender discrimination, First Amendment issues of religion and freedom of speech and the press, and the rights of criminal defendants. Judicial conservatives are more solicitous of business interests and exertions of governmental power, usually siding with the executive branch over Congress and with states in conflicts with the federal government.

Looking at the Court's current (early in 2011) makeup, most court watchers place Justices Stephen Breyer, Ruth Bader Ginsburg, Sonia Sotomayor, and Elena Kagan in the liberal bloc, with Chief Justice John Roberts, and Justices Antonin Scalia, Clarence Thomas, and Samuel Alito as the conservatives. This leaves Justice Anthony Kennedy as the swing vote on the Court's most sharply divided decisions in recent years. He is perhaps best labeled a moderate-conservative. For example, in the Court's 2008–2009 term, twenty-five cases were decided by 5–4 votes. Justice Kennedy sided with the four conservatives in thirteen of these cases and with the four liberals in five, placing him on the conservative (and winning) side more than twice as often.

In the 2009–2010 term, Justice Kennedy joined the four conservatives in eight of the sixteen 5–4 decisions and the four liberals in three, again slightly more than a 2–1 margin.

We can also measure the gulf between the liberal and conservative justices by the percentage of agreement in their voting. During the 2009–2010 term, the current four liberals voted together in 69 percent of nonunanimous cases, while the four conservatives stuck together in 67 percent. Another way of looking at the Court's ideological divisions is to see how often individual justices agree in their votes. In that same recent term, for example, Justices Stevens (the most consistent liberal) and Scalia (the most conservative) voted together in only 17.6 percent of nonunanimous decisions, differing in almost five out of every six cases that split the Court. Justice Kennedy, by contrast, voted with Justice Stevens in 45.6 percent of nonunanimous decisions and with Justice Scalia in 52.2 percent, making him the Court's real "man in the middle," whose vote every lawyer who argues before the Court hopes to gain. The current split among the justices, which may shift at any time through death or retirement, is nothing new. Profound and almost irreconcilable differences in judicial ideology have marked the Court since its early decades and remain to this day, as we will see in several of the cases discussed in this book.

Needless to say, no judicial nominee in his or her right mind would confess to being an ideologue of any stripe; the one charge a nominee wants to avoid is being labeled a "judicial activist," which has become an epithet. Ever since Judge Robert Bork doomed his nomination to the Court in 1987 by frankly expressing his opposition to abortion, Supreme Court nominees have steadfastly refused to tell senators how they might vote on any issue. They stick to the "mainstream," although everyone knows this is a charade. During his confirmation hearings in 2005, Chief Justice John Roberts likened the judge's role to that of an impartial "umpire" in a ball game. "Judges are like umpires," he said. "The role of an umpire and a judge is critical. They make sure everybody plays by the rules. But it is a limited role. Nobody ever went to a ballgame to see the umpire." This was disingenuous, to say the least. Every major-league pitcher and coach keeps "books" on umpires and knows which ones have wider strike zones, favoring pitchers, and narrow zones, giving batters an advantage. During her confirmation hearings in June 2010,

Justice Elena Kagan displayed admirable candor in calling Roberts out, although not by name. Saying that the judging process is "easy, and that we call ball and strike and everything is [so] clear-cut that there is no judgment in the process," Kagan replied, would make the process "a kind of robotic enterprise." In the hard cases, she added, "there are frequently clashes of constitutional values." That's why "not every case is decided 9–0."

This exchange harks back to an opinion of Justice Owen Roberts, writing for a majority in striking down a key New Deal statute in 1936, the Agricultural Adjustment Act. Roberts applied what I call a "mechanical" test of judicial interpretation in saying the Court's only duty was "to lay the article of the Constitution which is invoked beside the statute which is challenged and to decide whether the latter squares with the former," effectively relegating the judge to the role of a carpenter with a T-square. This prompted Justice Harlan Fiske Stone to excoriate Roberts's opinion as a "tortured construction of the Constitution" that substituted "judicial fiat" for the judgment of Congress. That debate, as we see in the statements of John Roberts and Elena Kagan, still goes on and shows no signs of abating. Judges are not "automatons," to use Kagan's term, but come to the bench with judicial philosophies that can differ radically. This debate is worth keeping in mind when we look at the cases we'll follow in this book and the divisions between the justices (and the lower-court judges as well) over their outcomes.

As noted previously, federal judges at all levels, after their confirmation, are protected from electoral retaliation for unpopular decisions and can be removed only through impeachment for "treason, bribery, or other high crimes and misdemeanors," the latter term left undefined by the Constitution's Framers. Impeachment is actually the first step in the removal process, which begins when one or more members introduce an impeachment resolution in the House of Representatives. Dozens of such resolutions have been introduced in recent decades, most of them never acted on by the full House. However, a majority of representatives can vote to adopt "articles of impeachment," specifying the charges against the judge. The process then moves to the Senate, which sits as a trial court, with evidence and testimony presented by House "managers" who act as prosecutors and by lawyers who defend the impeached judge, with a two-thirds vote of the senators required for conviction and removal from judicial office.

During the last two centuries, only a tiny number of federal judges—fifteen out of more than three thousand who have sat on federal courts—have been impeached by the House. Of these, only eight have been convicted and removed from office, although about twenty judges have resigned their posts to avoid probable or certain impeachment. The first to be convicted was John Pickering of New Hampshire in 1804; his main offense was having angered President Jefferson by using the Sedition Act to punish Jefferson's supporters for allegedly "seditious" speech and writings. Pickering's supposedly "unlawful rulings" in these cases, although they displayed his partisan bias, were really political offenses against the ruling party and hardly met any legal definition of "high crimes and misdemeanors," unless those terms are stretched beyond common meaning. Pickering was also an alcoholic and mentally unstable, however, making him unfit for judicial service and his removal more defensible. (Fortunately, the federal courts have now adopted procedures for removing judges who are physically or mentally disabled from presiding over cases, leaving them with their salaries and pensions.)

Having removed one political opponent from the federal bench, President Jefferson went after bigger game, persuading the House to impeach Supreme Court justice Samuel Chase of Maryland. Chase had campaigned against Jefferson's election in 1800, denouncing the Jeffersonian "Mobocracy" for imperiling the nation's "peace and order, freedom, and prosperity." However, Jefferson overreached himself, although his Republican (later Democratic) party controlled the Senate by a 25–9 margin. The political basis of the eight impeachment charges against Chase was clear; one Republican senator boasted that "we want your offices, for the purpose of giving them to men who will fill them better." Likely fearing that impeachment was a double-edged sword that could be used against their own judicial supporters, the Republican-dominated Senate fell short of the two-thirds majority needed to convict Chase and remove him from the Supreme Court; five of the eight charges did not gain even a simple majority.

In recent decades, politically motivated impeachments have ended. The most recent judges to be removed, Alcee Hastings of Florida in 1989 and G. Thomas Porteous of Louisiana in 2010, were both charged with corruption and accepting bribes. Hastings achieved some measure of revenge, winning election to the House of Representatives in 1993 and every succeeding election through 2010, thus outlasting all but a few of the colleagues who voted to impeach him.

However, calls to impeach federal judges who render unpopular decisions have not abated, despite the slim chances of winning impeachment and conviction. Recently, conservative groups demanded the impeachment of Alfred Goodwin, a Ninth Circuit appellate judge who ruled in 2002 that the words "under God" in the Pledge of Allegiance violated the First Amendment's "Establishment of Religion" clause. This prompted President George W. Bush to denounce Goodwin's decision as "ridiculous." In 2010, district judge Vaughn R. Walker in San Francisco drew similar calls for impeachment with his ruling that California's controversial "Proposition 8," adopted by a 52–48 percent margin of the state's voters to prevent the legalization of same-sex marriages, violated the federal Constitution's Due Process and Equal Protection clauses.

It seems unlikely that empty threats of impeachment will have a "chilling effect" on federal judges who rule on controversial issues such as the Pledge and same-sex marriage. However, judges in most states do not enjoy the same protection of life tenure on the bench. Only twelve states provide lifetime appointments for their judges, while the rest require judges to stand for election at the polls. Seven states conduct partisan elections for judicial candidates, while fourteen elect judges through supposedly "nonpartisan" contests, although political parties often make clear to voters which candidates they support or oppose. The remaining states use what are called "retention" elections, in which judges who have been appointed (usually by governors) go before the voters after serving terms that range from six to ten years, with the prospect of being removed from the bench. Such removals are rare, though, and most voters pay little attention to judicial elections.

In some states, however, particularly those with partisan elections, judicial contests become heated, most often when voters are faced with choosing (or retaining) judges who campaign as conservatives or liberals. Such elections often feature television and newspaper ads that portray candidates in political terms, with conservatives painting themselves as defending "law and order" or attacking opponents as "soft on crime." Liberal candidates profess to protect the "little people" from corporate-dominated lawmakers or to defend abortion rights. Interest groups such as the Chamber of Commerce and the AFL-CIO raise millions of dollars in some states to promote their favored judicial candidates. A recent poll showed that 76 percent of voters and 26 percent of state judges as well believe that campaign contributions to judges have at least some influence on their decisions. The same poll showed that nine in ten voters and eight in ten state judges "say they are quite concerned about special interest groups buying advertising to influence the outcomes of judicial elections." Even retention elections often draw large sums to promote or oppose candidates. For example, in 2010, opponents of same-sex marriage poured more than a million dollars into a successful campaign to unseat three members of Iowa's supreme court—including its chief justice—who faced retention at the polls, in retaliation for their votes to legalize same-sex marriage in Iowa.

The question of whether judicial elections are a good or bad method of selecting judges has provoked heated debate for more than a century, with supporters arguing that it promotes democracy, while opponents point to the growing influence of "special interest" groups and campaign contributions as damaging to judicial independence. Nonetheless, it seems clear that in many states these elections have turned less on judicial qualifications such as experience, legal knowledge, and temperament than on which candidate can raise the most money to gain office.

The Importance of Turning Points and Discretion in the Legal System

Although few cases reach the Supreme Court, every case must begin with a lawyer (or sometimes a private party) filing a claim or charges. Thus, the first turning point in any case comes even before a case begins. In a civil case, regardless of its facts and the laws or the constitutional provisions that might apply, the prospective plaintiff and his or her lawyers must decide whether there are sufficient grounds for a lawsuit. Merely being upset about something that someone else (whether it's an employer, a neighbor, or a government official) has done to you or failed to do does not warrant a lawsuit, unless there is some damage to you that merits some judicial remedy, provided by law. Lawyers are supposed to know about the possible grounds for a lawsuit and what remedies are available and to advise their clients about their options.

For example, let's say you work in a store as a clerk, and you get upset when your manager says, "You wear the ugliest clothes I've ever seen. In fact, some of our customers have complained that you look like a hippie, so I want you to dress more appropriately. You know, a little more conservatively." When you tell your boss that other customers have actually complimented you on your colorful outfits, he says, "That's not a suggestion, it's an order. If you don't meet our company's standard of appearance, I'll have to let you go." You go to see a lawyer, and she says, "I understand your being upset, but we'll need more facts to decide whether there's a lawsuit here. Does your company have an employee manual that lays out what kind of apparel is okay and what isn't? And you haven't actually been fired. Maybe you could work it out with your boss and ask him whether what you're wearing today is acceptable to him. But if he threatens to fire you or actually does, come back to see me. And we'll need some documentation, such as pictures of what you wear to work or copies of a manual, if there is one."

This may seem like a trivial matter, hardly worth the cost and time of bringing a lawsuit, but there might be grounds, if it turns out that the boss was simply imposing his own personal dislike of your outfits, and he fired you for not conforming. The facts of every situation differ, as does the law that might apply, which both affect this initial decision point. But let's assume you did get fired, your lawyer advises you that this sounds like a "wrongful termination" case, and she says she'll take it.

The next turning point in this hypothetical (as law professors call these made-up cases to stimulate thought and discussion) is to determine whom to file suit against (the manager or the company?), what facts and legal grounds your lawyer can allege, and what court to file in. The manager is the company's agent, but the corporate "suits" might not even be aware of what happened in your store, or they may have approved his firing of you. There are laws in most states to protect employees against various forms of "wrongful termination," such as racial or gender or religious bias, but your case doesn't seem to fit into any of these categories. Still, your lawyer says, "We can find a hook; there have been other cases where bosses said that women can't wear even dress pants to work and insisted on skirts or dresses." Lawyers are cautious by training (no lawyer wants to be ridiculed or possibly sanctioned for filing a "frivolous" lawsuit), but good lawyers are also creative. That's how old law is expanded or new law created. This doesn't sound like a federal case, so your lawyer will probably advise filing in a state court and naming both the manager and the company as defendants.

Assuming a lawsuit is filed, the next step in our "hypo" (as law students call these brain-teasers) shifts to the defendants. How do they answer your suit, and what legal defenses can they raise? They might even allege that you were fired because you were consistently getting into squabbles with everybody, including your fellow employees and customers, and that you were fired "for cause." They would probably ask a judge to dismiss your suit for lack of any legal ground. Assuming the defendants do file a **motion to dismiss**, the next decision shifts to the judge, who has the discretion to grant the defendant's motion or deny it, thus allowing the case to proceed. Granting a motion to dismiss doesn't mean your case is over, because these decisions can be appealed, although most are upheld by appellate courts.

At this point, with cases that survive dismissal motions or are not settled by the parties, the next step is for the judge to hold a **hearing**, at which only lawyers appear and argue, or set the case for a **jury trial**, which both plaintiffs and defendants are entitled to demand. Following the hearing or the trial, depending on the outcome, the judge then reaches a decision point. If the plaintiffs have prevailed, the judge has discretion to award monetary damages or injunctive relief (or both) and to accompany his or her order with a written opinion, laying out the reasons for the order and citing legal precedent from the decisions of higher appellate courts, including the Supreme Court.

The next turning point belongs to the losing party in the case, whether plaintiffs or defendants, who must decide whether to appeal the jury verdict or the judicial order to the appellate court (state or federal) that has jurisdiction over the trial court. This is an important decision point, because the losing parties and their lawyers must specify in an appeal the **clear errors** committed by the trial judge, such as allowing the admission of testimony or evidence that should have been excluded (or barring testimony and evidence that should have been admitted). You cannot appeal a case simply because you don't like the outcome. You must convince an appellate court that something fundamental went wrong on the way to that outcome.

Another ground for appeal is that the trial judge's opinion relied on **precedent** that did not properly apply in the case. As noted previously, only about one in five district court decisions are appealed to the courts of appeals, which generally uphold the trial court's decisions. Appeals cost money and can drag out for two or three years. The winning party in the trial court must also decide how to respond, most often by arguing that the trial judge correctly applied relevant precedent.

Cases in the federal appellate courts are normally assigned for hearing and oral argument to **panels** of three judges, chosen at random by computers. Following the oral arguments (which can be dispensed with or conducted by phone or video-conferencing, an increasingly popular method of hearing arguments), the panel members decide cases by majority vote, usually with opinions (both majority and dissenting in divided votes). Appellate judges have discretion in their rulings: they can simply affirm or reverse the trial judge's decision, ordering judgment to be entered for the winning party, or they can **remand** the case to the trial judge for further proceedings, which include new hearings on issues the appellate judges specify. The same process applies in state courts, although eleven states (all of them with smaller populations) do not have intermediate appellate courts, with appeals from trial courts going directly to the state's supreme court.

The losing parties in federal appellate courts then face another turning point: one option is to ask for an **en banc** review of the panel's decision by a larger number of judges. In the small number of cases in which an en banc review is granted, which requires a majority vote of the circuit's active judges, the larger panel can affirm or reverse the decision of the three-judge panel. An en banc review is rarely granted, most often in cases in which the three-judge panel's decision conflicted with precedent within the circuit or from the Supreme Court. Only a handful of states provide for an en banc review of decisions by intermediate state appellate courts.

Another option for the losing party in the courts of appeals, one that few lawyers pursue, involves asking the U.S. Supreme Court to review the appellate court's decision. Losing parties in state supreme courts also have this option. As noted earlier, the reason so few certiorari petitions are filed with the Supreme Court is that the justices have almost complete discretion to choose the cases they review, limiting their docket to cases of "extraordinary importance." With the chance of winning review at less than 1 percent, most lawyers advise their losing clients to take their lumps and end the litigation. In cases that the justices do review, they have discretion to either affirm or reverse the lower-court ruling or to remand the case for further proceedings on issues the justices specify in an order.

We'll now discuss the turning points and the role of discretion in the criminal-justice system, which are different up to the steps of appeals from verdicts, where they merge with those in the civil system. As noted previously, the vast majority (roughly 98 percent) of criminal cases begin and end in state courts, with only a small fraction even going to trial. This is largely because most criminal cases, from traffic offenses to murder cases, are resolved before trial with guilty pleas by defendants and the imposition of fines or decisions by judges to place those who plead guilty to probation, supervised by county or state officers, or short terms of imprisonment.

Every initial stage in the criminal-justice system involves great latitude for discretion, by police officers, prosecutors, and judges. These discretionary decisions are largely unreviewable by appellate courts. Let's begin with another hypo, in which a police officer responds to a report of a bar-room brawl. He or she can assess the situation and say, "Okay, everybody, break it up, and you all go home." Or the officer can arrest one or more of the brawlers, especially if someone has been injured. The officer has discretion in which charges to file, from disorderly conduct to simple assault or to aggravated assault. After an arrest, a prosecutor has discretion to drop the charges, if he or she doesn't think they can be sustained in court. The prosecutor also has discretion to either reduce or enhance the charges; some prosecutors routinely "overcharge" defendants, giving them more bargaining chips in **plea-bargain** negotiations with defense lawyers. The primary goal of a defense lawyer is, if possible, to keep the client from serving jail time, preferably through a probationary sentence. If that fails, defense lawyers press for the shortest possible term to which the prosecutor and a judge will agree. Criminal defendants, of course, must decide whether to accept the terms of a plea bargain that his or her lawyer has made with a prosecutor, or whether to insist (which is the defendant's right) on risking a jury trial and the possibility of conviction and a harsher sentence, although most defendants heed their lawyers' advice.

Assuming a criminal case goes before a judge, he or she has discretion to dismiss the charges or reduce them. If a defendant is found guilty at trial, the judge normally has considerable discretion in imposing sentences, within ranges set by law (some state and federal laws require mandatory sentences, which most judges oppose because it makes their job mechanical). In criminal appeals, judges have discretion in affirming or reversing a conviction, and, as we've seen, the Supreme Court has complete discretion in deciding whether to hear and decide an appeal. Discretion can obviously be abused (as in prosecutorial "overcharging"), but it is an essential element in the legal system.

The first turning point in a criminal case rests with a police officer, who can make an arrest or simply decide that no crime has been committed. Assuming an arrest is made, the next decision lies with prosecutors, who decide what charges to bring (often differing with police officers, after looking at the reports and the evidence). In cases that involve serious charges, prosecutors then must decide whether to seek an **indictment** from a **grand jury** and for what charges. Securing an indictment is usually a formality, because grand jurors almost always follow a prosecutor's advice to issue one. In first-degree murder cases, prosecutors also have discretion to seek the death penalty, except in the fifteen states without capital punishment.

Following a Supreme Court decision in 1985, every state with the death penalty requires that prosecutors must specify "special circumstances" that make the defendant "death-eligible." These "circumstances," laid out by statute, include multiple homicides; murder of law-enforcement and other "public safety" officers, such as firefighters; particularly "heinous" or "atrocious" murders, such as leaving a stabbing or shooting victim to bleed to death; murder for hire or for financial gain (such as collecting insurance on the victim); cases that involve more than one violent crime, such as kidnapping or rape, in addition to the murder; and cases in which the defendant has been previously convicted of a violent crime. If the defendant is convicted of first-degree murder, prosecutors must persuade the jurors, in a separate "sentencing hearing," that each of the alleged "special circumstances" has been proved beyond a reasonable doubt. Even though the same jurors had unanimously voted to convict the defendant, they can vote not to impose the death penalty, which in most states results in a sentence of life imprisonment without the possibility of parole.

In most states, the next step after indictment is the holding of a preliminary hearing, at which judges listen to arguments from prosecutors and defense lawyers (who often choose not to present a case, to avoid tipping their hands about their defense strategies). At these hearings, judges have discretion to dismiss the indictment for lack of sufficient evidence in persuading jurors to find a defendant guilty "beyond a reasonable doubt," although judges rarely exercise this discretionary power.

Assuming that an indictment is upheld, the next steps in the system involve the trial, most often before a jury, although defendants can ask for a trial before the judge. Following the trial, if the defendant is convicted, defense lawyers face a turning point in deciding whether to file an appeal, almost always in a state appellate court, because judicial rules require the "exhaustion of remedies" in state courts before defendants can ask the Supreme Court for review and relief. The "exhaustion" rule also applies in cases where defendants seek a review of their convictions in a federal district court through a **petition for a writ of habeas corpus**, a procedure that I'll explain in the next chapter on the Paul House case. As noted earlier, the Supreme Court may affirm or reverse a state-court decision or remand the case to lower state or federal courts for further proceedings. It's worth repeating here that the justices review only a tiny number (five to ten in each recent term) of criminal convictions, leaving intact the outcomes in some seventeen million other cases. Those that the justices do review, they do so primarily to settle lower-court confusion about the law or to correct serious errors by judges, not because they intend to second-guess the jury.

So, with this background that provided a historical review of the drafting of the Constitution's judicial articles and provisions, described the influence of political factors on the American legal system, and explained the role of decision points in civil and criminal cases, we'll begin our tour in the small town of Luttrell, Tennessee.

PART I

"No Reasonable Juror"

The Death-Row Ordeal
of Paul House

1

The Murder of
Carolyn Muncey

O ur guided tour of the American criminal-law system and its procedures begins in the small town of Luttrell, Tennessee, a village of
some one thousand residents in rural Union County, about twenty-five
miles east of the state's third-largest city, Knoxville. On July 13, 1985,
sometime between 9:00 and 11:00 P.M. on a hot Saturday night, Carolyn
Muncey disappeared from her home on isolated Ridgecrest Road, about
two miles from Luttrell's town center,. A twenty-nine-year-old mother
of two children, ten-year-old Lora and eight-year-old Matthew, Carolyn
lived with her husband, William Hubert Muncey Jr. (known to friends
and neighbors as "Little Hube" to distinguish him from his father, "Big
Hube"). Their unpainted, four-room house lacked running water (which
they carried from the houses of family members and neighbors), indoor
plumbing, and a telephone, although it had electricity and a television
set. The Munceys were dirt poor, supplementing Little Hube's sporadic
income from odd jobs with food stamps and welfare grants.

Let me begin with a brief summary of the events that started with
Carolyn's disappearance, followed by the discovery of her battered

body the next afternoon. and ended with the arrest of Paul House for her murder, four days later. This account is drawn from the testimony and the evidence presented by prosecutors at House's murder trial in February 1986, in their scenario of the events surrounding Carolyn's disappearance and murder. As we'll later see, much of what the jurors considered in deciding whether to convict House was highly disputed, both at the trial and in later judicial proceedings.

Jurors first heard that Carolyn and her children visited with their across-the-road neighbor, Pam Luttrell, on that Saturday night. Carolyn told Pam that Little Hube had spent the day "digging a grave some-where" with friends whose grandmother had died but had promised to take her fishing the next day. Carolyn and the kids went back home sometime around 8:00 or 8:30 P.M., then she made dinner and put Lora and Matthew to bed.

Shortly after 1:00 A.M., Little Hube knocked on the Luttrells' door, told Pam that he had come back from a weekly square-dance at the local recreation center, discovered Carolyn missing, and couldn't find her anywhere around the house. Using Pam's phone, he called his parents and other relatives to come and help look for Carolyn, leaving Lora and Matthew with Pam. Someone then called the Luttrell police depart-ment to report Carolyn missing, and Chief Dennis "Dink" Wallace came to the Munceys' house, helped Little Hube look some more, without finding Carolyn, and then left. Little Hube told Wallace that he thought someone had kidnapped Carolyn.

The next afternoon, on Sunday, with Carolyn still missing, her cousin Billy Ray Hensley drove to the Munceys' house to help with the search. As he rounded a turn onto Ridgecrest Road, about five hundred feet from the Munceys' driveway, Hensley took a "glance" down the road and saw someone come "out of nowhere" from an embankment about a hundred yards across the road from the Munceys' driveway, wiping his hands on a "black rag." When Hensley got near the driveway, he was "flagged down" by a man driving an old white Plymouth, who told Hensley he was looking for Little Hube to help with the search for Carolyn. The two cars, going in different directions, wound up at the house of Bill Silvey, a couple of miles away, where Hensley saw Little Hube and the man who flagged him down, both in the white Plymouth. With his "suspicions" aroused, Hensley and a friend, Jackie Adkins, returned to Ridgecrest

Road and looked over the embankment, where Adkins spotted the body of Carolyn Muncey, loosely covered with brush and tree branches. From a neighbor's house, they called the Union County sheriff's office to report their discovery.

Returning to the spot where Carolyn's body lay, Hensley saw the white Plymouth drive up, with both Little Hube and the man who flagged him down inside. Hensley then told Union County sheriff Earl Loy, who was at the scene, that the Plymouth's driver was the man he had seen near the embankment. That man was Paul Gregory House, then twenty-three years old, who had moved to Luttrell a few months earlier and was living with his girlfriend, Donna Turner, in her trailer, about two miles from the Munceys' house.

After Hensley pointed out House at the scene where Carolyn's body was found, Sheriff Loy asked him to come for a talk at the sheriff's office in Maynardville, which House did that evening. He was questioned by Charles Scott, an agent with the Tennessee Bureau of Investigation (TBI), who had come to Luttrell to assist local police in the investigation of Carolyn's murder. Asked about his whereabouts on Saturday night, House told Scott he had been at Donna Turner's all night and Sunday morning. Sheriff Loy also asked House whether the jeans he was wearing, which were clean and creased, were the same ones he had worn the night before; House said they were. The next day, Scott went to Donna Turner's trailer and—with her consent—searched her laundry hamper, finding at the bottom a pair of jeans that had several small "brownish-reddish" spots on them that Scott suspected were blood. Scott took the jeans with him and gave them to Bill Breeding, Union County's criminal investigator.

Following the discovery of Carolyn Muncey's body, an autopsy was performed by a pathologist, Dr. Alex Carabia, who concluded that she had died, sometime between 9:00 and 11:00 P.M. on Saturday night, from a blow or blows to her head, causing a cerebral hemorrhage. Dr. Carabia also extracted four vials of blood from the body. On Monday evening, Bill Breeding and a Maynardville police officer, Joe Ed Munsey (no relation to Carolyn or Little Hube Muncey), packed the blood vials in a Styrofoam box and put it into a cardboard box, along with House's jeans, a blood sample he had volunteered, and the clothing— a housecoat, a nightgown, a bra, and panties—Carolyn Muncey had been wearing when her body was found. With the cardboard box in their trunk, Breeding and Munsey then drove from Maynardville to Washington, D.C., a ten-hour trip, where they delivered the evidence to Paul Bigbee, an FBI agent who did "blood and body fluid" analysis in the FBI lab.

On Tuesday, July 16, Bigbee reported to the Union County prosecutor, Paul Phillips, that his analysis of the blood spots on House's jeans showed they had a "93 percent" probability of matching Carolyn Muncey's blood typing, and that semen stains on her nightgown and panties came from a man who matched House's blood group. While this testing was being done, Donna Turner was grilled by TBI agents, and she confessed that Paul House had not spent all of Saturday night with her but had gone out for a walk around 10:45 P.M. and returned an hour later "hot and sweaty" and without his tank-top shirt or tennis shoes. Armed with this information, Bill Breeding went to Turner's trailer on Wednesday, July 17, and placed House under arrest for the first-degree murder of Carolyn Muncey, then took him to the Union County jail in Maynardville.

Paul House certainly seemed like a plausible suspect. Born in Oklahoma in 1961, he moved with his parents as a child to Salt Lake City, Utah, where his father, James, worked as an airline mechanic and his mother, Joyce, held various office jobs. Although Paul was bright and did well in school, he became a heavy marijuana smoker as a teenager and dropped out of high school, claiming that it was too boring. In 1981, he was arrested and charged with "aggravated sexual battery," allegedly for forcing a young woman to have sex with him while he held a knife to her throat, although House claimed they had consensual sex after smoking pot. Pressured by his lawyer, who said he would get a lighter sentence if he pleaded guilty, Paul agreed and was sentenced to five years to life in the Utah state prison, where he behaved himself and was released on parole after four years, in March 1985. He then moved to Luttrell, first living with his mother, who had divorced House's father in Utah and was now married to Bill Silvey. Paul House and his step-father had fought over Silvey's annoyance with House, who spent most of his time watching television and smoking marijuana. House then moved in with his new girlfriend, Donna Turner, a divorced mother of three young children, who lived in a double-wide trailer about two miles from the

Munceys. House had met the Munceys through Bill Silvey and had visited their home two or three times.

The Turning Points in a Criminal Case

In every criminal case, police officers, prosecutors, and judges face turning points at which they weigh their options on whether and how to proceed, keeping in mind that the vast majority of cases drop out of these systems at one or another step. To help readers follow Paul House's trial in 1986, I will outline the steps that are common to all criminal trials, followed by those in cases in which prosecutors have sought the death penalty, and the jury has found the defendant guilty of first-degree murder.

The Report of a Crime

It seems obvious that every criminal case begins with the report of a crime, whether actually observed in progress or reported to the police or other law-enforcement officials. If someone calls 911 to report a disturbance at a neighbor's house, the police may simply advise the caller to close her windows. But if the caller says she hears screams and loud thumping noises, the police will probably respond. Many reports of possible crimes turn out to be baseless. Some reports, however, involve more serious crimes. When Little Hube Muncey called the Luttrell police to report that his wife was missing, telling Chief Wallace he thought she had been kidnapped, there was no evidence of a crime or even the basis for a "missing person" report. But when Jackie Adkins and Billy Ray Hensley found her body the next day, it was obvious a murder had been committed and must be investigated, the first major decision point in the case.

The Investigation of a Crime

Once a crime has been reported, police and other law-enforcement personnel conduct an investigation, looking for evidence and possible suspects. Viewers of television programs such as the popular *CSI* and

Law and Order series might assume that crime-scene investigators have state-of-the-art equipment and that detectives can make suspects squirm and confess. In many big cities this is true, but small-town officers and even state investigators often lack basic training and equipment. In Paul House's case, as we will see, examples of sloppy investigation abound. For example, when Chief Wallace first responded to Little Hube Muncey's report that his wife was missing, Wallace took a cursory look around their house and saw no evidence of disorder or signs of a struggle, and later investigators did not use tools such as Luminol, which can detect even tiny spots of blood. After Carolyn's body was found, the scene was not cordoned off by crime-scene tape or rope, people tramped around the scene (perhaps wiping out footprints), and no log was kept of people entering the scene. When TBI agent Scott retrieved House's jeans from Donna Turner's laundry hamper, he used his bare hands and did not wear latex gloves, leaving traces of his skin and DNA on the jeans. The jeans were then placed in a cardboard box, along with the poorly stoppered blood vials and Carolyn Muncey's clothing, creating the probable blood spillage onto the jeans. The case against House was compromised, as the Supreme Court later ruled, by this "evidentiary disarray."

Arresting a Suspect

The Fourth Amendment to the U.S. Constitution provides that "no Warrants shall issue, but upon probable cause, supported by oath or affirmation . . ." Despite this provision, courts have created numerous exceptions that allow police to arrest and detain suspects on mere "suspicion" that they have committed a crime. For example, the Supreme Court upheld the arrest and conviction of a man whom a Cleveland, Ohio, plainclothes officer suspected was planning to rob a jewelry store because the suspect had been pacing back and forth along the block and looking into the store window. When he was stopped and his overcoat was "patted down," the officer found a handgun. The Fifth Amendment also provides that no person "shall be compelled in any criminal case to be a witness against himself. . . ." Once a suspect is under arrest or is being detained without the opportunity to leave, the police must provide him or her with the famous (or infamous, depending on your viewpoint) *Miranda* warning (called such because it originated in that famous Supreme Court case): "You have the right to remain silent. Anything you say can and will be used in a court of law. You have the right to a lawyer. If you cannot afford a lawyer, one will be provided to you." But the Supreme Court has gradually whittled down this right, ruling in 2010 (by a 5–4 margin) that suspects under detention must speak up to claim their *Miranda* right to remain silent and consult a lawyer; how many suspects will even know of this is highly speculative. The record does not show whether Paul House was given the *Miranda* warning after his arrest, but the statements he made to police before his arrest were not protected from use in his trial, although House had denied any involvement in Carolyn Muncey's murder.

Arraignment and Bail

An arraignment is a largely formal proceeding in which a judge informs the defendant of the charges against him or her, ascertains whether the defendant is represented by counsel, and then appoints a lawyer, usually a public defender, if the defendant has none. In Paul House's case, his mother, Joyce, had hired a Knoxville criminal defense lawyer, Charles "Chuck" Burks, to represent her son. Arraignment judges also set bail or schedule a later bail hearing. The Eighth Amendment to the Constitution provides that "excessive bail shall not be required" in criminal cases, but setting bail for a defendant is not mandatory; its purpose is to ensure that defendants appear for the proceedings, and many defendants who face minor charges are released without bail, on what is known as **"personal recognizance,"** on their promise to appear. In most states, defendants in murder cases are routinely denied bail, because they pose a high risk of fleeing before trial, although exceptions are sometimes made, as in the notorious O.J. Simpson case. Because the prosecutor was seeking the death penalty in House's case, he was remanded to the Union County jail to await trial.

Although every criminal defendant is entitled to arraignment and bail decisions, the steps that follow this process usually depend on whether the case falls into one of two categories: **misdemeanors** or **felonies**. In most states, misdemeanors are minor crimes, such as "disorderly conduct" or traffic offenses, punishable by maximum jail terms of a year or less or by fines less than a certain amount. Felonies are major crimes that carry prison sentences of more than a year or substantial fines. Charges in both categories allow defendants the right to a jury trial, although most misdemeanor defendants (the minority who plead "not guilty") waive this right and opt for trial before a judge. Misdemeanor cases are generally prosecuted on filing of an **information** by the prosecutor and never reach the step of a grand jury proceeding or indictment.

Preliminary Hearings and Grand Jury Proceedings

A preliminary hearing is sort of a "mini-trial" at which a judge will listen to witnesses called by the prosecution and decide, on the basis of this testimony, whether there is sufficient **probable cause** of the defendant's likely guilt to send the case to a grand jury. Defendants can **waive** a preliminary hearing, but defense lawyers generally like to see and hear the prosecution's witnesses and get a sense of their demeanor and credibility at a trial. Preliminary hearings almost always result in sending the case to a grand jury; prosecutors usually have already exercised their **discretion** to drop charges at an earlier stage if they decide the case is too weak to secure a guilty verdict at trial. **Prosecutorial discretion** is probably the most important factor in the criminal justice system, weeding out the weak cases and sparing defendants (and the public) the cost and time of trying such cases, even if the prosecutor believes the defendant is guilty. Ethical prosecutors will exercise their discretion wisely, although some (often with an eye on the ballot box) will risk embarrassing defeats to polish their "law and order" credentials.

The **grand jury** is one of our oldest legal institutions, stemming back to the twelfth century in England and formalized in the Magna Carta in 1215. Ironically, grand juries were initially designed to protect the monarchy and the nobility from decisions by local juries that favored defendants who were charged with offending the "King's Peace." Composed largely of wealthy landowners, the early grand juries brought charges that were prosecuted before judges who owed loyalty to the king. Transported to the American colonies, the grand jury system became a favorite tool of prosecutors; grand jurors were generally chosen by judges from among people they knew and trusted as "upstanding" citizens, who would almost always do the prosecutor's bidding; in fact, defendants and their lawyers are excluded from the closed-door proceedings. The function of a grand jury is to decide whether, on the basis of testimony by the prosecution's witnesses, sufficient evidence was presented to warrant an **indictment** against a defendant, a formal charge that would be read to the trial jurors. Prosecutors assume, usually correctly, that trial jurors would reason that "if the grand jury thinks this defendant is guilty, they must be right." (As a bit of legal trivia, Sol Wachtler, the former chief justice of New York's highest state court, once said offhandedly to a reporter that any decent prosecutor could persuade a grand jury "to indict a ham sandwich.")

In Tennessee, grand juries are composed of thirteen members, twelve of whom are sufficient to issue a **true bill** against a defendant, a formal charge that must include every element of the crime. If the grand jury declines to issue an indictment, it returns a **no true bill,** and the charges are dismissed and the defendant released from custody. In Paul House's case, a Union County grand jury heard testimony from only two witnesses, Tennessee Bureau of Investigation agent Charles Scott and Sheriff Earl Loy, and returned, on September 23, 1985, a "true bill" that read: "The Grand Jurors for the State of Tennessee, duly elected, impaneled, sworn and charged to inquire in and for the body of the County of Union in the State of Tennessee, upon their oath present: That PAUL GREGORY HOUSE prior to the finding of this indictment, on or about July 13, 1985, in the County and State aforesaid, did unlawfully, feloniously, willfully, deliberately, maliciously and premeditatedly, with malice aforethought, murder and kill one Carolyn Muncey, by striking, beating, and choking her, and did thereby commit murder in the First Degree, against the peace and dignity of the State of Tennessee." In this archaic and formalistic language, the grand jury set the stage for Paul House's murder trial.

Following the indictment, the Union County prosecutor, Paul Phillips, reached another turning point and used his discretion to file papers that he would seek the death penalty, under the Tennessee law (similar to those in other death-penalty states) that provided for capital punishment if prosecutors allege so-called **special circumstances,** such as murders with multiple victims; killings that are especially **heinous** or **atrocious** in their manner, such as torture or mutilation; murders of law-enforcement officers; those committed by defendants with prior convictions for violent crimes; and murders committed in the course of another felony, such as rape, robbery, or kidnapping. In seeking the death penalty for Paul House, Phillips alleged that Carolyn Muncey's murder by a brutal beating was atrocious and left her bleeding to death; that House had a prior rape conviction; and that she was murdered in the course of kidnapping and an attempted rape, because an actual rape could not be proved.

Pretrial Motions and Discovery

Criminal defense lawyers almost always file **pretrial motions** with the judge, often seeking rulings that would reduce or eliminate certain charges (for example, reducing first-degree murder charges to second-degree murder or manslaughter or dropping charges such as weapons or drug possession), if the judge feels the evidence presented at preliminary hearings or other proceedings would not support the original charges. Other pretrial motions ask for rulings that would **suppress** the prosecution's introduction of evidence that was allegedly obtained illegally, such as drugs or weapons that were seized in violation of Fourth Amendment protections, or of statements or confessions that were allegedly coerced. Rulings on "suppression" motions are often vital to a defense case and, if granted, might persuade prosecutors to reduce charges (which they can do any time before trial) or even dismiss them.

Defense lawyers also routinely file **discovery** requests with prosecutors, seeking what is called **Brady material**. In 1963, the Supreme Court ruled in *Brady v. Maryland* that prosecutors have an affirmative duty to disclose to defense lawyer any **exculpatory** evidence that would be favorable to the defense. Failure to hand over such material would violate the Due Process clause and the defendant's right to a fair trial. In **Brady motions**, defense lawyers can specify certain evidence they know or suspect to be exculpatory or can file requests for "all Brady

material." In later cases, the Supreme Court expanded the *Brady* ruling to cover exculpatory material that was inadvertently or negligently
withheld by prosecutors and imposed on them a **duty to learn** of such
material, even if it was held by other government agencies or officials.
Under Tennessee court rules, prosecutors are also required to allow
defense lawyers or experts to "inspect" any "tangible objects" in the
state's possession that are "material to preparing the defense," as well as
reports of "scientific tests or experiments" on such items.

In Paul House's case, his lawyer Charles "Chuck" Burks had filed
discovery requests with the prosecution, and, as we will see, later courts
ruled that prosecutors had failed to turn over "Brady material" to Burks
during House's initial trial.

Jury Selection

The U.S. Constitution provides, in the Sixth Amendment, that "In all
criminal prosecutions, the accused shall enjoy the right to a speedy and
public trial, by an impartial jury of the State and district wherein the
crime shall have been committed. . . ." The Constitution doesn't specify
how many jurors are required, but English law set the number at twelve
(based perhaps on the number of disciples at the Last Supper), and that
number has remained constant, at least in felony cases; some states
allow smaller numbers in misdemeanor trials.

Well into the twentieth century, the constitutional requirement of
an **impartial jury** was hard to obtain or enforce. Particularly in small
and rural counties, sheriffs would select potential jurors from "reputa-
ble" citizens whom they knew (all men and almost always white). Jurors
often knew both the victim and the defendant, as well as the witnesses.
Today, jurors are selected from **jury panels** that are randomly chosen
from lists of registered voters or licensed drivers, which excludes many
people, especially the poor or the politically unconcerned. Many people
also ignore notices for jury service and are rarely forced to appear or
fined for their failure to show up.

Once those good citizens who do show up for jury service are
selected for a trial panel, they face questioning from judges and
lawyers during the **voir dire** process, a French term that means "to
see them say." Voir dire (sometimes conducted by judges alone) is

designed to weed out potential jurors who express some bias in the case, toward either the prosecution or the defendant; who know or are related to the victim or the defendant or any of the lawyers or the witnesses; or on whom jury service would impose a burden, such as people who have to care for small children or disabled relatives. Jury panelists who simply refuse to serve (despite laws that make such refusal a misdemeanor offense) or who seem unduly eager to serve are often excused.

Both prosecution and defense lawyers are allowed to ask judges to excuse jury panelists **for cause**, such as expressing a bias or a prejudgment of the case; granting or denying such requests is up to judges, who vary in their willingness to comply. Lawyers are also permitted to exercise **peremptory challenges**, which judges cannot question. A lawyer might suspect that a potential juror has concealed his or her bias during voir dire or simply "looks" disposed toward the other side. The Supreme Court has ruled that prosecutors may not use peremptory challenges to remove jurors solely on the basis of their race or ethnicity (most often used to get rid of black jurors in cases with black defendants, based on notions of "racial sympathy"), requiring prosecutors to present a plausible argument for such racially based challenges. The number of peremptory challenges allowed to each side varies from state to state; Tennessee law currently allows fifteen such challenges in death-penalty cases.

Once a twelve-member jury is seated, judges generally select one or two panel members to serve as **alternate jurors**, who will sit through the trial in case a regular juror becomes ill or is excused for some other reason; if this doesn't happen before the jury begins its deliberations, the alternates are excused, with the judge's thanks for their service.

Reading the Indictment

Once a jury has been seated in a criminal case, the next step is the judge's reading of the indictment to the defendant. This follows the requirement in the Sixth Amendment that the accused "be informed of the nature and cause of the accusation" against him or her. It's a purely formal step, because defendants and their lawyers have already received copies of the indictment.

Opening Statements by the Lawyers

After the indictment has been read, lawyers are allowed to make opening statements to the jury, beginning with the prosecution. These statements, designed to lay out a road map of the evidence the lawyers will present to the jury, are optional, and defense lawyers often decide to forgo them or defer them until after the prosecution has rested its case. Judges instruct jurors that nothing said in opening statements should be taken as "proof" of the evidence they will consider through witnesses and exhibits, but these statements do give lawyers, especially prosecutors, a chance to let the jurors hear an obviously biased preview of their case.

Presentation of Prosecution and Defense Witnesses

The next step in criminal cases is the presentation of prosecution witnesses. Between them, the prosecution's witnesses are required to present evidence to support every element of the case against the defendant; their cumulative testimony and the exhibits they present must convince all of the jurors, beyond any reasonable doubt, of the defendant's guilt. Their testimony begins with **direct examination** by a prosecutor, followed by **cross-examination** by a defense lawyer, who may choose to forgo such examination. Based on questions during cross-examination, prosecutors may engage in **redirect** examination, followed by **recross** questions from the defense, subject to the judge's rulings on the relevance of such follow-up questioning.

After the prosecution completes its questioning of the state's witnesses and **rests its case** against the defendant, defense lawyers are allowed to (and normally do) offer a **motion for a directed verdict of acquittal** to the judge, based on arguments that the prosecution has failed to present sufficient evidence of the defendant's guilt. Such motions are almost always denied but are offered for the record, in case of a future appeal.

If the defense lawyer does not move for a directed verdict of acquittal, or the judge denies one, the next step is the presentation of defense witnesses. This step is optional, and in some cases, the defense lawyer chooses not to put on a case, resting the defense on an argument to the jury (even if the judge has denied a directed acquittal motion) that the state has failed to prove the defendant guilty beyond a reasonable doubt. This is obviously a risky strategy, but there are sometimes no witnesses, including the defendant, who can offer credible testimony on the defendant's behalf. If the defense does call witnesses, they undergo the same sequence of direct examination, cross-examination, redirect, and recross questioning.

Closing Arguments by the Lawyers

After the defense rests its case, assuming its attorneys present witnesses, the next step is for both sets of lawyers to make closing arguments to the jury. In most courts, the prosecution goes first, the defense follows, and the prosecution then gets the last word. Again, closing arguments are optional, but lawyers rarely pass up this last chance to convince the jurors that all of the testimony and the evidence, put together and considered in full context, should result in the verdict for which they argue, of "guilty" or "not guilty." Anyone who has watched television crime dramas such as *Law and Order* has witnessed fictional closing arguments that are hard-hitting and often dramatic, playing on the emotions of the jurors. As we will see, the closing arguments in Paul House's murder case, especially those of the prosecutors, pulled out all of the stops.

The Judge's Charge to the Jury

Following the closing arguments, the judge makes a charge to the jury, in which he or she stresses the presumption of innocence given to criminal defendants, reminds jurors that the prosecution bears the burden of establishing the defendant's guilt beyond a reasonable doubt, lays out the elements of the offense that must be proved, and urges jurors to approach their deliberations with open minds and a willingness to listen to one another in the jury room.

Jury Deliberations

If no jurors have been excused for illness or family emergencies, the judge then dismisses the alternate jurors, and those who remain begin their deliberations in the case. The outcome of these deliberations, needless to say, represents a major (and usually final) turning point in a criminal case.

The jurors first elect a foreperson, charged with tallying the votes and reporting the verdict to the judge. Jury deliberations have no time limit; they are sometimes concluded very quickly, after only one vote, and other times drag on for days or even weeks. Jurors are allowed to inform the judge that they are unable to reach a unanimous verdict; the judge usually sends them back, sometimes with a **dynamite charge** to keep deliberating, with an admonition that jurors in the minority (especially just one or two holdouts) should carefully listen to the majority and reconsider their position. Movies such as the 1957 classic *Twelve Angry Men* have portrayed jury deliberations in which jurors engage in shouting, crying, and browbeating. This does sometimes happen, but most often the debates are civil, despite often sharp divisions revealed in early votes on the verdict.

The vast majority of cases end with a unanimous verdict of "guilty" or (less often) of "not guilty," but there are occasional cases of **hung juries** in which, even after a dynamite charge from the judge, unanimity cannot be reached. In such cases, the judge will declare a **mistrial**, giving the prosecution the choice of trying the case once again or dismissing the charge, which frees the defendant. Jurors are generally allowed, after a trial has concluded, to discuss their votes with lawyers and the media (although most judges caution them against this), and prosecutors who learn that only one or two hold-out jurors voted for acquittal are more likely to opt for a retrial.

Delivering the Jury's Verdict

Following their deliberations, the jurors return to the courtroom to report their verdict, which is usually delivered by the foreperson. If the verdict is "not guilty," the judge immediately frees the defendant from custody; in cases with "guilty" verdicts, the judge can impose a sentence on the spot but more often defers the sentencing until he or she receives reports from probation officers and recommendations from prosecutors and defense lawyers on what sentence they consider appropriate.

Sentencing Hearings in Death-Penalty Cases

In most cases, the jury's verdict and the judge's sentence, if the defendant is convicted, end the judicial proceedings, unless defense lawyers file an appeal with a higher court. In death-penalty cases, however, such as that of Paul House, a **sentencing hearing** is conducted in the trial court, before the same jury that convicted the defendant. These separate hearings were required by the U.S. Supreme Court in the 1972 case of *Furman v. Georgia*, which ruled that placing "unguided" discretion in the hands of trial jurors in deciding whether to impose the death penalty was likely to produce "arbitrary and capricious" decisions. In *Gregg v. Georgia*, decided in 1976, the Court ruled that states could impose death sentences only if jurors considered both **aggravating** and **mitigating** factors, through testimony presented at a separate hearing. Examples of aggravating factors are those listed earlier as factors in the prosecutor's decision to seek the death penalty for Paul House: the "atrocious" manner of Carolyn Muncey's murder, House's prior rape conviction, and the allegations (although not proved at the trial but suggested to jurors by Paul Phillips) of kidnapping and attempted rape. Prosecutors are required to prove such aggravating factors beyond a reasonable doubt, and jurors must decide on them unanimously. Mitigating factors include such things as the defendant's age, mental state, and capabilities; lack of a previous criminal record; evidence of childhood sexual or physical abuse; and records of psychiatric conditions, such as bipolar disease. Defense lawyers are not bound by the rules of evidence at sentencing hearings and can introduce any testimony or records they choose, including pleas for mercy by defendants, parents, and friends. Jurors are directed to "weigh" the aggravating and mitigating factors against each other and can recommend a death sentence only if the former outweigh the latter, although such a balancing is obviously subjective.

In most states, sentencing hearings in capital cases follow the same format as "guilt" trials, beginning with witnesses for the prosecution, followed by those for the defense, and with closing arguments in the prosecution, defense, and prosecution sequence. The jurors then deliberate and reach a verdict that must be unanimous; most states offer only the choices of death or life imprisonment, either with or without the possibility of parole, depending on each state's death-penalty law. Once a verdict is reached, the judge then imposes the sentence; a small number of states allow judges to disregard a death verdict and impose a life sentence instead.

2

The Murder Trial
of Paul House

The murder trial of Paul House began on February 3, 1986, in the Union County courthouse in Maynardville, Tennessee, and concluded five days later, on February 8. The following account is based on 1,726 pages of the trial transcript, from which I have excerpted and quoted, in their own words, questions by the lawyers and answers from the most important witnesses. During the six days of Paul House's trial and sentencing hearing, the prosecution offered the testimony of sixteen witnesses, with six called by the defense. I have included excerpts from the testimonies of eleven of the state's witnesses and two for the defense. What I have left out is primarily testimony from witnesses (most of them law-enforcement officers and staff) who provided details about such matters as calls to the sheriff's department.

Much like a play or a movie, every criminal trial has a cast of characters, with leading roles played by the presiding judge, the prosecutors, and the defense lawyers. In Paul House's trial, the judge was J. Kenneth Porter, who was **sitting by designation** in this case, presumably because the Union County judge who normally would have presided had recused himself because of ties to the prosecutors. Porter was a 1957 graduate of the University of Tennessee Law School in Knoxville.

The prosecution team in the House case was headed by Paul Phillips, a 1975 graduate of Vanderbilt Law School in Nashville, who was first appointed to the post of district attorney general for the five-county judicial district that includes Union County and then elected to that position in 1982 and for three successive eight-year terms. With a folksy manner (addressing jurors as "y'all," which the court reporter used in the trial transcript) and a bulldog tenacity, Phillips bonded with jurors and intimidated defense witnesses. He was assisted in the House case by Clifton "Sonny" Sexton, a long-time deputy and a 1952 graduate of the University of Tennessee Law School. Facing Phillips and Sexton was Charles "Chuck" Burks, hired by Paul House's mother, Joyce, to defend her son. A 1973 graduate of the Memphis State University Law School, Burks had a practice in Knoxville and had handled several murder cases. Like Phillips, he also adopted the "y'all" manner with jurors.

Setting a Time Frame for Carolyn Muncey's Disappearance

The prosecution's case in Paul House's trial began with testimony from Pam Luttrell, who lived with her husband, Jerry, their young daughter, Angie, and a baby, across the road from the Munceys' house. Paul Phillips and Sonny Sexton opened their case with Pam Luttrell to establish a time frame for Carolyn Muncey's disappearance on the night of her death. Sexton conducted her direct examination.

Pam first said that Carolyn and her children, Lora and Matt, had come over to visit about 8:00 P.M. on that Saturday night. The two women chatted while Pam fed her baby and the children played. According to Pam, Carolyn said that "Little Hube had gone to dig a grave, and he hadn't come back, but that was all right, because she was going to make him take her fishing the next day." Carolyn and her kids left about an hour later, when it was getting "dusky dark," although Pam couldn't be sure about the time.

Around 1:00 A.M., while Pam was up for another baby feeding, Little Hube knocked on the Luttrells' door and came in with Lora and Matt.

Little Hube said that "Carolyn was gone and he couldn't find her." He used Pam's phone to call his father and brother to come over and look for Carolyn, then left the children with Pam when his relatives arrived at the Munceys' house. While the children were at Pam's house, she said, "Lora was talking to me and then Matt kept butting in, and he said— sister, they said Daddy had a wreck, they said Daddy had a wreck."

During her cross-examination by Chuck Burks, Pam recalled her conversation with Lora, who told Pam that someone had come to the Munceys' house after Carolyn brought them home, that Lora "thought she heard a horn" blowing. When Carolyn answered the door, Lora heard from her bedroom someone ask for "Bubbie," a nickname that Little Hube's family and relatives called him. Pam also told Burks that Lora had told her that the voice "sounded like my Paw-Paw," which is what the Muncey children called Little Hube's father. Burks then asked Pam whether she had heard anything else that night, after Carolyn and her children left. "I heard a car rev its motor as it went down the road," Pam replied, putting the time she heard this at about 10:00 P.M. This "revving" was something, Pam explained, that Little Hube habitually did as he turned into his rather steep driveway, although Pam added that other people also "revved" their vehicles at the driveway. Burks obviously meant to suggest to the jurors that Little Hube might have come home at some time before Carolyn disappeared, although Pam's testimony gave Burks no evidence to suggest that Little Hube had anything to do with her disappearance.

After Burks finished with Pam, Sonny Sexton took over with the redirect examination, going back to Lora's visit at 1:00 A.M. Pam recounted that Lora had first been woken up when "she thought she heard a horn blow, and somebody asked if Bubbie was home, and her mama told them—no. And then she said she didn't know if she went back to sleep or not, but then she heard her mama going down the steps crying, . . . and she told me that she heard her mama say—Oh God, no, not me." Sexton's point with these questions was that whoever might have driven up to the Munceys' house and asked for "Bubbie," it was unlikely to have been Little Hube, and that Carolyn's exclamation after she later left the house, crying, might be related to Matt's statement to Pam that "they said Daddy had a wreck," presumably to lure Carolyn out of her house.

After Pam Luttrell was excused, Sexton called Lora Muncey to the witness stand. The jurors undoubtedly felt sympathy for a child who had lost her mother, and some probably cast glances at the burly young man who was accused of Carolyn's brutal murder. Sexton asked Lora whether anything had happened after she returned from the Luttrells' house "that caused your mother to be upset or did you hear anything?" Lora replied that when someone first came to house, "It sounded like Paw-Paw said—where's Daddy at, and she said, 'Digging a grave.'" Some time after that, Lora continued, someone came and said "that Daddy had a wreck down the road, and she started crying. . . ."

When asked what she and Matt had next done, Lora said, "We waited a few minutes, and then we got up, and we went down to Pam's and they was in bed, and then we went up to Mike Clinton's, and she wasn't up there." Mike Clinton and his wife, Patricia, lived next door to the Munceys' house, about a hundred feet away. Clinton later testified, as a defense witness called by Chuck Burks, that Lora and Matt had come to his door just before 11:00 P.M., while Clinton was watching television and waiting for the nightly news. After she and Matt went back home, Lora continued, "Daddy came in and fixed him a bologna sandwich, and he took a bite of it, and he says—'Sissy, where is Mommy at?' and I said—'She hasn't been here for a little while.'" At that point, after looking around the house and outside, Little Hube took Lora and Matt to the Luttrells' house.

In his brief cross-examination of Lora, Chuck Burks asked her whether Carolyn had left the house "in a car or truck," to which Lora answered, "I ain't for sure." Burks intended with this question to antici- pate the later defense testimony of Donna Turner, in whose trailer Paul House lived, that House had left her place that night on foot, sometime between 10:30 and 10:45 P.M., and had not driven her car. If Carolyn had left her house in a car or a truck, as Burks suggested, the person who lured her out with a story of Little Hube's "wreck" could not have been House, although this point was probably lost on the jurors.

Between them, the testimony of Pam Luttrell and Lora House estab- lished a time frame for Carolyn's disappearance as sometime between 8:30 and 10:45 that Saturday night, considering that it would likely have taken Lora and Matt at least ten minutes to get dressed, go down the driveway and across the road to the Luttrells' house, and then walk back up to the Clintons' before 11:00 P.M. Neither Pam nor Lora, of course, had mentioned Paul House or implicated him in any way in Carolyn's murder. The defense case, as we shall see, rested almost entirely on the credibility of House's alibi for his whereabouts during this time frame.

Billy Ray Hensley Takes a "Glance" Down Ridgecrest Road

After Lora Muncey left the witness stand, Sonny Sexton called Billy Ray Hensley to testify. Hensley, who tended tobacco fields and was a part-time truck driver, was Carolyn's first cousin. To set the scene, the Munceys' house was off Ridgecrest Road, which ran uphill for about two miles from Tazewell Pike, a two-lane state highway that connected the town of Luttrell with Knoxville, some twenty miles to the west. Ridgecrest Road intersected with Bear Hollow Road about six hundred feet from the Munceys' driveway. If you were driving on Bear Hollow Road, there was a left turn onto Ridgecrest.

Sexton first asked Hensley how he had learned of Carolyn's disappearance on Saturday night. About 2:00 P.M. on Sunday, Hensley said, his wife got a phone call and said, "It was Little Hube's wife, and she's missing." Deciding to look for Little Hube and offer his help in searching for Carolyn and thinking that Little Hube might be home, Hensley headed in his car to the intersection of Bear Hollow Road and Ridgecrest. "I went to the top of the ridge" where the two roads intersected, Hensley said, "and just before I rounded the curve on Ridgecrest, I saw Mr. House come out from under a bank, wiping his hands on a black rag. And I went on down to Little Hube's driveway. I pulled up in the driveway where I could see up toward Little Hube's house, and I seen Little Hube's car wasn't there, and I backed out in the road and come back towards" Bear Hollow Road. "And that is when Mr. House flagged me down . . . through the windshield" of the car he was driving in the opposite direction. The two cars stopped beside each other, and Hensley and House had a brief conversation. According to Hensley, House "said that he was looking for Little Hube Muncey, he heard that he was over there [at a spot off Tazewell Pike] getting drunk, and I said—yes, I am looking for him, too."

After this conversation, House continued down Ridgecrest toward Tazewell Pike, and Hensley went back up to Bear Hollow Road, thinking that Little Hube might be at this father's house. As he drove, Hensley said, "I got to thinking to myself—he's hunting Little Hube—what would he be doing off that bank . . . And I went over to Big Hube's house . . . and saw Little Hube's car." When he arrived at Big Hube's, Hensley spotted his friend Jackie Adkins, just as House pulled in. Telling Adkins of his "suspicion" that House would not have looked for Little Hube down the embankment on the other side of the road from the Munceys' house, Hensley and Adkins headed back in Hensley's car to Ridgecrest Road. When they arrived at the spot where Hensley said he saw House coming up from the embankment, he and Adkins stopped and looked over the side. At the bottom, out of view from the road, they saw Carolyn Muncey's body, covered loosely with brush and tree branches. Hensley then said that he and Adkins got back in the car, went to a nearby house, and called the sheriff's department to report their discovery.

Later that afternoon, Hensley returned to the spot where he and Adkins had discovered Carolyn's body. The Union County sheriff, Earl Loy, was directing the deputies and the police officers who conducted a search for any physical evidence and took photographs of the scene. A few minutes later, Paul House arrived in Donna Turner's car, accompanied by Little Hube Muncey. Hensley then told Sheriff Loy that House was the man he had seen coming up from the embankment, which prompted Loy to ask House to come in that evening for an interview at the sheriff's office in Maynardville, which House agreed to do. At this point, House became the primary suspect in Carolyn's murder.

After Sonny Sexton completed his questioning of Billy Ray Hensley, Chuck Burks began his cross-examination. Burks questioned Hensley about an obvious discrepancy between Hensley's assertion on direct examination that he first saw Paul House before he reached the intersection of Bear Hollow and Ridgecrest roads and his earlier statement to the police that he had traveled some five hundred feet before he saw House. Burks then handed Hensley some photographs taken by the police at the site where Carolyn's body was found.

"Do any of those pictures depict the view that you had when you saw Mr. House?" Burks asked, referring to the view from Bear Hollow Road.

"Not from where I was at, no," Hensley replied.

Burks then handed Hensley a photograph looking up Ridgecrest toward Bear Hollow Road. "And up and down this road you do have some things that block your view from [Bear Hollow Road], do you not?" Burks asked. "You have a barn, you have a big tree, you have got other items throughout here, do you not?"

"I'd say you do," Hensley agreed.

Burks continued. "Isn't it a fact that if a person was down in the embankment or at any point on the embankment, you couldn't see them from the roadway, could you?"

"No, not on the bank," Hensley conceded.

"So, you couldn't see someone walking up or climbing up the bank, could you?" Hensley then gave Burks ammunition for another shot at his credibility. "What I saw was somebody appear out of nowhere," he replied.

Burks next returned to Hensley's account of first having seen House from Bear Hollow Road. "How long of a period of time did you keep your eyes fixed up there, or was it just a glance up and glance back? . . . How much time did you take to look over there and turn back? Tell the jury."

"I don't know," Hensley replied, "just a second or two."

"Just a glance?" Burks suggested.

"Yeah," Hensley conceded.

Whether this aggressive cross-examination swayed any jurors to question Hensley's credibility would await their verdict at the trial's end. Yet there are two points worth mentioning here, which cast doubt on the thoroughness of Chuck Burks's trial preparation. First, he did not produce a photograph, taken from Bear Hollow Road, that would have made it clear that Hensley's view of the spot where he said he observed House coming up from the embankment was in fact obstructed by a large barn and trees, as well as overhanging foliage. Burks could have hired a photographer to take such pictures and then introduced them into evidence. Hensley did concede to Burks, looking at photos the police made from the opposite direction, that his view from Bear Hollow Road would have been obstructed, but photos made from Hensley's alleged viewpoint would have been more likely to impress jurors. Why Burks did not introduce such photos remains a mystery.

Second, Burks did not call an expert witness in eyewitness testimony, who might have undermined Hensley's testimony that he would have had great difficulty in identifying House as the person he allegedly saw "coming up" from the embankment, from a distance of five hundred to six hundred feet, during a "glance" of just one or two seconds. At such a distance, a person who was six feet tall would have an "apparent height" of only one inch; that person's head would have an apparent height of about one-sixth of an inch. Burks could easily have found an expert witness, from as nearby as the University of Tennessee in Knoxville, to make this point, aided by photographs showing the great reduction in the "apparent height" of people viewed from a distance of some five hundred to six hundred feet, as opposed to close-up viewpoints. To be fair, Burks probably didn't think of hiring an expert witness to make this argument, which might not have impressed the jurors in any event.

Paul House's Phony Alibi and the Discovery of His "Blood-Spotted" Jeans

Billy Ray Hensley's account of Paul House's "suspicious" behavior on Ridgecrest Road on Sunday afternoon did not connect House to Carolyn Muncey's disappearance and murder the night before, but it prompted investigators to question House about his activities and whereabouts on that night. After Hensley left the witness stand, the next four prosecution witnesses told jurors of the events that led to House's arrest for the murder.

Paul Phillips first called Earl Loy, the Union County sheriff. Loy had spoken with House during an interview at the jail on the night after Carolyn disappeared. Phillips asked Loy only one significant question, which led to the most important piece of physical evidence in the case, the blue jeans that Paul House had worn the night of Carolyn Muncey's death, and which were later discovered at the trailer where House lived with his girlfriend, Donna Turner. Loy said he noticed during this interview that House "had on clean blue jeans with a crease ironed in them, and I asked him if that was the same clothes he wore Saturday, the day before. He hesitated just said, 'Yeah, the blue jeans are,' but said— 'I have changed shirts.'"

Loy had possibly been tipped off about the jeans by Donna Turner, who had been pressured to reveal what she knew by the state's next witness, Bill Breeding, the criminal investigator in the Union County Sheriff's Department. Sonny Sexton conducted Breeding's examination, beginning with his discovery of House's jeans, which Breeding had found at the bottom of Turner's laundry hamper. Breeding noted that he had observed several "brownish-reddish" spots on the jeans, which he suspected were blood, so he took them for evidence.

Considering the crucial importance of the jeans to the prosecution's case, as the only piece of physical evidence that supposedly connected Paul House to Carolyn Muncey's murder, it seems puzzling that if House had murdered her, he would have simply dumped the jeans in Turner's laundry hamper. If he knew that Carolyn's blood was on the jeans, he could have washed them himself or disposed of them by burning or burying them in the woods. This is even more puzzling, given the prosecution's suggestion, during closing arguments, that House had taken the risk, during broad daylight, of returning to the spot where Muncey's body was found to retrieve the blue tank top he had worn the night of her murder, which prosecutors also suggested (without ever having found the missing tank top) was the "black rag" that Billy Ray Hensley said he observed in House's hands when he supposedly climbed up from the embankment. If the tank top linked House to the murder, the blood-spotted jeans would have provided even more incriminating evidence against him.

On cross-examination, Chuck Burks did not question Breeding about his discovery and retrieval of House's jeans. He focused instead on the statement Breeding had taken from Billy Ray Hensley about having seen Paul House on the afternoon when Carolyn Muncey's body had been discovered. In that statement, Hensley had told Breeding that he first spotted Paul House after Hensley had rounded the turn from Bear Hollow Road and traveled some five hundred feet down Ridgecrest. This was a crucial issue, in light of Hensley's statement about the "black rag" in House's hands and the prosecution's suggestion (verging on an assertion) that it was the missing tank top that House had supposedly come to retrieve, making him the primary suspect in Carolyn Muncey's murder. Burks asked whether Breeding had reviewed the statement after it was prepared or had made any corrections or changes to it, to which Breeding replied, "I don't think I did." Given the obvious discrepancy between Hensley's trial testimony and his statement to Breeding, jurors were left to decide which was more credible.

House's status as a suspect was further driven home to the jurors by the testimony of Ray Presnell, an agent of the Tennessee Bureau of Investigation, who took a statement from House on the day after Carolyn Muncey's death. Sonny Sexton conducted Presnell's examination, asking him to read from House's statement, which was not recorded or taken down verbatim but was later reconstructed from Presnell's notes of the interview. "I have known Carolyn Muncey since approximately April 1985," Presnell quoted House as saying. "I met her through my step dad, Bill Silvey. . . [House] said that he became friends with [Carolyn and Little Hube] and went to their house at least three times. He stated that he did not have sex relations with Carolyn, did not touch her sexually, said the last time he had seen Carolyn was at Little Hube's residence . . . at least a month ago. . . ."

Presnell then read from House's statement about his activities on the day of Carolyn's disappearance. "I stayed at Donna's and slept until about 5:30 P.M., got up . . . I read a book until about 7:00 P.M. Then watched the AIDS concert [on TV] until about 7:40 P.M., then watched *Wild, Wild West* until 9:00 P.M., then watched *Welcome to Hard Times*, it was a Western, until 11:00 P.M. Then went to bed and got up at 10:00 A.M., today, July 14th, on Sunday." If this detailed account was true and could be confirmed by Turner (and assuming the jurors found it credible), then House had an alibi for his whereabouts during the time frame of Carolyn's disappearance. Sexton then asked whether Turner had backed up House's alibi. "Well, that night it was confirmed with Donna Turner," Presnell answered, "but she later changed her story." With that statement, House's credibility vanished, along with that of Turner's later account of his second alibi, during her testimony as a defense witness.

Presnell then moved on to House's account of his activities on Sunday, July 14, on which House said he spent the morning helping his mother, Joyce, move to Knoxville (she was splitting up with her husband, Bill Silvey) and came back to Donna Turner's trailer about noon. His mother came over about 2:00 P.M. and told House that Carolyn had disappeared. House took Donna's car and drove to the Munceys' house, missed the driveway, parked up the road, went back and saw that Little Hube's car wasn't there, got back in the car, and was driving toward Tazewell Pike when he saw Billy Ray Hensley's car parked on the road. He asked Hensley, whom he hadn't met before, if he knew Little Hube and said he was looking for him, to offer help in searching for Carolyn. The two men parted, going in opposite directions, and House went to Bill Silvey's, where he saw Little Hube. House concluded by telling Presnell that "I swear I have not seen Carolyn Muncey for over a month. I did not ever have sex with her, I knew Little Hube better than her." This last statement suggests that Presnell suspected that House had at least had an affair with Carolyn or even that rape was a motive for her murder. In his brief cross-examination of Presnell, Chuck Burks elicited that Presnell asked questions of House and wrote down answers, not always verbatim.

The state's next witness, Charles Scott, also a Tennessee Bureau of Investigation agent, interviewed House the following day, on Monday, July 15. His account of that interview tracked House's statement to Presnell almost exactly. Scott was questioned by Sonny Sexton, who asked whether House "told you he was home all night [on Saturday] with Donna Turner?" Scott replied that he had. Sexton next asked if Donna Turner had confirmed that alibi. Scott responded that she had not, adding that she first told him that House had been at her trailer all of Saturday night. Sexton continued, "Then later did she come back to you after you had told her about the seriousness of covering up for homicide, did she tell you about 10:30, maybe 10:45, that being a 'guesstimate'?" "That's true," Scott replied. This exchange makes it clear that House, even before any physical evidence linked him to Carolyn Muncey, was considered a suspect in her murder.

Nailing Down the Time Frame and the Cause of Carolyn Muncey's Death

It is important in murder cases for the prosecution to establish, as nearly as possible, the cause and the time of the victim's death, both to rule out accident, suicide, or natural causes for the death and to confirm or question the alibis of suspects. This is sometimes difficult, given the decomposition of bodies that are not found for some time after the death. In the case of Carolyn Muncey, however, her body was discovered the day after her death, and witnesses testified that she had disappeared from her house some sixteen hours earlier. To establish the cause and the time of her death, the state called Dr. Alex Carabia, a pathologist who performed the autopsy on her body, at a morgue in nearby Oak Ridge, about nine hours after her body was discovered.

Paul Phillips conducted the examination of Dr. Carabia, who had performed hundreds of autopsies and had practiced forensic pathology for twenty-six years. Phillips first asked Carabia to describe the injuries he found on the body. "I found on Mrs. Muncey an abrasion on the left side of the forehead. . . . I found that she had a black eye on the left side. . . . She had several bruises on the anterior aspect of the neck and also a bruise on the posterior aspect of the neck, the back of the neck. She had abrasions on both thighs. . . . She had blood stained hands, both hands were stained. . . . The blood was also on her fingers and up to the wrists, both wrists. Those were the most important findings when I examined the body previous to the autopsy." Phillips asked whether the bruises could be "consistent with a struggle, a fight?" Carabia agreed that they could, although none of these injuries could have caused Carolyn's death.

Phillips then asked about the cause of death. Carabia said he found "a large hemorrhage under the skin of the left side of her forehead." Would that be consistent with being hit? Phillips inquired, to which Carabia answered "Yes. . . . I think she died of [a] blow to the head," between one and two hours after receiving the blow. Carabia then agreed with Phillips that the "abrasion" on the left side of Carolyn's forehead was "consistent with having received a hard blow with a fist." As we shall see, the word *abrasion* would, thirteen years later, become highly disputed as the proper term to describe this wound and its possible connection with the cause of her death. Based on the digestive state of the contents of Carolyn's stomach, Carabia estimated her time of death as between 9:00 and 11:00 P.M. on the day she disappeared.

In his cross-examination of Dr. Carabia, Chuck Burks asked about the blow to the left forehead that the pathologist concluded had caused Carolyn's death. "You are not suggesting how she received this blow, whether it be by an instrument, by a fist, or her head striking some object, are you? It would be consistent with all three of those, would it not?" When Carabia agreed, Burks asked, "And, of course, the point is we just really don't know what caused that blow, do we?"

"I don't know," Carabia answered. Burks had no evidence to back up his suspicion that Carolyn Muncey received the fatal blow by being shoved or thrown against some hard object, such as the corner or the edge of a table; he simply wanted to suggest that maybe the blow didn't come from a fist, a suggestion that was probably lost on the jury.

The "93 Percent Probability" That Carolyn Muncey's Blood Was on House's Jeans

The state's most important witness, along with Billy Ray Hensley, was Paul Bigbee, an FBI serologist and specialist in blood analysis. Early on Tuesday, July 16, Bigbee had received a cardboard box that Bill Breeding had driven to the FBI lab in Washington, D.C. The box contained the blue jeans Breeding had retrieved from Donna Turner's laundry hamper, packed in a paper bag; a Styrofoam container that held four vials of blood that Dr. Carabia had taken from Carolyn Muncey's body; a vial of Paul House's blood, which he had volunteered to provide; an envelope with two or three hairs that Breeding had found in her hand; and bags that held the clothing Carolyn had been wearing when her body was discovered: a cotton bra, panties, a nightgown, and a nylon housecoat.

Significantly, as would become clear thirteen years later, the vials of blood were closed with plastic stoppers but not sealed by tape to the vials, nor were they protected from "degradation" with a preservative. Testimony during a later hearing would show that the stoppers had come loose, and an entire vial was empty, but the trial jury never learned of this crucial point.

After receiving the material from Breeding, Bigbee examined the pair of blue jeans that belonged to Paul House. He also examined Carolyn's clothing and found semen stains on her nightgown and panties. The prosecution wanted to impress on the jurors that five spots of blood on House's jeans had most likely come from her body, during a fatal struggle with House, and that he had deposited the semen on her clothing during an attempt to rape her.

Paul Phillips examined Bigbee, asking him first what he found on House's jeans. "I found blood on these blue jeans that was consistent with that from Carolyn Muncey," Bigbee answered. Phillips then led Bigbee through a lengthy explanation of blood group typing, in which Bigbee used terms such as *phosphoglucomutase* and *haptoglobin*, which were undoubtedly lost on the jurors but probably impressed them with his expertise. Based on the blood characteristics that Bigbee described, Phillips asked an important question: "So, what percentage of the population would [have] the same characteristics that Carolyn does and that the jeans show? When you take all of the characteristics into account." Bigbee's answer was precise: "If I compared those, only the items found on the jeans, approximately 6.75 percent of the population would have the same series of characteristics."

Phillips then moved to another important point in the prosecution's case: "Now, in addition to the blood on his blue jeans . . . did you also examine her clothing for the presence of any other body fluids?" Bigbee replied that "I found semen in the panties and on the gown." His testimony got technical again, after Phillips asked whether his testing could determine "the person that semen is from?" Bigbee replied that "if the person who deposited the semen is a secretor, which means 80 percent of the population secrete the ABO blood group substances in other body fluids, such as semen and saliva, if that person is a secretor, then the ABO blood type can be determined from the semen." He added that "the person who deposited that semen was a blood type A." Paul House, Bigbee noted, was both a secretor and had blood type A.

In cross-examining Bigbee, Chuck Burks did elicit one admission: he asked whether Bigbee could say how long the blood stains had been on House's jeans, to which Bigbee answered that his testing could not determine that. Burks also pointed out that Bigbee had received a sample of Little Hube Muncey's blood but could not determine whether he was a secretor and could have deposited the semen on his wife's clothing. Bigbee said he would have needed a saliva sample to determine Little Hube's secretor status. "And did you ever get a saliva sample from the state to determine whether or not he was in fact a secretor?" Burks asked.

"No, I did not," Bigbee replied.

Burks finally showed Bigbee an article from a law enforcement journal, written by another FBI forensic specialist, and read to Bigbee this quote: "At the present time, no serologist, including those at the FBI laboratory, can state unequivocally that a stain was deposited by one individual to the exclusion of all others." Bigbee agreed that "there is no serologist that can do that."

Taken together, Bigbee's examination by Phillips and his cross-examination by Burks undoubtedly left jurors impressed with the FBI technician's expertise and inclined to accept Phillips's suggestion that the blood on Paul House's jeans must have come from Carolyn Muncey, during a struggle for her life with a man who intended to rape her, and that House had deposited his semen on her clothing before killing her with a blow to her head.

Two points about Bigbee's testimony deserve mention here. First, although it seemed almost certain that the blood on Paul House's jeans came from Carolyn Muncey's body, Bigbee could not say how, when, or where that blood had been deposited on the jeans. Second, Bigbee's testimony about the semen on Carolyn's clothing hardly offered conclusive evidence that it came from House. Bigbee stated that 80 percent of the population are "secretors" of the most common "A," "B," and "O" blood types, and that both House and the blood on his jeans came from the "A" type. Given the fact, which Bigbee did not mention, that about 40 percent of the U.S. population belong to the "A" type, a little simple math demonstrates that some 36 percent of the male population could just as likely have deposited that semen. The jurors in House's trial, however, most likely concluded that because House had type "A" blood and the semen on Carolyn's clothing was also type "A," that the semen came from him, during the attempted rape that provided the motive for the prosecution's theory of the case.

This latter point, in retrospect, offers a sad irony in the House case. Paul Bigbee conducted his testing of the semen stains in 1986, without the benefit of the DNA testing that would have proved conclusively that the semen did not come from House. Although DNA testing, matching samples of blood and semen to establish or disprove their genetic connection, had been developed in England a few years earlier, not until 1987 did American courts accept DNA testing as scientifically valid and admissible in evidence. Had House's trial taken place a year later than 1986, and if Chuck Burks had retained an expert witness on DNA testing, he could have shown that House had not deposited the semen on Carolyn's clothing, thus demolishing the prosecution's rape motive. After all, if House had not lured Carolyn from her house with the intention of raping her, what other motive could there be? Certainly not ransom, given the Munceys' poverty.

But the whole case turned on the rape motive.

Paul House's Defense against the Murder Charge

After the prosecution rested its case against Paul House, it was time for Chuck Burks to call his defense witnesses. He could not put House on the stand to defend himself, however, because prosecutors would have been able to question him about his prior rape conviction in Utah, which would have made a guilty verdict a virtual certainty. Defense lawyers in murder cases rarely subject their clients to cross-examination, largely because most of them have criminal records that jurors would hold against them, despite judicial instructions not to do so. Burks probably knew or at least suspected that most of the jurors were already aware of House's rape conviction, given the rapid spread of gossip in small towns and rural counties, but putting House on the stand was a risk he could not take.

From the beginning of the case, Burks framed his defense strategy around one main issue, the time frame of Carolyn Muncey's disappearance and Paul House's whereabouts at that time. Pam Luttrell had testified for the prosecution that Carolyn had left the Luttrells' house around 8:30 or 9:00 on the night of her death. Dr. Carabia had testified that she had most likely died between 9:00 and 11:00. To commit the murder, House would have had to arrive at the Munceys' house during those two hours. In order to nail down this time frame, Burks called as a defense witness Mike Clinton, the Munceys' neighbor, who testified that just before 11:00 that night, Carolyn's children, Lora and Matt, "came up to the house and knocked on the door and asked if we had seen their mother." Clinton was sure of the time because he was waiting to watch the 11:00 news on television and "looked at the clock" when the children knocked on his door. Clinton was a credible witness, and Paul Phillips did not challenge his testimony. From the testimony of Lora Muncey, it was also clear that she and Matt had noticed their mother's absence even earlier than 11:00, because they first got dressed, went down the driveway, crossed the road, and knocked on the Luttrells' door, although no one answered. It seems reasonable that the children would have left their house sometime around 10:45.

Given this time frame, Burks hoped to convince the jurors that House had been at Donna Turner's trailer, almost two miles from the Munceys' house, until 10:45 that night, making it impossible for him to have committed the murder. Burks called Turner to make this assertion, hoping that jurors would believe her account, despite her admission that she had initially lied to investigators in claiming that House had stayed in her trailer that whole night. But this thin reed was all that Burks could rely on, unless the jurors had a "reasonable doubt" as to the testimony of Billy Ray Hensley and Paul Bigbee, which seemed unlikely. So Burks did what he could in questioning Donna Turner, beginning with the night of Carolyn Muncey's disappearance.

Donna said that she and House had been watching television, listing the same programs (the Live Aid concert and a western starring Henry Fonda) that House had claimed to watch in his statement to Charles Scott, while Donna was ironing clothes in the living room. "I had just got through finishing ironing," she said, "and I have got a VCR . . . that has a clock on it, and I looked down, and it had 10:45 on it, and he got up [and] said—'I believe I will go for a walk.' And I said—'When will you be back?' and he—I turned around to go into the hall of my trailer with the clothes, and when I was going into the hall, he was going out the door."

After House left for his walk along the dark country roads, Donna watched a movie on the VCR until House returned about an hour later, around midnight. He was sweaty and out of breath and was missing the blue tank top he had been wearing, along with his tennis shoes. "Donna, somebody tried to kill me," House blurted out. According to Donna, House told a story of a truck pulling up behind him, with at least two men who got out and came after House. House told Donna that the men "called him some names and then they told him he didn't belong here anymore. And he said that he didn't pay no attention to it, that he kept on walking and then he said that they stopped, pulled in behind him . . . and that one of them got out and grabbed him by the shoulder . . . and he said he swung around with his right hand and he hit something. And then he said that he took off down the bank and started running, and they fired two shots at him. . . . I tried to get him to see if he could tell who done it, 'cause I kind of thought my ex-husband had something to do with it." House told Donna the men had torn his tank top during this altercation "to where it wouldn't stay on him and he said—'I just throwed it off when I was running.'"

Chuck Burks asked Donna why she had first told the police that House had not left her trailer that night. "I was scared for him," she replied. "They was telling me that they believed that I was withholding something from them and that, you know, they scared me. . . . [T]hey brought my sister in there and she said, 'Please tell them the truth,' and I started crying, and she said that they told her that they had an eyewitness that saw him walking at the time I said he was here and she said— 'You had better tell them the truth.' I told them the truth. I told them exactly what I have said here." During his lengthy and aggressive cross-examination of Turner, Sonny Sexton could not shake her story, except to get her to admit that it might have been closer to 10:30 when House left for his walk, although she professed to be sure it was 10:45. Donna's testimony confronted the jurors with a classic "either-or" choice: if they believed her, Paul House could not have murdered Carolyn Muncey; if they didn't, they were almost certain to convict him. Her admission that her first alibi for House was false and the rather bizarre story of his second alibi made House's conviction almost certain, assuming the jurors credited the testimony of Billy Ray Hensley and Paul Bigbee.

Closing Arguments from the Lawyers

Once Chuck Burks rested his defense, the trial moved to closing arguments to the jurors. Sonny Sexton began for the prosecution. To better appreciate its emotional delivery and its likely impact on deeply religious jurors in rural Tennessee, portions of Sexton's summation are worth quoting at some length: "July thirteenth was a very fateful occasion for Carolyn Muncey. She was a woman in her late twenties, and when she put her children to bed that night, I am sure she didn't anticipate that would be the last time she would see them. Nor did she realize that the last meal she had would be her last supper. But at some time after that she was deceived, not unlike Eve was in the Garden of Eden [with] the serpent and leaving the children in the dark—and going off with someone, because of the concern she had for her husband. She had been told he had had an accident. At that time I'm sure she hadn't anticipated that she would be brutally beaten, battered, and strangled, and have her body dumped into a brush pile to be found by the insects and the rodents. There is one good thing about that, because she doesn't have to endure the pain in this world any longer. See, some other people aren't quite that fortunate. Because you have got her son, Matthew, who [won't] experience the warmth of a mother's touch, he won't know what it is like when he brings his finger or a skinned knee to have her . . . kiss the hurt away. Of course, you have got Lora who will maybe someday understand why her mother left crying that night and left her alone, her and her brother. Without explanation."

Sexton concluded with these words: "Mr. House has an excellent attorney, Mr. Burks, and that is his job. He has put on a good defense. He has cross-examined our witnesses, and he represents the defense side of this. Carolyn Muncey doesn't have anybody but us, there is nothing she can say. It is circumstantial because our eyewitness is in the cemetery somewhere out at Luttrell. We have to represent her, and we want justice done, we want justice done for her, Lora, Matthew, Little Hube, the Luttrell community of Union County." Observers at the trial noticed tears streaming down the faces of several jurors when Sexton took his seat.

Chuck Burks spoke next. Like most defense lawyers, he stressed to the jurors the concept of **reasonable doubt** in assessing the prosecution's case and the **circumstantial** nature of the state's case against Paul House. "When the evidence is made up entirely of circumstantial evidence," he said, "you must find that all of the essential facts are consistent with the state's theory, the hypothesis of the defendant's guilt, consider all of the evidence, and compare it with this hypothesis. Of all the facts proven, the facts must exclude—and I think that is a key word—must exclude every other reasonable theory or hypothesis except that of guilt. And the facts must convince the mind beyond a reasonable doubt that the defendant is the one who committed the offense."

Burks next discussed the testimony of Billy Ray Hensley and his claim that he saw Paul House "coming out of the embankment" at the spot where Carolyn Muncey's body was found. "That's the single most crucial element in this entire case as it relates to Paul Gregory House," Burks said. He continued, "Where is the photograph of what Bill Hensley saw if the state relies so heavily on what he saw? Where is it? Is it [missing] because it really shows that you couldn't see much, over one and a half football fields' distance, with a dark shaded, green background. . . . What did he see about Paul Gregory House? And where is the photograph? . . . That is the case that the state asks you to convict Paul Gregory House and send him to the penitentiary or kill him."

Donna Turner's second alibi for House was the only hope for his acquittal. Burks told the jurors that the state had "the problem of the time of [Carolyn Muncey's] death and the time that we know she was missing. We know that she is missing at 11:00 P.M. We know that she has been gone for some point in time before that. Everybody agrees on that. . . . Donna Turner . . . has come in here, under oath, and has told you the best she can that [House did not leave her trailer] until 10:45. And not only that, but when he left, he took no car. . . . [Y]ou have to totally disregard what she has to say, what she has sworn to under oath in this case, before you can consider the rest of the state's proof. If you get to that one point, and you say—'I believe her,' the state's case is over with. That's the facts. If you say—'I am not sure whether I believe her or not,' the state's case is over with, because that is reasonable doubt."

Burks finally discussed a crucial issue in the case: "Why was Carolyn Muncey killed? We don't know. Is it important to have some motive? In your minds? What motive did Paul Gregory House have to go over and kill a woman that he barely knew? Who was still dressed, still clad in her clothes. What motive have they shown? . . . Paul Gregory House had no motive to do this. . . . All we ask [is] that truth and justice serve in this case. If the state hasn't proved their case beyond a reasonable doubt, or if you just don't know, justice dictates a verdict of not guilty."

Paul Phillips had the last word in the closing arguments, telling the jurors seventeen times that Paul House had "lied" in his statements to the police and the investigators and in telling Donna Turner the "wild story" about being attacked by unknown assailants during his late-night walk. "All the way down—lies, lies, lies," Phillips shouted to the jurors.

Chuck Burks had expressed doubt to the jurors that House would return "in broad daylight" to retrieve the blue tank top (which was never found). The prosecution had suggested it was the "black rag" that Billy Ray Hensley said he saw in House's hands when he came up from the embankment. Phillips said in a scornful voice: "Well, I will answer that, Mr. Burks. Here is why you would do that in broad daylight. Because, folks, he committed this crime at night, as fast as he could, he got back to Donna Turner's trailer to try to create for himself an alibi. But then, something happened and he realized that he had lost his tank top, and when he realized that, he started thinking. 'Where did I lose that tank top?'—and he remembered it being torn off of him. . . . So, there is a tank top, he is afraid, at the scene of the crime. That tank top he knows can be linked to him. . . . So, he has got to go over there and get that tank top, or it is discovered. He has got to. What do you mean—broad daylight? You can't let that body be found with that tank top there. . . . So, what do you do? Well, you say— 'Donna, let me go see Little Hube, let me have your car. . . . To see—is the coast clear, is anybody at Carolyn's, is anybody going to see me? . . . I have gone down the road, there is nobody around. No patrol cars. No Munceys. Glory hallelujah—I am going to get my tank top, and nobody will know what I did to Carolyn.' Well, do you know what happens when evil men and evil spirits are bent on mischief? Something intervenes. Something happens that allows a jury to find out who committed a terrible crime. Something happened, like a ray of sunshine. . . . And that ray of sunshine in this case was Billy Ray Hensley. He told you on this stand, he doesn't know what caused him to go down that road. I don't know either. But I can tell you this. It was a providential event because it allowed this jury to know who killed Carolyn Muncey, because that is what started the clues unfolding to prove him guilty beyond a reasonable doubt. The best he could do in his evil design to conceal this crime was undone when Mr. Hensley came down this road."

Phillips then addressed the question of motive for the murder. "Why did Mr. House kill Carolyn Muncey? . . . The evidence at the scene which seemed to suggest that he was subjecting this lady to some kind of indignity, why would you get a lady out of her house, late at night, in her night clothes, under the trick that her husband has had a wreck down by the creek? Why do you want to get her down by the creek? . . . Why is it that you choke her? Why is it that you repeatedly beat her? . . . Well, it is because either you don't want her to tell what indignities you have subjected her to, or she is unwilling and fights against you, against being subjected to those indignities . . . , to do something that she nor any other mother on that road would want to do with Mr. House, and you kill her because of her resistance. That is what the evidence at the scene suggests about motive."

Phillips concluded with these words about Paul House: "If he walks out of this courtroom a free man, and he is guilty, can you rest easy about that? Not only has Carolyn's goodness not been rewarded, but if he leaves the courtroom a free man, when in fact he is guilty and it has been proven beyond a reasonable doubt, then evil and trickery and deceit has succeeded today, and the shameful abuse of a good mother has gone unchallenged, and unpunished."

Judge Porter's Charge, the Jurors' Verdict, and the Sentencing Hearing

After Phillips concluded his closing argument, Judge Porter delivered his charge to the jury, laying out the legal principles the jurors must follow in deciding the case. He said this about reasonable doubt: "The state has the burden of proving the guilt of the defendant beyond a reasonable doubt, and this burden never shifts but remains on the state throughout the trial of the case. The defendant is not required to prove his innocence. Reasonable doubt is that doubt engendered by an investigation of all the proof in the case, and an inability after such investigation, to let the mind rest easily as to the certainty of guilt. . . . Absolute certainty of guilt is not demanded by the law to convict of any criminal charge, but moral certainty is required . . . as to every proposition of proof requisite to constitute the offense. . . . If you find from the proof beyond a reasonable doubt that the defendant is guilty of murder in the first degree . . . then it shall be your duty, after a separate sentencing hearing, to determine whether the defendant shall be sentenced to death or life imprisonment, but you will not consider punishment for this offense at this time."

Following Judge Porter's charge to the jurors, they accompanied the court's bailiff to the jury room for their deliberations on Paul House's fate, beginning at 3:13 P.M. on February 7, 1986. According to one juror, they began with a prayer for divine guidance. They returned to the court-room with their verdict at 4:47, a little more than an hour and a half later. The jury's foreperson announced the verdict to Judge Porter: "We, the jury, find the defendant, Paul Gregory House, guilty of murder in the first degree." It's not hard to imagine how the jurors reached this verdict. In its essence, they had to weigh the blood on House's jeans against an alibi given by someone who had already admitted lying to the police.

Sheriff's deputies escorted House back to his cell, to await the sentencing hearing the next day. His mother, Joyce, recalled his reaction to the verdict. "Paul was devastated," she said. "When I went back to see him, he was in shock, and he said, 'Evidently, the justice system doesn't work, does it, Mom?'" The next morning, House attempted suicide, slashing his wrists with the blade from a disposable razor. After paramedics rushed him by helicopter to a hospital in nearby Knoxville, jail officers found a handwritten letter in his cell, addressed to his mother. House's wounds were not serious, and he was transported back to the courthouse for the sentencing hearing, which began with a motion by Chuck Burks to dismiss all three of the aggravating factors the state had alleged in seeking the death penalty, making House eligible only for life imprisonment.

Burks argued to Judge Porter that the records of House's prior conviction in Utah for "aggravated sexual assault," to which he had pleaded guilty, did not show that "it involved the use of threat or violence." He next said that Carolyn Muncey's murder was not especially heinous or atrocious, given Dr. Carabia's testimony that the blow to her head—which caused her death—had most likely immediately rendered her unconscious. Burks finally argued that the state had not proved the murder was committed during the course of other felonies, such as kidnapping or rape, because Muncey might have left her home voluntarily, and there was no proof that House had raped or attempted to rape her.

Paul Phillips responded that rape does not necessarily "involve the sexual organs of the female," whether in the Utah conviction or in the attempted rape of Carolyn Muncey. Phillips next argued that whether or not Muncey was rendered unconscious by the blow to her head, "just leaving her out there to the elements" without medical attention was a heinous act, and that "no matter how brief a period of time that this lady was held against her will" constituted kidnapping.

Judge Porter gave his decision to Burks: "I am going to overrule you in all of those matters."

With that decision, which Burks must have anticipated and admitted he made "for the record" on appeal, should House be sentenced to death, the sentencing hearing began, before the same jurors who had convicted him a day earlier. The hearing lasted less than an hour. Paul Phillips called only one witness, Guy Marney, a Tennessee parole officer, who told the jurors that House's parole supervision had been transferred to Marney after House moved to Tennessee, and that he had been convicted of aggravated sexual assault and had received a sentence of five years to life. Marney was on the stand for less than five minutes.

On his part, Chuck Burks called only two witnesses to offer "mitigation" testimony on Paul House's behalf. The first was his father, James, an airline mechanic in Utah, from whom House's mother was divorced. His testimony did little to help his son, portraying a "very strained" relationship between them. House's father also said that when Paul "had to be punished for something, it was hard to get him to show remorse or anything like that." Chuck Burks asked, "Does that mean that he wasn't having remorse?" Jim House answered that "It doesn't mean that he is not having remorse, and it does not mean that he is not sorry, and I know, after talking with Paul Gregory last night for some great length, that Greg is very sorry that this thing happened to Mrs. Muncey. He feels sorry for those two little kids."

Burks then called Joyce House, to make a final plea to the jurors to spare her son's life. "Is there anything that you would like to say to this jury?" Burks asked her.

"I just—I believe he is as innocent as you guys think he is guilty," she replied.

"Mrs. House," Burks said, "we are not dealing with innocence or guilt now, but as far as this sentencing is concerned, is there anything you would like to ask this jury?"

"Just to give me my son's life."

For reasons he did not explain, Paul Phillips then asked Joyce House to read to the jury the letter her son addressed to her when he cut his wrists that morning, which she did in a quavering voice: "Dearest Mom: I really don't know what to say or how to say it. But I am going to try. I didn't kill Carolyn, I don't think I could ever kill anyone. . . . I told you my feelings about being sentenced to life or death. . . . Either way I would be punished for something I didn't do. I won't go back to prison for even one day for someone else's crime. It is nothing but a living death and I refuse. When they found me guilty they ended my life. . . . I don't have anything left to live for. . . . They don't have the right to make the decision about my life, so, I am taking it out of their hands. It hurts so much to have people believe I could do something like that. I know you won't like what I am going to do, but I think it is best for me. . . . I thought for a long time that I would be found guilty. I wasn't afraid. I am still not. All I wanted was justice. I found that there isn't any to be had. If I could have seen the future and known positively I would be found guilty, I still wouldn't have run. They would have taken it as an admission of guilt and I am not guilty. . . . Love forever and always, your son, Paul Gregory."

Chuck Burks then made a final plea to the jurors: "Ladies and gentlemen, I tried to think of some way of telling you maybe a life sentence would be justified in this case. How can you justify a life sentence in this case? And I thought about it last night, and when I came in this morning, and I heard about [House's suicide attempt] and I read the note [to his mother] and I realized—that maybe in this case life would be worse than death for Paul Gregory House. It may be that that is the appropriate sentence, for him to serve the rest of his life, knowing that he can't escape the conviction, he can't escape what has happened. . . . Because if you give him his life, if you have sentenced him to [a] life of living death, you also have given him the one thing that nobody else can give him, and that is, the opportunity to maybe salvage it. . . . [I]f God loves him, and God can see a chance in him, I just pray that y'all can, and I just pray that your verdict on this sentence will be tempered with mercy.

In his final remarks to the jurors, Paul Phillips did what many prosecutors, especially those in the "Bible Belt" states, frequently do, telling the jurors that God will make the final decision on Paul House's ultimate fate: "There was some mention by defense counsel that Mr. House should be given—his life should be spared by this jury, because he should have the opportunity . . . for reconciliation with his God. He has an opportunity, and that is not what this case is about. The law is to protect society, and we have to have law, and Christ said that He didn't come to add anything or take anything away from the law. The grace that is available to him through his mediator, he can have today or tomorrow, whenever his heart decides. That is not a matter for you or me to interfere in. That is a matter between him and his God, and that has no effect upon whether his punishment is life imprisonment or his punishment is death. He has that opportunity. That is up to him, that is up to his Creator, that is not a consideration for us. We have to consider the law that is recognized in both the Old and the New Testaments, that is necessary for society to be civilized and not chaotic."

The jurors went back to the jury room for their deliberations at 3:05 p.m. on Saturday, February 8, 1985. They returned to the courtroom at 5:17, a little more than two hours later, once again having begun their deliberations with a prayer for divine guidance, this time with a man's life in their hands. The foreperson announced their verdict: "We, the jury, unanimously find that the punishment for the defendant, Paul Gregory House, shall be death."

Judge Porter then imposed the sentence on Paul House: "Mr. House, would you stand up, please? Mr. Paul Gregory House, it is the verdict of the jury that your punishment for first-degree murder is death. Therefore, under my duties as Judge, I pronounce that your life shall be taken by electrocution, at a date which will be set by the [State] Supreme Court. May the Lord have mercy upon your soul, and may His Holy Spirit bring solace to the remainder of your life. You may sit down."

Paul House was then escorted from the courtroom by the bailiffs and transported the next day to the Riverbend Maximum Security Prison, some twenty miles west of Nashville, where he was placed on death row with about a hundred other condemned murderers, to await his execution. However, before the Tennessee Supreme Court set his execution date, House filed the first in a long series of appeals from his conviction and sentence in both the state and the federal courts, a process that would last for another twenty-two years.

3

Paul House's Appeals in the Tennessee State Courts

Every state and federal court allows criminal defendants to appeal their convictions and sentences to appellate courts; however, the grounds for such appeals are limited. Convicted defendants cannot challenge the jury's verdict simply on assertions that it reached the wrong verdict. Jurors are considered "fact finders" of the evidence presented to them, both in testimony from witnesses and in physical and documentary evidence. Potential grounds for appeal in a criminal case are limited to claims of **legal error** on the part of judges, **juror misconduct, prosecutorial misconduct,** and **"ineffective assistance of counsel."**

In deciding postconviction claims of legal errors by trial judges, appellate courts apply two standards: if the alleged errors are deemed to be **"plain"** or **"clear"** from the trial record, of such magnitude that they deprived the defendant of a fair trial, and would—had they not been made—most likely have resulted in a "not guilty" verdict, appellate courts may order a new trial or, in rare cases, order the trial judge to dismiss the charges and free the defendant. However, even if the trial judge committed errors, if the appellate court finds that they were **harmless** in their effect on the trial's outcome and would not have resulted in a different verdict, the conviction will be affirmed. Needless to say, the appellate court's ruling as to whether alleged legal errors are "plain" or "harmless" effectively decides the case. Appellate judges look for precedent in similar cases in making such rulings, either from their own prior decisions or from those of other state and federal courts, including the U.S. Supreme Court. What may strike the majority of one court as plain error, however, might be seen by another as harmless in its effect. There is clearly some element of subjectivity in making such determinations.

Claims of juror misconduct include such allegations as visiting the scene of the crime (unless such visits are approved and conducted by the judge, with prosecution and defense lawyers present), drug or alcohol use by jurors during the trial or jury deliberations, improper communications between jurors and witnesses or lawyers, reading or viewing newspaper or television accounts of the trial, and discussing the case with family members or friends.

Claims of prosecutorial misconduct include allegations that prosecutors withheld "exculpatory" evidence from the defense (material that would tend to support the defendant's innocence), presented testimony of witnesses that prosecutors knew or should have known was false, or made inflammatory or prejudicial comments about defendants, such as references to their race or religion.

Finally, claims of ineffective assistance of counsel (or IAC) must show that the conduct of defense lawyers fell below the standard required of a "reasonably competent" attorney; the bar is set fairly low in assessing such claims. This standard was first defined by the U.S. Supreme Court in the 1984 case of *Strickland v. Washington*, in which the defendant, sentenced to death for three murders, claimed that his lawyer had failed to locate and present witnesses at his sentencing hearing who could have testified about his character and psychiatric problems. The Supreme Court set out a two-part test in what lawyers call IAC cases: First, did the defense lawyer's performance fall below an "objective standard" of competence? And second, was there a "reasonable probability" that had the lawyer performed competently, the trial or the sentencing outcome would have been different? Examples of successful IAC claims include lawyers who slept through portions of the trial, those whose performance was impaired by alcohol or drug abuse, and lawyers who failed to search for or present witnesses whose testimony would have aided the defendant. IAC claims are rarely granted, however, except in cases of "egregious" misconduct or incompetence.

Paul House's state court appeals of his conviction and sentence went through eight steps, during an eight-year period, which I'll briefly outline and summarize. First, Chuck Burks filed an appeal in early 1987 with the Tennessee Supreme Court, as authorized by state law in all death-penalty cases. Defense lawyers generally employ one of two strategies in such appeals: one is a "shotgun" approach, raising any possible issue they can find in the trial record and the judicial rulings, hoping that at least one or two pellets will find their mark; the other is a more focused "rifle" approach, aiming at the most likely targets for appellate reversal of the conviction. Burks adopted the shotgun strategy, raising ten issues. Most of these were hardly likely to convince any judge to reverse House's conviction or to order a new trial; for example, Burks claimed that court personnel allowed several jurors to visit a lounge and drink alcohol between the guilt and sentencing phases of the trial. A few raised more serious issues, including a claim that prosecutors violated Tennessee criminal procedure rules by not providing the defense with a "timely" opportunity to conduct independent tests on Paul House's "bloodstained" jeans. All in all, Burks was really just going through the motions with this appeal, because he had no "new" evidence to show House's innocence.

After reviewing the trial transcript and the briefs filed by Chuck Burks and the state's lawyers, the Tennessee Supreme Court didn't take long to decide this appeal. In a unanimous 5–0 ruling on December 14, 1987, the court rejected almost all of Burks's challenges, finding them to be unsupported by the trial record or "harmless" to the defense. Conceding that this was an "entirely circumstantial" case, the court nonetheless concluded that there was "strong" evidence of House's guilt. The only claim the judges found worthy of discussion was that prosecutors should have allowed Burks to conduct an independent examination of House's jeans. However, they found no "deliberate withholding" of the jeans from such testing and no "serious question" of the reliability of the FBI's testing. As a result, the court concluded, "We find no reversible error" in admitting those test results at the trial.

After this ruling, Chuck Burks bowed out of the case, leaving Paul House on his own in any further appeals. Two months later, from his death-row cell, House filed a **pro se** (a Latin term meaning "on my own behalf") appeal with the trial court, claiming that Burks had provided ineffective assistance of counsel at his trial and sentencing hearing. House alleged that Burks had failed to give him proper advice; had not conducted a thorough pretrial investigation; had not made necessary and timely objections to Judge Porter's rulings; had not prepared adequately for the trial and the sentencing hearing; had not objected to Judge Porter's "improper" jury instructions; and had not challenged a biased juror at the sentencing hearing. In filing this petition on his own, House had obviously gone through his trial transcript and gotten the assistance of **jailhouse lawyers** in the prison. Every prison has inmates who burrow into law books and assist others in preparing legal papers, although most pro se appeals are promptly tossed out by judges for lack of merit or a violation of procedural rules.

Judge Porter appointed a new lawyer to assist House in his pro se appeal, who added several claims to his petition, including a revised challenge to the jury instructions. However, this lawyer did not raise the ineffective assistance of counsel claim. At a hearing before Porter, House's new lawyer did not offer any new evidence, relying only on the trial transcript. Not surprisingly, because his own trial rulings were challenged, Porter dismissed the petition. On an appeal to the Tennessee Court of Criminal Appeals, Porter's denial of relief was upheld in 1989.

Following this judicial setback, House filed a second petition, this time with an ineffective assistance of counsel claim, aided by a second court-appointed lawyer. This petition also asked for investigative and expert witness assistance in pursuing the original postconviction claims. The state's lawyers argued in response that the claims in the second petition were barred from consideration by the doctrines of **waiver** and **default,** which preclude judicial rulings on issues that were not raised in an original petition or had been decided against the defendant. The Court of Criminal Appeals initially affirmed Judge Porter's denial of the first petition, but the legal precedent on which the judges relied on the waiver and default issues had been subsequently reversed by the Tennessee Supreme Court, which remanded House's second petition to the Court of Criminal Appeals in 1993.

Following this remand, in March 1994, the Court of Criminal Appeals reversed the earlier dismissal of House's petition, ruling that he could raise the ineffective assistance of counsel claim in a subsequent hearing. Eighteen months later, in September 1995, after the state's appeal from this reversal, the Tennessee Supreme Court changed its mind and reinstated the dismissal of the second postconviction petition, holding that House had received "a full and fair hearing" before Judge Porter on the "ineffective assistance of counsel" claim in his first petition. House was not entitled under the "waiver" doctrine to pursue it in any further appeals, because it had not been raised in the second petition, even if his court-appointed lawyer had been at fault and had provided House with more "ineffective assistance of counsel" in failing to raise this claim.

If this account of House's efforts to challenge his conviction and death sentence in the Tennessee state courts sounds complicated and convoluted, it is. State courts are generally inclined to uphold jury verdicts in criminal cases and to shield their trial judges and prosecutors from claims of improper conduct. In addition, they set a very low bar for challenges to the competence of trial lawyers, granting relief only in "egregious" cases of misconduct. After eight years of fruitless appeals in the Tennessee courts, Paul House—now without any lawyer to help him—was left with only one avenue for exoneration, the federal courts.

4

Paul House's Federal Habeas Corpus Petition and Hearing

Rebuffed in his repeated appeals at every level of the Tennessee state courts and by the U.S. Supreme Court's refusal to review these decisions, Paul House took a further step in his quest for exoneration, by moving his appeals to the federal courts. On September 30, 1996, House filed a **petition for a writ of habeas corpus** with the federal district court for the Eastern District of Tennessee in Knoxville. Again acting pro se, House asked the court to grant him a hearing on his claim of "actual innocence," arguing that the evidence at his original trial in 1986 had failed to establish his guilt of Carolyn Muncey's murder.

Rooted in English common law, the "ancient writ" of habeas corpus (loosely translated from Latin as "bring the body before us") was originally designed to protect Englishmen from arbitrary arrest and imprisonment by the king's agents. The writ allowed supposedly independent and impartial judges to determine the lawfulness of the incarcerated

person's detention. If they found no legal basis for this arrest or imprisonment, judges could order the prisoner's release.

The American colonists, often subjected to detention by the
king's agents, demanded the same protection as their English broth-
ers, and the writ of habeas corpus was frequently invoked and zeal-
ously defended. Following the Revolution and American independence,
the Constitution's Framers provided, in Section IX of Article I, that
"The Privilege of the Writ of Habeas Corpus shall not be suspended
[by Congress], unless when in Cases of Rebellion or Invasion the public
Safety may require it." During the Civil War, President Abraham Lincoln
did suspend the writ in several places, to prevent accused Confederate
sympathizers from challenging their arrests and detention by military
authorities, but the Supreme Court emphatically rejected this usurpation of congressional power by the executive branch.

The current federal habeas statute was first enacted by the
Reconstruction Congress in 1867, designed primarily to protect African
American freedmen in Southern states from arrest and imprisonment
on trumped-up charges, on the assumption that federal judges would be
more fair and impartial in reviewing such cases. The statute (now codified in federal law in Section 2254 of Title 42 of the U.S. Code) allows
state prisoners who have exhausted their state appeals to seek federal
court review of their convictions, but only when such challenges allege
a violation of protected constitutional rights to a fair trial, largely under
the "due process" clause of the Fourteenth Amendment.

In recent years, state prisoners have filed roughly twenty thousand
federal habeas petitions each year, although only about two hundred
are filed by death-row inmates. More than two-thirds of these petitions
are summarily dismissed, without a hearing, most often on procedural
grounds, such as failing to exhaust state appeals. In the minority of petitions that reach the hearing stage, virtually all result in affirmance of
state court judgments. However, the success rate for death-row inmates
is some 40 to 50 percent, most often resulting in orders for new trials
and rarely in release of the inmates. That success rate has risen sharply
during the last two decades, largely as a result of DNA testing that conclusively established the prisoner's innocence.

Paul House hoped to become one of these fortunate habeas petitioners, although at the time that he sought review, he did not yet have

any DNA evidence to rebut the state's allegation of rape or attempted rape of Carolyn Muncey, based on the semen stains found on her nightgown and panties. This alleged rape had been the "aggravating factor" that persuaded the trial jury to sentence him to death. Having read about DNA testing, however, House was convinced that persuading a federal judge to permit such testing would at least release him from death row and allow him to challenge other evidence in his trial. House's habeas petition was assigned to District Judge James H. Jarvis, a native of Knoxville and a graduate of the University of Tennessee Law School, who had engaged in private practice and served as a state judge before President Ronald Reagan named him to the federal bench in 1984.

House was fortunate when Judge Jarvis appointed Stephen Kissinger to represent him in the habeas proceedings. A graduate of the University of Wyoming's law school, Kissinger served as a law clerk for a federal judge in Wyoming and then took a job as a public defender. In the early 1990s, he moved to Florida to work in the federal defender's office, primarily on death-penalty appeals. After leaving Florida because it was "too hot" and too hostile toward public defenders, Kissinger took a job with the Federal Defenders Service in Knoxville, with the House case as one of his first assignments. He enlisted the volunteer services of Michael Pemberton, a Knoxville lawyer with extensive criminal defense experience. Kissinger spent the year between his appointment and the evidentiary hearing scheduled by Judge Jarvis in February 1999 putting together, with the aid of Pemberton and their investigator, Mike Lee, what would in effect become the trial that Paul House should have received in 1986.

After reviewing the trial record, of both witness testimony and physical exhibits, and interviewing their client, Kissinger and Pemberton decided to focus on five issues for the evidentiary habeas hearing. First, they decided to follow up rumors that Little Hube was a chronic wife abuser and might have killed Carolyn in a more deadly assault. He was, in their minds, the most logical suspect in her murder, if Paul House had not committed the crime.

On this issue, prompted by a tip from Pam Luttrell, the Munceys' across-the-road neighbor and the last person, aside from Carolyn's two children, to see her alive on the night of her murder, House's lawyers and Mike Lee struck gold, so to speak. Lee found two witnesses—both of them long-time friends of Little Hube Muncey—who were prepared to bolster the case that he had killed his wife, with testimony that Little Hube had "backhanded" Carolyn the night of her murder and had asked one of them, even before Carolyn's body was found, to concoct a phony alibi for him.

Pam Luttrell also pointed Mike Lee to two women, Kathy Parker and her sister, Penny Letner, who told him that Little Hube had not only regularly abused Carolyn but had also, at a party shortly before or during Paul House's trial, drunkenly and tearfully confessed to killing her, supposedly by accident, during an argument that turned violent. If Judge Jarvis accepted their testimony as credible, the state's case against House would crumble.

Prosecutors had suggested to jurors at House's trial that rape was the motive in Carolyn Muncey's murder. So a second issue, and the easiest to prove, was that DNA testing showed that House was not the source of the semen found on Carolyn Muncey's nightgown and panties. This would eliminate rape as a motive and also as an aggravating factor in the jury's decision to impose the death penalty. Kissinger and Pemberton found a DNA specialist, Lisa Calandro, to testify that the DNA did not match House's.

The third issue for the habeas hearing involved the most incriminating piece of physical evidence against House at his original trial: the blue jeans that were seized from Donna Turner's laundry hamper. FBI serologist Paul Bigbee testified that the jeans had been stained with Carolyn Muncey's blood, presumably—as prosecutors argued and the jury obviously believed—during a struggle with Paul House while he was killing her. Muncey's blood, however, had been extracted from her body at least twenty-four hours after her death, had not been placed in the vials with a preservative, had not been properly stoppered, had been transported to the FBI lab in Washington, D.C., in the trunk of a car, in the same cardboard box with House's jeans, and had leaked from the vials at some point—with an entire vial discovered to be empty. Based on these facts, Kissinger and Pemberton hoped to convince Judge Jarvis that the evidence had been tainted by these mistakes in its handling, either through deliberate tampering or by inexcusable negligence. House's lawyers were delighted to secure the report and the testimony of their "star" witness for the habeas hearing, Dr. Cleland Blake, the assistant chief medical examiner for Tennessee. With more than thirty years of experience as a forensic pathologist, Dr. Blake had testified for the prosecution in hundreds of assault, rape, and murder cases. In this case, he was willing to give his expert opinion that the blood on House's jeans had not come from Carolyn Muncey's body while she was alive—presumably struggling with House—but from the vials of "degraded" blood. If Judge Jarvis credited Dr. Blake's testimony, the case against Paul House would collapse.

Kissinger and Pemberton also wanted to discredit the trial testimony of Billy Ray Hensley, who had first pointed to House as a suspect. Hensley had told police that he had seen House "coming up from the embankment" where Carolyn Muncey's body was found, wiping his hands on a "dark rag." Prosecutors suggested to the jury that this was the tank top House had been wearing and had claimed to have discarded after a struggle with two men who assaulted and shot at him. Hensley's statements to the police about where he had been when he first saw House contradicted his trial testimony. Kissinger and Pemberton produced exhibits, based on maps and aerial photographs, showing that Hensley's view, supposedly from a distance of some 450 feet, had been blocked by a large barn and foliage overhanging the embankment, rendering his trial testimony—the only "eyewitness" account placing House near Muncey's body—completely unbelievable.

Finally, in preparing for the habeas hearing, Kissinger and Pemberton decided to ask House's trial lawyer, Chuck Burks, to testify that several crucial pieces of evidence, including statements obtained from potential witnesses by the police and the state detectives, had been withheld from him by prosecutors, evidence that Burks had properly requested through "discovery" motions and that would have been essential for House's defense. In securing Burks's agreement to testify, Kissinger and Pemberton were walking a fine line, because calling Kathy Parker, Penny Letner, and other witnesses to Little Hube Muncey's confession that he killed his wife and his efforts to concoct a phony alibi for his whereabouts at the time of her death would suggest that Burks had been negligent—meeting the legal standard of ineffective assistance of counsel—in not locating and presenting those witnesses himself at House's trial. However, Burks didn't seem to mind, assuming he knew that Kissinger and Pemberton would question his professional competence.

Preparing for what they expected would be an all-out, guns-blazing attack on the prosecution's case at Paul House's original trial, the state's lawyers were placed on the defensive, as defense lawyers always are. Tennessee's then attorney general Paul Summers assigned two lawyers from his staff, Alice Lustre and Glenn Pruden, to represent Ricky Bell, the warden of the Riverbend state prison and the ostensible defendant in House's habeas petition (stemming back to English law, officials with custody of the prisoner's "body" were generally named as defendants in habeas cases).

Little Hube Muncey's Abuse of Carolyn, His Concocted Alibi, and His Confession

Mike Pemberton opened the habeas hearing by calling Mary Adkins to the stand. When asked about her relationship with Little Hube Muncey, she said, "We grew up together" and never had any disagreements or conflicts. Pemberton began with questions about the night Carolyn Muncey had been killed. Adkins said she had been at the Rec Center dance that Saturday night and saw Carolyn and Little Hube in the parking lot during a break. They seemed to be having an argument, but Adkins wasn't close enough to hear what they said. Yet she saw that Little Hube "grabbed her and he just backhanded her." Asked whether she had "any firsthand knowledge of whether or not Little Hube had physically abused Mrs. Muncey," Adkins said, "I have seen bruises on her, yes, in the past. . . . I have asked her, and she would just make fun and say, you know, she had bumped into something."

Pemberton next called Artie Lawson, who told Judge Jarvis that Little Hube "is a good friend" and that they had no disagreements. Pemberton again began with the weekend of Carolyn's death. She recounted that Little Hube "come to my house that Sunday morning, and he asked me if anybody come to say anything, you know, talk to me, that he was there at six o'clock. He asked me if anyone, you know, come and ask me anything to tell that that I . . . was at the dance that Saturday night—but I was not. He said that he had eat breakfast [at my house] at six o'clock that Sunday morning, and he did not. It's not true. He wanted me to say that he was at the dance and I . . . saw him at the dance, but I was not at the dance. I didn't see him. That is all I know."

Having elicited "warm-up" testimony from Mary Adkins and Artie Lawson, Mike Pemberton called the first of his two "strike-out" witnesses, Penny Letner. She said she went to an informal party at the trailer in which her sister, Kathy Parker, lived. Penny said that she arrived while Little Hube "was sitting there, and he was pretty well blistered. I could tell by the way he was talking. . . . He was sitting there, and he went to crying and was talking about his wife and her death, and he was saying that he didn't mean to do it. . . . He said he didn't mean to do it. That she was 'bitching him out' because he didn't take her fishing that night, that he went to the dance instead. He said when he came home that she was still on him pretty heavily, 'bitching him out' again, and that he smacked her, and that she fell and hit her head. He said, 'I didn't mean to do it, but I had to get rid of her, because I don't want to be charged with murder.'"

Penny continued, "When he said that he had to get rid of her, it scared me quite badly. I was nineteen-year-old with a small child. I got out of there immediately. After he made those statements, I was ready to leave there." Asked about Little Hube's state, Penny said, "He was crying. He was very upset."

Alice Lustre conducted the cross-examination of Penny Letner. "Did you report this to the police?" Lustre asked. "No. I didn't. I was nineteen-year-old. I was kind of scared. I was frightened, you know. I didn't know how to take it. I figured me being nineteen-year-old, they wouldn't listen to anything I had to say."

Lustre pressed Penny: "How is it that you came to give a statement now?"

Penny answered firmly: "Because it's not right. The gentleman [Little Hube] stood right up there in my face in front of several people and owned up to doing it. It's not right for a man to be in jail for something he didn't do." She again described the scene: "He was sitting there crying and going on sobbing, he didn't mean to do it. I replied, 'Didn't mean to do what?' That is when he started, you know, making the statement that she was bitching him out for not taking her fishing, that he smacked her and she fell and she hit her head."

A "confession" heard by only one person clearly has less impact than one that is corroborated by another witness, assuming they have not colluded and are testifying from their independent recollection. Mike Pemberton's next witness was Penny's sister, Kathy Parker, who hosted the "get-together" at which Little Hube showed up, uninvited and with a beer can in his hand. Asked by Judge Jarvis how long she had known Little Hube, she said, "I dated him when I was fourteen-year-old" and never had any arguments or fights with him. Pemberton asked her to recount that night: "Me and some family members and some friends was sitting around drinking, and he just walked in and sit down. . . . He was there ten or fifteen minutes, and he started crying and going on and rambling off. Talking about what happened to his wife and how it happened and he didn't mean to do it. . . . He said they had been into an argument, and he slapped her and she fell and hit her head, and it killed her, and he didn't mean for it to happen." Pemberton also asked Kathy about Little Hube's state: "He was drinking real heavily."

Pemberton then asked, "What did you do when you heard Little Hube say he hit his wife and she died?"

"I freaked out and run him off," Kathy replied.

Pemberton continued, "After the party, did you tell anybody about this?"

Kathy explained what she did: "Not that night. The next day I went to Union County . . . to the Sheriff's Department, I tried to speak to the sheriff, but he was real busy. He sent me to a deputy. The deputy told me to go upstairs to the courtroom and talk to this guy, I can't remember his name. I never did really get to talk to anybody."

Pemberton had a question about Carolyn Muncey: "Are you aware of whether or not Little Hube had ever abused her or beat on her?"

"She was constantly with black eyes and busted mouth."

A final question: "Why are you here today?"

"Because I don't think what happened is right," Kathy said. "It needs to be taken care of. An innocent man is in jail."

In her cross-examination of Kathy Parker, Alice Lustre wondered about the timing of her testimony, receiving in return a lesson in "brush-offs" by officialdom. Lustre asked, "Now, what prompted you to come forward at this point with this statement now when you say you reported it to the sheriff or tried to at the time of the trial and then, you know, thirteen years later we have now got this statement?"

Kathy replied, "There wasn't anybody talk to me. I couldn't give a statement to anybody. They didn't want to hear it. . . . They had it all signed, sealed, and delivered. We didn't know anything to do until we heard that they reopened this trial."

Lustre remained skeptical in this exchange: "You didn't try going to the paper and saying, 'You know, hey, an innocent man has been convicted and sentenced to death'?"

"Didn't figure it would do any good," Kathy replied.

"Well, you are here today," Lustre shot back.

"I would have been here thirteen and a half year ago, if I would have known where to go." It would be up to Judge Jarvis to decide the winner in this verbal spat.

Pemberton's next witness, Hazel Miller, had known Little Hube "all his life" and said "he has always treated me decent." She recounted a visit from him some two or three months before Carolyn's death, saying that he wanted "to get my daughter to go out with him." This took place, of course, while Little Hube was still married to Carolyn. Pemberton asked Hazel to recall her conversation with Little Hube. "He was upset with his wife, that they had an argument, and he said he was going to get rid of that woman one way or the other. He was going to get rid of her one way or the other. I presume he meant he was going to get a divorce."

"What did you say?" asked Pemberton.

"Told him he ought to go home to his wife and kids and take care of them." Judge Jarvis asked Hazel if Little Hube had ever said anything like that before. "Well, sometimes he would make the remark, you know, that he was going to run her off or something like that."

Pemberton next called Dennis "Dink" Wallace, who had been the Luttrell police chief at the time of Carolyn Muncey's murder. Wallace said that he had provided security at the Rec Center dance the night Carolyn Muncey disappeared, and that Little Hube was there. However, he recalled that Little Hube left the dance sometime between 9:30 and 10:30 that evening, and Wallace did not see him return.

Alice Lustre cross-examined Chief Wallace. She did not ask about Little Hube having left the dance and not returning. She focused on Wallace's visit to the Munceys' house at about 1:40 in the morning, having been dispatched there by the sheriff's department after Little Hube had called to report that Carolyn was missing. When he arrived, Wallace said, he noticed that Little Hube was "intoxicated," and told Wallace that he had come home, found his wife gone, "and went to the kitchen to fix him a sandwich or something to eat." After the two men looked around the outside of the house, without finding Carolyn, Wallace continued, "I said, 'Have you uns been a fussing or a fighting?' He said no. I asked him—he had told me she had been kidnapped. I asked him why did he think his wife had been kidnapped? . . . He said he didn't know. I asked, 'Has she run off from home before?' He said no." Wallace apparently did not ask Little Hube who might have kidnapped his wife and for what reason, and Lustre did not inquire about this.

Lustre then asked whether Wallace had looked around the inside of the house while he was there and had seen "anything out of place or that looked odd to you?"

"Not that I can recall," he replied.

"See any blood around the house, any furniture knocked over, shoved out of the way?"

"Not as I know of," Wallace said. The point of these questions was obviously to establish that Carolyn had left the house voluntarily—presumably, after being lured out with the story of Little Hube's car wreck—and had not been assaulted before she left. Of course, between the time Little Hube said he had returned home from the dance, shortly after midnight, and Chief Wallace's arrival some two hours later, Little Hube could have straightened any knocked-over furniture and cleaned up any blood in the kitchen, if he had "smacked" and killed her in the house, although the deadly assault might have taken place on the porch or farther from the house. Given Wallace's cursory look around the premises, it's impossible to say whether he might have noticed anything suspicious.

Lustre asked Wallace if he had been at the scene where Carolyn's body was discovered the next afternoon, and he said he had. "Were you there when Mr. Muncey, Little Hube, was there?" Lustre asked.

"I was there when he come there," he replied. "House drove him up. Little Hube was riding with him. Hubert, he got out and House run up in front of him and grabbed him and went to holding him back there. They was looking back over where the body was at."

Referring back to the previous night, Lustre asked this about Little Hube: "How did he appear, other than intoxicated, how did he appear to you? Was he upset, happy?"

"He didn't seem to be upset," Wallace replied.

"How about the next day when you saw him . . . where they found the body? How was he that day?" Lustre continued.

"He didn't seem to be upset to me," Wallace answered. Lustre did not explain her reason for asking these last two questions. Perhaps, knowing that Little Hube would testify later at the hearing, she anticipated that Steve Kissinger or Mike Pemberton would ask him why, when he first saw his wife's murdered body, he seemed calm and displayed no shock or grief. On the other hand, Little Hube might simply have been too intoxicated to display any emotion.

Little Hube's Semen and Carolyn Muncey's Blood

After Mike Pemberton completed his questioning of the Luttrell witnesses, Steve Kissinger took over with the scientific expert witnesses. Kissinger already knew, from the police interview with Little Hube Muncey, that he admitted having sex with his wife on the morning of her death (later testimony would show that House's trial lawyer, Chuck Burks, had not been given this report before the trial). Kissinger wanted to nail down the point that DNA testing cleared House as the source of the semen on Carolyn Muncey's nightgown and panties, demolishing the prosecution's claims at trial that rape was the motive for her murder. Kissinger's witness on this issue was Lisa Calandro, a DNA expert with a forensic testing company in California, who performed DNA testing on the nightgown and the panties, comparing what she found against a sample of Paul House's blood. Calandro found semen stains on both items, including the "inside crotch area" of the panties. Of course, if Paul House had, in fact, raped Carolyn Muncey, the presence of semen on the inside of the panties meant that he would have had to replace them on her body.

Knowing how damaging Calandro's testimony was to the state's rape claim, Glenn Pruden tried to cut it off and concede this crucial point. "We are willing to stipulate the source of the semen is not petitioner," he told Judge Jarvis. Kissinger, however, was determined to get this testimony into the court record.

"Your Honor, this testimony is quite brief," he replied. "We do not accept the stipulation."

"Make it brief," he told Kissinger, who did, with one question: "Were you able to come to a conclusion as to whether Mr. House was a possible donor of the semen on the nightgown or the panties?"

Calandro's reply was equally brief: "He was eliminated as the semen donor."

Much as Hazel Miller and Artie Lawson had been "warm-up" witnesses for the "strike-out" testimony of Penny Letner and Kathy Parker about Little Hube Muncey's confession that he killed his wife, Lisa Calandro was a warm-up for what Steve Kissinger hoped would be the strike-out testimony of his star witness, Dr. Cleland Blake. His credentials were impressive. As the assistant chief medical examiner of Tennessee and consultant in forensic pathology for the Tennessee Bureau of Investigation for twenty-two years, Dr. Blake had conducted, he said, more than five thousand autopsies and had testified in several hundred cases, almost always for the prosecution.

Kissinger first directed Dr. Blake to the autopsy report of Dr. Alex Carabia on Carolyn Muncey's body. In reviewing that report, Kissinger asked, "Did you come to some conclusions which were inconsistent with the conclusions reached by Dr. Carabia?" Turning to the "pathological diagnosis" in the report, Blake read ,"an abrasion of the left upper forehead, 19 mm in length, 3.4 inches." An abrasion, Blake explained, "is a scrape or scruff, rub off of the surface of the skin. The wound I see on the left forehead is not an abrasion. It's a laceration. Further in his report he describes that as a bruise."

Kissinger then asked whether the terms *abrasion* and *laceration* were interchangeable. "No, they are not. They are absolutely not," Blake replied. "A laceration is a tear, it can be a puncture tear, rip tear, or a blow on the head by a heavy iron object or against a solid or hard object. This is clearly a laceration, a vertical laceration. This has all the features of a laceration. The skin around it is compressed, there is a hole punching through the skin. However, he says it does not go full thickness through the skin. There is a dark hole indicating to me that this is clear-cut full thickness laceration of the skin. Besides that, [it] is the source of bleeding, and there is a lot of deep scalp arteries present there that in my opinion gave rise to virtually all of the blood that we see on this person. It is not an abrasion."

Kissinger asked Blake's opinion on the source of the laceration. "Impact against a hard object or a hard edge," he replied.

"In your opinion, could that have been caused by a fist?" Kissinger inquired.

"No. That would never be a fist injury. This is a relatively small area of contact between two hard objects. One hard object being the edge or point of some structure, not a fist, and the other hard object is the skull itself. . . . It is a surface with an edge, a corner, if you would, a hard surface with a corner."

Kissinger then asked, "Doctor, in your opinion, is this injury that we observe on Mrs. Muncey's forehead consistent with a blow from a fist?"

"No, not at all. I am absolutely certain. The most you can have [from a fist] is a bruise there. You cannot split the scalp open with standard knuckles against the skull."

Kissinger's point in this line of questioning was to suggest to Judge Jarvis that the laceration on Carolyn Muncey's forehead, as the source of the blood that covered her face, hands, and clothing, might well have been caused by Little Hube's "smacking" his wife's head against a sharp object, such as the edge of a table. Kissinger had no evidence to support this inference, but there was also no evidence from the crime scene that Paul House had used a metal bar, a tree branch, or a rock to inflict the laceration. Whether Judge Jarvis followed this logic was something Kissinger could only hope for.

Having made this point, Kissinger moved to a much more important issue in the case: "Your report also addressed the packaging of blood, fluid scrapings, and other biological specimens by Dr. Carabia. You indicated that his handling of those materials was inappropriate. Can you explain to the court why you have concluded that those materials were not handled appropriately?"

Blake replied that the autopsy report indicated that when the blood specimens were picked up from the morgue in Oak Ridge for transport to the FBI lab in Washington, D.C., "they apparently were left on a table or simply left in the morgue area, and they were given to Mr. Breeding by someone there. There was no total chain of custody where these were locked up and in [Dr. Carabia's] possession until they were transferred to the persons who were going to take them to the laboratory, wherever they were going. Each one has to be labeled separately, sealed, either with tape or paraffin, and name, date, time, name of person, the name or initials of the person who packaged the blood, who took the blood has to be recorded and preferably on an accompanying sheet to go with the material wherever it goes. I don't see in the record where they personally transferred the specimens to either of the two agents, Breeding or Presnell or whoever else picked them up."

Blake continued, "They were not sealed. . . . They were not packaged individually such that they would be protected during any transit time. . . . The chain of custody is clearly not kept." Kissinger asked why it is important to seal the tubes. "Because if they get warm they will blow the stoppers, they can blow the stoppers, and blood can come out. You can lose your specimen." This was a crucial point in Kissinger's argument to Judge Jarvis. The blood vials had been transported to the FBI lab in the trunk of Bill Breeding's car, on a very hot night, with no refrigeration or ice in the Styrofoam box that contained the vials, along with Paul House's jeans. If the unsealed stoppers in the vials had "blown" from the heat or become dislodged from bouncing on the roads, the blood might have spilled on the jeans. This was speculation, of course, but other testimony made it clear that by the time the vials were returned to Tennessee, one vial was entirely empty and another was missing a quarter of its contents. Because Paul Bigbee, the FBI serologist who tested the blood on House's jeans, had testified that he used only a few drops of blood from one vial, the "missing blood" became an important issue.

In addition to the question of how the blood got onto the jeans, equally important was the question of when this happened. Judge Jarvis took over from Kissinger with questions of his own on an issue he said was "pretty important to me." Jarvis read to Blake from his report on the "deterioration" of certain blood enzymes in the autopsy vials and on the jeans. Blake had written, from his review of Bigbee's report, that "the same amount of enzymes deteriorated on the jeans as in [the] known blood sample of Carolyn Muncey. If victim's blood had spilled on to the jeans while victim was alive, the identical deterioration of enzymes would not have occurred." Jarvis then asked, "Does that mean what I think it means, that you have . . . concluded from that the blood of Mrs. Muncey that was on those jeans was part of this batch of blood that was tested [from the vials that were sent to the FBI laboratory]?" Blake said that Jarvis had correctly read his report: "There was a similar deterioration, breakdown of certain of the named numbered enzymes on the jeans, as in the blood [in the vials]. They had been subjected to the same environment, but now, if the victim's blood had spilled on the jeans while the victim was alive and this blood had dried, the deterioration would not have occurred. . . ."

Judge Jarvis then inquired, "Indicating what, Doctor, the blood came from where? Was the victim alive when the blood got on there, or was it blood that was [in the vials] that had deteriorated?" Blake replied, "I think what was on the jeans that they were testing had been altered by putting it in close proximity with the [vials]. The enzymes were equally deteriorated in both, the sample and the jeans."

Jarvis asked for more clarification: "If the blood had come from the victim while she was alive and dried, as you talked about a little while ago, then the enzymes would have been different?" Blake answered his seeming eager student, "That is correct. Because they would have been preserved on the dried garment and the blood tubes that . . . had no proper preservation and had no refrigeration, had no preservation and got bacterial growth in them, that is why they would have been different." Jarvis seemed to have grasped the significance of Blake's conclusion. "That is really important. That is really a crux of some of this." If the blood on House's jeans had come from the vials, rather than from Carolyn Muncey while she was still alive and bleeding from the laceration to her forehead, then the only piece of physical evidence linking House to her murder would have been seriously undermined.

Prosecutorial Misconduct, Ineffective Counsel, or Both?

A confession from Little Hube Muncey, made before two long-time friends who had no reason to fabricate a story to favor Paul House, whom Penny Letner and Kathy Parker had never met, and the opinion of an experienced forensic pathologist, who had worked for the state of Tennessee for twenty-two years, that the blood on House's jeans had not come from Carolyn Muncey before she died: what more could Judge Jarvis need to order House's release from death row or at least grant him a new trial with the new evidence before the jurors? Steve Kissinger and

Mike Pemberton, however, were not ready to rest their case. Testimony to support a claim of prosecutorial misconduct or to show that House had received the "ineffective assistance of counsel" at his trial would strengthen an already strong case. This all assumed, of course, that Judge Jarvis found the testimony of the witnesses credible.

Having completed his questioning of Lisa Calandro and Dr. Blake, whose testimony Glenn Pruden was unable to shake on cross-examination, Kissinger turned over the next witness, Chuck Burks, to Mike Pemberton. He asked Burks about Little Hube Muncey as a suspect in his wife's death. "During the course of the investigation, it appeared that Little Hube and his wife, Carolyn, were not getting along," Burks said. "The whereabouts of Little Hube that night were somewhat in question in terms of what information that we had about where he was. I guess really the sort of absence of Little Hube throughout the whole process raised a question, but, yeah, he was, in my mind anyway, a suspect in this case."

Pemberton continued, "So you were left to your own investigation in respect to determining the whereabouts of Little Hube on that Saturday and what he did and who he talked to and who he saw and so on and so forth?"

"That is correct," Burks replied. Pemberton left unsaid the implication that Burks had failed to properly investigate Little Hube's whereabouts during the time after he left the dance that night and before arriving at his house sometime after midnight. Neither did Burks locate and produce witnesses, such as Chief Wallace, who might have testified that Little Hube did not remain at the dance until it ended around midnight.

Pemberton moved on to another crucial issue, whether prosecutors had failed to provide him, before the trial, with documents that would have been "exculpatory" and would have allowed Burks to challenge the prosecution's rape allegations and other evidence that would have undermined the state's case. Pemberton's goal in this line of questioning was to show that "prosecutorial misconduct" in the case had concealed crucial evidence from Burks and deprived Paul House of a fair trial. He first asked whether Burks had filed discovery motions before the trial. "I filed a motion for discovery and inspection, and within that motion is also a paragraph requesting exculpatory evidence," Burks replied, adding that his motion would have included any material relating to the prosecution's rape allegations. Later in his questioning, Pemberton handed Burks a report on a TBI interview with Little Hube Muncey.

"Anything of importance in that to you?" he asked.

"Yes," Burks said. "In the sentence where it said that the last time he had sexual relations with v, I guess is victim, was Saturday morning 'before I left for work.' The same day she was found to be missing."

During the trial, Pemberton continued, the prosecutors "put on Agent Bigbee to talk about semen and secretor status and Mr. House. That was a big issue?"

"It was," Burks replied. "The state introduced it for the purpose of suggesting that the semen had something to do with this murder. Certainly, information that Mr. Muncey had had sex with his wife the very day would certainly, I think, be important to suggest that he could have been the secretor."

In his discovery motion, Pemberton then asked Burks, "was this the type of information that you were seeking? Of an exculpatory nature?"

"Yes," Burks said.

"This material was not turned over to you?" Pemberton inquired.

"That is my recollection, that is correct," Burks recalled.

Pemberton moved to the question of House's tennis shoes, discovered by Donna Turner several months after Carolyn Muncey's murder, and showed Burks the Tennessee Bureau of Forensic Service Crime Laboratory report on the shoes. "The results on that laboratory report say what?" Pemberton asked.

"That the serological testing failed to indicate the presence of blood-stain [on the shoes]," Burks replied.

"Did you have this report prior to trial?"

"I don't recall ever seeing this report," Burks said.

"If you had had this report, what would you have done with it, if anything?" Burks answered that he would have tried "to show the jury that there was no blood on the shoes they alleged he was wearing at the time of this offense." This may have seemed to Judge Jarvis a minor issue, but because blood had been found on the cuff of Paul House's jeans, it was likely that some would also have been found on the tennis shoes.

Pemberton then showed Burks the plastic bag in which Paul House's jeans were placed after they arrived at the FBI lab in Washington, having been removed from the paper bag in which they arrived at the FBI lab. "Does that bag have some blood or staining on it?" Pemberton asked.

"It appears to have something on the bag that is brownish in color," Burks replied.

"Did you ever see that bag, the state ever show you that bag prior to trial?"

"I was never shown that bag at any time."

"Would that have been important to you, if you had known it existed?"

"If this is the bag that the blue jeans were in, I would have introduced it, I think, at trial to argue the question of possible contamination." Again, this may appear to be a minor issue, but the prosecution's withholding the report from Chuck Burks raised the issue of prosecutorial misconduct.

Pemberton next handed Burks a TBI report of an interview with Kathy Parker. If Burks had seen this report before the trial and had located Parker, he might have learned from her of Little Hube's confession that he killed his wife. Burks said he had never seen the interview report, and that if he had, "I would have pursued this witness to try to find out any information that I could as to the context of that statement and try to introduce that testimony at trial." Given Little Hube's confession to Kathy Parker and Penny Letner, this report—if Burks had followed up and interviewed Kathy himself—might well have changed the outcome of the trial.

When Mike Pemberton finished his examination of Chuck Burks, Judge Jarvis asked, with a touch of humor, "May this witness be excused and go back and earn a living? He is a good lawyer." At that point, Pemberton and Steve Kissinger concluded their habeas case, hoping that Jarvis had been impressed with testimony about Little Hube Muncey's confession and his efforts to concoct a phony alibi, the state's concession that no rape had been committed or attempted, Dr. Blake's assertion that Carolyn Muncey's blood had not wound up on Paul House's jeans while she was still alive, and finally by the state's withholding of "exculpatory" evidence from Chuck Burks.

The State's Lawyers Counter the Claims of a Flawed Trial

In the final session of the three-day hearing, the state's lawyers countered Paul House's claims of "actual innocence" with testimony from nine witnesses, including three expert witnesses. In sum, their testimony added nothing to the state's case against House; in fact, much of it undermined that case and supported the claims of the experts called by Kissinger and Pemberton.

Dr. Alex Carabia, who performed the autopsy on Carolyn Muncey after her death, was asked during cross-examination by Kissinger about the wound on Muncey's forehead that his autopsy report had called an "abrasion," and that Dr. Blake had said was a "laceration" caused by a sharp object and not a fist. Dr. Carabia now agreed the wound was a laceration. Paul Bigbee, the FBI serologist who had testified at the original trial that based simply on blood typing, there was a 93 percent probability that the blood on House's jeans matched that of Carolyn Muncey's blood, simply repeated at the habeas hearing his earlier claim that he saw no evidence of leakage from the blood vials when they arrived at the FBI lab.

The only new expert witness for the state was Paulette Sutton, a "blood spatter" analyst at the University of Tennessee in Memphis who had no medical training or expertise in serology. Most of her work looked at the patterns of blood on walls, floors, and victims' bodies, to determine such things as the distance from which guns had been fired at a victim and the angle from which shots had been fired, which were important questions in cases that questioned whether a death was caused by homicide or suicide, or where a victim was positioned (standing, sitting, or prone) when shots were fired. Based on her examination of House's jeans, Sutton said the stains appeared to have resulted from "smearing" or "wiping" some bloody object on the jeans, rather than from blood dripping or leaking onto them, as Dr. Blake had testified. During his cross-examination of Sutton, Steve Kissinger asked a telling question: "You don't know when any of these stains were placed on any of these objects, do you?"

"No, sir, I do not," she replied. Judge Jarvis made it clear that he didn't find Sutton's testimony relevant. He interrupted several times to

say, "Let's go on to something else," and noted that she couldn't determine who might have done the smearing.

Little Hube Muncey and Paul House
Finally Take the Stand

The state's lawyers did, however, call two witnesses whose testimony
everyone in the courtroom, especially Judge Jarvis, listened to intently.
These new witnesses were Little Hube Muncey and Paul House,
neither of whom had testified at the original trial and whose accounts
of their whereabouts and actions on the night of Carolyn Muncey's
murder the jury had never heard from them. In a real sense, Jarvis
served as a one-person jury at the habeas hearing, and his verdict—
and House's fate—might well depend on what the two men had to
say and his assessment of their demeanor and credibility. Of course,
no one in the courtroom expected either man to blurt out a confession to the murder. Whatever Little Hube and Paul House might or
might not say, their appearance at the hearing produced a buzz of
anticipation.

Alice Lustre began with Little Hube, asking about his activities the
day of his wife's disappearance. "Well, I helped dug a grave that day, and
I just went on over there to the dance and things and stopped and hung
around over there and things, and after the dance I went home. When I
went home, the door was standing partially open, and I went on in and
looked around and things. I went to the bedroom. My kids was still in
the bedroom."

"Do you recall leaving the dance at any time?" Lustre inquired.

"Not as I know of. I do not recollect leaving the dance that night."

"When you would go, would you ever leave and come back or
anything?"

"Yeah, we would probably run up to the package store or something
and back."

Lustre then began this exchange: "Now, after you came back, you
looked in the bedroom, and you couldn't find your wife. What did
you do then?"

"Well, I looked around the house and things on the outside, for we did not have no inside bathroom, and she wasn't out there. I got the kids, and I went down to the neighbors and seed if they had seen her."

"When you were looking around the house, did you see anything out of the ordinary?"

"No. Sure didn't."

"You went to a neighbor's after you had looked around, and what did you do then?"

"Well, I went back to the house, and the best I can remember I got the kids, and I went around over to my dad's. . . . I just started to looking and seeing if anybody had seen her or whatever."

"Did you try to contact the authorities?"

"Well, yeah, I took and we called them that night . . . and told them that my wife was a missing and . . . they said they could not do nothing until the next day or whatever."

"Had your wife ever done this before?"

"No, she never had no bad habits."

Lustre opened another issue: "Had you been drinking that Saturday night?"

"Sure."

"How much, if you can, about how much do you think you had to drink that night?"

"Well, I would say during the all day it was over a six pack anyway."

"Would you say you were drunk at that point?"

"No, not drunk, on account it takes quite a bit to really get me drunk."

Judge Jarvis took over the questioning: "Were you drinking a lot then?"

"Well, I drank some about every day."

"How many [were] you drinking a day?"

"Twelve, six to twelve."

Lustre then asked Little Hube to "tell the court a little bit about your relationship with your wife."

"Oh, we would go fishing and hunting, we work together out in the field and stuff like that. That is about it."

"Did you ever fight?"

"Oh, we had a few quarrels and stuff, but nothing major."

"Did any of these fights ever get physical in terms of pushing, shoving, hitting, basically touch one another when you were angry?"

"No, we didn't have no problems beating on one another."

Jarvis broke in again, "But you never hit your wife that night?"

"No."

"At the dance?"

"No."

"You say she wasn't there?"

"No, she wasn't."

"How long did you stay there?"

"Well, I stayed until the dance was over. It was around 12:00."

"How much schooling do you have?"

"I just went four years."

Lustre returned to her questioning: "Mr. Muncey, do you know Kathy Parker?"

"Yes, I used to date her back when we was younger."

"Do you remember ever being at a gathering at her house at about the time of the trial?"

"No. Sure don't."

"Do you remember being at a gathering where there would be a lot of people with Kathy being there, maybe at Penny's house?"

"No, sure didn't."

Lustre had one final question: "Mr. Muncey, did you kill Carolyn Muncey?"

"I sure did not."

Mike Pemberton, in his brief cross-examination of Little Hube, simply confronted him with the testimony of witnesses who had painted him as the most likely suspect in his wife's death. Pemberton expected, and got, nothing more than a series of denials of this testimony.

Lustre then called Paul House to the stand as a **hostile witness,** which allowed her to ask **leading questions**. Lawyers are normally not allowed to ask their own witnesses questions to which the lawyer suggests the answer, such as "You didn't kill Carolyn Muncey, did you?" But such leading questions are allowed when asked of hostile witnesses, such as Paul House, who was not testifying for the prosecution. House had not testified at his original trial; Chuck Burks had kept House from the stand because of his Utah rape conviction, although most, if not all, jurors probably already knew of this through the small-town grapevine. Correctly assuming that Lustre wanted Judge Jarvis to hear House's bizarre "late-night walk and assault" alibi from his own mouth, Steve Kissinger and Mike Pemberton felt as if they had nothing to lose. Jarvis already knew about this story, so they allowed their client to waive his Fifth Amendment right not to testify at the hearing.

Lustre began by asking House about his account of looking for Little Hube Muncey, the day after Carolyn's death, and of meeting Billy Ray Hensley. "Mr. House, you had some statements that you gave to the authorities at the time concerning your activities on Sunday in terms of driving up and down [Ridgecrest Road], is that correct?"

"Yes."

"You also talked about a little blue car that you saw."

"Bill Hensley, I guess that is the name, was in the car. I saw him, and he was coming towards me. I was going toward him. I waved him over. He stopped. . . . I asked him if he knew Little Hube. He said he did. Asked him if he had seen him, he said he hadn't, didn't see him around there anywhere. . . . I went back up to my mom and Bill Silvey's house."

"Did you know Billy Hensley before that day?"

"No, I never met him. I never seen him. I don't believe I had ever seen him before that day on the road."

Lustre asked her next question with pointed emphasis: "Mr. House, what were you doing down in the ditch?"

"I was not down in the ditch."

"You were never walking around that area?"

"The closest I got to what you call the embankment was when I ran up from the dirt road up to the Clinton's driveway, looked up and saw Little Hube's car was not there, and walked back on the other side of the road."

"Mr. House, are you also saying that . . . while you are going up and down this road [you were not] wiping your hands on any kind of rag?"

"No."

Lustre pressed House on the lies he had told authorities, beginning with Sheriff Earl Loy. "He asked you what you were wearing on Saturday night, correct?"

"Yes."

"You told him you were wearing the jeans that you had on at that time, didn't you?"

"Yes."

"Those were not the jeans you were wearing on that Saturday, were they?"

"No."

House also admitted that he lied when he first told TBI agents that he had not left Donna Turner's trailer that Saturday night.

In his questioning of House, Mike Pemberton asked him to expand on his alibi story, hoping Judge Jarvis might find it credible or at least to get House's story on the court record if the case reached the federal appellate courts. [This account is stitched together from the question-and-answer exchanges between Pemberton, House, and Judge Jarvis for the sake of brevity.] "I went for a walk. It was between 10:30 and 11:00. While I was walking, I had only been walking about twenty minutes at the most, it seems like. A truck pulled up behind me with, I remember it as being like 4-wheel drive. It sat up high, you know. Headlights were on. It had lights across the roof of the cab, and they were on. I couldn't see anything other than that about the truck. I looked back over my shoulder. I was looking at the lights. I turned around, and I kept walking. I believe there were at least two guys in the truck. I know the driver got out on his side, one guy got out on the passenger side. . . . The driver came up. I can remember he said something, but I don't know if I even heard him correctly at the time. He grabbed me by my arm. He started to jerk me around. I turned around and threw back with my left hand. I hit him. He let go. I started running. I ran kind of diagonally across the road into some trees, bushes, whatever it was. I heard a shot, at least one. There might have been two. I am not sure. I ran around through those woods for a while. I don't know how long. When I came out, [I saw] a house that sat up on the hill behind Donna's sister and brother-in-law's trailer on the same property. As soon as I saw that, I knew where I was. I went back across the road up to Donna's house. I stepped on something, a sharp rock or something. When I looked down, I only had one shoe. I lost one of them when I was running. I took the other one off and threw it across the road.

"I went up onto the porch of the trailer. The sliding glass door was locked. I walked around to the side door [and] knocked on it. She

came out and took me in. I went and got a soft drink out of the refrig-
erator. I started drinking that. I was breathing hard. I was sweating.
I needed to cool off and get something to drink. Then we went and
talked on the couch in the living room. I didn't even notice my shirt
was gone until I got up to the trailer. I noticed my shoe was gone, and
[Donna] may have pointed it out, 'Where is your shirt?' but I don't
remember."

After this account, Mike Pemberton questioned House: "Paul, did
you have anything to do with Carolyn Muncey's murder."

"No, I did not."

"Did you have anything to do with the sexual assault or a rape or
however the state wants to categorize it now? Did you have anything to
do with that?"

"No. I did not kill her. I did not ever contemplate killing her. I did
nothing to her other than be an acquaintance, I guess. I considered us
friends. I considered Little Hube my friend, but I guess we were just
acquaintances."

Alice Lustre took a final shot at House's story: "Mr. House, you
stated you heard at least one shot, maybe two?"

"Yes."

"You have just been shot at, possibly twice. Why did you not call the
police immediately upon getting home?"

"I was on parole."

"Somebody tries, potentially tries to kill you, and you are not going
to report it because you are on parole?"

"Yes."

"So it is your position that your being harassed and shot at was more
damaging to your parole than lying to police in investigating a murder?"

"I was too deep by then," House answered, in a tone of resignation
after thirteen years on death row.

Judge Jarvis Delivers His Verdict

On February 3, 1999, after three days of testimony from twenty witnesses and the submission of dozens of maps, photographs, and other
exhibits, Paul House's habeas corpus hearing concluded. In ruling

on his petition, Judge Jarvis had three choices: he could issue an **unconditional writ** and order House's release from prison and a dismissal of the murder conviction and the death sentence; he could issue a **conditional writ**, under which the state would be given the choice of retrying House (with defense lawyers able to present the "new" evidence from the hearing and any further investigation) or dismissing the murder charge on the state's own motion; or, finally, Jarvis could **deny** the petition, leaving House on death row, pending any appeal of his ruling.

It took Judge Jarvis more than a year to review the hearing transcript and the post-hearing briefs of both sets of lawyers and to prepare his ruling and opinion, which were issued on February 16, 2000. His written opinion, covering some fifty pages, adopted the state's position on every contested issue and discounted the testimony of all of the witnesses Kissinger and Mike Pemberton had called. Jarvis wrote this about the testimony of Kathy Parker and Penny Letner, recounting Little Hube Muncey's confession to them that he had "smacked" his wife, killed her, and dumped her body over an embankment along the road: "The court is not impressed with the allegations of individuals who wait over ten years to come forward with their evidence. This is especially true when there was no physical evidence in the Munceys' kitchen to corroborate his alleged confession that he killed her there." Jarvis, however, made no mention of Kathy Parker's account of her effort to report the confession the next day and her "brush-off" at the sheriff's office.

Judge Jarvis also discounted the testimony of the state's own assistant medical examiner, Dr. Blake, that the similar enzymatic deterioration of the blood in the autopsy vials and on House's jeans meant that Carolyn Muncey's blood had not gotten onto the jeans while she was still alive but almost certainly came from the vials, either accidentally or intentionally. On this issue, Jarvis wrote, "Without question, one or more tubes of Mrs. Muncey's blood spilled at some time. . . . Based upon the evidence introduced during the evidentiary hearing, however, the court concludes that the spillage occurred after the FBI crime laboratory received and tested the evidence." Some doubt certainly existed on this disputed issue, but Judge Jarvis took FBI agent Paul Bigbee's word that the vials arrived in his lab with no evidence of spillage or tampering.

Steve Kissinger called Paul House with the bad news: Jarvis had denied the petition, leaving his conviction and death sentence intact. By this time, House had been on death row for fourteen years and had become fatalistic about his chances of ever being released. Kissinger urged him not to lose hope, telling House that he and Mike Pemberton would file an appeal with the U.S. Court of Appeals for the Sixth Circuit in Cincinnati, Ohio. What the two lawyers could not foresee was that it would take more than four years before that court finally ruled on House's case.

5

Paul House Seeks Relief from the Sixth Circuit Court of Appeals

Following Judge Jarvis's denial of Paul House's habeas corpus petition, Steve Kissinger and Mike Pemberton filed an appeal in early 2000 with the United States Court of Appeals for the Sixth Circuit, whose jurisdiction covers the federal district courts in Michigan, Ohio, Kentucky, and Tennessee, with its headquarters in Cincinnati, Ohio. At that time, the Sixth Circuit had fifteen judges in active service, and appeals from district courts were normally assigned to three-judge panels, randomly selected by computer.

Kissinger and Pemberton based their appeal on two related grounds: first, that Judge Jarvis had committed **clear error** in ruling that the new evidence presented at the evidentiary hearing in 1999 did not justify a retrial in the case.

Appellate judges are generally reluctant to overturn the findings of trial judges on factual issues, because those judges have the opportunity to observe the "demeanor" of witnesses and assess their credibility.

Kissinger and Pemberton made the second point, however, that the new evidence in the case, considered as a whole, established that House had met the standard of **actual innocence** set by the U.S. Supreme Court in recent cases and deserved the dismissal of the murder charge against him or—at the least—an order that the state provide House with a retrial.

House's lawyers based this argument on two Supreme Court decisions. In the first, decided in 1993 in the case of *Herrera v. Collins*, the Court considered the challenge of a Texas inmate, Leonel Herrera, to the death sentence imposed after his conviction for having killed two police officers during a traffic stop. In a habeas corpus petition in federal court, Herrera's lawyers presented newly discovered testimony of witnesses who claimed that his brother, Raul, had actually killed the officers. Herrera's lawyers argued that the Eighth Amendment's ban against **cruel and unusual punishment** barred the execution of defendants who could prove actual innocence of the charges against them, and that such evidence should not be excluded because it had not been available at trial, even if the trial had been fairly conducted. Although the Supreme Court did not adopt the Eighth Amendment argument, a majority of the justices held that a "truly persuasive demonstration of 'actual innocence' made after trial would render the execution of a defendant unconstitutional, and warrant habeas relief if there were no state avenue open to process such a claim." The Court did not, however, specify in any detail a judicial standard for judging claims of "actual innocence" in other cases. Unfortunately for Herrera, the Court found his evidence of innocence too weak to warrant a new trial, and he was executed two months after the Court's decision.

The second case on which Kissinger and Pemberton relied in their Sixth Circuit appeal was *Schlup v. Delo*, decided by the Supreme Court in 1995. Lloyd Schlup was a Missouri inmate, serving a life sentence for murder, who had been convicted and sentenced to death for killing another inmate. After the state courts upheld his conviction and sentence, Schlup filed a habeas petition in federal court, pointing to newly discovered evidence—including the testimony of prison guards and a video of the assault—showing that he was not involved in the murder. This was much more convincing evidence of his innocence than Herrera had presented. The Supreme Court ruled that even if an actual innocence claim had been **defaulted** by not raising it in an original habeas petition, inmates might qualify for a new trial if they could establish, in light of the new evidence, that "it is more likely than not that no reasonable juror would have found [the defendant] guilty beyond a reasonable doubt." The Court described this standard as one that would apply only in the "truly 'extraordinary'" case, in which the new evidence "raise[s] sufficient doubt about [the defendant's] guilt to undermine confidence in the result of the trial." Ironically, Schlup later pleaded guilty to a murder the evidence showed he did not commit, in a plea bargain to avoid the possibility of another death sentence. He reasoned that a second life sentence would not add any time to the one he was already serving.

Armed with the *Herrera* and *Schlup* cases, Steve Kissinger and Mike Pemberton asked the Sixth Circuit's three-judge panel to follow those rulings and hold that Paul House met the standards for dismissal of the murder charge or to grant him a new trial. In March 2002, the panel affirmed Judge Jarvis's denial of House's habeas petition by a 2–1 vote, but its opinion was withdrawn after a majority of Sixth Circuit judges granted **en banc** review, deciding by a 6–5 majority the following November to submit three **certified questions** to the Tennessee Supreme Court, in response to arguments by the state's lawyers that the **procedural default** of House's first court-appointed lawyer in his habeas petition—in failing to challenge allegedly erroneous jury instruction and to raise the "actual innocence" claim—barred any federal court review under Tennessee law. The first certified question asked the Tennessee Supreme Court: If an "aggravating" factor—Paul House's supposed attempted rape of Carolyn Muncey—had been "disproven by new DNA evidence, does a defendant lose his current eligibility for the death penalty and require a new sentencing hearing?" The second question—really another form of the first—asked, in the jury's "weighing" of aggravating and mitigating factors during the sentencing hearing, "does the [Tennessee Supreme Court's] review process now permit it to remedy any error in the weighing process by the jury in light of newly discovered evidence?" And third: "Does Tennessee law require a new trial when newly discovered evidence of actual innocence . . . creates a serious question or doubt that the defendant is guilty of first degree murder?" In November 2003, a year after it received these questions, the Tennessee Supreme Court, at the urging of the state's attorney general, declined to answer them (perhaps to head off similar petitions from the state's death-row inmates) and returned the case to the Sixth Circuit.

Eight Judges Uphold Judge Jarvis's Denial of Habeas Relief

On March 10, 2004, Steve Kissinger made an oral argument to the full fifteen-member bench of the Sixth Circuit's active-service judges, opposed by a newly assigned lawyer from the Tennessee attorney general's staff, Jennifer Smith, a graduate of the University of Mississippi Law School. Seven months later, on October 6, the Court handed down its decision; by the narrow margin of 8–7, the judges upheld Judge Jarvis's denial of Paul House's original habeas petition. (It seems significant to me that all eight judges in the majority had been placed on the Sixth Circuit bench by Republican presidents and all seven in the minority by Democrats.)

The majority opinion was written by Judge Alan Norris, an Ohio native who spent twenty years in private practice (during which he served as a Republican member of the Ohio House of Representatives) and later as a state appeals court judge. After reviewing the facts in Paul House's case, accepting without question the state's version of the evidence, Norris wrote that "Although the evidence against appellant was circumstantial, it was quite strong . . . [and] clearly is sufficient to support the conviction." Norris added that "Certainly the sentence of death was not disproportionate to that imposed in other cases in view of the violent and brutal nature of the homicide shown in this record."

Moving to the newly discovered evidence produced at the evidentiary hearing before Judge Jarvis, Norris conceded that "it is fair to say that [House] has presented a colorable claim of actual innocence. However, as the Supreme Court has made clear, that is not the standard that we are bound to apply." That standard, drawn from the Supreme Court's *Herrera* and *Schlup* decisions, required (in Norris's view) that "in weighing the new evidence we [also] review the factual findings of the district court for clear error." Norris didn't find any errors in Judge

Jarvis's rulings. The most he would concede to the new evidence was that in House's "attacks on the scientific evidence that incriminated him, he has succeeded in showing that the semen attributed to him during the trial was that of Mr. Muncey and that, at some point, the blood evidence appears to have been mishandled, resulting in spillage."

Beyond those concessions, neither of which the prosecutors disputed at the habeas hearing, Norris echoed Jarvis on every point, agreeing with his finding that the testimony of Penny Letter and Kathy Parker about Little Hube Muncey's confession that he killed his wife was "not credible." In discussing Billy Ray Hensley's claim to have seen House "coming up" from the embankment with a "black rag" in his hands, Norris erroneously wrote that "two witnesses" (presumably, Hensley and Jackie Adkins) had seen House emerge from the embankment; this error, although minor, reflects sloppy work by Judge Norris or his law clerks. Norris also followed Jarvis in discounting Dr. Blake's unrebutted testimony that the identical "enzyme deterioration" of the autopsy blood from Carolyn Muncey and on House's jeans resulted from the "spillage" that Jarvis agreed had to have occurred, which Jarvis said "does not negate the fact . . . that the blood was in fact from Mrs. Muncey." (The question, of course, which neither Norris nor Jarvis addressed, is when and how her blood got onto House's jeans). Judge Norris ended his opinion with these words: "Despite his best efforts, the case against House remains strong. We therefore conclude that he has fallen short of showing, as he must, that it is more likely than not that no reasonable juror would have convicted him in light of the new evidence. All of the issues before us having been decided, the judgment of the district court is affirmed."

Seven Judges Dissent from the Majority's Ruling

In a blistering dissent, almost twice as long as Norris's and joined by five colleagues, Judge Gilbert Merritt dissected the majority opinion with a pathologist's scalpel. Merritt, a Tennessee native and a graduate of Vanderbilt Law School in Nashville, had served as a U.S. attorney in Tennessee before President Bill Clinton named him to the Sixth Circuit in 1997. His dissent began with these words: "I regard this as the rare or extraordinary case in which the petitioner through newly discovered evidence has established his actual innocence of both the death sentence and the underlying homicide. The Court's opinion . . . regards as 'undisputed' old evidence and inferences that are now contradicted by other evidence in the case. It fails to describe adequately the persuasive case of actual innocence that the petitioner's newly discovered evidence raises. Nor does it adequately describe the legal standards to be applied."

Judge Merritt addressed, point by point, the state's evidence against Paul House at the original trial and the new evidence from the habeas hearing before Judge Jarvis. First, he wrote, in both the trial and the sentencing hearing, "the State relied on rape as the motive for the kidnapping and murder of Carolyn Muncey. There was no other motive offered. It relied on a semen specimen on her nightgown as proof that House tried to rape her. Newly discovered DNA evidence now conclusively establishes that the semen was her husband's. . . . The new evidence disproves the motive the jury accepted as the basis for the kidnapping and murder and the aggravating circumstance the jury found as the basis for the death penalty. Second, . . . the State introduced at the trial one other piece of highly incriminating scientific evidence: evidence of Carolyn Muncey's blood on House's blue jeans worn on the night of the murder. . . . Dr. Blake, the State's medical examiner, testified at length that he had no doubt that the blood on House's pants was spilled from one of [the] four vials of blood shipped to the [FBI] lab by local law enforcement agents—spilled either accidentally or intentionally. . . . The new body of evidence shows conclusively that the vials of blood were not properly handled and shipped by law enforcement and that the blood that spilled from the vials cannot otherwise be accounted for.

"Third, testimony from five new witnesses offered at the habeas hearing implicates Mr. Muncey in his wife's murder. . . . The State offered no evidence that any of these witnesses was biased in favor of House or prejudiced against Mr. Muncey. Fourth, the evidence completely undermines the reliability of the testimony of Billy Ray Hensley, the witness who said that on Sunday afternoon before the victim's body was found, he saw House coming up the embankment on Ridgecrest Road where the body was later found that day. Based on his own testimony and an examination of the record, it would have been impossible for Hensley to have seen House as he claimed."

After a lengthy review—close to ten thousand words—of testimony from both the original trial and the habeas hearing, Judge Merritt concluded that House met the actual innocence standard of the *Schlup* decision, which provided a **gateway** to further hearings on the claims in his original habeas petition. "At a minimum," Merritt wrote, "based on the newly presented evidence we should allow House to pass through the gateway so that his constitutional claims of ineffective assistance of counsel at the guilt and penalty phases of the case become cognizable again. The remedy for passing the gateway test is a remand for further proceedings on the underlying constitutional claim. In this case, however, I would go further and issue the writ of habeas corpus because the prisoner has affirmatively established a free-standing case of actual innocence. . . . The new evidence so completely turns the case around that the proof is no longer constitutionally sufficient to warrant a conviction or imposition of the death penalty. Thus House should be immediately released."

In a prescient statement, however, Judge Merritt reminded readers of his opinion (perhaps with Supreme Court justices in mind) that "officials who have prosecuted, sentenced and reviewed the case, are inclined to persevere in the belief that the state was right all along. They tend to close ranks and resist admission of error. . . . This case is a good example of how these errors can lead to the execution of a defendant who is actually innocent." As we shall see, during the next five years, one state official—Paul Phillips, who prosecuted Paul House in 1986 and still serves as Union County's district attorney—refused to make any admission of error in the case.

One of Judge Merritt's colleagues, Judge Ronald Gilman—another Tennessee native and a graduate of Harvard Law School—took a bemused attitude in his brief dissent from the majority's ruling. "After reading Judge Norris's majority opinion and Judge Merritt's dissent," he wrote, "I am convinced that we are faced with a real-life murder mystery, an authentic 'who-done-it' where the wrong man may be executed. Was Carolyn Muncey killed by her down-the-road neighbor Paul House, or by her husband Hubert Muncey? . . . At the end of the day, I am in grave doubt as to which of the above two suspects murdered Carolyn Muncey. I am also puzzled as to why more of my colleagues are not similarly in doubt after evaluating the well-written but diametrically opinions by Judges Norris and Merritt. Be that as it may, the question becomes what is a federal judge to do when faced with such grave doubt? . . . The proper disposition of this case, in my opinion, is to issue a conditional writ that would free House unless he is provided a new trial by the state of Tennessee. . . . Under circumstances where we face the execution of a man who might well be innocent, I believe that our system of justice requires no less."

Faced with a majority opinion that upheld the denial of Paul House's habeas petition but encouraged by the close division on the appellate court and the forceful tone and the exhaustive review of the record in Judge Merritt's dissent, Steve Kissinger and Mike Pemberton began to prepare the next step in this now eighteen-year-old case, a writ of certiorari to the U.S. Supreme Court.

6

Paul House's Appeal to the United States Supreme Court

On March 5, 2005, five months after the Sixth Circuit ruled by a one-vote margin to uphold Judge Jarvis's denial of Paul House's habeas corpus petition, Steve Kissinger filed a petition for a writ of certiorari with the United States Supreme Court. Mike Pemberton, who had provided pro bono assistance to Kissinger in the habeas hearing and the subsequent Sixth Circuit appeal, continued in that role but relinquished his formal representation in the case. Pemberton was replaced in the Supreme Court appeal by George Kendall, a partner in a prestigious New York law firm who had done pro bono work in dozens of death penalty cases, including several that reached the Supreme Court, and Theodore Shaw, the general counsel of the NAACP Legal Defense and Education Fund. With this power-house legal team, Kissinger felt that he had a good chance of convincing the justices to review (and hopefully overturn) the Sixth Circuit ruling.

As with the lower courts, you cannot appeal a decision to the Supreme Court because of the outcome of the case. You must argue that the process by which that outcome was reached was flawed, but for the Supreme Court, you must argue that this flaw was a judge misapplying a Supreme Court precedent. The questions put before the Supreme Court may be nationally important, but they also tend to be, at least in presentation, very narrow.

Cert petitions are governed by the Rules of the Supreme Court of the United States, and it's worth quoting here from Rule 10: Considerations Governing Review on Certiorari, which reads, "Review on a writ of certiorari is not a matter of right, but of judicial discretion. A petition for a writ of certiorari will be granted only for compelling reasons. The following, although neither controlling nor fully measuring the Court's discretion, indicate the character of the reasons the Court considers: (a) a United States court of appeals has entered a decision in conflict with the decision of another United States court of appeals on the same important matter; has decided an important federal question in a way that conflicts with a decision by a state court of last resort; or has so far departed from the accepted and usual course of judicial proceedings, or sanctioned such a departure by a lower court, as to call for an exercise of this Court's supervisory power; (b) a state court of last resort has decided an important federal question in a way that conflicts with the decision of another state court of last resort or of a United States court of appeals; (c) a state court or a United States court of appeals has decided an important question of federal law that has not been, but should be, settled by this Court, or has decided an important federal question in a way that conflicts with relevant decisions of this Court."

As we can see, the Supreme Court views its power and discretion in deciding which petitions to review as largely that of resolving conflicts between lower courts, on both the state and the federal levels. The guiding principle behind such review is that of establishing uniformity and predictability in the law, so that lower courts and litigants will know "what the law is," as Chief Justice John Marshall called the Court's main duty more than two centuries ago.

The Supreme Court rules specify in detail the format and the contents of cert petitions, down to page lengths, type size, and the color of their covers. One rule requires the parties (designated as "petitioner" and "respondent") to list the "Questions Presented" in the case, for the convenience of the law clerks and the justices who read the petitions.

Once a cert petition has been filed, the Court's rules provide for a **Brief in Opposition** from the respondent. Both documents then go before the justices for their decision on whether to grant the petition and set the case for oral argument. Readers should not be surprised to learn that no justice reads all petitions and opposition briefs before casting his or her vote on review. Considering that some eight thousand petitions are submitted during each term, this would be physically impossible. So, beginning in 1973, when the annual number of petitions was growing rapidly, Chief Justice Warren Burger instituted what became known as the **cert pool**. Justices are allotted four law clerks each, and every current justice except Samuel Alito participates in the pool, in which every petition and opposition brief is randomly assigned to a law clerk, who reads them and writes a memorandum, usually of just a few pages, summarizing the facts and the legal issues in the case, and ending with a recommendation on whether the Court should grant cert. These memos are then circulated to all justices for consideration at their periodic cert conferences.

Critics of the cert pool argue that it gives law clerks, who are recent law school graduates with no experience in law practice, too much power to decide the fate of cases, because the justices almost always adopt the clerks' recommendations. One lawyer complained that "I write petitions for clients that are read by someone no older than my daughter." On the other hand, supporters answer that bright clerks (and they're all bright) can easily spot petitions that are totally lacking in merit, saving the overburdened justices much time in reviewing them. Also, the justices aren't bound by the cert pool recommendations, and most justices personally review petitions that raise important and unresolved legal questions. As Justice Alito has noted, "There are plenty of cases where the clerks recommend a grant, and we deny, and plenty where they recommend we deny, and we grant." Whatever its virtues and flaws, the cert pool has become an established part of the Court's procedures. It's also important to note here that in their cert conferences, the justices follow the unwritten but long-followed **rule of four**, which means that it takes the votes of any four justices—one short of a majority—to grant cert. In practical terms, this means that a majority bloc of five justices, whether liberal or conservative, can't keep cases off the Court's docket and frustrate the minority, which might be able, had cert been granted, to persuade one or more justices in the majority bloc to change their minds and join a majority opinion or to win the vote of a "swing justice," such as Anthony Kennedy on the current Court.

Every cert petition to the Supreme Court argues that the lower state or federal court "erred" in its decision, and petitions begin with a statement of the **Questions Presented** for review. Steve Kissinger submitted two questions: "I. Did the majority below err in applying this Court's decision in *Schlup v. Delo* to hold that Petitioner's compelling new evidence, though presenting at the very least a colorable claim of actual innocence, was as a matter of law insufficient to excuse his failure to present that evidence before the state courts—merely because he had failed to negate each and every item of circumstantial evidence that had been offered against him at the original trial? II. What constitutes a 'truly persuasive showing of actual innocence' pursuant to *Herrera v. Collins* sufficient to warrant freestanding habeas relief?"

In their **opposition** to Kissinger's petition, Tennessee's lawyers— headed by attorney general Paul Summers, with associate deputy attorney general Jennifer Smith as lead counsel for the state—rephrased the questions presented to remove Kissinger's quotation, from the Sixth Circuit's majority opinion, that Paul House had made a "colorable claim of actual innocence" and suggested that the "new evidence was insufficient to excuse his procedural default in the Tennessee state courts" and thus did not warrant Supreme Court review.

Despite the state's opposition, the Supreme Court granted Kissinger's petition on June 28, 2005 (near the end of the Court's term) and set a briefing schedule, with oral argument set for the next term on January 11, 2006. During the summer and into the fall of 2005, Kissinger and Smith labored on their **merits briefs**, those submitted by parties to a case. Not surprisingly, Kissinger's brief relied heavily on the dissenting opinion of Judge Gilbert Merritt to the Sixth Circuit's opinion, while Smith urged the justices to focus on the majority opinion of Judge Alan Norris, from which she quoted at length. Both lawyers also solicited **amicus briefs** from legal groups that supported their side and whose views and supporting data might impress the justices.

Kissinger's prize catch in the contest for amicus briefs was one from the Innocence Project, a group founded in 1992 by Barry Scheck and Peter Neufeld, who both taught at the Benjamin N. Cardozo School of Law in New York City. The Innocence Project brief described its purpose as providing *"pro bono* legal services to indigent prisoners for whom post-conviction DNA testing can provide conclusive proof of innocence." Their work, Scheck and Neufeld claimed, had "freed dozens of citizens from our nation's prisons and death rows, scientifically proving their innocence beyond any doubt. . . . It has also exposed grievous flaws and shortcomings of various 'old' methods of forensic science, ones that directly caused many of these wrongful convictions." DNA evidence, the brief argued, had in dozens of cases—many of which it cited and discussed at length—discovered "false facts" from poorly conducted or even fabricated "forensic evidence that likely carried great weight with the original jury, but which is now known, to a scientific certainty, to have been erroneous." In Paul House's case, the Project's brief stated, "the jury was told by an expert witness for the prosecution that the defendant was 'definitely' a potential donor of semen on the victim's clothing . . . yet DNA has now definitely excluded him as the source."

Kissinger was also supported by an amicus brief submitted by seventeen former federal prosecutors and eight criminal law professors, who noted the growing erosion of public confidence in capital punishment. They cited a poll showing that 88 percent of respondents "were concerned that innocent people may be put to death" and suggested that this lay behind the decline in death sentences from 320 in 1996 to 144 in 2003. The American Bar Association also weighed in with a brief that criticized the procedures that failed to provide juries with adequate guidelines in deciding capital cases. On her side, Jennifer Smith was supported by an amicus brief signed by fifteen state attorneys general, which claimed that many of the death-row "exonerees" cited in the Innocence Project brief and later granted new trials were in fact guilty of the charges against them and were later convicted on the basis of "untainted" evidence. How much weight the justices give to amicus briefs is hard to determine, although they are occasionally cited in opinions. It seems likely, however, that the Innocence Project's brief was carefully read and considered by the justices who would decide whether the new evidence presented at Paul House's habeas hearing warranted a reversal of his conviction and death sentence or at least a new trial.

Oral Argument in the Supreme Court

"We'll hear argument next in *House v. Bell*," Chief Justice John Roberts announced as he called Steve Kissinger to the lectern in the Supreme Court's chamber at 11:08 A.M. on January 11, 2006. The justices had before them on the bench the briefs filed by the parties and those of amicus groups, along with copies of the **joint appendix** filed by both parties, which included the agreed-upon excerpts from the trial and habeas transcripts, as well as **bench memos** in which the justices' law clerks had summarized the issues in the case and the citations to important parts of the case record.

After the traditional opening, "Mr. Chief Justice, may it please the Court," Kissinger plunged into his argument, wasting no time with a review of the case's procedural history: "The jurors who convicted Mr. House of first-degree murder heard that semen stains on the clothing matched Mr. House. They didn't hear the DNA evidence which showed that not to be the case. The jurors who convicted Mr. House [also] heard that bloodstains on Mr. House's blue jeans matched the blood belonging to the victim. They didn't hear the assistant chief medical examiner for the State of Tennessee testify that the source of those bloodstains was a sample taken during Ms. Muncey's autopsy.

After two brief questions from Justice Sandra Day O'Connor about whether DNA testing was available at the time of the original trial, Justice Antonin Scalia took over with eleven successive questions, grilling Kissinger with an almost prosecutorial tone. Kissinger had probably anticipated this early inquisition from Scalia. Judge Jarvis had considered the evidence about the semen and the blood on the jeans, Scalia noted. "And didn't believe it. Right? Found as a matter of fact that the blood was not the result of the spill." Kissinger and Scalia then sparred over whether Jarvis made this ruling as a matter of fact or only as a legal conclusion, a difference probably lost on spectators in the chamber.

"I don't care" which one it was, Scalia retorted. "That's what the district court believed, having heard the testimony. . . . On that one point, do you claim that the district court was clearly erroneous?"

"If indeed it was a finding of fact, yes, that finding of fact was clearly erroneous," Kissinger replied.

After some eight minutes of Scalia's interrogation, Justice Anthony Kennedy finally broke in, asking Kissinger about the missing blood from the four vials taken during Carolyn Muncey's autopsy. "That question goes actually to the substance of our constitutional ineffective assistance of counsel claim," Kissinger said. "Trial counsel's expert had in his possession the photograph that showed an entire tube of blood missing. Therefore, he had evidence that there was something wrong with the blood. . . . Here's trial counsel with evidence that blood is missing. He knows it's a critical issue in the case, and he failed to go out and hire someone like the assistant chief medical examiner for the State of Tennessee who came into Federal court and testified that the source of this blood [on House's jeans] was, in fact, that empty tube."

Impatient during Kennedy's interruption, Scalia jumped back into the questioning: "That would be an important point if, in fact, it conclusively established that the blood was not the blood of the victim, but I don't think it does conclusively establish that, and if it doesn't, the less than perfect performance of counsel is no basis for setting aside the conviction." Scalia's statement gave Kissinger an opening to raise the crucial legal question in the case: "Again, the proof of innocence does not have to be absolute. This Court stated in *Schlup* that the fact that there . . . still exists even substantial evidence of guilt does not prevent a defendant from passing through the *Schlup* gateway."

Justice Stephen Breyer broke into this exchange to ask Kissinger a helpful question: "And you're saying yes, any reasonable juror would have had to have a reasonable doubt [on the blood evidence], irrespective of what the trial judge found."

"That's correct, Justice Breyer," Kissinger replied.

Justice Scalia could not resist a final dig: "Oh, but surely he's supposed to make factual determinations. . . . I do think we have to accept his factual findings as accurate unless they're clearly erroneous. And here, he made the factual finding that the blood was there [on the jeans] before the transport. I think I'm bound by that unless you can show that it is clearly erroneous, which I don't think you can."

With more than half of Kissinger's thirty minutes taken up by the "blood" issue, Justice Ruth Bader Ginsburg tried to move the argument ahead: "If you get through the [*Schlup*] gateway," she asked, "what are your constitutional claims that lie behind it? What is it that you would say if you got through the gate?"

Kissinger was grateful for this change of topic: "Justice Ginsburg, we believe that we have numerous instances of ineffective assistance of counsel. First, counsel's failure, knowing of the importance of the blood evidence [and] knowing of the photograph showing the missing blood, he failed to go forward and basically do what we did in federal court, which was hire an expert to look at the results of the FBI testing and to determine whether there was a viable defense strategy available there, which he did not." Kissinger went on: "Also, if we look at the record in this case, . . . where trial counsel also pointed toward Hubert Muncey Jr. as the actual perpetrator of this crime . . . we see five witnesses, many of whom were friends of Mr. Muncey, who presented evidence that showed that on the night of Ms. Muncey's murder, Mr. Muncey and Ms. Muncey had a fight at the C&C Recreation Center, that Ms. Muncey went home, that Mr. Muncey followed her there, that he confessed that when he returned home, he was angry and drunk, that they began to argue again, that he struck her in the head, that she fell, that he checked her lifeless body and found she was dead, and that he hid her body in the bushes."

Breyer then asked about the prosecution's withholding from Chuck Burks "evidence that they had that showed that Mr. Muncey had sexual relations with his wife the morning of the killing, and therefore, the semen that they found didn't necessarily belong to your client, but rather belonged to him. As it turned out, it didn't. . . . So you're going to make that Brady claim," referring to the prosecution's duty to provide the defense with all "exculpatory" evidence in its possession.

"We are also going to make the Brady claim," Kissinger replied. "In addition, Your Honor, if indeed that evidence was available to trial counsel, . . . it's one of those situations, Justice Breyer, where there is either [a Brady violation] for the state's failure to turn it over, or, if it was available, it's another instance of ineffective assistance of counsel."

Chief Justice Roberts joined the questioning: "You started out by talking about what the first jury knew and didn't know, but we are in a sense reviewing that jury determination. Correct?"

"That is correct, Justice Roberts," Kissinger agreed.

Roberts stated the issue before the justices: "We are supposed to look at all of the evidence, the new evidence and the old evidence, and determine simply whether or not it would be unreasonable for any juror to convict on the basis of all of that evidence. Is that right?" Kissinger once again agreed: "Your Honor, what *Schlup* says is that we are to step back and see whether it is more likely than not [given all the evidence, old and new] that any reasonable juror would vote to convict."

When Jennifer Smith replaced Steve Kissinger at the lectern, she began her argument with an attack on the habeas hearing testimony of her fellow state employee Dr. Blake: "The evidence presented in the district court fails to raise sufficient doubt about Mr. House's guilt to justify review of his procedurally defaulted claims because reasonable jurors would not ignore that Mr. House's jeans were stained with the blood of Carolyn Muncey. That is a fact that has not been undermined by any of the evidence presented in the federal habeas proceeding. The enzymatic degradation theory of Dr. Blake was so thoroughly discredited in the federal evidentiary hearing that it is highly unlikely that any reasonable juror, viewing all the evidence, would be convinced by it, let alone that everyone would vote to acquit in light of it."

Justice Breyer expressed doubt about this claim. Much like Justice Scalia's grilling of Kissinger, Breyer asked Smith twenty-three questions about the blood evidence. He and Smith sparred for almost fifteen minutes over the disagreements between FBI serologist Paul Bigbee and Dr. Blake about "enzymatic degradation." It was Bigbee's report, in fact, on which Blake based his conclusion that the blood in the autopsy vials had degraded to the same extent as that on House's jeans and could not have come from Carolyn Muncey's body while she was still alive. This was, of course, a crucial issue in the question of how, when, and where the spots of Carolyn Muncey's blood got onto House's jeans (and one that Judge Jarvis had dismissed without any discussion). Referring to the record, Breyer stated, "I read that Dr. Blake said, Look, there are tiny little specks of blood on the jeans and we test them. They were tested. And they show that a certain enzyme deteriorated to degree X, and that's true of the test tube blood as well. Both deteriorated to degree X. But if you take fresh blood and spatter it [on the jeans], there will be no deterioration. So conclusion: the blood on the jeans came from the test tube. Now, you say that was discredited, but I didn't read anywhere that discredited it. What was the discrediting of that?" Smith replied that Dr. Blake's conclusion "was specifically discredited by the testimony of Agent Bigbee," without discussing why this was not shown in the record.

Justice John Paul Stevens took issue with Smith: "But does that finding rest on the conclusion that Dr. Blake was not credible and Agent Bigbee was credible?"

Smith backed away just a bit: "I think that that conclusion implicitly includes a finding that Agent Bigbee was credible and Dr. Blake was not credible."

Questions went on for another ten minutes on the blood evidence before the justices tired of the subject and shifted to another issue, initiated by Justice Scalia: "Ms. Smith, I'm interested in Mr. Muncey's confession. What do you say about that?"

"Your Honor," she replied, "I think that the confession evidence is perhaps the least reliable in terms of the *Schlup* analysis."

"What did the jury hear about Muncey's confession?" Justice O'Connor then asked.

"The jury was never informed of Muncey's confession," Smith conceded.

"I thought not," O'Connor said, with a verbal raising of her eyebrows.

Smith went on: "The fact of Muncey's confession didn't come up until thirteen to fourteen years after the trial had already been concluded. And that's one of the things that the district court found was significant." Justice David Souter was not impressed: "But wasn't the district court incorrect in that? Because as I understand it, there was evidence from one of the two witnesses who put in the confession evidence that she had gone to the sheriff's department to tell them about the confession and had simply gotten a runaround and finally left. So as I understand it, the record would not support a finding that the sources of evidence simply kept silent for over a decade."

Smith dug in her heels: "Your Honor, regardless of whether the witness waited or not, the court examined the credibility of the testimony and found that it wasn't credible. . . . In addition, the court also heard live testimony from Hubert Muncey Jr. himself, explaining his whereabouts and actually denying ever having made [the confession]. . . . So this confession, which has absolutely no corroborative support in the record, the court found that the [confession] testimony simply wasn't credible."

Justices Souter and Kennedy continued with questions about the semen evidence and the rape motive. "I assume," Souter began, "that any reasonable juror would have found the evidence of the semen stains extremely significant because not only did the state argue rape as a motive, possible motive, but there was a specific finding of an aggravated circumstance that the murder occurred in the course of kidnapping and rape. If that juror had heard the DNA evidence, that juror would have said the only positive evidence that a rape was committed here would be evidence that pointed to the husband, not in fact to the defendant House. And if a juror had heard that evidence, it seems to me it is highly unlikely that any reasonable juror would have concluded that the aggravating circumstance was found, and I suppose that would play a significant role in the ultimate conclusion. . . . But my understanding is that there is no evidence from which one would reasonably infer that House did this."

"Your Honor, the motive is well supported by the circumstances," Smith replied, without elaboration.

"But the semen was used to connect it to the defendant, and we now know that's wrong," Kennedy stated.

"If a reasonable juror knew that the semen belonged to Mr. Muncey and not Mr. House," Smith asserted, "the result would be exactly the same because Carolyn Muncey's blood was all over Mr. House's pants. That is an indisputable fact." With that logical twist, Smith concluded her argument. She left unanswered the question of how, if Paul House had not intended to rape Carolyn Muncey and killed her when she resisted, her blood would have wound up on his jeans.

After a brief rebuttal from Steve Kissinger, in which he stressed the undermining of the "old" evidence by the "new" evidence from the habeas hearing, Chief Justice Roberts concluded the arguments at 12:08 P.M. "Thank you, counsel. The case is submitted."

Unlike most Supreme Court arguments, in which the lawyers and the justices discuss the legal issues and precedents that apply to the case, the House case arguments focused almost exclusively on the facts of the case, both the "old" and the "new" evidence. The main issue the justices seemed to consider crucial in the arguments can be summed up in one word: blood. More than half of the questions to both lawyers related to the blood on Paul House's jeans: when, where, and how did

Carolyn Muncey's blood get on the jeans? If it got there, as the state claimed, at the time of her murder, House was almost certainly guilty and did not deserve a new trial. But if the blood was spilled on the jeans from the autopsy vials, as Dr. Blake had testified, the most incriminating piece of evidence for House's guilt was compromised. The legal question before the justices was not whether House had proved his "actual innocence" at the habeas hearing, but whether Judge Jarvis had committed "clear error" in denying the habeas petition, warranting a new trial in the case.

The Supreme Court Decides the House Case

On June 12, 2006, five months after the oral arguments, the justices issued the ruling and opinions in *House v. Bell*. Reporters who cover the Court are handed copies of the opinions at 10:00 A.M. on "decision days" (opinions are now also posted at the same time on the Court's website). They first look at the last page to see the outcome. In the House case, it read, "reversed and remanded." The Court had reversed the 2004 ruling of the Sixth Circuit, remanding the case to the district court in Tennessee "for further proceedings consistent with this opinion."

The Supreme Court was essentially ordering that House be tried all over again, in front of a jury, to allow them to hear all of this new (exculpatory) evidence. Of course, the state of Tennessee could decide not to bother with the new trial and simply drop the charges.

Justice Anthony Kennedy wrote for himself and four colleagues— Justices John Paul Stevens, Ruth Bader Ginsburg, David Souter, and Stephen Breyer—in the 5–3 majority opinion. (Justice Sandra Day O'Connor, who participated in the oral arguments, had retired and did not vote; her replacement, Justice Samuel Alito, took his seat in January 2006 and chose not to vote, although Court rules would have allowed him to do so.) Chief Justice John Roberts wrote for the three dissenters, who included Justices Antonin Scalia and Clarence Thomas.

Because both the majority and the dissenting opinions tracked very closely the Sixth Circuit opinions of Judges Alan Norris and Gilbert Merritt, although reversing their outcomes, I will summarize and quote the most significant excerpts of Justice Kennedy's majority opinion and Chief Justice Roberts's dissent. The first half of Kennedy's thirty-six-page opinion related the facts of the House case, drawn largely from the original trial transcript, and the case's procedural history, from House's appeals in the Tennessee courts through the habeas hearing and the appeals of Judge Jarvis's denial of the habeas petition to the Sixth Circuit.

Justice Kennedy then moved to the *Schlup* "gateway" standard, which held that a habeas petitioner must present "new reliable evidence—whether it be exculpatory scientific evidence, trustworthy eyewitness accounts, or critical physical evidence—that was not presented at trial," and which, had such evidence been available and presented to a jury, would establish that "it is more likely than not that no reasonable juror would have found [the defendant] guilty beyond a reasonable doubt." Kennedy held that considering both the "old" and "new" evidence, "There is no dispute in this case that House has presented some new reliable evidence" that cast doubt on his guilt, adding that "the State has conceded as much" in respect to the semen evidence. Kennedy also stressed that "the *Schlup* standard does not require absolute certainty about the petitioner's guilt or innocence," but just enough reliable evidence to cast doubt on the jury's guilty verdict.

Kennedy looked at three crucial issues in the case record: the new DNA evidence about the source of the semen on Carolyn Muncy's clothing; the bloodstains on House's jeans; and testimony that Little Hube Muncey had confessed to killing his wife. On the DNA evidence, Kennedy wrote that "we consider the new evidence of central importance," because "it was the only forensic evidence at the scene that would link House to the murder." In addition, it had provided the prosecution with rape as a motive for the crime. "When the only direct evidence of sexual assault drops out of the case," Kennedy wrote, "so, too, does a central theme in the State's narrative linking House to the crime," for which rape was the only motive suggested by the prosecution.

Kennedy devoted seven pages of his opinion to the "small, even minute stains in scattered places" on House's jeans, which he called the "only other relevant forensic evidence" in the case. Citing testimony at the habeas hearing about the "poor evidence control" of the jeans, from the time they were discovered in Donna Turner's laundry hamper, through their delivery to the FBI lab and then to defense examiners, Kennedy said this "evidentiary disarray surrounding the blood, taken together with Dr. Blake's testimony and the limited rebuttal of it in the present record, would prevent reasonable jurors from placing significant reliance on the blood evidence."

Kennedy then turned to testimony at the habeas hearing about Little Hube's confession to Kathy Parker and Penny Letner. During the habeas hearing, Kennedy wrote, "House presented troubling evidence that Mr. Muncey, the victim's husband, himself could have been the murderer." Dismissing Judge Jarvis's finding that Parker and Letner were "not credible" because they waited "too long" to tell their stories in court, Kennedy said "the record indicates no reason why these two women, both lifelong acquaintances of Mr. Muncey, would have wanted either to frame him or help House." Kennedy emphasized that "Parker's and Letner's testimony is not comparable to the sort of eleventh-hour affidavit vouching for a defendant and incriminating a conveniently absent suspect, . . . nor was the confession Parker and Letner described induced under pressure of interrogation." Conceding that the "evidence pointing to Mr. Muncey is by no means conclusive," Kennedy wrote, added to "the challenges to the blood evidence and the lack of motive with respect to House, the evidence pointing to Mr. Muncey likely would reinforce other doubts as to House's guilt."

Kennedy summed up the majority's conclusion in these words: "This is not a case of conclusive exoneration. Some aspects of the State's evidence . . . still support an inference of guilt. Yet the central forensic proof connecting House to the crime—the blood and the semen—has been called into question, and House has put forward substantial evidence pointing to a different suspect. Accordingly, and although the issue is close, we conclude that this is the rare case where—had the jury heard all the conflicting testimony—it is more likely than not that no reasonable juror viewing the record as a whole would lack reasonable doubt." Kennedy added that House had not met the *Herrera* standard of meeting the "extraordinarily high" burden of proving his "actual innocence," but that he "has satisfied the gateway standard set forth in *Schlup* and may proceed on remand with procedurally defaulted constitutional claims" that he received the "ineffective assistance of counsel" at his original trial. In effect, the majority instructed Judge Jarvis to take a second and closer look at the case, with findings that were "consistent with this opinion."

In his dissenting opinion, half as long as Kennedy's, Chief Justice Roberts chided the majority for "second-guessing" Jarvis, who had "attentively presided over a complex evidentiary hearing, often questioning witnesses extensively during the presentation of critical evidence." Roberts accused the majority of having "done little more than reiterate the factual disputes presented below" and engaging in "unbridled speculation" about the possible impact on trial jurors of the new evidence presented at the evidentiary hearing. Noting that *Schlup* had required a habeas petitioner to present "new *reliable* evidence" to support an "actual innocence" claim, Roberts used the words *reliable* and *reliability* nineteen times in his opinion to underscore his assertion that Jarvis had "observed the witnesses' demeanor, examined physical evidence, and made findings about whether House's new evidence was in fact reliable."

On each of Jarvis's rulings on the disputed issues of the blood evidence and Little Hube's confession, Roberts sided with Jarvis's "finding that [House's] new witnesses were not credible." Roberts asserted that Dr. Blake's testimony at the evidentiary hearing had been "rebutted" by Agent Bigbee and agreed with Jarvis that the testimony of Kathy Parker and Penny Letner was "not credible." The Chief Justice read *Schlup* as holding that a habeas petition based on "new" evidence must be denied if the judge decides that even *one* hypothetical juror might vote to convict the defendant. Concluding that the "new" evidence from the evidentiary hearing "is not substantially different from that considered by House's [trial] jury," Roberts found it "more likely than not that in light of this new evidence, at least one juror, acting reasonably, would vote to convict House. The evidence as a whole certainly does not establish that House is actually innocent of the crime of murdering Carolyn Muncey, and accordingly I dissent."

The accuracy of Roberts's prediction would be tested if Judge Jarvis ruled—as the Court's majority virtually ordered—that Paul House deserved a new trial, and if the jurors heard the testimony of Dr. Blake, Kathy Parker, Penny Letner, and the other witnesses from the evidentiary hearing. It would, of course, take the unanimous vote of all twelve jurors to convict him once again.

Given the Court's holding in favor of Paul House, its decision attracted widespread media attention. A *Washington Post* editorial applauded the ruling, saying that "in cases where an inmate has a particularly strong claim of innocence, procedural barriers sometimes have to give way to prevent a miscarriage of justice. . . . Given how many innocents have been wrongly convicted and later freed from death row and lengthy prison terms, opening the door for review makes a great deal of sense." The *Post* editorial, however, noted that "Mr. House still has a long way to go to get his conviction overturned."

7

The House Case Returns to the Federal and State Courts

The Supreme Court's remand of the House case to Judge Jarvis came with an admonition that his reconsideration of the habeas petition must be "consistent" with the majority's ruling. However, the lawyers on both sides never got the chance to learn whether Jarvis would, in effect, overrule himself and grant the petition. Jarvis had been diagnosed in 2002 with lung cancer, which was treated with chemotherapy and radiation. In early 2007, he decided to stop the treatment because it made him ill, and he relinquished his judicial duties. On May 15, 2007, the House case was reassigned to District Judge Harry S. "Sandy" Mattice, three weeks before Jarvis died. A 1981 graduate of the University of Tennessee Law School, Mattice spent twenty years in private practice (and was active in state Republican politics) before his appointment as U.S. attorney for the Eastern District of Tennessee, after which President George H. W. Bush named him to the federal bench in that district. Known as a cautious and careful judge, Mattice spent several months reviewing the record in the House case before he issued his order on the habeas petition on December 20, 2007, giving Paul House an early Christmas present. It was also House's forty-sixth birthday, making the decision doubly welcome.

In cases in which the parties agree that all "material evidence" is available to the court and not in dispute, leaving the judge solely with issues of law to decide, either or both parties are allowed under federal rules to file what are called **motions for summary judgment**. After reviewing the numerous claims in the summary judgment motion that Steve Kissinger had filed after the Supreme Court's decision, Judge Mattice denied the majority on grounds of procedural default at earlier stages of the case, but he found merit in four claims. First, he ruled that prosecutors at House's original trial should have disclosed to Chuck Burks the admission by Little Hube Muncey that he had sex with his wife the morning of her death, which "would have assisted defense counsel in refuting the prosecution's theory that the semen [on Carolyn Muncey's clothing] came from petitioner" and would have undermined the rape motive in the case. The failure to disclose this "exculpatory" evidence constituted prosecutorial misconduct, Mattice concluded.

Second, Judge Mattice ruled that prosecutors should have disclosed to Burks the TBI report that no blood was found on House's tennis shoes, which would "have been relevant to his defense, especially since blood was found on the hem of [House's] jeans." Third, Mattice said, "the prosecution should have disclosed, and trial counsel should have discovered, the mishandling of the blood evidence," casting blame on both sides. Finally, quoting the Supreme Court's discussion of the habeas testimony of Kathy Parker and other witnesses to Little Hube's regular abuse of his wife, Mattice found that Burks had provided "ineffective assistance of counsel" in failing to "discover and present all witnesses who could testify as to the husband's abuse of his wife and thus lend credence to the defense theory" that Little Hube might be implicated in Carolyn's death.

Based on these findings, Mattice concluded that House "is entitled to a new trial on all the evidence and therefore will be granted a conditional writ of habeas corpus that will result in the vacation of his conviction and sentence unless the State of Tennessee commences a new trial against him within 180 days after this judgment becomes final."

The reaction on both sides to Judge Mattice's ruling was predictable. "I've spoken with Mr. House," Steve Kissinger told a reporter. "He's pleased with the judge's decision. I am as well. It's been a long time coming."

On his part, Paul Phillips vowed to go forward with a new trial, although he hedged his bet. "I expect we would do that," he said. "I am satisfied there is proof beyond a reasonable doubt of [House's] guilt. Obviously, we would have to get in touch again with all of the witnesses and make sure we could put on adequate proof." The House case had become a political issue as well in Tennessee. State representative Mike Turner, a Democrat, sent a letter to governor Phil Bredesen, a fellow Democrat, signed by thirty-two state lawmakers of both parties, urging him to pardon House. Undoubtedly aware of death-penalty support among his constituents, Bredesen declined to intervene. Turner also said he would ask Tennessee's attorney general, Bob Cooper, not to appeal Mattice's ruling. Judicial rules gave Cooper thirty days—until January 19, 2008—to file an appeal with the Sixth Circuit. "I expect he probably won't," Turner said of Cooper's possible appeal. "And I think the local prosecutor probably won't pursue it. He'd have to be crazy because there's not any evidence. I think [Paul House] will be home in 180 days."

Turner was wrong in his prediction about Cooper. On January 18, 2008, the attorney general filed an appeal with the Sixth Circuit. At the same time, Cooper's office asked Judge Mattice to grant a **stay** of his order, pending the outcome of the Sixth Circuit appeal, which would effectively delay a new trial for another 180 days after the Sixth Circuit ruling (assuming that court denied the appeal). In response to the state's appeal and stay motion, Steve Kissinger filed a motion with Mattice, asking him to order Paul House's release from state custody until the state's appeal was decided, and also filed a **cross-appeal** with the Sixth Circuit, arguing that Mattice had erred in ruling against a relatively minor issue in Kissinger's summary judgment motion. The cross-appeal was intended to preserve that issue for briefing and argument before the appellate judges.

What followed these dueling appeals and motions, during the following six months, was a flurry of some thirty motions, briefs, arguments, and judicial orders and opinions before Judge Mattice and the

Sixth Circuit, sometimes crossing paths and creating judicial frustration and annoyance. Discussing each motion—with such captions as "Amendment to Pending Motion to Reconsider And/Or Clarify Order and Motion for Order Enforcing the Writ"—would unduly extend this account of the proceedings and bury readers in legal maneuverings, so only the most important will be discussed in this chapter. Summed up, the state's lawyers were seeking to delay any new trial as long as possible, giving Paul Phillips time to rebuild his damaged case, while Steve Kissinger sought to get Paul House released from prison as soon as possible, confident that the Sixth Circuit would eventually uphold Judge Mattice's order. One cynical columnist for the Nashville *Tennesseean* suggested that the state's lawyers were hoping that Paul House would die in prison before their delaying tactics were exhausted.

The first judicial response to the opposing motions came on February 28, 2008, when Judge Mattice heard arguments from Steve Kissinger and Jennifer Smith on the release and stay motions. Mattice had ordered that House's prison doctor, Madubueze Nwozo, appear and testify as to House's medical condition. For the past four or five years, House had suffered from an incurable and progressive case of multiple sclerosis, leaving him confined to a wheelchair. Dr. Nwozo affirmed that House could not walk or bathe himself without assistance. Kissinger called House's mother, Joyce, who told Mattice that she could care for her son at her home in Crossville, Tennessee; that she had taken a course in caring for disabled persons; that friends had volunteered to look after Paul while she was at work as a clerk in a nearby resort; and that a doctor had offered to give Paul his medications and injections. In response, Smith claimed that House, if released, posed a "risk of flight" and a "danger to the community," asserting—to Judge Mattice's obvious skepticism—that House might find someone to drive him to an airport for an escape to a foreign country or could lure an unsuspecting woman close enough to his wheelchair to assault her. On the stay motion, Smith conceded that the state would "probably not" prevail in its Sixth Circuit appeal. In his opinion on April 7, 2008, Judge Mattice granted Kissinger's motion to release House from prison, pending a recommendation by federal probation officers on "the appropriate conditions for petitioner's release." Splitting the baby, however, Mattice granted Smith's stay motion, saying it would "be a waste of judicial resources to require the State to retry petitioner in state court while simultaneously pursuing an appeal to the Sixth Circuit," effectively delaying any new trial until 180 days after the Sixth Circuit decided the state's appeal.

After an oral argument by Kissinger and Smith on April 30, 2008, a three-judge Sixth Circuit panel—including two judges who had voted in 2004 to uphold Judge Jarvis's habeas denial—waited only five days to unanimously affirm Judge Mattice's "conditional" habeas grant. The panel's three-paragraph opinion, issued on May 5, revealed its members' annoyance about the waste of judicial time on an appeal that Jennifer Smith had conceded would "probably not" succeed. "Having had the benefit of the guidance provided by the Supreme Court," the panel said, "and the extensive consideration that this case has received in the course of its twenty-year history, a detailed opinion by this court would serve no useful purpose and would only further delay resolution of this matter. The judgment of the district court is affirmed."

Judges rarely speak to the media about cases that come before them, but circuit judge Gilbert Merritt—whose 2004 dissent had been largely adopted by the Supreme Court and who sat on the panel that affirmed Judge Mattice's habeas grant—broke with protocol in an interview with a Nashville *Tennessean* reporter. "The blatant prosecutorial misconduct in this case shows two things," Merritt said. "First, the local district attorney in East Tennessee should never have prosecuted House in the first place, but certainly should have released him more than ten years ago once he received the exculpatory DNA evidence. Second, the local district attorneys, rather than the Attorney General or the Governor, exercise almost complete control over the system of criminal justice in Tennessee. They are frequently mistaken and frequently abuse their power. This is a case where the local DA made an egregious error twenty-two years ago and refuses to this day to admit the error in the face of clear evidence that someone other than House committed the crime." This judicial tongue-lashing did not sway Paul Phillips. "I'm looking forward to giving [House] a new trial," he said. "I am confident we will be ready within 180 days," hinting that he would produce new evidence and witnesses to prove House's guilt.

The Final Rounds in the Federal and State Courts

With the original retrial date of June 17, 2008, fast approaching, and with no word that state officials had appointed a new lawyer to represent House in the Union County court, Kissinger (who was limited to appearing in federal courts) asked Judge Mattice to bar any retrial, arguing that House was prejudiced by having no lawyer to prepare for trial in such a short time. At a hearing before Mattice on May 28, Kissinger learned for the first time that a Union County judge, Shayne Sexton, had issued, six days earlier, an **ex parte** order at the request of Paul Phillips, ordering that House remain in state custody until his retrial. An ex parte order is one granted by a judge without an opportunity for a defendant to be heard and is highly improper, especially when a defendant has no lawyer. Outraged by this development, Kissinger filed an **emergency motion** with the Sixth Circuit, asking again for an order barring any retrial and for House's release on bail to his mother's custody, as Judge Mattice had already ruled. After a quickly arranged hearing in Nashville, the Sixth Circuit panel ordered Judge Mattice to "supplement the record" on whether the state had complied with the conditions he set for a retrial.

Kissinger was further enraged after Judge Sexton held a hearing at the Union County courthouse on June 6, at which he appointed Dale Potter, an assistant public defender, to represent House. Potter, a former police officer and state prosecutor, had no time to prepare for this hearing, at which Sexton also ordered that House remain in state custody until the next hearing, unless he posted bail of $500,000, an amount that House's mother could not raise, and which would require a nonrefundable $50,000 payment to a bondsman. House became eligible for bail after Paul Phillips announced he would not seek the death penalty at a retrial, citing House's declining health and the time he had already spent in prison.

Judge Sexton also disclosed that he had granted an ex parte order to Phillips, allowing him to send three pieces of evidence to the FBI for DNA testing: cigarette butts found at the scene where Carolyn Muncey's body was discovered, scrapings from underneath her fingernails with traces of blood on them, and strands of hair recovered from her hands.

Dale Potter responded with a motion that Judge Sexton **recuse** himself from the case, noting that Sexton had worked for eleven years as a prosecutor under Paul Phillips, including times during House's early appeals. On June 25, after Sexton stepped aside, the Tennessee Supreme Court appointed a retired judge from Memphis, Jon Kerry Blackwood, to preside over the case.

Two days later, at a hearing in the Union County courthouse, Blackwood slashed House's bail to $100,000 and set the conditions for his release to his mother's custody in Crossville: House must register with local officials as a convicted sex offender, wear a GPS-tracking ankle monitor, and leave home only for medical appointments and court appearances. After an anonymous donor donated the $10,000 cash bond to secure the bail, Paul House finally left prison on July 2, 2008, after more than twenty-two years on death row. Television crews filmed him being wheeled to a waiting van, where his mother waited with a can of Pepsi and a Snickers bar. The media followed them to her home in Crossville, for his favorite meal of chile verde and cherry cheesecake. House spoke briefly with reporters on his arrival in Crossville. "It's been okay," he said. "I get to watch movies and eat whatever I want."

For all practical purposes, his release from prison ended Paul House's death-row ordeal, although he remained under indictment and house arrest. But there was still unfinished business in both federal and state courts, as Steve Kissinger continued to urge Judge Mattice to bar a retrial, and Dale Potter continued to prepare for one that was now scheduled to begin on October 13, 2008. In the meantime, Judge Blackwood ordered House and Little Hube Muncey to submit new blood and saliva samples for DNA testing of the cigarette butts, fingernail scrapings, and hair strands; however, Blackwood also ruled that this evidence should be submitted for testing to an independent lab, rather than to the FBI.

At a hearing before Judge Mattice on September 18, over strenuous objection from Jennifer Smith, Paul Phillips conceded that DNA testing on the hair excluded Paul House, as well as Little Hube Muncey, as the source. "It came from some other male," he said, also admitting that the lab found no usable DNA on the cigarette butts and the fingernail scrapings. Phillips insisted, however, that this negative finding in fact supported a new prosecution theory. "We have statements suggesting

Mr. House was with other males on the night of Carolyn Muncey's death," he said. "The fact that this hair in her hand was not [House's] or her husband's is consistent with [House] being with other males that night." Kissinger scoffed at Phillips's odd logic that the lack of proof that the hair came from House somehow proved his involvement in the murder. "There's some evidence that just doesn't pass the smell test." Despite this blow to the prosecution's case, Judge Mattice refused to bar a retrial, leaving further proceedings to Judge Blackwood, who scheduled a retrial—the third date—for June 1, 2009.

We will never know whether the Supreme Court majority, for which Justice Kennedy wrote in 2006, was correct in holding that "no reasonable juror" would vote to convict Paul House at a retrial. Nor will we learn what "new" evidence or witnesses Paul Phillips would have presented, as he had promised. At a hastily arranged hearing on May 12, 2009, Phillips asked Judge Blackwood to dismiss the murder charge against House, which Blackwood promptly did. Phillips knew he had no chance of securing a conviction at a second trial. Paul House did not attend the hearing that finally ended the murder charges against him after spending twenty-two years on death row. "Court is the last place I want to be," he told a reporter. Asked for his reaction to the dismissal, which meant he could remove the ankle bracelet and visit his grandfather in California, House revealed his lingering bitterness. "I guess they handled it pretty bad," he said. "I could say all kinds of things, but I will keep my mouth shut." House's mother, Joyce, was not so reticent. "We are just floating around here on Cloud Nine," she said. "I am just glad it's over. It has been too long in coming." Steve Kissinger, aided by Mike Pemberton and joined at the end by Dale Potter, had devoted thirteen years of his career to the House case and says he does not ever want to handle another one like it.

An Evaluation of the House Case

The final step in the criminal justice process takes place outside the courtroom, as lawyers, judges, commentators, and concerned members of the public evaluate that process and how it worked in a particular case. In the vast majority of criminal cases, whether defendants are found "guilty" or "not guilty" after a trial, a review of their outcomes reveals little or no doubt that the outcome was correct and that the process worked as it was designed to do. We can even conclude that the process worked in Paul House's case, with his eventual release from death row and dismissal of his murder charge. But his case also reveals many flaws in the criminal justice system, from the very beginning, and which are documented in this account of the case: sloppy police work, unprofessional and even unethical conduct by lawyers on both sides, credulous jurors, and biased judges. This is not an indictment of the legal system as a whole; most police officers, lawyers, judges, and jurors take their jobs seriously and do their best. But the failures of even one person in this system can result in a "miscarriage of justice" that may cost a fellow citizen his or her freedom or life.

This section has recounted one of these "miscarriage of justice" cases, not because it's typical, but rather because it almost cost Paul House his life for a crime he almost certainly did not commit. I say "almost certainly" because it's still possible—although unlikely—that he did murder Carolyn Muncey, that Paul Phillips was correct when he convinced a jury that House went to Carolyn's home with the intention of raping her, killed her when she resisted, got her blood on his jeans during their struggle, dumped her body over an embankment, returned the next day to retrieve his incriminating tank top, and was fortunately spotted by Billy Ray Hensley on this return to the crime scene. The question for the jury, however, was whether Phillips proved these "circumstantial" allegations beyond a reasonable doubt, at a fairly conducted trial. He obviously did not, failing to carry out his prosecutorial duties in a professional and ethical manner.

It's possible as well—and more likely—that Little Hube Muncey killed his wife, "smacking" her during an argument that turned violent, causing a fatal cerebral hemorrhage, dumping her body, and trying to fabricate a false alibi even before her body was discovered. This more likely circumstantial case can no longer be proved beyond a reasonable doubt, however, given the passage of time and the absence of reliable evidence and witnesses. If Little Hube was indeed guilty and escaped prosecution and punishment, the local and state police and Paul Phillips bear responsibility for not considering him a suspect (after Paul House was in their sights) and not conducting a thorough investigation.

It's even possible that Carolyn Muncey was murdered by someone else or by more than one person. There are clues, never followed up by police or lawyers, that someone named "Jackie" might have killed her. There was Jackie Adkins, who found the body, and Jackie Beeler, about whom Chuck Burks questioned Lora Muncey at the trial, although Lora said she didn't know him. Chuck Burks even discovered that Janice Savage, who was then staying next door to the Munceys with the Clintons, heard Carolyn loudly say, "No, Jackie, no," that evening, but apparently Janice refused to testify and couldn't have identified "Jackie" if she had.

My point is that in Paul House's case, none of these possible scenarios could be proved to a jury beyond a reasonable doubt, because the system failed at every level. More correctly, some of the people who make up this system failed in their duties. Whatever its genuine strength in protecting the rights of citizens accused of crime and in protecting the public as well, human failure and error are bound to occur. Making sure these failures and errors are prevented as much as possible and are corrected when they do cost someone his or her liberty or life is a difficult but necessary task, one to which we should all devote thought and time as responsible citizens.

Perhaps the most perceptive evaluation of the House case and of the magnitude of the reformative tasks that still confront us came from David Dow, a law professor at the University of Houston, who has represented some fifty death-row inmates in their appeals. Writing in the *Washington Post* after the Supreme Court's decision in 2006, in an op-ed column titled "The End of Innocence," Professor Dow recounted the story of his client Johnny Joe Martinez, who was executed in Texas in 2002, "because his court-appointed lawyer neglected to file a proper appeal—a mistake he freely admitted to, attributing it to inexperience. When the Martinez case reached the federal courts, those courts . . . said too bad for Mr. Martinez; the mistake of his lawyer was attributable to him."

Professor Dow also wrote that "of the fifty death-row inmates I have represented, I have serious doubts about the guilt of three or four—that is, 6 to 8 percent, about what scholars estimate to be the percentage of innocent people on death row." Considering that in 2011 there were some 3,270 death-row inmates in thirty-five states with death-penalty laws, there would be at least 190 and perhaps 260 who are innocent.

That's a troubling number, even if a few may later be cleared and released through DNA and other evidence of their innocence. Among his fifty death-row clients, however, Professor Dow added, "In 98 percent of the cases, 49 out of 50, there were appalling violations of legal principles: prosecutors struck jurors based on their race; the police hid or manufactured evidence; prosecutors reached secret deals with jailhouse snitches; lab analysts misrepresented forensic results. Most of the cases do not involve bogus claims of innocence, . . . but the government corruption that the federal courts overlook so that the states can go about their business of executing."

Professor Dow concluded that death-penalty opponents "should shift their focus from the question of innocence, but that is what they ought to do. They ought to focus on the far more pervasive problem: that the machinery of death in America is lawless, and in carrying out death sentences, we violate our legal principles nearly all of the time." These comments provide a chilling but hopefully thought-provoking reflection on the serious flaws in America's criminal justice system.

PART II

"An Establishment of Religion"

The Ten Commandments and Crosses in the Courts

8

A Tale of Two Cities
and Two Cases

Our guided tour of the American civil law system and its legal procedures begins in the small town of Whitley City, the governmental
seat of rural McCreary County, Kentucky. Whitley City is not really a
city at all. Just eleven miles from the state's southeastern border with
Tennessee, it is barely more than a village, with only eleven hundred
residents, spread out on both sides of the Norfolk & Southern Railway
tracks and Highway 27, a two-lane road that stretches from Miami to the
Canadian border in northern Michigan. Whitley City is the county seat
of McCreary County, which itself has only seventeen thousand citizens
and houses the county's government in a two-story brick courthouse on
Main Street, topped by a white spire and fronted with an American flag.
The county's residents visit the courthouse to pay their property taxes,
obtain copies of birth and death records, and perform jury service in
cases that rarely generate headlines outside the local newspapers.

Before the fall of 1999, no big-city reporters or television crews
had covered anything from McCreary County. But they descended on
Whitley City in droves after county officials provoked a legal battle that

began in the Main Street courthouse and wound up in the chamber of the United States Supreme Court in 2005. Visitors to Whitley City pass a billboard on Highway 27 that reflects the deep-rooted beliefs of its people: "WARNING. Jesus is coming. RU ready?" This is hard-shell Baptist country. Some 3,400 of McCreary County's 4,000 church-goers attend services at one of the nine Southern Baptist churches, while another 300 are Methodists, and most of the rest belong to the Church of God and smaller Pentecostal churches. The county has only one Catholic church, with 55 members, and a small Mormon congregation. The nearest Jewish synagogue is more than sixty miles away, across the county's border in Knoxville, Tennessee.

Not only are most of McCreary County's residents evangelical Protestants, they are unabashedly patriotic and politically conservative. During World War II, more than half of the county's young men volunteered for service; of these 923 soldiers, 32 lost their lives in battle. Seven died in the Korean War, another 8 in Vietnam. More recently, 162 men and women have served in the conflicts in Afghanistan and Iraq. Members of American Legion Post 115 conduct annual memorial services for those who died in the nation's wars, featuring patriotic speeches and Christian prayer. Not surprisingly, fundamentalist religion and fervent nationalism have combined in McCreary County to make it a conservative Republican stronghold, a political tradition that goes back to the Civil War. Although Kentucky was a slave state, the people in the eastern counties backed the Union and voted for Abraham Lincoln. Virtually all of the region's elected officials are Republicans, and McCreary County voters backed John McCain over Barack Obama in 2008 by a 3–1 margin.

McCreary County is also mountain country, and many of its residents proudly trace their ancestry to the settlers who followed Daniel Boone across the Cumberland Mountains in the early nineteenth century. Until the 1960s, the county had a thriving economy, as railroad cars and trucks carried away millions of tons of coal and lumber from the mines and the forests in the region. Competition from strip mines, however, along with the federal government's purchase of 70 percent of the county's land for the Daniel Boone National Forest, closed most of the mines and the sawmills, leaving the county and state governments and the Forest Service as the leading employers.

Although tourism, spurred by the opening in 1974 of the Big South Fork River National Park, has created some jobs, McCreary County remains an economic backwater. The per capita income of the county's residents is less than half the national average; close to half of families with children under eighteen live below the poverty line, rising to 72 percent of those with children under five. More than a third of the county's adults lack high school diplomas, and the high school drop-out rate is double the state average. With few prospects of well-paying jobs in the county, many of those who do graduate move to more prosperous areas. Those who stay are often unemployed, but they remain loyal to their ancestral home.

In short, McCreary County's residents are deeply religious, patriotic, and conservative. These factors help explain why Jimmie Greene did not anticipate any objections when he posted the Ten Commandments on the courthouse wall on September 14, 1999. Greene, who headed the county's governing board, the Fiscal Court, had the title of judge-executive, although he performed no judicial functions. The posting ceremony, attended by American Legion members and local pastors, was featured in the local newspaper, the *McCreary County Record*. Greene was surprised when he received a letter, a few weeks later, from the American Civil Liberties Union office in Louisville. The ACLU's state director, Jeff Vessels, warned Greene that posting the Commandments in the courthouse was unconstitutional and demanded that the framed copy be removed. Vessels cited a 1980 Supreme Court decision, *Stone v. Graham*, which struck down a Kentucky law requiring public schools to post copies of the Ten Commandments on classroom walls. The national ACLU had recently launched a legal campaign against Ten Commandments displays in schools, parks, and public buildings, and its Kentucky branch had been monitoring the state's newspapers for reports of postings such as that in McCreary County.

Jimmie Greene bristled when he received Vessel's letter. Greene was born in 1928, and his family's roots were deeply planted in the county's rugged terrain. He left as a young man to enlist in the air force, served in both the Korean and the Vietnam wars, and retired after twenty-four years with the rank of master sergeant. When he returned home, Greene became active in Republican politics and was elected in 1978 to head the county's government. A lifelong Baptist and a long-time American Legionnaire, Greene viewed the ACLU's demand as challenging both his faith and his patriotism. "America was based on Christianity," he later said. "I respect other religions, but historically they had nothing to do with the founding of America." Greene noted that he posted the Ten Commandments next to other records of the county's history on the courthouse wall. "I spent twenty-four years of my life defending those documents," he added, "and it hurts me, angers me that we have liberal institutions that are trying to rewrite American history."

Jimmie Greene was not the only Kentucky official who received a letter from Jeff Vessels. The ACLU had collected reports that more than a dozen counties had posted the Ten Commandments on courthouse walls and warned them of possible lawsuits if these were not removed. Darrell BeShears, whom Greene knew well as judge-executive of neighboring Pulaski County, also received Vessel's threat of litigation. The two men did not respond to the letters, but they soon learned that Vessels had not issued an idle threat. On November 18, 1999, the Kentucky ACLU filed suits in federal court against both McCreary and Pulaski counties, naming Greene and BeShears as defendants.

Greene was surprised to learn that he had been sued for an act of which he was proud. He was even more surprised that one of the two plaintiffs in the suit against McCreary County was his own cousin, Louanne Walker. A McCreary County native, Louanne was a divorced mother with two grown sons and worked in a state agency that helped county residents with benefits such as food stamps and welfare payments. Prodded by her older son, whom she called a "pistol" on civil liberties issues, Louanne had called the ACLU office in Louisville and alerted Jeff Vessels to the Ten Commandments display in the courthouse. Louanne confessed that she had expected criticism from family and neighbors. "You know, this is a small county, and I'd say most of the people here are in favor of having the Ten Commandments posted in the courthouse," she said. "I hope they realize this is not a statement about the Ten Commandments. I'm not against the Ten Commandments. I'm just a firm believer in separation of church and state."

Louanne was joined as a plaintiff in the suit by a long-time friend, Dave Howe. Raised in upstate New York, the son of a Baptist minister, Howe had moved to McCreary County in the 1960s, where he and his wife ran a pottery shop. Dave also hosted a weekly program on the local radio station, playing bluegrass and country music (and slipping in his favorite jazz recordings). Despite his twenty-year residence in the county, Howe said many people still considered him an outsider and a radical. "I'm not a member of the twelve tribes of McCreary County," he joked. On a more serious note, Howe explained his reasons for challenging the Ten Commandments display. When he saw the Commandments on the courthouse wall, he said, "I felt that they were violating the law." Howe, like Walker, had no quarrel with the Commandments as a moral guide. "Don't take them out of your heart, don't take them out of your home, don't take them out of your church," he said. "But don't put them in my face in the courthouse."

On his part, Jimmie Greene professed shock at his cousin's decision to sue him and the county over the Commandments display, telling a reporter that "her mother and father are my aunt and uncle, who happen to be buried in a little plot on the family property. I went out there the other day to visit them, 'cause I thought they might be rolling over in their graves." Greene vowed to keep the Commandments in the courthouse lobby. "I think with the moral decay of America and the filth we see on television and read in print has reached a degree that folk, whether they believe in the Ten Commandments or not, say we have to put a stop to it," he said. "I'm not going to take them down. It's going to take the big man in the black robe to tell me to take them down." Despite the belligerent tone on both sides, however, the suit did not provoke the kind of community tension and personal animosity that marked similar disputes in other towns. Greene calls Dave Howe "a fine friend" and is a welcome visitor at Howe's home in Parkers Lake, next to the Baptist church that Greene attends every Sunday. Howe says he never faced any hostility during the six-year legal battle over the Commandments. "People down here have been very Christian," he said. "They disagree with my position, but they're tolerant." But Louanne and Dave took up Jimmie's challenge when the ACLU filed a lawsuit in federal court.

The Ten Commandments
Case from Austin, Texas

The next stop on our tour takes us from Whitley City, Kentucky, to Austin, Texas. It would be difficult to find any place in the United States more unlike Whitley City than Austin, the state capital of Texas.

For one thing, Austin is six hundred times larger in population, with 657,000 residents, making it the fourth-largest city in Texas and the sixteenth-largest in the nation, circled by a metropolitan area that includes another 800,000 people. Austin's colorful history has shaped its growth from a small town, first settled in the 1830s by what are now called "Anglos," into a diverse and very distinctive city. Originally part of Mexico, Austin became the capital of an independent nation when the Anglos broke away from Mexico and established the independent "Republic of Texas" in 1836. Austin remained the capital after Texas relinquished its independence and was annexed by the United States in 1845. The Civil War made Austin the capital of a Confederate state, after Texas seceded from the Union in 1861. The city's fourth role as a state capital came in 1870, when Congress readmitted Texas to the Union.

Austin's history and its diverse population have contributed to the city's present composition and culture and to its status as a liberal enclave in a conservative state. More than a third of Austin's residents are Hispanic and 10 percent are black; in fact, non-Hispanic whites constitute just 53 percent of the city's population. The biggest institution in Austin and the main influence on its economy, politics, and culture is the University of Texas, established in 1883 and now enrolling some 49,000 students. With almost 3,000 faculty and 17,000 staff members, the UT campus dominates Austin and is the city's largest employer. The university's science and technology programs have attracted high-tech industries to Austin and its suburbs, including Dell, IBM, Apple Computers, and National Instruments. The people who work in these businesses are well-educated and affluent. More than half of Austin's white residents have college degrees, and the median family income is $54,000. Only 9 percent of Austin's families, mostly Hispanic and black, live below the poverty line.

Whitley City and Austin also differ in religion and politics. Catholics, most of them Hispanic, are the largest religious group in Austin, but the city also has more than ten thousand Jewish residents who attend eleven synagogues, along with Buddhist and Hindu temples. Texas, of course, is now a solidly Republican state, and creative gerrymandering has given the GOP control of its legislature and congressional delegation. But Austin remains a Democratic bastion. In the 2008 presidential election, almost 70 percent of its voters supported Barack Obama over John McCain. In short, unlike those in Whitley City, Austin's residents are diverse in race and ethnicity, affluent and well-educated, and liberal in politics. The only link between the big Texas city and the small Kentucky town is that the Supreme Court heard arguments, on the same day in March 2005, over Ten Commandments displays in both places.

Every day, thousands of people enter the Texas state capitol building in Austin, a domed edifice that was erected in 1888. Some are legislators, others work in state offices, and many are tourists who gather in the giant rotunda and take guided tours around the building. Many of these people also stroll around the capitol's parklike grounds, which cover twenty-two acres in the city's center. Scattered around the grounds are seventeen monuments and twenty-two historical markers. The monuments, some exceeding thirty feet in height, include statues that celebrate the "Heroes of the Alamo," the fabled Texas Rangers, Confederate soldiers, Pioneer women, and Texas cowboys. Somewhat out of place, in this commemoration of Texas history, is a replica of the Statue of Liberty in New York City. Also out of place, in the mind of one frequent visitor to the capitol grounds, is a granite slab, six feet high and three feet wide, shielded by hedges from sight of the surrounding monuments. Carved into the slab is the text of the Ten Commandments, headed by the words, "I AM the LORD thy God." The inscription at its base reads, "Presented to the People and Youth of Texas by the Fraternal Order of Eagles of Texas 1961."

Thomas Van Orden is an unusual man and seemingly an unlikely person to file a lawsuit that could wind up in the Supreme Court. At that time, he was homeless and jobless and slept in a tent, where he stored his bedding and belongings. Every couple of weeks, he visited the Austin Resource Center for the Homeless, where he showered and washed his laundry. He got by, as the Beatles song goes, "with a little help from my friends," who donated food and a little cash. Van Orden, however, was not a stereotypical homeless person, strung out on alcohol or drugs. Until 1999, in fact, he was a member of the Texas state bar, a 1970 graduate of Southern Methodist University's law school. During 1971 and 1972, he served in Vietnam, first as a helicopter door gunner and later in the Judge Advocate General's corps. After his discharge, Van

Orden returned to Texas, got married, and practiced criminal defense law in Houston and Dallas.

After Van Orden got divorced and moved to Austin in 1993, however, things turned bad. He fell into a deep depression and got behind in his legal work. The state bar suspended his license in 1995, charging him with failing to perform work for clients and to pay his bar dues. The bar order also required Van Orden to submit a psychiatric report, certifying that his "current state of mental health does not render him incapable of routine law practice," as a condition of regaining his license. After a three-month suspension, followed by forty-five months of probation, he returned to practice but was again disciplined in 1999 for failing to report to bar officials who supervised his probation. Van Orden's license was lifted for another forty-five months, until September 2003, but he decided not to return to law practice. "I went through a real hard period and I'm not going back there," he told a reporter, declining to discuss any aspect of his personal life, except to say that he had overcome his depression.

Jobless and homeless, Van Orden began to spend his days in the Texas state law library, housed in the state supreme court building, just a few hundred feet from the capitol building. He kept up with legal decisions, especially First Amendment cases. "I'm happy when I get to the library in the morning," he said. "The ordeal of the night is over, and I'm back in a nice environment doing something I enjoy."

Two things happened in the fall of 2001 that gave Van Orden something to enjoy. First, he read a decision in which the Seventh Circuit federal appellate court had ruled unconstitutional a Ten Commandments monument on the Indiana state capitol grounds. That got him to thinking about the granite slab he passed every time he walked through the capitol grounds to the law library. Van Orden delved into law books, found other cases ruling against Ten Commandments monuments and displays, and decided to file a lawsuit in Austin's federal court. Texas governor Rick Perry, a conservative Republican, headed the list of defendants, along with state officials who administered the capitol grounds. Van Orden filed his suit in February 2002, claiming that the Ten Commandments monument violated the Establishment of Religion clause of the First Amendment (which reads, "Congress shall make no law respecting an establishment of religion") and that he was harmed by having to pass it on his trips to the law library. The district court clerk waived the filing fee, certifying that Van Orden was a pauper, and he used a $4 disposable camera to take pictures of the monument that he attached to his complaint. Raised as a Methodist and later a member of Austin's Unitarian Church, Van Orden later explained his motives in bringing the suit. "I didn't sue the Ten Commandments," he said. "I didn't sue Christianity. I sued the state for putting a religious monument on capitol grounds. It is a message of discrimination. Government has to remain neutral." The only thing that connected Louanne Walker, Dave Howe, and Thomas Van Orden was that all three strongly believed that the First Amendment barred the display of the Ten Commandments on public property.

Filing the Complaints in the Kentucky and Texas Cases

After our visits to Whitley City and Austin, we'll now move to the turning points that govern the civil process. The first of these decisions is whether to file a suit, based on an assessment of whether the facts and the legal grounds, in laws and judicial precedent, justify a suit. One of the most basic differences between civil and criminal cases is that whereas attorneys for the state decide whether there are grounds and evidence to support criminal charges, civil cases are initiated by the complaining party and his or her counsel.

Most conflicts between people and groups with differing values and interests are resolved without recourse to litigation, through discussion between the contending parties or through such procedures as **mediation** and **arbitration**, which mirror civil trials but are conducted quickly as private transactions, without opportunities for appeals. **Settlement without litigation** is most often reached in conflicts over money, such as contract disputes, in which the parties can agree on a compromise that satisfies both sides. The Ten Commandments cases, however, did not lend themselves to settlement through any of these options. Jimmie Greene in McCreary County and the state officials in Texas were confronted with "either-or" choices when they received demands to remove their Decalogue displays: either take them down, which they refused to do, or accept the risk of litigation.

The first formal step in a civil case is filing a **complaint** in a court with jurisdiction over the parties to the suit and the subject matter of the dispute. Complaints and all subsequent filings (known as **pleadings**) in federal court civil cases are governed by the rules and the procedures set out in the **Federal Rules of Civil Procedure**. Most state courts have adopted their own civil rules, which generally track the federal rules, with occasional deviations. Both federal and state courts also have **local rules**, dealing with matters such as time limits, serving documents, and forms.

The basic concept of a complaint, as the name indicates, is to set out the legal claims that plaintiffs bring against defendants. Every pleading, beginning with the complaint, must include the following: a **caption** indicating the **name of the court** in which it's filed; the **title** of the action (which must include the names of all parties, both plaintiffs and defendants); the **file number** assigned to the case by the court clerk; and a designation of the **type of pleading** (such as complaint, answer, or motion). To satisfy pleading requirements (and avoid an embarrassing dismissal before a complaint reaches a judicial hearing), a complaint must include the following: a reference to a state or federal statute or a constitutional provision that confers **jurisdiction** on the court to consider the case; an averment of proper **venue** (generally, the judicial district where the parties reside or the acts giving rise to the suit took place); a "simple, concise, and direct" **statement of the basic facts** in the case (to which documents can be appended, such as contracts); and a **statement of the relief sought** from the court. In most civil cases, the relief sought is a claim either for **monetary damages** from the defendants or for **injunctive relief**, a judicial order that a defendant perform certain acts or refrain from taking actions against the plaintiffs (many civil cases ask for both types of relief). Parties may also ask for a **declaratory judgment,** a judicial finding that one party is entitled to judgment as a matter of law. All pleadings must be signed by an attorney representing the parties or by a **pro se** party (from the Latin for "on behalf of oneself"), filing the suit without a lawyer.

It's important to note two points here. First, parties to a civil suit come in various kinds, which include **personal** (John Smith or Sarah Jones); **corporate** (Sam's Plumbing or British Petroleum); **organizational** (the ACLU or the National Rifle Association); or **governmental** (a local, county, state, or federal body or officials, from police officers to the U.S. president). Complaints can also list multiple parties and are often filed as **class actions**, in which large groups of people (such as corporate shareholders or employees who share a common interest and a common set of facts) combine their claims in one suit. Second, complaints may include multiple claims, such as negligence, fraud, or misrepresentation. The federal rules also provide (although it's rarely enforced) that all **averments** in a pleading be listed in numbered paragraphs, for the convenience of judges and other parties. With that brief outline of pleading rules for a civil complaint, and following the old adage of "show, don't tell," let's now look at the actual complaint in the McCreary County case (I have eliminated some paragraphs and renumbered the others). The complaint filed by Thomas Van Orden followed this standard outline as well.

UNITED STATES DISTRICT COURT
EASTERN DISTRICT OF KENTUCKY
London Division

AMRICAN CIVIL LIBERTIES UNION OF KENTUCKY; LOUANNE WALKER and DAVE HOWE,
Plaintiffs

v.

MCCREARY COUNTY, KENTUCKY; and JIMMIE GREENE, in his official capacity as McCreary County Judge Executive,
Defendants

COMPLAINT
Preliminary Statement

This is a suit for injunctive and declaratory relief under 42 U.S.C. Sec. 1983, challenging the continued posting of an unadorned version of the Ten Commandments in the McCreary County courthouse. The plaintiffs—a civil liberties organization whose McCreary County members use the courthouse for civic business and McCreary County residents who use the courthouse to transact civic business—contend that these unadorned displays endorse and favor religion, in violation of the establishment clause of the First Amendment to the U.S. Constitution.

Jurisdiction and Venue

1. The Court has jurisdiction over this case under 28 U.S.C. Sec. 1331, which provides for original district court jurisdiction over cases presenting federal questions.
2. Venue is proper in the Eastern District of Kentucky under 28 U.S.C. Sec. 1391, because the defendants reside there and events transpired there.

Parties

3. Plaintiff American Civil Liberties Union of Kentucky (ACLU) is a membership organization whose sole purpose is defending citizens' constitutional rights.
4. Plaintiff Louanne Walker (Walker) is an adult citizen of Kentucky, residing in McCreary County, Kentucky.
5. Plaintiff Dave Howe (Howe) is an adult citizen of Kentucky, residing in McCreary County, Kentucky.
6. Defendant McCreary County, Kentucky, is a local governmental entity organized under Kentucky law. It operates and controls the courthouse located in Whitley City, Kentucky.
7. Defendant Jimmie Greene (Judge Greene) is the County Judge Executive for McCreary County. As such, he serves as the county's chief executive branch officer and as a member of the county's legislative branch. In those capacities, he sets county policy, including the policy challenged here.

Factual Allegations

8. McCreary County owns, and the McCreary County defendant operates and controls, the McCreary County courthouse.
9. Displayed on the walls of the McCreary County courthouse is a framed copy of one version of the Ten Commandments. The display is located in the common areas of the courthouse, where it is readily visible to citizens. The Ten Commandments display is unadorned by any surrounding text, documents, or similar displays. It is not part of any larger historical or educational display.
10. The version of the Ten Commandments posted in the McCreary County courthouse is [a] uniquely Christian version; its text differs from the literal translation of the Hebrew.

11. The version posted in the McCreary County courthouse contains expressly sectarian and religious commands, such as observing the Sabbath, not worshipping idols, believing in a deity, and not taking the deity's name in vain.

12. The ACLU has members in more than 90 Kentucky counties, including McCreary County. These members must use their courthouse to transact civic business, such as obtaining and renewing licenses, registering property, paying local taxes, and (for some) voting. When transacting this civic business, they have occasion to view the Ten Commandments display in their courthouse. The ACLU appears as an organizational plaintiff to articulate and enforce the interests of each McCreary County ACLU member.

13. Plaintiffs Walker and Howe live in McCreary County. They must use their courthouse to transact civic business, such as obtaining and renewing licenses, registering property, paying local taxes, and registering to vote. When transacting this civic business, they have occasion to view the Ten Commandments display in their courthouse.

14. Each plaintiff is committed to defending and preserving the American form of democracy. Each supports and is proud of the individual freedom and limited government secured by the Bill of Rights. Each believes in the "separation of church and state" and "freedom of religion" guaranteed by the free exercise and establishment clauses of the First Amendment.

15. Each plaintiff believes that religious freedom can best be preserved if government remains strictly neutral toward religion, neither favoring nor disfavoring religion or any religious sect. Each plaintiff therefore believes that government veers from its proper limited role when it favors or endorses particular religious views, even if the plaintiffs share those views. Specifically, each plaintiff believes that government has no business supporting or opposing religious views about a deity, Sabbath observance, or idolatry.

16. For these reasons, each plaintiff opposes the specific display of the Ten Commandments in the McCreary County courthouse.

17. Each plaintiff perceives this Ten Commandments display as a violation of the Constitution inconsistent with the American form of democracy and as an assault on religious freedom. Each plaintiff therefore is offended by the continued display and by having to view this display when transacting civic business in the McCreary County courthouse. The unwelcome exposure to the government's religious message diminishes each plaintiff's enjoyment of the courthouse.

18. The ACLU has asked McCreary County and its policymaking officials to cease their unlawful and offensive displays, but these officials have failed and refused to do so.

19. The continued unadorned display of the Ten Commandments in the McCreary County courthouse therefore constitutes the policy of the defendants.

20. The plaintiffs are now suffering, and will continue to suffer, irreparable harm for which they have no adequate remedy at law.

Claim for Relief

21. The defendants' acts, practices, and policies constitute an endorsement of, and favoritism toward, religion.

22. The defendants therefore have deprived the plaintiffs of rights secured by the establishment clause of the First Amendment, applied to the states through the Fourteenth Amendment to the U.S. Constitution.

WHEREFORE, the plaintiffs request that this Court:

A. Declare unconstitutional the McCreary County Ten Commandments display;

B. Issue preliminary and permanent injunctions against the continuation of these defendants' display;

C. Award plaintiffs their costs, including reasonable attorney fees, pursuant to 42 U.S.C. Sec. 1988; and

D. Grant any additional relief to which the plaintiffs may be entitled.

/s/ *David Friedman*
General Counsel
American Civil Liberties Union of Kentucky

One part of the *McCreary County* complaint is worth noting here. David Friedman based the court's subject-matter jurisdiction on both the First Amendment and **Section 1983 of Title 42 of the U.S. Code**. Constitutional provisions are not normally **self-enforcing** but require a **statutory basis** for their enforcement. Most civil rights and liberties cases rest the court's jurisdiction on Section 1983, which reads, "Every person who, under color of any statute, ordinance, custom, or usage, of any State or Territory or the District of Columbia, subjects, or causes to be subjected, any citizen of the United States or other person within the jurisdiction thereof to the deprivation of any rights, privileges, or immunities secured by the Constitution and laws, shall be liable to the party injured in an action at law, suit in equity, or other proper proceeding for redress . . ."

This section of federal law was enacted by Congress in 1871, to protect newly freed slaves from arbitrary arrests, imprisonment, and often torture by sheriffs and other officials in Southern states and to provide a **safe haven** in federal courts when local and state officials refused to curb these lawless acts, because state judges almost always dismissed the few indictments that were brought, and all-white juries refused to convict those officials who did face trial. During the last half-century, no other provision of federal law has proved more effective in protecting citizens from official misconduct, and almost every civil rights and liberties lawyer uses Section 1983. Jimmie Greene posted the Ten Commandments in his courthouse **under color** of his official position and thus became subject to the suit against him.

Before the McCreary and Pulaski cases reached their first court-room hearing, Jimmie Greene and Darrell BeShears took identical steps that would later prove significant in judicial decisions. Their respective county attorneys, who mostly handled criminal matters and state law cases that raised no federal constitutional issues, stepped aside in the Commandments cases. On December 8, 1999, Greene and BeShears announced that Ronald D. Ray would represent the counties in federal court. A retired Marine Corps colonel, with Bronze and Silver Stars from Vietnam combat service, and a former deputy assistant secretary of defense during the Reagan administration, Ray was also a vocal supporter of Alabama judge Roy Moore. Known as the "Ten Commandments judge," Moore was then embroiled in controversy over posting the Commandments in his courtroom and would later be removed as Alabama's chief justice for defying federal court orders to remove a two-ton granite Commandments monument from the state supreme court rotunda.

Although Ray believed the Commandments should remain in the courthouses, he advised Greene and BeShears that their displays would more likely survive judicial scrutiny if they were enlarged to include other "historical" documents. Ray knew that ACLU lawyers would rely on the Supreme Court's 1980 decision in the *Stone* case, which ruled against display of the Ten Commandments in Kentucky schools. He also knew the Court had later ruled in 1984 that officials in Pawtucket, Rhode Island, could allow the Christmas season display of a Nativity crèche in a city park, along with such "secular" symbols of the holiday season as candy canes, reindeer, and Santa Claus. And in 1989, although the Court found unconstitutional a stand-alone Nativity crèche in a Pennsylvania courthouse, the justices upheld the nearby display of a Jewish menorah, flanked by a Christmas tree. These were not permanent displays, of course, and reindeer and candy canes did not send the "undeniable" religious message of the Ten Commandments, as the Court said in its *Stone* decision. But these later cases offered Ray a chance to argue that "expanded" courthouse displays would pass constitutional muster.

Yielding to Ray's advice, Greene and BeShears first persuaded each county's governing body to adopt identical resolutions, stating that the Ten Commandments were "codified in Kentucky's civil and criminal laws," saying that they "agree with the arguments set out by Judge Moore" in defending his courtroom Commandments display, and citing "the duty of elected officials to publicly acknowledge God as the source of America's strength and direction." Greene and BeShears then placed eight framed documents on either side of the Commandments in their courthouses. They included excerpts from the Declaration of Independence, the national motto of "In God We Trust," a statement by Abraham Lincoln that "the Bible is the best gift God has ever given to man," and the Mayflower Compact. These documents, though, unlike reindeer and candy canes, all contained references to God. They added, in fact, even more religion to the Commandments displays. Ray, however, assured his clients that the expanded displays were protected by Supreme Court precedent and promptly filed a motion to dismiss the ACLU lawsuits, arguing that Greene and BeShears had "done nothing wrong" in posting the expanded displays.

The second major turning point in a civil lawsuit, once a complaint has been filed and properly served on the defendants (either by mail or personal service by a "process server"), shifts from the plaintiffs to the defendants, who are required to file an **answer** to the complaint. Defendants who fail to file an answer run the risk of having a **default judgment** entered against them, meaning that the plaintiff is entitled to judgment and the relief requested. Normally, such answers respond to the numbered paragraphs in the complaint and may include **admissions** or **denials** of the plaintiff's averments. Matters that are admitted are usually undisputed facts (such as "Jimmie Greene was the judge-executive of McCreary County when he posted the Ten Commandments in the courthouse"). Matters that are disputed by defendants are almost always denied (such as "posting the Ten Commandments violated the Establishment Clause"). Failure to deny a claim is almost always held to be an admission. Defendants may also, and often do, answer a claim by saying they are **"without knowledge or information to form a belief as to the truth of the averment,"** which has the same effect as a denial. Defendants are also allowed to bring **counterclaims** against plaintiffs (such as "the plaintiff falsely claims the widgets he sent to defendant met the contract specifications and is liable to defendant for the cost of securing another supplier"). In addition, defendants may add **third-party defendants** to an answer through a **cross-claim** (such as "the wholesaler knew that plaintiff was unreliable in meeting shipping dates and is liable for our costs in finding another widget supplier").

Another form of answer (in effect, a preemptive move to derail the case before any judicial hearings or a trial on its merits) is a **motion to dismiss the complaint**. In federal courts, this procedure is governed by Rule 12(b), which lists seven grounds for such motions: that the complaint should be dismissed for (1) lack of **subject matter jurisdiction**; (2) lack of **personal jurisdiction** over the parties; (3) **improper venue**; (4) **insufficiency of process**; (5) **insufficiency of service of process**; (6) **failure to state a claim upon which relief can be granted**; and (7) **failure to join a party** that is necessary to resolve the claims in the complaint. Of these Rule 12(b) provisions, the most important and frequently invoked is 12(b)(6), failure to state a claim upon which relief can be based. What this means, in effect, is that—even granting the truth of the plaintiff's factual allegations in the complaint—there is no legal ground for a judgment in plaintiff's favor. A Rule 12(b)(6) motion, if granted by a judge, effectively throws the case out of court.

Ronald Ray filed a motion to dismiss in his answer to David Friedman's complaint in the McCreary County case. Ray's Rule 12(b) motion covered thirty-two pages, along with a lengthy legal memorandum, some fifty pages of exhibits, and an eighty-page supporting

affidavit (a sworn statement) from Alabama judge Roy Moore. Given the memorandum's length, and following the "show, don't tell" adage, I offer the following edited version that includes its main points; I have also eliminated the exhibits and Judge Moore's affidavit.

DEFENDANTS' MOTION TO DISMISS

Come now the Defendants, McCreary County, Kentucky and Jimmie Greene in his official capacity as McCreary County Judge Executive by counsel, and move the Court, pursuant to Rule 12(b)(5) and (6) of the Federal Rules of Civil Procedure, to dismiss the instant complaint for failure to state any claim upon which relief may be granted. As grounds therefore, Defendants state the following grounds:

1. The case is moot, and there is no present justiciable controversy giving the court jurisdiction to render a declaratory judgment accordingly.
2. The Plaintiffs lack standing to bring the action.
3. Service of process was inadequate.

A Memorandum in support of this motion to dismiss is tendered herewith and incorporated herein by reference.

Wherefore, Defendants respectfully move the court to dismiss this action with prejudice.

MEMORANDUM IN SUPPORT OF DEFENDANTS
Motion to Dismiss

This action arises out of a Complaint filed on November 18, 1999 by the American Civil Liberties Union of Kentucky ("ACLU"), Lorraine [sic] Walker and Dave Howe (hereafter "the Plaintiffs"), against McCreary County, Kentucky and Judge Jimmie Greene, in his official capacity as McCreary County Judge Executive (hereafter "the Defendants"). That complaint alleges generally that the Defendants have "displayed on the walls of the McCreary County courthouse a framed copy of one version of the Ten Commandments," and that this plaque "is not part of any larger historical or educational display." . . .

In their Complaint, Plaintiffs assert that "The Ten Commandments display is unadorned by any surrounding text, documents, or similar displays. It is not part of any larger historical or educational display." This statement is not true and was not true on November 18, 1999, when

Plaintiffs filed their verified Complaint. As shown in the Resolution of the McCreary County Fiscal Court (Exhibit 1), the Ten Commandments is only one of a number of historical documents displayed in the hallway of the McCreary County Courthouse. The Plaintiffs' Complaint, therefore, is not "well grounded in fact," cf., Rule 11, F.R.C.P. . . .

Statement of Facts

Since this action was filed, as responsible public officials, the McCreary County Fiscal Court has reviewed the ACLU's Complaint against its display of the Ten Commandments in a courthouse . . . , has drafted a resolution to clarify its position and avoid any possible misunderstanding, and has supplemented the Ten Commandments with six (6) other historic documents of civil government. Further, after review the said Fiscal Court finds the ACLU's First and Fourteenth Amendment endorsement of religion allegation totally unfounded and nearly "absurd," as the Ten Commandments in a courthouse constitute a "state" document, rather than a "religious" document, because of the Ten Commandments' central role in the formation of American Civil Government and American common law, and as the foundation of the civil and criminal legal codes of each state, including Kentucky, and also as the foundation legal code of the American Republican form of civil government. . . . The Fiscal Court does not concede any wrongdoing or improper action in displaying the Ten Commandments as part of their larger duty to educate the public concerning the early history and foundational documents upon which American law and government rest. . . . Accordingly, the McCreary County Fiscal Court has now supplemented the (allegedly) offending display of the Ten Commandments with a display of six (6) other American historic documents and its Resolution reflecting a few of the many authorities cited by the United States Supreme Court when it found in 1892, as a matter of law, fact, and history, that America is a "Christian Nation". . . .

Such a historic display of state and national governmental documents, which necessarily contain Christian references for reasons recognized by the Supreme Court, are now somehow alleged by the ACLU to be suddenly transmuted ipso facto into "religious" or "church" documents because of these references to God, the Bible, or the Ten Commandments. Leaders of the federal and state governments, presidents, congressmen, senators, judges, have repeatedly recognized this as historically true, and that censorship of American legal and governmental history is not authorized by the First or Fourteenth Amendments because of religious references or even etiology in those historical state documents. . . .

As shown below, this ill-advised effort by the Plaintiffs to censor or suppress American history because of putatively "religious" references in historic "state" documents must be dismissed as failing to state a claim, and this intervening development of clarification and resolution of the Fiscal Court has also rendered the case moot. Accordingly, the Defendants have moved the Court to dismiss the action. . . .

Conclusion

As shown above, the controversy alleged in the Complaint is now moot, and the case must be dismissed. . . . Defendants pray for an order of the court so holding.

/s/ Colonel Ronald D. Ray

A Side Trip to a Law School Classroom

The third major turning point in civil lawsuits, once a complaint and an answer have been filed, shifts from the parties to the judge assigned to the case. Judges who are confronted with a motion to dismiss, as were those in both Ten Commandments cases, must first decide whether to grant or deny the motion. If dismissal motions are denied, cases move to the next judicial step, in which judges set the case for a further hearing or a trial. Because neither Commandments case involved the kinds of disputed facts that are presented for jurors to decide in many civil cases, both judges scheduled hearings at which the contending lawyers presented arguments on issues of law. Following these hearings, both judges prepared orders and wrote opinions that discussed the legal reasoning on which they based their decisions.

Before we look at these hearings and the orders and opinions the two judges issued, we're going to "zoom out" and examine the body of Supreme Court precedent in Establishment Clause cases that was available to both judges and on which they were expected (but not required) to rely in their opinions. This is important and relevant, because this body of precedent established the framework for the opinions, much as an architect's drawings provide the framework for a building that is constructed in accordance with them. Let's now imagine ourselves sitting in a law school classroom in a constitutional law course, listening as the professor delivers a lecture on Supreme Court precedent in Establishment Clause cases. As your tour guide and as a law professor, I've delivered this lecture so many times that I practically have it memorized.

Surprisingly, not until 1947 did the Supreme Court decide its first Establishment Clause case, some 156 years after ratification of the First Amendment. The reason for this lengthy delay requires a brief explanation of the so-called **incorporation** doctrine. By its terms, the First Amendment applies only to congressional enactments, presumably leaving state and local government free to legislate on issues of religion, speech, press, assembly, and petition, which many did in ways that allowed punishment for supposedly harmful expressions of religious and political beliefs. Challenges to such laws on First Amendment grounds were uniformly rejected by federal judges until 1925, when the Supreme Court, in the case of *Gitlow v. New York*, held that "we may and do assume that freedom of speech and of the press—which are protected from abridgement by Congress—are among the personal rights and 'liberties' protected by the due process clause of the Fourteenth Amendment against impairment by the States." Ironically, the Court in *Gitlow* affirmed the conviction and prison sentence of a communist activist who had distributed a "manifesto" advocating a future—but not immanent—revolution against the capitalist system.

This "incorporation" of the Free Speech and Free Press clauses into the Due Process clause of the Fourteenth Amendment, thus allowing federal judicial review of state and local laws challenged as First Amendment violations, was followed in 1940 by a similar incorporation of the Free Exercise of Religion clause in *Cantwell v. Connecticut*, in which the Supreme Court struck down a state law requiring official licensing for the public distribution of religious literature, enforced only against Jehovah's Witnesses.

It was only a matter of time, after the *Gitlow* and *Cantwell* rulings, until the Supreme Court incorporated the Establishment Clause into the Fourteenth Amendment and applied it to state laws. This happened in 1947 in the case of *Everson v. Ewing Township*. At that time, the New Jersey township had no high schools, either public or private, so high-school students attended public or Catholic parochial schools in the neighboring city of Trenton. Because the township also lacked school buses, students whose parents or friends did not drive them to school used public buses. To cover the bus-fare costs, Ewing Township offered tax-funded subsidies to parents who requested them, an average of $40 per family and a yearly outlay of less than $1,000.

Arch Everson, a taxpayer in the township, challenged the subsidies in state court, arguing that they violated the Establishment Clause. After the New Jersey courts ruled against him, Everson sought review in the Supreme Court. The resulting decision produced an odd split between the justices. Writing for the majority in a 5–4 decision, Justice Hugo Black upheld the reimbursement program, analogizing the bus-fare subsidies to such taxpayer-funded "public safety" services as police and fire protection, although he conceded that the subsidies provided aid to parents with children in church-run schools and thus indirectly to the churches themselves. The four *Everson* dissenters, in an opinion by Justice Wiley Rutledge, answered that the subsidies "give aid and encouragement to religious instruction" in parochial schools. In Rutledge's view, the purpose of the Establishment Clause was "to create a complete and permanent separation of the spheres of religious activity and civil authority by comprehensively forbidding every form or public aid or support for religion."

However, and herein lies the enduring significance of the *Everson* case, not a single justice took issue with Black's exposition—seemingly at odds with his approval of the bus-fare subsidy program—of the essential meaning of the Establishment Clause. After a lengthy historical review of the persecution inflicted on religious dissenters by the established churches of England and the American colonies and the First Amendment's Framers' revulsion about these practices, which included fines, imprisonment, torture, and even death, Black quoted the words of Thomas Jefferson. In his famous letter in 1802 to the Baptists of Danbury, Connecticut, who had complained about being taxed to support the established Congregational Church, President Jefferson replied that the Establishment Clause was designed to erect "a wall of separation between Church and State." That wall, Justice Black added, "must be kept high and impregnable." The most important sentence in Black's opinion affirmed that the Establishment Clause "requires the state to be a neutral in its relations with groups of religious believers and non-believers; it does not require the state to be their adversary." Nor, he might have added, their advocate.

Fourteen years after the *Everson* decision, the Court decided an important case that expanded the "neutrality" principle from the *Everson* case into a more precise judicial "test" of laws challenged on Establishment Clause grounds. In 1971, the Court struck down laws from Pennsylvania and Rhode Island that provided tax-funded subsidies to private schools—almost all Catholic—for textbooks and teacher salaries, limited to supposedly "secular" instruction. Writing for the Court in *Lemon v. Kurtzman*, Chief Justice Warren Burger cited Justice Black's *Everson* opinion in devising what became known as the *Lemon* test: "First, the statute must have a secular legislative purpose; second, its principal or primary effect must be one that neither advances nor inhibits religion; finally, the statute must not foster an excessive government entanglement with religion." Laws that failed any one of the three so-called prongs of the *Lemon* test would be held unconstitutional. The vice of the Pennsylvania and Rhode Island laws, Burger reasoned, was that they "entangled" state officials in deciding how much—if any—religious content was provided by teachers and textbooks in religious-school classes. During the years since the *Lemon* decision, the "entanglement" prong has rarely been employed, while the "purpose" and "effect" prongs have been applied in dozens of Establishment Clause cases.

A final pair of Supreme Court rulings will set the stage for the Ten Commandments cases discussed in this section. Both cases involved challenges to Christmas season displays on public property. Christmas, of course, is a holiday with both sacred and secular meanings. Christians celebrate the birth of Jesus, and even non-Christians cannot avoid exposure to such trappings of the holiday season as Nativity crèches. Such displays on private property do not offend the Constitution, but their placement on public property has offended some people enough to file lawsuits seeking their removal.

The first challenge to Nativity displays reached the Supreme Court in 1984, from the city of Pawtucket, Rhode Island. For some forty years, city workers had erected a city-owned crèche as part of a Christmas season display in a downtown park. Surrounding the crèche were such traditional items as candy-striped poles, a giant teddy bear, a Santa's sleigh, and a large banner that offered "Seasons Greetings" to all who viewed the display. Ruling on a suit filed by local ACLU members, with supporting briefs from Jewish groups, the Supreme Court upheld the Pawtucket display by a 5–4 margin. Writing for the majority in *Lynch v. Donnelly*, Chief Justice Warren Burger conceded that "the crèche is identified with one religious faith," but he shied from banning its display "at the very time people are taking note of the season with Christmas hymns and carols in public schools and other public places." Christmas, he suggested, was so embedded in the nation's heritage that it had become as much a secular as a religious holiday. Although Burger cited both the *Everson* and the *Lemon* cases, the latter written by himself, he focused on the "context" of the crèche among its secular trappings in finding that the display "engenders a friendly community spirit of goodwill" during the Christmas season. Writing for the dissenters, Justice William Brennan noted that the crèche "retains a specifically Christian religious meaning" and reminded the majority that the *Lemon* test remained as "the fundamental tool of Establishment Clause analysis," arguing that the Pawtucket display violated both its "purpose" and "effect" prongs.

More significant than the majority and dissenting opinions in *Lynch*, however, was the concurring opinion of Justice Sandra O'Connor. Although she joined the majority to uphold the display, O'Connor wrote separately to offer a "clarification" of the *Lemon* test. She proposed to focus the "purpose" prong on "whether the government's actual purpose is to endorse or disapprove religions" and the "effect" prong on "whether, irrespective of government's actual purpose, the practice under review in fact conveys a message of endorsement or disapproval." O'Connor put her "endorsement" test in these words: "The Establishment Clause prohibits government from making adherence to a religion relevant in any way to a person's standing in the political community. . . . Endorsement sends a message to nonadherents that they are outsiders, not full members of the political community, and an accompanying message to adherents that they are insiders, favored members of the political community." Applied to the Pawtucket display, O'Connor reasoned that the city did not "intend to convey any message of endorsement of Christianity or disapproval of non-Christian religions" by including a Nativity scene in its holiday display.

The Court's most recent foray into Christmas season displays produced more shifting alignments of justices than coaches employ in football games. The primary reason for judicial discord in *Allegheny*

County v. ACLU, decided in 1989, was that this case involved two separate displays in downtown Pittsburgh, Pennsylvania. One display, located in the rotunda of the county courthouse, consisted solely of an elaborate Nativity scene, topped by an angel holding a banner that proclaimed "Gloria in Excelsis Deo." The second display, outside the nearby City-County Building, featured an eighteen-foot Jewish menorah, flanked by a forty-five-foot Christmas tree, along with a banner declaring the city's "Salute to Liberty."

Ruling on the city's appeal from lower-court rulings against both displays, the Supreme Court ordered the crèche removed and allowed the menorah to remain. The difference seemed to be the Christmas tree and the somewhat less sectarian nature of the menorah. Candy canes and teddy bears might have saved the crèche, but its placement as "the single element" of the courthouse display made its "religious meaning unmistakably clear" to Justice Harry Blackmun, who wrote for the five-justice majority in the Nativity case, with several justices joining one or more parts of his opinion. In contrast, Blackmun said, in a separate opinion for six justices, the effect of "placing a menorah next to a Christmas tree is to create on 'overall holiday setting' that represents both Christmas and Chanukah—two holidays, not one."

The Supreme Court's first Ten Commandments case—and the one most relevant to the judicial opinions in the McCreary County and Van Orden cases—was so "easy" for a majority of five justices that it was decided in 1980 with an **unsigned, per curiam** decision, without benefit of briefs and oral argument. In seven paragraphs, the Court's opinion struck down, in *Stone v. Graham*, a Kentucky law that mandated the posting of the Decalogue on the walls of all of the state's public-school classrooms. The statute provided that the documents should be paid for by private contributions, collected by the state treasurer, and that each copy should include, in "small print" after the last commandment, the following statement: "The secular application of the Ten Commandments is clearly seen in its adoption as the fundamental legal code of Western Civilization and the Common Law of the United States."

Armed with the *Lemon* test, the *Stone* majority rejected the state's claim, in its petition for certiorari, that this addendum to the Decalogue copies expressed a valid secular purpose for their classroom display.

"The preeminent purpose for posting the Ten Commandments on schoolroom walls is plainly religious in nature," the majority held. "The Ten Commandments are undeniably a sacred text in the Jewish and Christian faiths, and no legislative recitation of a supposed secular purpose can blind us to that fact." The Decalogue's prohibition of murder, theft, adultery, and perjury could not conceal its primary concern with "the religious duties of believers: worshipping the Lord God alone, avoiding idolatry, not using the Lord's name in vain, and observing the Sabbath Day." The majority concluded that the law violated the "purpose" prong of the *Lemon* test "and thus the Establishment Clause of the Constitution."

Chief Justice Warren Burger and three colleagues dissented from this summary disposal of the *Stone* case, but only Justice William Rehnquist issued a dissenting opinion. Rehnquist made two points in his reply to the majority. He first argued that the Court should defer to the "secular purpose articulated by the State" and the decision of its legislators. He then agreed with the state's claim that "the Ten Commandments have had a significant impact on the development of secular legal codes of the Western World" and dismissed the majority's "emphasis on the religious nature of the first part of the Ten Commandments" as "beside the point."

9

The Hearings and the Opinions in the *McCreary County* and *Van Orden* Cases

As I noted earlier, the third major turning point in a civil lawsuit, after a complaint and an answer have been filed, shifts to the judge. After a judge reviews the complaint and the answer in a civil case and disposes of any pretrial motions, he or she generally schedules either a **hearing** (at which only lawyers appear and argue), a **bench trial** before the judge (at which witnesses may be called and may testify), or a **jury trial**. The *McCreary County* case came before federal district judge Jennifer Coffman, at a hearing on April 20, 2000. Colonel Ray—the title he insisted on using—would certainly not have picked Coffman to decide the Commandments cases. Named by President Bill Clinton in 1993 as Kentucky's first female federal judge, she was a Democrat and had represented plaintiffs in employment discrimination cases before joining the bench. Ray also faced a formidable courtroom adversary in David Friedman, who argued for the ACLU's plaintiffs. A partner in a prestigious Louisville firm, Friedman had fifteen years of experience as an ACLU volunteer counsel, defending clients who ranged from Republican state officials to Ku Klux Klan members. "My client is the Bill of Rights," Friedman said.

Ray had a hard row to hoe in the hearing before Judge Coffman and probably hurt his clients by asking her to consider the eighty-page affidavit from Judge Roy Moore, who was then campaigning for election as Alabama's chief justice. On his part, Friedman cited the affidavit and the county resolutions praising Moore as evidence of the religious motives behind the Commandments displays. "There's no question here why these were put up," he said of the documents that Greene and BeShears had posted along with the Commandments. "The ACLU threw everything but the kitchen sink at Judge Moore, and the Ten Commandments are still on his courthouse wall," Ray replied. "There's no difference between a courtroom in Alabama and a courtroom in Kentucky." Ray also charged the ACLU with "censorship" of the nation's religious history. "The history speaks for itself," he said. "If you stand on history, it's clear we're a Christian nation."

Ray's overtly religious appeal did not impress Judge Coffman. Two weeks after the hearing, on May 5, she handed down an opinion that gave Friedman a hands-down victory, denying Ray's motion to dismiss the cases and ordering McCreary and Pulaski county officials to "immediately" remove the courthouse documents and not erect any "similar displays" in the future. "While a display of some of these documents may not have the effect of endorsing religion in another context," she wrote, "they collectively have the overwhelming effect of endorsing religion in the context of these displays. Each and every document refers to religion. Several have been edited to include only their religious references. Indeed, the only unifying element among the documents is their reference to God, the Bible, or religion."

Judge Coffman's ruling in the *McCreary County* case relied on the Supreme Court decisions we examined previously for precedent, which she enforced with an order that McCreary and Pulaski county officials must remove the Ten Commandments displays from their courthouses. Faced with this order, they had little choice but to comply. "I believe in obeying the rules," said Darrell BeShears, who removed his county's display with no fanfare. Jimmie Greene, however, refused to do the job himself. "I said early on that I would not remove them, and

I will not," he told reporters. "I'll go to jail before I take them down. This is one order I will not obey. I'm a law-abiding citizen, but there is a higher power. Could you think of a better reason to go to jail than standing up in defense of the Ten Commandments?" Greene left the unpleasant task to Paul Worthington, the commander of Whitley City's American Legion Post, who removed the courthouse display at a ceremony attended by three hundred people, many wearing T-shirts bearing the Ten Commandments. Worthington moved the display to the Legion's building, while Greene vowed to appeal Coffman's order to the Supreme Court, if necessary. "We're either going to win and America is going to be the winner," he said, "or America is going to hell in a hand basket. We've got to win this."

Van Orden's Day in Federal Court

Two years after Judge Coffman ruled in the *McCreary County* case, Thomas Van Orden walked to the federal courthouse in Austin for the first hearing on his suit in July 2002, to argue the case himself. The case was assigned to Harry Lee Hudspeth, a senior district judge who had been named to the bench in 1979 by President Jimmy Carter. Although he denied the state's motion to dismiss the case, Hudspeth ruled for the state in his decision, which was handed down three months later in October. He applied the three-pronged test established by the 1971 Supreme Court ruling in *Lemon v. Kurtzman*, a decision that struck down public funding for religious schools. The first prong of the *Lemon* test required the state to show a "secular purpose" for erecting the Ten Commandments monument. The state's lawyer referred Judge Hudspeth to a 1961 legislative resolution, commending the Eagles for their efforts "to reduce juvenile delinquency." Presumably, young people who viewed the monument would heed its admonitions and behave properly. In his opinion, Hudspeth gave the state a passing grade on this part of the test; the resolution, he wrote, "makes no reference to religion" and showed "a valid secular purpose" in placing the monument on capitol grounds. The second *Lemon* prong bars government actions that have the "primary effect" of promoting religion. Noting that the monument was only one of seventeen on the capitol grounds, Hudspeth ruled that a "reasonable observer" would not "conclude that the state is seeking to advance, endorse, or promote religion by permitting the display." The final *Lemon* prong prohibited "excessive government entanglement" with the monument, which Van Orden conceded it did not.

The Counties' Appeal to the Sixth Circuit Court of Appeals

The next important decision in a civil lawsuit falls on the losing parties in the trial court, who must decide whether to file an appeal from the ruling against them. Most of these losing parties—about 80 percent in federal courts and even more in state courts—choose to throw in the towel, so to speak, and accept the trial court's ruling against them, however reluctantly.

Deciding whether to file an appeal involves several factors, including the cost of further litigation and the time it will take to obtain an appellate ruling, which can drag out a case for one or two years and sometimes longer. Lawyers for losing parties must first advise their clients on what legal grounds would justify an appeal, which require a claim of **clear error** on the part of the trial court. Just as in criminal trials, this is a significant hurdle to clear, because a bare claim that a jury did not correctly decide the facts in the case won't suffice, nor will a claim that a judge made an error in his or her rulings that did not affect the outcome of the case. Appellate courts apply the **harmless error** standard to deny a majority of appeals, and lawyers are supposed to know the difference between clear and harmless errors in the trial courts.

Both the *McCreary County* and the *Van Orden* case reached the appellate level, with filings in two different federal courts of appeal, the Sixth Circuit in the former and the Fifth Circuit in the latter. We'll look first at the appeal that was filed in the *McCreary County* case by the losing side. Winning the battle to return the Ten Commandments to the McCreary and Pulaski courthouses seemed a daunting task, considering the firm legal foundation of Judge Coffman's opinion on Supreme Court precedent in Establishment Clause cases. Compounding the problem was the realization by Jimmie Greene and Darrell BeShears that Robert Ray had virtually handed David Friedman a victory with his

"Christian nation" argument. If the counties appealed from Coffman's ruling, federal appellate judges were unlikely to give any weight to the clearly sectarian argument that Ray had offered to defend the displays. Ray had, however, filed an appeal with the Sixth Circuit court of appeals in Cincinnati, Ohio, which gave Greene and BeShears time to ponder their next move. Out of the blue, they received an offer of help from a Florida lawyer, Mathew Staver.

Like their adversaries in the ACLU and other groups committed to church-state separation, lawyers in Religious Right groups monitor the media for news of cases that fit their agendas. Staver headed Liberty Counsel, a legal group founded by Jerry Falwell, the Baptist preacher and televangelist who gained prominence in the 1980s by creating the Moral Majority, whose evangelical Christian members became a political force in Republican politics. "The idea of separation of church and state," Falwell charged, "was invented by the Devil to keep Christians from running their own country." Mat Staver, who left a successful law practice in 1994 to pursue his Christian goals through Liberty Counsel, has focused most of his efforts on campaigns against gay marriage and abortion. But the Ten Commandments cases struck him as a chance to open another front in the "cultural war" in which he had enlisted as a legal warrior. With a staff of twenty lawyers (including volunteers who donate their services on a pro bono basis) and an annual budget of $1.4 million, Liberty Counsel could offer Jimmie Greene and Darrell BeShears more clout than Robert Ray's one-man practice did.

Staver also had an idea the Kentucky officials found attractive. He proposed a third courthouse display, in which the Ten Commandments would be flanked, not by religious statements, but with "documents that played a significant role in the foundation of our system of law and government." Greene and BeShears liked Staver's idea and erected new displays on their courthouse walls, including copies of the Magna Carta, the Declaration of Independence, the Bill of Rights, and all four verses of the "Star Spangled Banner." Posters next to each courthouse exhibit identified the documents as "Foundations of American Law and Government Display."

After the third display was in place in both courthouses, Staver dismissed the Sixth Circuit appeal that Ronald Ray had filed and asked Judge Coffman for a "clarification" of her order, which she denied in September 2000, saying the order "speaks for itself." David Friedman, angered by what he considered an obvious ploy to return the Commandments to the courthouses, countered with a motion to hold the county officials in contempt of the order that barred them from erecting "similar displays" that included the Ten Commandments. Ruling on March 30, 2001, Coffman denied the contempt motion and urged Staver and Friedman to settle the cases by April 30. Basically, she was asking Friedman to agree that the third display conformed to Supreme Court precedent that allowed religious symbols in public places, if they were flanked by "secular" items and images. Not surprisingly, Friedman did not agree, reporting that he and Staver could not settle the cases. After hearing arguments from both lawyers, Coffman issued another opinion on June 22, 2001, ruling that the new displays were a "sham," designed to shield the Commandments behind a facade of supposedly "secular" documents. Rather than shielding the Commandments poster, Coffman explained in her opinion, "placing it among these patriotic and political documents, with no other religious or moral codes, imbues it with a national significance constituting endorsement" of its religious message by county officials.

For a third time in a little more than a year, the Commandments were removed from the two Kentucky courthouses. David Friedman, who grew up in New York City and is a die-hard Yankees fan, knew that the baseball rule of "three strikes and you're out" does not apply to lawsuits. As he expected, Mat Staver filed a new appeal with the Sixth Circuit Court of Appeals, which handles appeals from federal district courts in Michigan, Ohio, Kentucky, and Tennessee, with its headquarters in Cincinnati, Ohio. However, the legal equivalent of a rain delay held up oral arguments in the cases for eighteen months, until December 2002, and another year passed before the three-judge panel issued its ruling on December 18, 2003. Just a month earlier, in what might be seen as an omen, Roy Moore had lost his post as Alabama's chief justice for defying federal court orders to remove the Ten Commandments monument he had placed in the state supreme court building.

The long-awaited Sixth Circuit ruling handed Friedman another victory, this time by a split decision. Judge Eric L. Clay, placed on the bench by President Clinton in 1997, wrote for the 2–1 majority. He upheld Judge Coffman's decision but focused on an issue her opinion had not addressed. Clay quoted from the poster the counties had placed next to their "Foundations" displays: "The Ten Commandments provide the moral background of the Declaration of Independence and the foundation of our legal tradition," words that Mat Staver had likely composed. Clay found nothing in the display that connected the two documents and cited historians who asserted that Thomas Jefferson, the Declaration's primary author, did not believe in "the God of the Bible (and thus the Ten Commandments), but the God of Deism." Jefferson "was most inspired by contemporaneous political writings as well as the musings of European philosophers and writers," Clay wrote, and he found a "patently religious purpose" behind the "Foundations" display.

The sole dissenter, Judge James L. Ryan, almost sneered at Clay's historical excursions. Named to the court by President Reagan in 1985, Ryan belonged to the Federalist Society, an influential group of conservative lawyers and judges. Clay's opinion, he wrote, attributed to viewers of the "Foundations" display, and by inference to Clay himself, "an utter lack of common sense, a profound ignorance of American history, and, arguably, an outright hostility to religion in our nation's public life." No courthouse visitor, Ryan continued, "could fail to appreciate what, apparently, my colleague does not: that from the founding of our republic, religion was and always has been, an inherent component of the law and culture of our pluralistic society, and that saying so in the public square *acknowledges* religion, but does not *endorse* it."

On his part, David Friedman exulted in his victory. "The court has rousingly endorsed the principles of religious freedom and rousingly endorsed the requirement that government remain neutral toward religion," he said. "We are delighted with the opinion." Telling reporters "the case is far from over," Mat Staver asked for an en banc review of the panel decision by the full court, but the judges refused him on March 23, 2004. The next step was to petition the Supreme Court for review of the Sixth Circuit decision, normally a long shot, because the justices turn down almost 98 percent of these petitions. But Staver's odds were about to improve dramatically.

Van Orden's Appeal to the Fifth Circuit
Court of Appeals

Judge Hudspeth's ruling meant that the Ten Commandments monument at the Texas state capitol had passed its first judicial test, and Thomas Van Orden kept passing the monument on his visits to the capitol grounds while he prepared an appeal to the Fifth Circuit, for a hearing in early 2003. He had little to lose in filing an appeal, because he had plenty of time on his hands, and the costs of an appeal were minimal to a "pro se" litigant. Van Orden recruited two University of Texas law students to help with research and hitched a ride with one for the arguments in New Orleans. The Fifth Circuit was notably conservative, and Van Orden drew a three-judge panel headed by Patrick Higginbotham, named to the court by President Reagan in 1982 and one of its most conservative members. Van Orden knew his Fifth Circuit argument would be a challenge. "It's like I'm appealing to the damn Southern Baptist Convention down there," he said. He was right. Ruling on November 12, 2003, Higginbotham spoke for all three judges in upholding Judge Hudspeth's decision, changing very few of its words. There was nothing in the legislative record, he wrote, "to contradict the secular reasons" for placing the Commandments monument on the capitol grounds to reflect the Eagles' "concern for juvenile delinquency." Higginbotham echoed Hudspeth in concluding that a "reasonable viewer" would look from the monument to the nearby capitol and supreme court buildings and recognize its message as "relevant to these law-giving instruments of state government."

10

The Supreme Court
Appeals in the Ten
Commandments Cases

After the conflicting rulings of the courts of appeals in the Kentucky and the Texas cases, the losing parties in both—the *McCreary County* defendants and Thomas Van Orden—faced another turning point in deciding whether to ask the Supreme Court to review those rulings. Again, factors of cost and time affect these decisions in most cases in which parties lose in the state and federal appellate courts. Lawyers must also advise their clients about the likelihood of gaining Supreme Court review, because the odds are heavily stacked against them, with the justices granting review in roughly 1 percent of the cases they consider for review. Since Mat Staver and Liberty Counsel were representing McCreary and Pulaski counties on a pro bono basis, and Thomas Van Orden was a "pro se" litigant, and because the parties in both cases were determined to press them to the Supreme Court, the factors of time and cost and the odds against them of gaining review did not deter them from a final appeal to the justices.

In considering the cert petitions in the *McCreary County* and *Van Orden* cases, the justices were confronted with what lawyers call a "circuit-split" between federal courts of appeals, with different outcomes in cases that involved the "same important matter" of the public display of religious messages and symbols. This circuit-split made it more likely that the two cases would be heard and decided by the Supreme Court. And because both the Fifth and the Sixth circuit decisions came down in the same Supreme Court term, it was also likely that if review was granted, the cases would be consolidated for argument and decision at the same time.

Mat Staver framed the questions in the *McCreary County* case in these words: "(1) Whether the Establishment Clause is violated by a privately donated display on government property that includes eleven equal size frames containing an explanation of the display along with nine historical documents and symbols that played a role in the development of American law and government where only one of the framed documents is the Ten Commandments and the remaining documents and symbols are secular. (2) Whether a prior display by the government in a courthouse containing the Ten Commandments that was enjoined by a court permanently taints and thereby precludes any future display by the same government when the subsequent display articulates a secular purpose and where the Ten Commandments is a minority among numerous other secular historical documents and symbols. (3) Whether the *Lemon* test should be overruled since the test is unworkable and has fostered excessive confusion in Establishment Clause jurisprudence. (4) Whether a new test for Establishment Clause purposes should be set forth by this Court when the government displays or recognizes historical expressions of religion." In his petition, Thomas Van Orden presented only one question: "Whether a large monument, 6 feet high and 3 feet wide, presenting the Ten Commandments, located on government property between the Texas State Capitol and the Texas Supreme Court, is an impermissible establishment of religion in violation of the First Amendment." Both petitions raised the "same important question" of displaying the Commandment on public property, but Staver's reached further, in urging the justices to jettison the *Lemon* test and substitute one that would presumably allow such displays.

The Court's votes on cert petitions at its cert conferences reflect a turning point in the legal process that cannot be underestimated, because the Court's denial of some 99 percent of these petitions leaves in place the rulings and the orders of the lower state and federal courts from which they were appealed. On October 12, 2004, both the *McCreary County* and the *Van Orden* case passed through this exceedingly narrow doorway to the Court's chamber, with oral arguments in both cases set for March 2, 2005.

During the months between the cert grant in the Ten Commandments cases and the date for oral arguments, the lawyers on both sides spent long hours in researching, drafting, and polishing their briefs. There was one change in lawyers during this period: Thomas Van Orden had first decided to argue his own case before the Supreme Court, but he reconsidered after the media got wind of the "homeless lawyer" and tracked him down in the basement of the Texas Supreme Court law library in Austin, just two hundred feet from the Commandments monument he had sued—thus far unsuccessfully—to remove from the capitol grounds. Reporters treated Van Orden like a side-show curiosity. A *Los Angeles Times* story set the tone, taking readers into the library. "Inside, a homeless man with tired eyes works at a corner carrel in the basement amid his belongings—a duffel bag with a broken zipper, reading glasses he found in a parking lot, chicken-scratch notes sullied with splashes of instant coffee. His carefully parted hair and striped shirt contrast with his stained teeth and dirty fingernails. Armed with scraps of paper and pens he digs out of the trash, he's been here for two years, trying to define, once and for all, the boundaries of a governmental endorsement of religion."

But the chicken-scratch notes turned into a petition the Supreme Court treated with respect, granting review and giving Van Orden a final shot in his case. After this unwelcome media attention, although he politely answered reporters' questions, Van Orden decided his case would be better argued by an experienced First Amendment advocate. Out of the blue, he called Erwin Chemerinsky, who then taught constitutional law at the University of Southern California, later moved to Duke University's law school, and is now dean of the newly established law school at the University of California in Irvine. Intrigued by Van Orden's case, he readily agreed to help with his brief and argue for him.

Initially, the two men communicated by e-mail, between Chemerinsky's office and the public computers in the Texas law library.

In November 2004, Chemerinsky flew to Austin to meet his client in person and view the Commandments monument on the capitol grounds. "I have nothing but the greatest admiration and respect for him," he later said of Van Orden. "He genuinely cares about this issue. He's extremely intelligent and articulate, and I think he did an excellent job of briefing and arguing the case on the trial level and the appellate level." On his part, Van Orden sounded bemused that his chicken scratches had led to the Supreme Court. "You can still do it with a piece of paper, a pen, and a law book," he said. "But that will be lost in all the hoopla of the Ten Commandments."

Oral Argument in the Supreme Court

There was plenty of hoopla when the Supreme Court met on March 2, 2005, for arguments in the Ten Commandments cases from Texas and Kentucky. Hundreds of people, including five busloads from McCreary and Pulaski counties, braved frigid weather and lined up before dawn for seats in the Court's chamber. "They'll stand out in the cold, and they'll do it gladly," declared Jimmie Greene, who had stepped down as McCreary County's Judge-Executive in 2002 and was accompanied by his successor, Blaine Phillips, and by Darrell BeShears, who still headed Pulaski's government. Of the two *McCreary County* plaintiffs, only Dave Howe came to Washington for the arguments; Louanne Walker decided to avoid the media frenzy at the Court and stayed home in Whitley City. Fearing that reporters and television crews would swarm around the "homeless lawyer" from Austin, Thomas Van Orden turned down Erwin Chemerinsky's offer of a plane ticket to Washington and sat on a park bench during arguments in his case.

Only eight justices sat behind the Court's mahogany bench when the session opened. Chief Justice William Rehnquist, suffering from thyroid cancer, remained home to recuperate from radiation treatment. By tradition, the Court's senior associate justice, John Paul Stevens, presided in his place. The Texas case was first on the docket, and Chemerinsky went first as counsel for the losing party in the lower court, with thirty minutes to make his argument and answer questions from the bench. Aware from experience that justices often pounce on lawyers with critical questions after only a few seconds, he began with a forceful statement: "On the grounds of the Texas state capitol, there is one evident religious statement that conveys a powerful religious message that there is a theistic God and that God has dictated rules for behavior. Of course, the government may put religious symbols on its property but must do so in a way that does not endorse religion or a particular religion."

Sure enough, Justice Antonin Scalia quickly pounced on Chemerinsky: "I suppose that opening statement suggests that you think that Thanksgiving proclamations are also unconstitutional, which were recommended by the very first Congress, the same Congress that proposed the First Amendment."

Chemerinsky gave up just an inch. "I think the Thanksgiving proclamations would be constitutional," he replied. "I think it's very different than this Ten Commandments monument. Here you have a monument that proclaims not only there is a God, but God has dictated rules of behavior for those who follow him or her."

Chemerinsky knew that Scalia would certainly vote against him, and he waited for questions from the Court's swing justices, who could tip its narrow balance in either direction. One of these justices, Sandra Day O'Connor, raised a concern that Chemerinsky had anticipated. "How about if they're packaged in a museumlike setting?" she asked of the seventeen monuments on the capitol grounds. "Of course, there can be Ten Commandments or any religious works as part of a museum setting," he conceded. "This isn't a museum setting. Every monument on the state capitol grounds is there because the state legislature wanted to convey a particular message. This is the only religious message anywhere on the capitol grounds. The Ten Commandments come from sacred texts."

Justice Anthony Kennedy, another swing vote in First Amendment cases, shifted to another issue that Chemerinsky had anticipated. "This is a classic 'avert your eyes,'" Kennedy said. "If an atheist walked by, he can avert his eyes, he can think of something else." Of course, most people would avoid looking at a message only if they already knew what it said. Chemerinsky, however, did not make this point, asking

Kennedy instead to "imagine the Muslim or Buddhist who walks into the State Supreme Court to have his or her case heard. That person will see this monument and realize it's not his or her government." Sharpening his point, Chemerinsky noted that the Texas monument was drawn from Christian versions of the Commandments. "A Jewish individual would walk by this Ten Commandments," he said, "and see that the first commandment isn't the Jewish version, 'I am the Lord, thy God, who took you out of Egypt, out of slavery.'" Justice Scalia jumped back into the argument. "When somebody goes by that monument," he retorted, "I don't think they're studying each one of the commandments. It's a symbol of the fact that government derives its authority from God. And that is, it seems to me, an appropriate symbol to be on state grounds."

Justice Steven Breyer, who normally voted with the Court's liberals on First Amendment issues, hinted that he might view the Kentucky and Texas cases differently. "I come to the conclusion very tentatively," he told Chemerinsky, that "making a practical judgment in these difficult cases" could best be done by looking at "the divisive quality of the individual display, case by case. And when I do that, I don't find much divisiveness here. I would love to hear what you think." Aware that he needed Breyer's vote to prevail, Chemerinsky took a bold step, moving outside the Court's hushed chamber. "The Ten Commandments is enormously divisive right now," he replied. "I don't think we can ignore the social reality. The chief justice of the Alabama Supreme Court resigned, there are crowds outside today. I got hate mail messages this week, not because people care about the Ten Commandments as a secular document, but people care about the Ten Commandments because it's a profound religious message." Whether Justice Breyer loved these thoughts when he voted on the case remained to be seen.

From the first to the last sentence of his argument, Chemerinsky stressed that the Commandments sent a "profound religious message" to viewers of the Texas monument. In his countering argument, the state's attorney general, Greg Abbott, stressed the "secular" message of the Commandments. The Commandments, he asserted, "send a secular message to all the people, whether they are believers or not believers, of the important role the Ten Commandments have played in the development of law."

Whatever his colleagues thought of this claim, it struck Justice Scalia as heresy. "It's not a secular message," he replied. "I mean, if you're watering it down to say that the only reason it's okay is it sends nothing but a secular message, I can't agree with you. I think the message it sends is that law and our institutions come from God. And if you don't think it conveys that message, I just think you're kidding yourself."

Watering down the religious message of the Commandments was, in fact, exactly what Abbott was trying to do. He knew Scalia would vote to retain the monument, but he also knew the Court's swing justices might be troubled by that message. Justice O'Connor was the most troubled of this group. She had developed a standard in earlier cases, under which governmental "endorsement" of religious practices or symbols violated the Establishment Clause. O'Connor noted that all seventeen monuments on the capitol groups had been placed there with legislative approval. "Is that not really some kind of endorsement for each one?" she inquired.

Abbott tried to duck the question. The state, he replied, "has specifically endorsed nine of those monuments by putting the state seal" on them. "This monument does not have that kind of endorsement on there." Whether or not this statement satisfied O'Connor, she remained silent for the rest of Abbott's argument.

Justice David Souter, however, remained troubled. "Anyone would reasonably assume that the State of Texas approved this message," he observed, "and thought it was appropriate to devote state property to its promulgation."

Abbott replied that "there is a very meaningful difference between acknowledging something and endorsing something." Texas, he added, simply wanted to acknowledge the Commandments "as a well-recognized historical symbol of the law. It is not endorsing the religious text of the Ten Commandments."

Abbott shared his thirty minutes of argument with Paul Clement, the acting solicitor general in the Justice Department, who appeared as a "friend of the court" in both the Texas and the Kentucky cases. Politics and religion had both influenced the Bush administration's decision to send Clement to the Supreme Court. President George W. Bush had won his second term the previous November, with his margin of victory over John Kerry provided by the votes of some three million evangelical Christians who had sat out the 2000 election, almost costing Bush his razor-thin electoral-college tally over Al Gore. Standing up for the Ten Commandments might help Bush retain the support of conservative Christians who questioned his commitment to their campaigns against abortion and the "creeping secularization" of American society. In addition, Bush himself was a "born-again" Christian, and his attorney general, John Ashcroft, belonged to the Assemblies of God church, the nation's largest Pentecostal denomination. Ashcroft had no trouble persuading Bush to back the defenders of the Commandments in Texas and Kentucky.

When he replaced Abbott at the lectern, Clement asserted that Texas was not "endorsing the religious text of the Ten Commandments" by placing the monument on its capitol grounds. But he also, perhaps unwittingly, walked through the door that Erwin Chemerinsky had opened with his reference to Judge Roy Moore. With Mat Staver sitting behind him, minutes away from arguing the Kentucky cases, Clement suggested that it might be unconstitutional to display the Commandments "in a way that it actually looks like a religious sanctuary within the walls of the courthouse." Justice Anthony Kennedy promptly asked Clement whether such a display would "cross the constitutional line" the Court had drawn in earlier cases. Clement conceded that placing the Commandments in a courthouse, at least by themselves, "probably does cross the constitutional line." He quickly stepped back from the metaphorical courthouse doorway, adding that "a display of the Ten Commandments in some appropriate way in the courthouse certainly wouldn't cross the line that we would have this Court draw."

Minutes after Clement sat down, Mat Staver stood at the lectern to defend the McCreary and Pulaski county officials who had first posted the Commandments on their courthouse walls in 1999, without any surrounding documents. Clement's tacit concession that such a display "probably" violated the Establishment Clause put Staver on the defensive with the first question from the bench. The Kentucky cases, Justice Souter noted, "started out with just the Ten Commandments alone," before other documents were added in the second and third displays. Souter did not conceal his skepticism about the motives behind these "expanded" displays. "Everybody knows what's going on," he told Staver. "Everybody knows that the present context is simply litigation dressing and that the object for what is going on was revealed in the first place. What is your response to that?"

Staver knew that defending the initial "stand-alone" Commandments displays was a lost cause, so he took the unusual tack of casting the blame on Jimmie Greene and Darrell BeShears, who were sitting behind him in the Court's chamber. "They were not jurists schooled in the law," he told Souter. "And admittedly they made a mistake." After the Kentucky ACLU sued them, Greene and BeShears "wanted to figure out how to display this particular document." Staver admitted that "they stepped, however, on a land mine" when they added religious documents to the courthouse displays.

"Well, they created the land mine," Souter shot back.

With his argument in danger of exploding, Staver tried to distance himself from the first and second Commandments displays. "What they have now," replied, "is the Foundations display, fundamentally different than any previous display." Souter agreed that the Foundations display "includes a lot of legal documents," but he did not let Staver off the hook. "Is there any reason for anyone to believe," he asked, "that display of legal documents or anything else would be there for any other purpose than the display of the Ten Commandments, including the overtly theistic part of the text?" Staver's reply was, at best, disingenuous. "That religious purpose has been buried and has been abandoned," he said. Jimmie Greene and Darrell BeShears, of course, had neither buried nor abandoned their purpose in posting the Commandments, from the first to the last displays.

Justice Souter was clearly skeptical that adding "secular" documents to the courthouse displays had "buried" the religious purpose behind placing the Commandments at their centers. Under the "purpose" prong of the *Lemon* test, such religious motives would cross the constitutional line. Returning to the lectern after Mat Staver sat down, Paul Clement argued that "a focus on purpose is probably not a prudent exercise of judicial resources." In effect, he urged the justices to ignore the first two Commandments displays and focus on the "secular" purpose of the Foundations displays. Justice Souter was not about to ignore reality. "It would be crazy law from this Court," he told Clement, "that said you can engage in religious endorsement, promotions, et cetera, so long as you hide the ball well enough." Clement made no effort to defend the first two displays, suggesting that "bad legal advice or simply frustration at the first lawsuit being filed" led the Kentucky officials into a constitutional minefield. But, he concluded, "municipalities should be rewarded, not punished, for trying to change their conduct to get things right."

When he replaced Clement at the lectern, David Friedman argued that the Kentucky officials had gotten things wrong from the outset. He pointed the justices to two documents in the case record. The first was the resolution adopted by the McCreary and Pulaski county governing bodies right after the ACLU filed its lawsuit in 1999. "In that resolution," Friedman said, "the counties make clear that they relied on and cited approvingly the Kentucky legislature's reference to Jesus Christ as the Prince of Ethics. They made clear that they supported the fight of Alabama Supreme Court justice Roy Moore against the ACLU. They made absolutely clear that they deemed this to be a Christian nation." Friedman noted that the resolution, designed to justify the second displays, with religious documents flanking the Ten Commandments, had not been rescinded or repealed by either county.

Friedman's second document was the framed text that had been placed next to the "secular" Foundations displays. "It asserts that the Ten Commandments, the revealed word of God, provides the moral background of the Declaration of Independence," Friedman said. In his Sixth Circuit opinion, Judge Clay had subjected the Foundations document to historical scrutiny, finding nothing that connected the Commandments and the Declaration. Putting the county resolutions and the Foundations document together, Friedman argued that "the current courthouse display reveals both a purpose and an effect to endorse religion."

Friedman spoke for more than five minutes before he fielded the first question from the bench. Most lawyers who appear before the Court get nervous if they are not quickly interrupted with questions, fearing the justices might be bored by their arguments or perhaps had all made up their minds about the case. One justice was clearly not bored, although he had obviously made up his mind. Friedman's argument that the Commandments did not provide "the moral background of the Declaration of Independence" drew a sharp retort from Justice Scalia.

"That's idiotic," he said. "What the Commandments stand for is the direction of human affairs by God. And to say that that's the basis of the Declaration of Independence and of our institutions is entirely realistic."

Another justice was not bored and had earlier hinted that he might view the Texas and Kentucky cases differently. Justice Breyer had told Erwin Chemerinsky that "I don't find much divisiveness" over the Texas monument. Friedman opened this issue in the Kentucky cases, noting "the public reaction" to the ACLU lawsuit, "the letters to the editor, the 'Keep the Ten Commandments' signs on yards throughout the county." Breyer seemed receptive to this issue, suggesting that "it's easy in this area to become far more divisive than you hoped and really end up with something worse than if you stayed out in the first place. In other words, it's a very delicate matter, and it's very easy to offend people." Friedman concluded by saying that McCreary and Pulaski county officials were "simply wrapping the Ten Commandments in the flag and, with all due respect, that constitutes endorsement" of religion.

The Supreme Court Opinions in the Ten Commandments Cases

Needless to say, the most important turning point in any case that reaches the Supreme Court for decision comes when the justices meet in their book-lined conference room to vote on cases that have been argued during the Court's "argument weeks." The procedures for these conferences follow a long-standing tradition that deserves some mention. The chief justice presides and generally begins the discussion of each case with a brief summary of its facts and legal issues. Following that, the most junior justice in length of service offers his or her thoughts on the case and indicates his or her vote on whether to affirm or reverse the lower-court ruling. Beginning the voting with the newest justice presumably helps him or her avoid the temptation to follow the lead of senior justices. The justices then go around the table until the senior associate justice casts his or her vote; the chief justice keeps a record of votes on a tally sheet. It's important to note that all conference votes are tentative and may be changed at any time before the decision becomes final.

After the voting is complete, the chief justice, if he's in the majority, designates a justice (which could be himself) to draft a **majority**

opinion, or an **opinion for the Court** in cases decided unanimously. If the chief is in the minority, the senior associate justice in the majority makes the opinion assignment. During the following weeks and sometime months, the justices who are assigned to draft majority and dissenting opinions put themselves and their clerks to work on these opinions, which are then circulated to all of the justices for their comments. There ensues a flurry of memos between the chambers, some as brief as returning a draft opinion to its author with the notation "I join," others with suggestions for changes, which range from adding or deleting a footnote to adding new sections. Justices who agree with the case's outcome but who differ with the opinion's author on its legal reasoning are free to write "concurring opinions," which often happens. Some justices also write opinions that concur in some parts with the majority but dissent on other issues. Putting together all of the possible alignments of opinions, there are a large number of permutations (although I haven't calculated the number) of majority, **plurality**, **dissenting**, **concurring**, and **concur in part, dissent in part** opinions in any case.

As I noted earlier, all votes and opinions are tentative and may be changed at any time before the decision is announced and becomes final. In some cases, the landmark abortion case of *Roe v. Wade* being the most recent notable example, what starts out as a majority opinion may wind up as a dissent, when one or more justices become persuaded that their initial votes were wrong, and they switch to the other side. It's also a dirty little secret, long known to Court insiders but publicly revealed by former justice Thurgood Marshall, that justices sometimes engage in the kind of "horse-trading" that is common in Congress. For example, one justice may offer another justice his or her vote in one case (usually one in which that justice has little interest) for a vote in a case in which the "trader" has a greater interest. Once the Court's ruling in a case and all of the opinions are handed down, however, all of the behind-the-scenes negotiations end, and the ruling becomes final.

Court watchers in the media and the legal community were divided over whether the Court would uphold or strike down the Commandments displays in the Kentucky and Texas cases. As it turned out, the justices were also divided, handing down conflicting decisions when they ruled on June 27, 2005. By two separate majorities of 5–4, the Court banished the Commandments from the McCreary and

Pulaski county courthouses but allowed the monument to remain on the Texas capitol grounds in Austin. The divergent outcomes of the two cases reflected the Court's continuing difficulty in defining a consistent judicial standard in Establishment Clause cases. Rather than finding any **bright line** to guide their interpretation, the justices—as they had in earlier cases—looked to the "context" and the "setting" of public displays of religious symbols and sentiments.

Ruling in *McCreary County v. ACLU of Kentucky*, the title for the two Kentucky cases, five justices agreed that the purpose behind the courthouse displays was to endorse the religious message of the Commandments. Writing for himself and Justices Ginsburg, Breyer, O'Connor, and Stevens, Justice Souter looked to past cases that mandated governmental neutrality in religious matters. That principle was violated "when the government's ostensible purpose is to take sides," Souter wrote. It was clear to him that the counties had taken sides by initially posting, by itself, a religious text that rested its prohibitions "on the sanction of the divinity proclaimed at the beginning of the text." It was also clear to Souter that subsequent displays of more secular documents did not erase the clearly religious purpose of the first, which displayed "an unmistakably religious statement dealing with religious obligations and with morality subject to religious sanction." Souter dismissed the revised displays as a "litigating position" adopted by county officials who "were simply reaching for any way to keep a religious document on the walls of courthouses constitutionally required to embody religious neutrality" and concluded that "no reasonable observer could swallow the claim that the counties had cast off the objective so unmistakable in the earlier displays."

The Court's swing justices in most religion cases, Sandra O'Connor and Anthony Kennedy, swung in opposite directions in the Commandments cases. O'Connor joined the *McCreary County* majority with a separate concurring opinion. "It is true that many Americans find the Commandments in accord with their personal beliefs," she wrote, tacitly acknowledging public support for their display. "But we do not count heads before enforcing the First Amendment," she added. The fact that virtually all McCreary and Pulaski county residents were Christians, although O'Connor did not mention this fact, could not allow that religious majority to proclaim its beliefs on courthouse walls.

The Constitution's religious clauses, she concluded, "protect adherents of all religions, as well as those who believe in no religion at all."

Although Chief Justice Rehnquist had not attended the oral arguments because of illness, he read the transcripts and joined Justice Scalia's dissent in the *McCreary County* case, along with Justices Kennedy and Thomas. Reflecting his view that the Establishment Clause did not protect religious minorities or nonbelievers from majoritarian sentiment, Scalia denounced "the demonstrably false principle that the government cannot favor religion over irreligion." He looked to tradition, beginning with the Thanksgiving proclamation of the First Congress, citing "the interest of the overwhelming majority of religious believers in being able to give God thanks and supplication *as a people.*" Scalia recognized the conflict between adherents of minority religions and nonbelievers and the majority that believes in the religious commands of the Decalogue. "Our national tradition has resolved that conflict in favor of the majority," Scalia wrote, adding his view that the Establishment Clause "permits this disregard of polytheists and believers in unconcerned deities, just as it permits the disregard of devout atheists." Unlike Justice O'Connor, Scalia counted heads and found more on the side of the Ten Commandments.

The Supreme Court also counts heads when its members vote on cases. The majority coalition in *McCreary County* shifted to the other side in the Texas case, *Van Orden v. Perry*, with Justice Steven Breyer casting the deciding vote. This case produced seven opinions among the nine justices, another reflection of judicial discord over the place of religion in the public square. Chief Justice Rehnquist, joined by Scalia, Kennedy, and Thomas, wrote a brief plurality opinion that conceded the "religious significance" of the Commandments, but that did not prohibit their public display. "Acknowledgments of the role played by the Ten Commandments in our Nation's heritage are common throughout America," he wrote. "We need only look within our own Courtroom," pointing to a depiction inside the Court's chamber of Moses holding tablets with the Commandments and to other displays of the Decalogue in federal buildings around the nation's capital. "Simply having religious content or promoting a religious message consistent with a religious doctrine does not run afoul of the Establishment Clause," Rehnquist concluded.

Justice Breyer did not join Rehnquist's opinion, explaining his position in a separate concurrence. "If the relation between government and religion is one of separation, but not of mutual hostility and suspicion, one will inevitably find difficult borderline cases," he wrote. "The case before us is a borderline case." During oral arguments in the Texas case, Breyer suggested that he was looking for a "practical" solution to the Commandments disputes, expressing concern about the "divisiveness" they created. The factor that most influenced Breyer's vote in the Texas case was that the Commandments monument had stood for more than forty years before Thomas Van Orden challenged its display. "That experience helps us understand that as a practical matter of *degree* this display is unlikely to prove divisive. And this matter of degree is, I believe, critical in a borderline case such as this one." The Texas monument "has stood apparently uncontested for almost two generations" without provoking any public division, Breyer also noted. In contrast, the Kentucky displays had been recently erected, and the *McCreary County* plaintiffs had promptly objected to them.

Breyer knew that hundreds of Commandments monuments stood outside courthouses and city halls in almost every state. Ruling against the monument in Texas, he wrote, "might well encourage disputes concerning the removal of long-standing depictions of the Ten Commandments from public buildings across the Nation. And it could thereby create the very kind of religiously based divisiveness that the Establishment Clause seeks to avoid."

Among the four dissenters, Justice Souter replied most directly to Breyer's reliance on the forty years that passed before Van Orden challenged the monument that he walked past on the capitol grounds in Austin. Breyer seemed to suggest, Souter replied, "that forty years without a challenge shows that the religious expression is too tepid to provoke a serious reaction. I doubt that a slow walk to the courthouse, even one that took forty years, is much evidentiary help in applying the Establishment Clause." Justice Stevens, in his dissenting opinion, decried Rehnquist's "simplistic commentary on the various ways in which religion has played a role in American life" and denounced "the plurality's wholehearted validation of an official state endorsement that there is one, and only one, God." The *Van Orden* majority, he wrote, "would replace Jefferson's 'wall of separation' with a perverse wall of exclusion—Christians inside, non-Christians out." Such a reading of the Establishment Clause, Stevens complained, was "plainly not worthy of a society whose enviable hallmark over the course of two centuries has been the continuing expansion of religious pluralism and tolerance." In the end, Justice Breyer played the role of Solomon in proposing to split the Establishment Clause baby in half, satisfying hardly anyone on either side, both on the Court and in the American public.

Quite predictably, the Court's divided rulings on the Commandments displays sparked divided reactions from those who brought and argued the two cases. On his part, Thomas Van Orden confessed that he was "not happy" about the ruling against him, saying he would spend the day reflecting "on the past three and a half years, including everything I went through." The lawyers who argued the Texas case responded with subdued words. Sitting before reporters in front of the capitol grounds monument in Austin, Greg Abbott said the Court "has made clear that Texas is a model of how governmental bodies across the country can constitutionally display religious symbols." Van Orden's lawyer, Erwin Chemerinsky, pointed to the Kentucky decision as the more significant ruling, calling it "an important victory" for church and state separation. "The government is still limited in what it can do with religious symbols on government property," he said.

People in McCreary County reacted with more emotion to the ruling in their case. Jimmie Greene had planned to lead a Fourth of July parade to return the Commandments display from the American Legion hall to the courthouse. "I woke up this morning, just convinced we were going to have a big celebration next week and put the commandments right back in the courthouse," he said. But the Court's decision ruined his plans. "All along through this process I have been optimistic and felt there was no way the Supreme Court could vote against us," Greene told reporters who sought him out in Whitley City. "But after hearing the decision I don't think I have ever felt more depressed in my life. It just broke my heart. I am not ashamed to tell you that I cried."

His cousin Louanne Walker, who had sued to remove the Commandments display, had a different reaction. "It was really a wonderful day," she said on learning of the decision. "Surprising, but wonderful."

Dave Howe, Greene's friendly adversary in the case, did not hold out an olive branch. "You don't establish a religion," he said. "They were trying to establish Lord Jesus Christ as founder of this country. Jimmie had never denied that. He said he wanted to get God back in the courthouse, and that is not acceptable."

David Friedman had some advice for those who still wanted to display the Commandments. "They should do it in their homes, in their religious institutions, on their cars, and not through the government," he said. "The government is all of ours, and it can only be all of ours when it remains neutral." Mat Staver, who had predicted victory in the case he argued, sounded bitter and defiant in defeat. "This battle is far from over," he said. "We're looking to take this case back to the Supreme Court."

The odds of obtaining a rehearing in the Kentucky cases were slim, but prospects for later decisions in other Commandments cases improved, just four days after the *Van Orden* and *McCreary County* rulings. After twenty-four years on the Court, Justice Sandra O'Connor announced, on July 1, 2005, that she would step down when her successor was confirmed by the Senate and sworn in. O'Connor's departure threatened to shift the Court's narrow balance in religion cases. President Bush first named John Roberts, a federal appellate judge, to replace O'Connor, but the death of Chief Justice Rehnquist, on September 3, prompted Bush to place Roberts in the Court's center seat. Roberts had served as a law clerk to Rehnquist and clearly shared his predecessor's conservative views. After Bush selected Samuel Alito, another conservative appellate judge, to fill O'Connor's seat, Religious Right groups and their lawyers were ecstatic. Mat Staver praised Alito's nomination, noting his appellate decision upholding a Nativity display in New Jersey. Alito's confirmation by the Senate, on January 31, 2006, added an almost-certain fifth and deciding vote to the Court's conservative majority in Establishment Clause cases, assuming the Court's ideological balance did not shift before another Ten Commandments case reached its docket. As we will see, however, Alito's vote made no difference when the *McCreary County* case returned to the Court after the Sixth Circuit ruling in August 2010 turned down Mat Staver's request for en banc review of a decision of a three-judge panel. The Supreme Court upheld the grant by Judge Coffman of a permanent injunction against display of the Decalogue in the county courthouse.

11

The Impact of Justice Breyer's Concurrence on Pending Ten Commandments Cases

Much subsequent litigation would have been avoided had Justice Stephen Breyer not switched sides in the *McCreary County* and *Van Orden* cases, joining the majority in the former and casting, through his concurring opinion, the decisive vote in the latter. This switch raises an important and intriguing question: Why did Breyer switch sides in these cases? A careful reading of his *Van Orden* concurrence reveals both the pretextual nature of his arguments in that opinion and the actual reason for his decision to uphold the Decalogue monument on the Texas state capitol grounds.

Justice Breyer's concurring opinion is important because it established what is known as **the law of the case**. In cases that are decided by a plurality of four justices, with one justice joining the "judgment of the Court" but not the plurality opinion, that justice's concurring opinion becomes the precedential guideline for lower-court judges in pending or subsequent cases on that issue. It may seem odd for one justice to wield such influence, but that's been the Court's historical practice.

In his *Van Orden* concurrence, Breyer conceded that this was a "difficult borderline" case. Looking for factors to distinguish it from *McCreary County*, he found three that influenced his decision. At five places in his concurrence, Breyer cited the "context" of the Texas monument. Unlike the Kentucky display, in which the Ten Commandments first stood alone on the courthouse wall and were the centerpiece in later displays, the Texas monolith was set aside "in a large park" that contained thirty-eight other monuments and historical markers, none with religious meaning. For Breyer, this "physical setting" provided "a strong, but not conclusive, indication that the Commandments text on this monument conveys a predominantly secular message" in a "context of history and moral ideas." It is hard to fault Justice Breyer for this emphasis on the physical setting and the "context" of the Texas monument, because that factor provided the basis for the Court's decisions on the Nativity scene and the menorah displays in the *Lynch* and *Allegheny County* cases, although he cited neither in his concurrence.

A second source of later confusion among lower-court judges lies in Breyer's repeated reference to the supposedly "secular" nature of the Ten Commandments. In fact, he contradicted himself in making this argument, because he had joined the *McCreary County* opinion of Justice Souter, who labeled the Decalogue "an unmistakably religious statement dealing with religious obligations and with morality subject to religious sanction." Nonetheless, Breyer claimed in his *Van Orden* concurrence that the Commandments conveyed "a secular moral message" about "proper standards of social conduct" and "a historic relation between those standards and the law."

A final distinguishing factor between the Kentucky and Texas cases lies in Justice Breyer's references in his *Van Orden* concurrence to the supposed community "divisiveness" engendered by the former and lacking in the latter. Citing the fact that forty years had passed between the Texas monument's installation and Thomas Van Orden's challenge to it, as evidence that it was "unlikely to prove divisive" in Austin (although perhaps not elsewhere in Texas), Breyer revealed in his concurrence his real fear that its removal "might well encourage disputes concerning the removal of longstanding depictions of the Ten

Commandments from public buildings across the Nation. And it could thereby create the very kind of religiously based divisiveness that the Establishment Clause seeks to avoid." As an aside, if past and potential "divisiveness" was a proper factor in judicial decisions, the Supreme Court might not have rendered its *Brown* and *Roe* decisions, striking down school segregation and upholding abortion rights, both of which created "divisiveness" that sparked decades of violence and even murder. In my view, by raising the "divisiveness" issue, Breyer was recoiling from the prospect of back-hoes and cranes ripping out dozens of Ten Commandments monuments, provoking (probably unfounded) scenes of resistance by their supporters.

In his *Van Orden* concurrence, Justice Breyer buttressed his claim that display of the Ten Commandments conveyed a "predominantly secular message" with the assertion that the "proper standards of social conduct" contained in the Decalogue reflected the "historic relation between those standards and the law." Similar statements have been made in the writings and the legal briefs of the Decalogue's defenders, including the *Van Orden* amicus brief of the United States. Breyer cited this amicus brief, which asserted that "historians" have supported the view that "the Ten Commandments influenced the development of American law." However, neither Breyer nor the Justice Department brief named a single historian or cited any scholarly publication to support these assertions.

If the Ten Commandments were, in fact, a source of American law, the burden should rest on supporters of their public display to produce some evidence of this purported linkage. They have produced none, beyond mere assertion. The best, and first, place to look for such evidence is in the proceedings of the Constitutional Convention in 1787. There is not one mention of the Ten Commandments or of the Bible, for that matter, in James Madison's almost verbatim notes of the convention's debates. Nor are there any mentions of the Commandments in reports (much more fragmentary) of the state ratifying conventions or in the *Federalist Papers*. To be sure, some of the laws in the American colonies were based on biblical precepts, such as laws in the Massachusetts Bay Colony that punished such crimes as idolatry, blasphemy, and witchcraft with death penalties. But such laws, even those that stayed on the books after the Constitution was ratified, have no legal force today. And the crimes of murder, adultery, theft, and perjury, forbidden by the Commandments, have more ancient roots than the Bible, stemming back to the Code of Hammurabi from the sixteenth century B.C. and the prebiblical laws of ancient Greece and Rome. Legal anthropologists have recorded such prohibitions in virtually every preliterate culture in the world.

Other legal scholars agree on these issues. Marci Hamilton, of Cardozo Law School, has written extensively on this issue "as a Christian, an American, and a scholar." She dismisses claims that the Commandments form "the ground for much of our criminal law, and therefore constitute a legal and historical document—not a religious one," as "so weak it ought to be rejected out of hand." Hamilton notes that the first four Commandments, as well as the admonitions to honor one's parents and not to covet one's neighbor's goods or wife, "simply *cannot* be enacted into law." In addition, a criminal prohibition against adultery, although still a ground for divorce in some states, "would likely be struck down as unconstitutional" by the Supreme Court, Hamilton wrote. That leaves only murder, theft, and perjury, which were crimes in most societies long before the Bible was written.

Another noted legal historian, Paul Finkelman, of Albany Law School, notes that it's even difficult to decide which of several versions of the Commandments (the Bible lists seventeen in two separate Old Testament books) is accurate, and that Catholics and Protestants have competing lists; even Protestant denominations have adopted different versions. Finkelman concludes that "the claim that the Ten Commandments, or even the Bible, are the moral foundation of American law simply does not stand up to careful scrutiny. Indeed, even in the colonial period the overwhelming majority of laws—which regulated land, crops, domestic animals, the sale of tobacco and rice, white-Indian relations, and slavery—had little or nothing to do with the Bible, let alone the Ten Commandments." Finkelman agrees with Marci Hamilton that "most of the Commandments could not be enacted into law and withstand a constitutional challenge."

Steven K. Green, of Willamette University Law School, who wrote his Ph.D. history dissertation on this topic, prepared a Supreme Court amicus brief in *McCreary County* that was signed by twenty-seven noted legal historians, a veritable "Who's Who" in this field. After an exhaustive review of all of the available sources on the drafting of the Declaration of Independence and the Constitution, the brief notes that "the Ten Commandments and biblical law received nary a mention in the debates and publications surrounding the founding documents." The brief's signers agreed that the "foundation of the law of the United States thus emanates from the nature of representative government— what Jefferson called 'the consent of the governed'—and needs no external or divine authority for its support." Hardly anyone disputes that most of the Constitution's drafters were Christians of various stripes, largely of heterodox views. But none, with the possible exception of James Wilson of Pennsylvania, subscribed to the biblical inerrancy and orthodoxy of today's Religious Right activists. This raises the question of why Justice Breyer cited the unsupported and conclusory Justice Department brief in his *Van Orden* concurrence, ignoring the well-supported brief of the nation's leading legal historians. My own suspicion is that Breyer wanted to avoid the "social conflict" that he feared would follow a decision to remove the Decalogue monument from the Texas state capitol grounds and simply closed his eyes to the relevant evidence in the case.

Justice Breyer's concurrence in *Van Orden* had the unfortunate (but easily foreseen) consequence of forcing lower-court judges to confront a difficult and "fact-intensive" question in deciding pending and future Ten Commandments cases: Is this case more like *McCreary County* or *Van Orden*? This inquiry required judges to examine a host of subsidiary questions. Was the display located inside or outside of a public building or even in a distant park? Was it standing alone or surrounded by other documents or monuments? Was it erected decades ago or recently? Was it initiated by public officials or private citizens? Was it paid for or maintained by public or private funds? Was its erection accompanied by religious comments from public officials, clergy members, or private citizens? How much time elapsed between its erection and a lawsuit challenging the display? In answering these questions and deciding on which side of Breyer's "borderline" they fell, judges were literally compelled to use a tally sheet, ticking off which factors had the most weight in helping them reach their decisions.

It is hardly surprising that federal appellate courts, given the conflicting decisions in *McCreary County* and *Van Orden* and the divergent political and social views among their judges, would reach different conclusions, almost guaranteeing an eventual "circuit-split" of the kind that had prompted the Supreme Court to grant review in the Kentucky and Texas cases. That split has now happened, as we shall see further on. We begin by examining two recent cases, from Nebraska and Washington state.

The Eagles Monument in Plattsmouth, Nebraska

Our Ten Commandments tour next takes us to Plattsmouth, Nebraska, a town of some sixty-five hundred residents on the state's eastern border, across the Mississippi River from Iowa. Back in 1965, the local Aerie of the Fraternal Order of Eagles donated a Ten Commandments monument to the town, which placed it in a forty-five-acre park, some ten blocks from city hall. Like the similar monument outside the Texas state capitol building, it was inscribed with two Stars of David and the Greek letters Chi and Rho to signify Christ. There are apparently no surviving records of the town's decision to accept the monument or of remarks made at its installation. Thirty-six years passed before a town resident, known as "John Doe" in court papers, filed suit in 2001 to seek its removal, with the Nebraska ACLU as lead plaintiff.

After a federal district judge ruled for "Doe" and the ACLU, holding that the monument violated the Establishment Clause, a divided panel of the Eighth Circuit Court of Appeals affirmed that decision. But an en banc review by all thirteen circuit judges, with only two dissenters, reversed the panel in 2005, holding that "*Van Orden* governs our resolution of this case." Citing Justice Breyer's concurrence in that case, the majority found that the monument's location in a park, the time that elapsed before it was challenged, and its donation by a private group combined to allow the "use of the text of the Ten Commandments to acknowledge the role of religion in our Nation's heritage." The two dissenters viewed the Decalogue as "a command from the Judeo-Christian God on how he requires his followers to live." Labeling the Commandments as simply "an 'acknowledgement of the role of religion' diminishes their sanctity to believers and belies the words themselves," the dissenters wrote in an apparent reference to the commandment against "graven images."

Another Eagles Monument in Everett, Washington

Everett, Washington, is a waterfront city, north of Seattle, whose seventy thousand residents mostly work in the timber, fishing, and shipping industries. In 1959, the Eagles donated a Ten Commandments monument to the city, inscribed like those in Plattsmouth and Austin with two Stars of David and the Chi and Rho symbols of Christ. City officials installed it in front of the city hall, at a ceremony attended by civic leaders and church leaders, who offered an invocation and a benediction, along with brief remarks that noted the religious nature of the. Decalogue.

After a local resident, Jesse Card, filed suit against the city, aided by volunteer lawyers from prestigious firms in Seattle and Washington, D.C., a federal district judge ruled for the city in 2005. Ruling on Card's appeal in March 2008, a three-judge panel of the Ninth Circuit Court of Appeals unanimously upheld this decision in a lengthy opinion that reviewed the *McCreary County* and *Van Orden* cases, focusing on Justice Breyer's concurrence in the latter. Citing such factors as the monument's private donor, the years that elapsed before Card filed suit, and the presence of other—although later-added—monuments around it, the appellate panel found, as Breyer had in *Van Orden*, that the Everett monument conveyed both "a secular moral message" and "a historical message." Dismissing *McCreary County* as factually dissimilar to the Everett case and looking to the "context" of the monument's history and surroundings, the panel found it "clear that *Van Orden* controls our decisions."

It's worth noting that in both the *Plattsmouth* and the *Everett* case, the plaintiffs' lawyers did not seek Supreme Court review of these unfavorable decisions, most likely fearing that the conservative justices might use the lower-court decisions as an opportunity to overrule the *McCreary County* case, following the replacement of Justice Sandra O'Connor by Samuel Alito.

Viewed in tandem, the *Plattsmouth* and *Everett* cases, with their primary focus on the factors that Breyer found "determinative" in his *Van Orden* concurrence, established what might be described—not entirely facetiously—as the "Breyer test." Under this test, if a Decalogue display is old, donated by a civic group such as the Eagles, and unchallenged for decades, it passes constitutional muster. But what if the display is new, donated by someone with clearly religious motives, and promptly challenged by a lawsuit? Does that make a challenge to the display a *McCreary County* case, governed by these factors? What if a Ten Commandments case involves some factors in *Van Orden* and some from *McCreary County*? These questions illustrate the dilemma faced by judges who were later called on to resolve the conflicts posed in Decalogue cases.

"The Lord Had Burdened My Heart"— The Ten Commandments Monument in Haskell County, Oklahoma

After our briefs stops in Nebraska and Washington state, we'll spend a longer time in Haskell County, Oklahoma, where the "Breyer test" met its stiffest challenge from appellate court judges. Haskell County has much in common with McCreary County, Kentucky. Both are small in population, with about fifteen thousand residents in each, and poor; the median income in both counties is roughly half the national average. Education levels in both lag well behind those in their states and the rest of the nation. Neither county is closer than sixty miles to a major city. Both are conservative in politics; more than 70 percent of the voters in each backed John McCain over Barack Obama in the 2008 presidential election. Both are fundamentalist in religion, with Baptists an overwhelmingly majority in each.

But, considering the similarities between the two counties, it is not surprising that Ten Commandments displays were installed in both places, with local residents expressing surprise and dismay that anyone would file a lawsuit to remove this symbol of the Christian faith. The Ten Commandments display in Haskell County was initiated in 2004 by

Mike Bush, who owned a small construction firm and served as a part-time lay Baptist minister. Bush told the county's three-member Board of Commissioners that "the Lord had burdened my heart" to install a Decalogue monument on the courthouse lawn in Stigler, the county seat and a town of some twenty-five hundred people. "The Board agreed that Mike could go ahead and have the monument made and Mike is taking care of all the expense," the minutes of this meeting recorded. The Haskell County monument was dedicated on November 7, 2004, at a ceremony attended by more than a hundred people, including all three commissioners and representatives of seventeen churches. Following the ceremony, one commissioner told a reporter, referring to the monument, "That's what we're trying to live by, that right there. I'm a Christian and I believe in this. I think it's a benefit to the community."

One person who did not think the monument was a benefit to Haskell County was a Stigler resident, James W. Green, who filed a suit against the Board of Commissioners in October 2005, aided by the Oklahoma ACLU and one of its volunteer lawyers, Micheal Salem of Norman. In response, Mike Bush organized a "Support the Ten Commandments Monument" rally at the courthouse the month after Green filed his suit. Attended by three to four hundred people, the rally featured local pastors and U.S. senator Tom Coburn, a conservative Republican, who said, "I wish this was in every courthouse on the lawn. We need more of this, not less." Mike Bush reported that 2,835 signatures had been collected on a petition supporting the monument. "My heart is thankful to see so many people coming out," he said. "All our laws are based on the ten laws up here on our courthouse lawn." One of the county commissioners stirred the crowd with a defiant pledge: "I'll stand up in front of that monument, and if you bring a bulldozer up here, you'll have to push me down with it," a pretty clear indication of the "divisiveness" the Supreme Court had deplored in *McCreary County* but that Justice Breyer did not find in the *Van Orden* case.

Jim Green's suit came before federal district judge Ronald A. White, named to the bench by President George W. Bush. Sitting in nearby Muskogee, White conducted a two-day bench trial in May 2006. Mike Salem appeared for Green; opposing him and representing Haskell County was Kevin Theriot, a staff lawyer in Kansas for the Arizona-based Alliance Defense Fund, a Religious Right legal group whose stated mission is to promote "the spread of the Gospel through the legal defense and advocacy of religious freedom" and that affirms the Bible as "the inspired, infallible, and authoritative word of God."

Ruling on August 18, 2006, Judge White relied on *Van Orden* in holding that the Haskell County monument did not "overstep the constitutional line demarcating government neutrality toward religion." He noted that the courthouse lawn included several other monuments, such as those honoring war veterans and recognizing the Choctaw Indians, who make up roughly 15 percent of the county's residents. "A reasonable observer would see that the [Decalogue] monument is not the focus of the courthouse lawn," White wrote. "The mélange of monuments surrounding the one at issue here obviously detract from any religious message that may be conveyed by the Commandments." Revealing his personal view that the *Haskell County* case was hardly worth his time, White dismissed it as a "kerfuffle," saying in effect that it was much ado about nothing.

Jim Green's appeal from Judge White's ruling was filed in the U.S. Court of Appeals for the Tenth Circuit in September 2006. Almost three years passed before a three-judge panel, all of its members named to the bench by President George W. Bush, issued its unanimous opinion on June 8, 2009. Writing for the panel, Judge Jerome Holmes reversed Judge White's ruling, finding this case more like *McCreary County* than *Van Orden*. Holmes focused on the facts that the Haskell County monument had been recently installed, that Green filed suit within a year of its erection, and that county commissioners had supported the monument with religious comments. Any "reasonable observer" of the monument, Holmes wrote, "would have been left with the clear impression—not counteracted by the individual commissioners or the Board collectively—that the commissioners were speaking for the government and the government was endorsing the religious message of the Monument." On this point, Holmes quoted the religious comments of the commissioners to reporters, noting that "in a small community like Haskell County, where everyone knows everyone," such statements of opinion would be perceived as government speech; indeed, one commissioner described his post as a "24/7" job. In this regard, Haskell County more resembled McCreary County than Austin, Texas.

After this judicial setback, Kevin Theriot asked the Tenth Circuit for an en banc review of the panel's decision by the full bench of twelve active judges. Ruling on July 30, 2009, the judges denied the request by a 6–6 vote, because a majority is required for such review. All six judges who voted to rehear the case had been named to the bench by Republican presidents (although, as noted previously, so had all three members of the panel that reversed Judge White's ruling). Between them, the six dissenters issued two lengthy opinions, while the six in the majority remained silent, as is normal in voting against an en banc review. In both opinions, the dissenters castigated the panel for finding the *Haskell County* case more like *McCreary County* than like *Van Orden*. Writing for himself and three colleagues, Judge Neil Gorsuch called the panel decision "simply inconsistent with the most analogous decision of the Supreme Court." The most important factors to Gorsuch were the secular monuments that surrounded the Ten Commandments on the courthouse lawn, which he felt diminished the Decalogue's religious message, and its donation by a private citizen, Mike Bush. Admitting that the conflicting decisions in *McCreary County* and *Van Orden* were difficult to reconcile and apply, Gorsuch said, "We should all be able to agree at least that cases like *Van Orden* should come out like *Van Orden*."

In an opinion joined by two colleagues, Judge Paul Kelly noted the inscription on the monument, "Erected by Citizens of Haskell County," and also cited the "context" of nearby monuments, then concluded that these factors left "little doubt that the government itself did not communicate a predominantly religious message but rather was merely providing space for yet another donated monument related to Haskell County's history." Kevin Theriot responded to the en banc denial with a thinly veiled broadside at Jim Green. "Americans should not be forced to abandon their religious heritage simply to appease someone's political agenda," he said. "The emotional response of a single, offended passerby does not amount to a violation of the Establishment Clause."

The Supreme Court had granted review in the *McCreary County* and *Van Orden* cases to resolve a circuit-split between the appellate courts that struck down the Ten Commandments display in the Kentucky courthouse and upheld the monument on the Texas state capitol grounds. As we have seen, circuit courts in the *Plattsmouth* and

Everett cases relied on *Van Orden* for guidance, while the Tenth Circuit panel in the *Haskell County* case found the challenged Decalogue monument more like *McCreary County.*

This subsequent circuit-split prompted Kevin Theriot to ask the Supreme Court, once again, to resolve the lower-court conflicts that Justice Breyer's concurrence had produced. On October 28, 2009, Theriot filed a certiorari petition in the *Haskell County* case with the Supreme Court. Not surprisingly, his petition quoted extensively from the opinions of Judges Kelly and Gorsuch, dissenting from the Tenth Circuit's denial of an en banc review of the unanimous panel decision. Theriot placed special emphasis on Gorsuch's statement that "cases like *Van Orden* should come out like *Van Orden.*" Downplaying the undeniable religious message of the Commandments, Theriot stressed instead the purported "historical significance" they represented in America's religious heritage, repeating this phrase six times in his thirty-three-page petition. Theriot summed up his appeal for Supreme Court review in these words: "Circuit courts need this Court's guidance on the proper analysis to apply to monuments passively acknowledging religion's historical significance that are part of historical displays on government grounds. Otherwise, these cases will continue to be decided on irrelevant facts like those that led to the finding of unconstitutionality in this case: age of the monument, how quickly it was challenged, whether it was displayed in a small or large town, and the personal religious views of the government officials who allowed it."

Jim Green's lawyers filed their brief in opposition to Kevin Theriot's certiorari petition in the *Haskell County* case with the Supreme Court on January 11, 2010. Primarily drafted by Daniel Mach of the ACLU's Washington, D.C., office, the brief urged the justices to deny review of the Tenth Circuit's panel decision on two main grounds. First, that the religious statements of Mike Bush and the county commissioners, before and after the Ten Commandments monument was installed, demonstrated an official endorsement of its sectarian message. Mach devoted eight pages of his brief to documenting these statements. Second, and not surprisingly, he argued that the overall context of the monument distinguished it from the one on the Texas state capitol grounds in the *Van Orden* case, making it more analogous to the Kentucky courthouse display in *McCreary County*, as the Tenth Circuit panel had concluded. In fact, Mach cited the words *context* and *contextual* forty-eight times in his thirty-two-page brief.

Even if the Tenth Circuit panel "had viewed this case solely through the lens of *Van Orden*," Mach argued, the Haskell County monument "still would not have passed constitutional muster because there are significant material distinctions between this display and the monument in *Van Orden*." Mach cited such factors as the recent erection of the Haskell County monument, the promptness with which Jim Green filed suit against it, and the community "divisiveness" it sparked. Mach did not rely solely on these factors, however, stressing that the Tenth Circuit panel had reviewed "the record as a whole" in the case and the "totality of the circumstances" that surrounded the monument's erection and had not singled out any factors as "determinative" in its ruling.

In contrast to Theriot's petition, Mach dismissed the asserted circuit-split with the decisions in the *Plattsmouth* and *Everett* cases with hardly a glance, conceding that those monuments satisfied the factors in Justice Breyer's *Van Orden* concurrence. In effect, the ACLU signaled its willingness to allow these and other "old" monuments, mostly donated by the Fraternal Order of Eagles, to remain standing. What Mach was saying, in essence, was that "cases like *McCreary County* should come out like *McCreary County*." This one did, Mach concluded, and thus did not warrant Supreme Court review or reversal of the Tenth Circuit's panel decision.

"We All Love Jesus Christ"— The Ten Commandments Display in Grayson County, Kentucky

Before we learn the fate of Kevin Theriot's certiorari petition in the *Haskell County* case, we'll take a brief detour to Grayson County, Kentucky. Ruling on January 14, 2010, two members of a Sixth Circuit three-judge panel reversed a district court decision that ordered the removal of a Ten Commandments display from the courthouse wall in the county seat of Leitchfield.

The case of *ACLU of Kentucky v. Grayson County* began in September
2001, when the Reverend Chester Shartzer, the pastor of the Clearview
Baptist Church in Leitchfield, appeared before the county's governing
body, the Fiscal Court, expressing "his desire for the County to place
the Ten Commandments in the County buildings." Located in the coal
fields of western Kentucky, Grayson County—much like McCreary
County in the state's eastern region—is small and rural and conservative in politics and religion. Its voters backed John McCain by a two-to-
one majority over Barack Obama in the 2008 presidential election, and
Southern Baptists outnumber other denominations by a similar margin. (With 120 counties, most of them small, rural, and conservative,
Kentucky is an ideal spawning ground for Ten Commandments cases,
with displays in more than a dozen counties.)

Reverend Shartzer had done his homework and knew that Judge
Coffman had ruled that a display of the Decalogue with other "historical documents" in the McCreary County courthouse was a "sham" and
violated the Establishment Clause. But he was not dissuaded, explaining to the Fiscal Court members that "the Civil Liberties [meaning the
ACLU] would look more favorable to it if [the Ten Commandments]
were hanging in a grouping with the other historical documents."
The county's attorney, Tom Goff, warned the Fiscal Court members "that there could be lawsuits filed against the County," but they
unanimously approved Shartzer's request to post the Decalogue in the
courthouse, along with the "historical documents" that Judge Coffman
had rejected in McCreary County, setting the stage for another Ten
Commandments lawsuit.

Shartzer's prediction that the ACLU "would look more favorable"
to the Grayson County display proved wrong. At the request of two
county residents, Ed Meredith and Ray Harper, the Kentucky ACLU
filed suit in 2002. Once again, as in the *McCreary County* case, Grayson
County was represented by Mathew Staver of Liberty Counsel, who
had no doubt provided Shartzer with the same "historical documents"
that were displayed in McCreary County. The Ten Commandments
were removed from the Grayson County courthouse after federal district judge Joseph McKinley granted the ACLU's preliminary injunction request, but further proceedings were placed on hold, pending the
outcome of appeals to the Sixth Circuit and the Supreme Court in

the *McCreary County* case. When he finally ruled in 2008, granting a permanent injunction against displaying the Ten Commandments in the courthouse, Judge McKinley held that county officials had "never considered a secular purpose" for their display, thus violating the "purpose" prong of the *Lemon* test.

When the county's appeal from Judge McKinley's ruling came before a three-judge panel of the Sixth Circuit, Mat Staver already had two sure votes in his pocket. Judge David McKeague was a long-time Republican activist and party official in Michigan and was also a member of the Federalist Society, an influential organization of conservative lawyers and judges. Senior district judge Karl Forester of Kentucky, who sat on the panel by designation, had already upheld a Ten Commandments display in his home state.

Writing for himself and Judge Forester, McKeague conceded that the documents in the Grayson County courthouse "match exactly" those in the McCreary County display the Supreme Court had ruled against. However, McKeague said, judges "must be alert to distinguishing facts" in similar cases. Lawyers and judges can always "distinguish" two cases if they try hard enough, and McKeague found two such facts to distinguish the *Grayson* and *McCreary County* cases. First, the Grayson display was donated by a private citizen, Reverend Shartzer; and second, no Grayson County officials made religious remarks at the display's installation. Finding both "historical and educational" value in the display, McKeague deferred to the county's "stated secular purpose" and held that the inclusion of the Decalogue "endorses an educational message rather than a religious one."

In a pointed dissent, Judge Karen Nelson Moore—named to the bench by President Bill Clinton—took McKeague to task for ignoring the clear evidence in the case record that posting the Decalogue in the courthouse was considered by county officials as separate from and unrelated to the "historical documents" that surrounded it. Citing the minutes of the Fiscal Court meetings, she said this record "clearly indicates that the predominant purpose was to post the Ten Commandments as a religious text and that the additional 'Historical Documents' were added merely to avoid violating the Constitution." Nothing was said at these meetings about the "historical" or "educational" nature of the Decalogue. "The County's asserted purpose here—that the Display was posted for educational or historical reasons—is a sham and should be rejected," Moore concluded, echoing the words of Judge Coffman in the *McCreary County* case.

The response of Grayson County residents to their victory in the Sixth Circuit made clear their religious motivation—dismissed by Judge McKeague—in displaying the Decalogue in their courthouse. On January 18, 2010, several hundred people gathered at the courthouse for a jubilant celebration. "Amid anthems, hymns, and plenty of 'amens,' a copy of the Ten Commandments was placed back on the wall at the Grayson County courthouse," one reporter wrote. "We all love Jesus Christ," she quoted one spectator as saying. "This represents our savior, and it's the law we have to go by." County magistrate Presto Gary said the long legal battle had been worth the effort. "If we don't get something back for Christian people to believe in, what kind of shape would our country be in?" he asked. "But we had faith and kept praying." After the Ten Commandments were placed back in their frame, the crowd spontaneously broke into singing "God Bless America" and "Amazing Grace." Afterward, everyone crowded around a big sheet cake emblazoned with the American flag. Fittingly, the celebration ended with a prayer by Reverend Chester Shartzer. "I'm so proud of the Christian leadership we've had in Grayson County," he said.

Needless to say, Kevin Theriot cited the *Grayson County* decision in his *Haskell County* reply brief, as further evidence of the circuit-split he asked the Supreme Court to resolve in his favor, noting that the Sixth Circuit "upheld a display identical to the one that this Court considered in *McCreary*." Despite his efforts to get the *Haskell County* case back to the Supreme Court, Kevin Theriot failed to persuade a single justice to review the Tenth Circuit decision. On March 2, 2010, the justices denied his certiorari petition with no recorded dissent. "We're very disappointed that the Supreme Court didn't take the case," he said but expressed his hope that the Court would review another Ten Commandments case "and help clarify that religious speech shouldn't be marginalized from the public square." Two weeks later, on March 18, with few spectators and no protests, a crew from the Muskogee Marble & Granite Company lifted the Haskell County monument from the courthouse lawn with a crane, moving it some hundred feet to adjoining property owned by the American Legion but still within sight of courthouse visitors.

Kevin Theriot's hope that the Supreme Court would review another Ten Commandments case was fulfilled, but with an outcome that disappointed him and other Decalogue supporters. The Supreme Court's decision in the *McCreary County* case in 2005 did not end that case. In ruling that McCreary and Pulaski county officials must remove the Ten Commandments from their courthouse lobbies, the Court had simply upheld the preliminary injunction issued by Judge Coffman in 2000, ordering removal of the displays. That injunction remained in effect and unchanged, while the counties appealed Coffman's ruling through the Sixth Circuit and the Supreme Court.

The later judicial proceedings in these cases highlight the procedural tangles that confront judges in long-running civil litigations. On October 15, 2007, David Friedman of the Kentucky ACLU asked Judge Coffman to "alter or amend" the preliminary injunction and to grant a permanent injunction that would end the cases for good, asserting in a summary judgment motion that no factual issues remained for her to decide. In response, Mat Staver of Liberty Counsel filed an opposing summary judgment motion, citing resolutions passed by the governing bodies of both counties, disavowing any "religious purpose" in posting the "Foundations of American Law and Government" displays that surrounded the Ten Commandments with supposedly "secular" documents. Friedman promptly moved to strike Staver's motion, arguing that the newly enacted resolutions came too late to meet a discovery order that Judge Coffman had issued, and that the resolutions had no effect on the pending issues. On August 4, 2008, Coffman granted Friedman's motion and issued the permanent injunction he sought. Mat Staver then appealed this ruling to the Sixth Circuit.

Friedman and Staver argued the appeal before the same Sixth Circuit three-judge panel that had upheld Judge Coffman's original ruling in 2003, in which two judges—Eric Clay and Julia Smith Gibbons—had sided with Friedman, with Judge James Ryan issuing a blistering dissent. The panel members had before them not only the Supreme Court's ruling in *McCreary County*, but also the decisions of two different—and more conservative—Sixth Circuit panels in the *Mercer County* and *Grayson County* cases, both upholding Ten Commandments courthouse displays, identical to those in McCreary and Pulaski counties, with both decisions relying on Justice Breyer's concurrence in *Van Orden* for authority.

Ruling on June 9, 2010, the *McCreary County* panel split the same way it had in 2003. Judge Clay again wrote for the majority in upholding Judge Coffman's grant of a permanent injunction. Noting that Mat Staver had "offered no new facts on remand that show that their purpose had changed from the one that the Supreme Court found to violate the Establishment Clause," Clay added that "Defendants have spent the time since the Supreme Court decision continuously seeking to accomplish their initial purpose of posting the Ten Commandments as a religious document." Clay also agreed that Judge Coffman had properly denied Staver's effort to present the resolutions that "repudiated" the earlier ones because he "attempted to admit new evidence more than one year after the close of discovery." Clay added that the resolutions "were adopted only as a litigating position." In effect, Judge Clay was reprimanding Staver for his failure to follow the rules of civil procedure. He also reprimanded his colleagues on the *Mercer County* and *Grayson County* panels for "essentially ignor[ing] the Supreme Court's reliance in *McCreary* on *both* the content of the display and the evolution of the evidence in determining that Defendants had a religious purpose in posting the Foundations Display." Such a public chiding of one's judicial colleagues, even in an opinion that few people would read, is rare in the clubby and collegial atmosphere of an appellate court.

Judge Clay's opinion prompted a brief but pungent dissent by Judge Ryan. "I cannot be too critical of my panel colleagues who feel *stare decisis*-bound by the Supreme Court majority's persistent hostility to religion and its refusal to acknowledge the historical evidence that religion, religious symbols, and the support of religious devotion were of the very essence of the values the Constitution's authors and the ratifying legislators thought they were preserving in the language of the First Amendment," he wrote. "The result, I fear, is that federal courts will continue to close the Public Square to the display of religious symbols as fundamental as the Ten Commandments, at least until the Supreme Court rediscovers the history and meaning of the words of the religion clauses of the First Amendment and jettisons the flawed reasoning of *Lemon v. Kurtzman*." Judge Ryan concluded with an appeal to the Sixth Circuit's conservative majority, urging them "to reconsider en banc what my colleagues have held today, from which I strongly dissent."

Within hours of reading Ryan's call to arms, Mat Staver issued a press release, announcing his intention to file a motion for an en banc review of the panel's decision. Staver issued his own call to arms: "This battle is far from over. The Ten Commandments are part of the fabric of our country and helped shape our laws. They are as much at home in a display about the foundations of law as stars and stripes are in the American flag. The Founding Fathers would be outraged that we are even debating the constitutionality of the Ten Commandments."

However, the Sixth Circuit denied the en banc request on July 29, 2010, with only Judge Ryan dissenting. Undeterred by this judicial rebuff, Mat Staver filed a certiorari petition with the Supreme Court three months later, on October 27. Much like Kevin Theriot's unsuccessful request for Supreme Court review in the *Haskell County* case, which the justices had denied just eight months earlier, Staver's petition cited the Sixth Circuit's "intra-circuit" split between its panel's *McCreary County* ruling and those of different panels in the *Grayson County* and *Mercer County* cases, as well as the "inter-circuit" split with the decisions of the Eighth and Ninth circuits in the *Plattsmouth* and *Everett* cases.

In a press release that alerted the media to his certiorari petition, Staver urged the Supreme Court to "issue a clear ruling that frees judges and lawmakers from the Establishment Clause purgatory created by its confusing rulings" in Ten Commandment cases. The lower-court decisions that followed the *McCreary County* and *Van Orden* rulings certainly reflected confusion among judges who struggled to reconcile them, but whether the Supreme Court would take up Staver's challenge remained to be seen.

That question was finally answered on February 22, 2011, when the Court denied the certiorari petition, without any comment or dissent. It's always hazardous to predict the outcome of future cases but I doubt the justices will once again wade into this divisive issue in the foreseeable future. Supreme Court decisions on such questions are supposed to provide consistency and predictability on constitutional issues, but the present justices seem inclined to let sleeping dogs lie on this one, regardless of how confusing their rulings have proved for lower-court judges and the general public as well.

12

The Influence of Politics in Religion Cases: The Mt. Soledad Cross Case

San Diego proudly bills itself as "America's Finest City." The second-largest city in California, after Los Angeles, and the seventh-largest in the United States, it is home to more than 1.3 million people, having doubled in population since 1970. San Diego is also the home of the nation's longest-running battle over religious symbols in public places, a lawsuit that was filed in 1989 and was still unresolved in 2011, after dozens of courtroom hearings, city council debates, and judicial rulings in state and federal courts.

The seemingly unending conflict in San Diego over the Mt. Soledad Cross—erected in 1954 in the center of a public park, at the summit of the city's highest peak—offers an instructive example of the power of religious symbols, both to inspire their adherents and to incite their antagonists. The longevity of *Paulson v. San Diego*, the case that sought to remove the cross from the park, illustrates the difficulty of ending a legal struggle between a stubborn and tenacious plaintiff on one side and equally stubborn and tenacious city officials on the other, backed by overwhelming majorities of the city's voters. Hardly any case in U.S. legal history has resulted in such a prolonged and contentious battle. It reflects the prescient observation of Justice Oliver Wendell Holmes, more than a century ago, that "we live by symbols."

On the surface, San Diego seems an unlikely setting for conflicts over religion. The city's last four mayors have been Catholic, Jewish, and Protestant, and election campaigns have never focused on a candidate's religious affiliation or beliefs. San Diego is a laid-back city, attracting more than thirty million visitors each year, drawn by the year-round temperate climate, seventy miles of Pacific Ocean beaches, and a raft of tourist attractions, including the world-famous San Diego Zoo, Sea World, and the newly renovated Gaslamp District in the city's downtown center. But along with its palm trees and sandy beaches, San Diego has long been a military center, beginning with the establishment in 1907 of the Navy Coaling Station. It is now the home port of the world's largest naval fleet, which includes two supercarriers, amphibious assault ships, and submarines. A huge Marine Corps base, Camp Pendleton, lies just north of the city. Since World War II, several million navy and marine troops have been stationed or trained in San Diego, and thousands have returned to the city to work or enjoy their retirement. Military veterans make up a substantial part of the city's residents, most are conservative in politics, and they vote in large numbers. However, San Diego is no longer the safe Republican city it was for many years. Partisan gerrymandering has given both Democrats and the GOP two safe congressional seats that include parts of the city, and several city council members in recent years have been notably liberal.

San Diego is justly proud of its many public parks, especially the 1,400-acre Balboa Park, whose Spanish-style buildings were constructed to host a World's Fair in 1915, and which shares its space with the zoo. Another park, some ten miles north of the city center, offers visitors a panoramic view of the city from the summit of Mt. Soledad, jutting 820 feet above the ocean at its foot. To the south, the view from the 170-acre park stretches to the border with Mexico and the adjoining city of Tijuana, another popular tourist attraction. To the north, visitors can see the campus of the University of California, San Diego, established in 1962 as an outgrowth of the Scripps

Institution of Oceanography. The Mt. Soledad Natural Park, which the city dedicated as a public park in 1916, is located in La Jolla, one of the wealthiest of San Diego's disparate neighborhoods. Before the UCSD campus was established, in fact, La Jolla was an exclusively Christian community, and its realtors kept out Jews with restrictive covenants. The university's first chancellor, however, called the realtors together and told them bluntly that "you can't have a world-class university without Jews." Bowing to this pressure, La Jolla slowly and grudgingly allowed Jews to purchase homes, but the town's leadership remained in the hands of wealthy Christians, whose outward civility barely concealed their religious prejudices.

Among La Jolla's most influential families were the Kelloggs, who owned the La Jolla Beach and Tennis Club, which had no Jewish members before the late 1960s. In 1952, during the Korean War, the Kelloggs were instrumental in founding the Mt. Soledad Memorial Association. This organization's well-connected leaders persuaded the San Diego city council to allow the construction, at the summit of the Mt. Soledad Natural Park, of a forty-three-foot-tall Latin cross as a memorial to World War II and Korean veterans. City officials granted permission to erect the cross but retained ownership of the cross site. Significantly, the cross was dedicated on April 18, 1954, an Easter Sunday, at a religious service that featured Bible readings and prayers and the singing of "Onward Christian Soldiers." During the next forty years, in fact, the Memorial Committee conducted services every Easter Sunday but never on Veteran's Day. Also significantly, the city's official maps and tourist brochures identified the site as the "Easter Cross."

The Legal Challenge to the Easter Cross

Not until 1989, thirty-five years after the Mt. Soledad Cross was erected, did anyone question the city's legal authority to allow a private group to place a Christian symbol on its property. That year, two San Diego residents, Philip Paulson and Howard Kreisner, informed city attorney John Witt that they were preparing a lawsuit to challenge the Easter Cross. The two men were professed atheists, and Paulson, who first proposed the lawsuit to remove the Easter Cross, was a Vietnam

combat veteran who objected to a war memorial that was nothing more
than a Christian symbol. I entered the case after reading about their
efforts through an article in the *San Diego Union*, the city's morning
newspaper, and contacted them with an offer to work together on the
lawsuit on a pro bono basis. Since 1982, I had taught constitutional law
in the political science department of the University of California in San
Diego and had an interest in issues of law and religion. At our first meeting, Paulson and Kreisner showed me the draft of the complaint they
had prepared to file in the San Diego federal court as pro se plaintiffs,
without legal counsel. Kreisner, who had done the legal research for the
lawsuit, was determined to argue the case himself.

The case of *Paulson v. San Diego* was assigned to one of the most conservative judges on the federal bench. Gordon Thompson was a native
San Diegan, born in 1929, who grew up and still lived in the affluent
Point Loma area, where he had attended the Presbyterian church since
childhood. Thompson began his legal career as a prosecutor in the district attorney's office, then left after three years to join a law firm whose
clients included many of San Diego's banks and businesses. He also
became active in Republican politics and was appointed by President
Richard Nixon in 1970 to the federal district court. Thompson was
certainly not the judge whom Paulson and Kreisner would have picked
for their case, but they hoped he would defer to the decisions of fellow
judges in similar cross cases.

During the first hearing on the Mt. Soledad case in 1991, Thompson
made clear his personal view that the Easter Cross should remain in the
park. But he also made clear his commitment to precedent established
in similar cases by the Ninth Circuit Court of Appeals, which bound
district judges to its rulings. In the most recent case, decided just a
few months earlier, the Ninth Circuit had invoked the "no preference"
clause of the California constitution to order the removal of Christian
religious statuary from a San Bernardino county public park. Howard
Kreisner, who argued for himself and Phil Paulson, sounded almost like
an accountant in dryly citing this and other judicial rulings that ordered
the removal of crosses from public property. It was undeniable, Kreisner
told Judge Thompson, that the Easter Cross was a sectarian religious
symbol, despite the city's efforts to portray it as a "secular" war memorial
with no sectarian meaning.

Appearing for the city, Mary Kay Jackson argued that the cross had "lost its religious symbolization" and had become "resymbolized" into a secular object. Jackson's effort to strip the cross of religious meaning clearly offended Judge Thompson, for whom the cross was the central symbol of his religious beliefs. In his ruling, issued on December 3, 1991, Thompson stressed that "the Latin cross is a powerful religious symbol" and represents "the Christian message of the crucifixion and resurrection of Jesus Christ, a doctrine at the heart of Christianity." He also noted the Memorial Association's use of the cross site only for Easter services and said that nothing in the park indicated to visitors "that the cross was intended to commemorate our country's war dead." Given this history, Thompson concluded, "the city's purported commemorative objective is a pretext" for its sectarian "preference" for Christianity. He concluded his opinion by ordering the city to remove the Easter Cross within thirty days.

Several factors affected the city's initial response to Thompson's ruling. First, the city attorney had assured the city council that the cross would survive judicial scrutiny and urged an appeal to the Ninth Circuit. Second, most council members sincerely believed that a Christian symbol could properly serve as a memorial to San Diegans who gave their lives to defend the nation. Third, Judge Thompson had suggested in his opinion that the Easter Cross might remain on Mt. Soledad if the site was no longer public property, a broad hint that the city might sell or donate a portion of land around the cross to a private group. Fourth, and perhaps most important, public reaction to Thompson's ruling was overwhelmingly critical. By a margin of more than ten to one, letters to the city's newspapers denounced the decision, and calls to council members demanded action to save the cross.

Putting the Easter Cross to a Vote

Responding to this pressure, the council adopted two measures by unanimous vote. The first authorized the city attorney, John Witt, to file an appeal with the Ninth Circuit, while the second placed a proposition on the ballot for the next election in June 1992. Proposition F asked voters to approve "the removal from dedicated park status of that portion of Mt. Soledad Natural Park necessary to maintain the property as an historic war memorial" and to transfer that parcel "to a private non-profit corporation for not less than fair market value." Under the city charter, approval of Proposition F required a two-thirds vote in favor. That hurdle was easily overcome. Mayor O'Connor headed the list of city officials who urged voters, in their official ballot pamphlet and in capital letters, to "SAVE THE CROSS." Not surprisingly, 76 percent of the voters supported the proposition.

Armed with voter approval to sell a portion of the Mt. Soledad park, including the Easter Cross itself, city officials decided to hold off until the Ninth Circuit ruled on their appeal of Judge Thompson's 1991 order, just in case it was reversed. Phil Paulson and Howard Kreisner asked me, because I was admitted to practice before the Ninth Circuit, to file a brief for them and argue the appeal. The hearing took place in 1993 at the court's picturesque Spanish-style chambers in Pasadena, California, before a three-judge panel, with Mary Kay Jackson leading off for the city. It was clear from the outset that all three judges had little sympathy with Jackson's argument. She had tried to buttress her case by attaching to her brief a batch of newspaper articles, reporting that veterans groups, including the American Legion, had taken part in Easter services sponsored by the Mt. Soledad Memorial Association. I objected that none of this material had been considered by Judge Thompson, and that Jackson was improperly bringing it before the appellate panel. Jackson became flustered as the judges grilled her on this issue, and I took just fifteen minutes in reply, pointing the panel to the Ninth Circuit case on which Thompson had relied for precedent.

In its unanimous ruling, written by Judge Thomas Tang, the appellate panel chastised Jackson's effort to introduce documents that "were not before the district court and therefore cannot be considered part of the record on appeal." But this made no difference in their decision. "Even if we were to agree that the cross has always been explicitly recognized and referred to as a war memorial," Tang wrote, "that would not obviate the appearance of preference" for the Christian religion. "A sectarian war memorial carries an inherently religious message and creates an appearance of honoring only those servicemen of that particular religion," he concluded.

Defeated in the first two rounds of the Mt. Soledad case, San Diego officials decided to keep up their fight to "save the cross," approving John Witt's request to seek an en banc review of Judge Tang's ruling by a larger panel of Ninth Circuit judges. This was a long shot, for three reasons: first, a majority vote of the twenty-eight Ninth Circuit judges was necessary to secure an en banc review of any three-judge panel decision; second, Witt would have to argue that Tang's opinion was "clearly erroneous" in its reasoning; and third, the Ninth Circuit—along with other circuits—rarely granted en banc review. But this effort, however unlikely to succeed, would at least buy time while city officials pondered their next move. Undeterred by these long odds, Witt filed his request in early 1994, only to be rebuffed by the unanimous vote of the Ninth Circuit judges to deny en banc review.

Down by three rounds after this defeat, the San Diego city council sent Witt back from his corner for a fourth round, granting his request to seek review of the Ninth Circuit ruling by the U.S. Supreme Court. Witt pinned his hopes on two slim reeds. First, under the Court's unwritten rules, it would require the votes of only four justices to hear the case. Back in 1989, four conservative justices—three still on the Court in 1994—had dissented in a case that challenged the display of a Christian nativity crèche in a county courthouse during the Christmas season. With the addition of Justice Clarence Thomas to the Court in 1991, Witt might pick up the four votes he needed to hear the Mt. Soledad case. Second, the Court had reversed more than 80 percent of the Ninth Circuit rulings that it had reviewed in recent years. In fact, the Ninth Circuit, considered the most liberal in the nation, had the lowest batting average of any appellate court.

Witt filed his Supreme Court petition and a supporting brief in September 1994, and I answered with a reply brief asking the justices to deny the city's request. Confined by the Court's rules to ten pages, both briefs did little more than review the Ninth Circuit's ruling, reaching opposite conclusions on its reasoning. I considered Witt's petition an exercise in futility and was not surprised when the Court denied it on October 10, without any recorded dissent. I was also not surprised when San Diego officials announced, shortly after their defeat in the fourth round of the Mt. Soledad case, that they had sold 222 square feet of the park, including the concrete base on which the Easter Cross rested and the iron fence surrounding it, about 15 feet on each side, to the Mt. Soledad Memorial Association for the "fair market value" of $14,500. This figure had been determined by the city's property appraiser, who based his calculations on prior sales of "undeveloped" land in La Jolla. This sale, arranged in advance and without any opportunity for other groups to bid for the property, allowed San Diego officials to claim they had complied with Judge Thompson's hint that selling the Easter Cross site to a private group might cure its constitutional violations.

Following this sale, the Mt. Soledad case returned to Thompson for round five in this protracted litigation, with a new party in the case. Thompson granted a motion by the Mt. Soledad Memorial Association to intervene and to protect its rights to the Easter Cross and the 222-square-foot portion of the park the city had sold to it. Paulson and Kreisner also filed a motion to void what they called the "sweet-heart deal" to sell the "postage stamp" plot. Even the small plaque the Memorial Association had attached to the fence surrounding the cross, which declared the area within the fence to be private property, did not remedy the constitutional violation, they claimed, arguing in addition that the city had violated its own regulations in failing to allow other groups to bid for the cross site.

Judge Thompson issued his ruling on September 18, 1997. His opinion found "most telling" the city's appeal to "Save the Cross on Mount Soledad" in campaigning for voter approval of Proposition F. "For the city to take the position of trying to 'save' such a preeminent Christian symbol," he wrote, "clearly shows a governmental preference for the Christian religion." Thompson also faulted the city's "no bid" sale of the cross site to the Memorial Association. "The exclusion of any other purchasers of or bidders for the land," he stated, "gives the appearance of preferring the Christian religion over all others." Finally, Thompson concluded, "the city's attempt to comply with this Court's order by selling only a small portion of the land underneath the Mt. Soledad cross still shows a preference or aid to the Christian religion," in violation of the California constitution's "no preference" clause. Once again, Thompson gave the city thirty days to remove the cross.

Before this ruling, Phil Paulson and I had explored the prospect of moving the cross to the nearby Mt. Soledad Presbyterian Church, about one-half mile down the hill. The church had plenty of outdoor space to accommodate the cross, and its pastor, Reverend Mark Slomka, had indicated his receptiveness to this idea. Despite this possible way to comply with Judge Thompson's order, there was a new obstacle to resolving the case, now in its eighth year of litigation. John Witt, the elected city attorney, had left office in 1996 and was replaced by one of his former deputies, Casey Gwinn. Unlike Witt, who delegated the case to his staff and never appeared at the courtroom hearings, Gwinn viewed the cross challenge as an affront to his evangelical Christian faith and handled the case himself. He regularly preached at local evangelical churches; in one sermon at the Mission Valley Christian Fellowship, Gwinn said, "I'm just here as a follower of Jesus. The way that we experience everlasting life is to accept a personal relationship with Jesus and to say I claim him as my way to eternal life. There's no other way to get there."

A Second Effort to Sell the Easter Cross

Following Judge Thompson's third order to remove the cross, the San Diego city council met on September 30, 1997, to consider its next move. Casey Gwinn urged the council to authorize a second sale of the cross site, this time with a larger portion of land and an open bidding process. During the public comment period, Phil Paulson stated that "I do not want to see the cross on Mt. Soledad defaced, demolished, or desecrated. I do not want the cross removed. But rather I want the cross moved from the Mt. Soledad public park to the Mt. Soledad Presbyterian Church." The council, however, approved Gwinn's proposal to conduct a "restructured" sale of the cross site.

Around this time, I informed Paulson that I was dropping out of the case, which had taken a toll on my family. After each newspaper and television report on the case, I received veiled threats on my telephone. "We know where you live, and we're going to get you," one said. Concerned for the safety of our two young daughters, my wife convinced me to withdraw from the case and turn it over to another lawyer. By that time in 1996, Howard Kreisner had also withdrawn as a plaintiff, moving to Austin, Texas. Phil Paulson then recruited James McElroy, a prominent San Diego lawyer and also the national board chairman of the Southern

Poverty Law Center, to replace me. Meticulous in his legal preparation but also brash and outspoken, McElroy was more than willing to take on the city in the Mt. Soledad case.

When city officials, responding to Judge Thompson's latest order, prepared their instructions to prospective bidders for the cross site, they extended its boundary to include the circular area around the cross, up to the sidewalk around it, an area a little more than one-half acre in size. The city's invitation for bids noted that the property was "presently the site of a large, concrete, Latin cross." Bidders would not be required to retain the cross but were required to submit evidence of their "experience and qualifications to maintain the property as an historic war memorial." This, of course, had long been the city's description of the Easter Cross. Five organizations submitted bids, three proposing to retain the cross and two—the National League for the Separation of Church and State, and the Freedom from Religion Foundation—proposing to replace it with secular war memorials. The Mt. Soledad Memorial Association's bid of $106,000 topped the list, $6,000 above the next-highest bid. There was no evidence that city officials had tipped off the association to the competing bids, but the odd figure did raise skeptical eyebrows. Significantly, the city's review committee gave the association extra points for having shown "a very strong track record over forty-six years of being involved in the existing memorial." Not surprisingly, the city council voted unanimously to approve the sale to the Memorial Association.

Round eight of the Mt. Soledad case was fought, once again, in Judge Thompson's courtroom. Jim McElroy filed a motion in August 1999 to void the second sale, arguing that requiring bidders to demonstrate prior experience in maintaining "an historic war memorial" gave the Memorial Association an advantage that other bidders could not match, and that the half-acre plot was still too small to distinguish the cross site from the surrounding park. Ruling on February 3, 2000, Thompson upheld the sale as a "neutral" process that had not favored any of the bidding groups. His brief opinion made clear Thompson's view that San Diego officials had now complied with his earlier orders and that the Easter Cross could remain in the Mt. Soledad park. As far as he was concerned, the ten-year-old case was now over.

Jim McElroy, however, was not about to throw his towel into the judicial ring. He promptly filed an appeal to the Ninth Circuit, ringing the bell for the ninth round in the Mt. Soledad case. McElroy faced off with Casey Gwinn, who claimed that San Diego was now a spectator in the case, having sold the cross site to comply with Judge Thompson's orders. But a third lawyer now joined the fight. The Memorial Association had retained Charles Berwanger, an experienced property lawyer with a big San Diego firm, to argue its claim as the legal owner of the half-acre plot on which the Easter Cross sat. Berwanger told the three-judge panel that any order to remove the cross from "private property" would violate the association's rights under the "free exercise of religion" and "freedom of speech" clauses of the First Amendment. McElroy replied to this Alphonse-and-Gaston routine by arguing that Berwanger was in fact the real spectator in the courtroom. By requiring prior experience in maintaining "an historic war memorial," McElroy argued, the city had given an unfair advantage to the Memorial Association. He lost the ninth round on August 22, 2001, however. The three-judge panel, headed by Chief Judge Procter Hug Jr., unanimously upheld Judge Thompson's approval of the "restructured" sale.

Hug made three points in his opinion. First, he said, the city's requirement that bidders demonstrate prior experience in maintaining "an historic war memorial" was "not only logical and reasonable, but indeed prudent considering the intended and required function of the property." Second, however small the half-acre plot within the 170-acre park, visitors would see the Memorial Association's plaques around the site and "quickly recognize that the cross sits on private property." And third, echoing Berwanger's First Amendment argument, Hug agreed that "requiring the removal of the cross from private property would infringe upon the Association's fundamental constitutional rights."

Jim McElroy still led in rounds by a 6–3 margin. He opened the tenth round with a counterpunch, asking the Ninth Circuit judges to grant an en banc review of Hug's ruling. Granting this request, the Court set a hearing for March 21, 2002, before an eleven-judge panel at its courtroom in Phoenix, Arizona. He was also lucky in drawing a panel that was heavily weighted in his favor. Eight of its members had been placed on the bench by presidents Jimmy Carter and Bill Clinton, including Chief Judge Mary Schroeder, who had replaced Procter Hug in that post after he moved to "senior" status in January 2002.

The same three lawyers who had argued a year earlier in Pasadena—McElroy, Gwinn, and Berwanger—largely restated their positions in Phoenix. In this round, however, McElroy won on points by a 7–4 margin, in a ruling handed down on June 26, 2002. Writing for the majority, Judge Susan Graber, named to the bench by President Clinton, held that the city's sale of the cross site to the Memorial Association "granted a direct, immediate, and substantial benefit in aid of a Christian message." She based her opinion, however, on what seemed a trivial issue. In selling the site to the association, she wrote, "the City gave away for free an economically valuable means of fulfilling the main condition of the sale." In contrast, Graber said, bidders who wanted to replace the cross "would be saddled with the costs of removing the cross and of constructing an alternative war memorial." In his brief opinion for the four dissenters, Judge Ferdinand Fernandez, placed on the bench by President George H. W. Bush, simply asserted that San Diego officials "did not stray from the path of neutrality" in selling the Easter Cross site to the Memorial Association.

Judge Graber's opinion returned the Mt. Soledad case to Judge Thompson, with instructions to "devise a remedy for the constitutional violation" he had found in 1991, eleven years earlier. Before any further proceedings, however, Casey Gwinn bought time for another year, fighting rounds eleven and twelve in this marathon battle. He first asked the Ninth Circuit judges to reconsider their ruling, which the court denied in October 2002. Gwinn then filed the city's second petition for review by the Supreme Court, losing again in April 2003. He tried to put a good face on his defeat, telling reporters he was "not terribly surprised" by the ruling but "felt we had to go through the process." On a conciliatory note, Gwinn suggested that he could sit down with McElroy and Berwanger and "try to find common ground" in resolving the case. On his part, McElroy sounded less conciliatory. "The city has been rather strident in their approach in the past," he said. But he did not reject the city's olive branch. "I'm hoping they now might come to the table with more of an open mind and a willingness to entertain the fact that we need to do more to make this work constitutionally."

The third lawyer in the case, Charles Berwanger, knew that Judge Thompson could hardly approve a third sale of the cross site and had little choice but to enforce his original order to remove the cross. He also realized that the Memorial Association had the most to lose in the case. During the last four years, the association had spent more than a million dollars to construct granite walls around the cross site, after collecting much of this money from the families of veterans who paid the association to place plaques with their names and pictures on the walls. If Thompson voided the second sale, ownership of the cross and the memorial walls around it would revert to the city. Faced with this dire prospect, Berwanger signaled his willingness to work out a settlement with McElroy, under which the cross would be relocated to the nearby Mt. Soledad Presbyterian Church. Presumably, the city would allow the association to maintain the memorial walls in the park.

During the next year, McElroy and Berwanger, along with Mark Slomka, the pastor of the Presbyterian church, worked out a settlement that satisfied all of them. Slomka told reporters in July 2004 that his church's elders had voted unanimously to accept the cross if the city council approved the deal. Carl Dustin, the Memorial Association's vice president and a former commander of the American Legion post that had raised funds in 1954 to erect the Easter Cross, said the post's members had also voted unanimously to support moving the cross. Jim McElroy joined the chorus, stating that the Mt. Soledad case would finally end if the cross were relocated to the Presbyterian church's grounds. All that remained was approval from the city council and Judge Thompson, who was unlikely to object to the settlement.

A Third Effort to Sell the Easter Cross

The city council met on July 19 to discuss the proposed settlement, but a wrench suddenly hit this well-greased machinery. Casey Gwinn urged the council to authorize a third sale of the cross site and to put another proposition in the ballot to secure voter approval. "The voters and taxpayers of San Diego have a right to weigh in on the future of this cross," he said. "Whether the cross comes or goes should be decided by a private property owner, not by the City of San Diego." Gwinn's proposal, if successful, would unravel the settlement that Jim McElroy and Charles Berwanger had reached and which they planned to submit to Judge Thompson, expecting his approval to end the fifteen-year-old lawsuit. The city attorney, however, did not want to end the litigation; he was determined to keep the Easter Cross on Mt. Soledad, counting on public support to back him.

With Gwinn's proposal on the agenda, the council meeting on July 27 drew a large crowd and unleashed a flood of heated rhetoric on both sides. Jim McElroy called on the council to "be a gracious loser" and bow to court rulings against the city. Bill Kellogg, who headed the Memorial Association, called the proposed sale "fraught with problems." Moving the cross, he said, "will allow us to return the focus to honoring our veterans, instead of debating the issues of separation of church and state." Cross supporters dominated the microphone during the public comment period. "The courts have been wrong," argued a Baptist minister, James Gilbert. "Stand up for what is right." On the other side, Vietnam veteran Bill Paul told the council "the cross may represent some people, but t doesn't represent me nor many of my fellow Marines." The prospect of further litigation obviously concerned some council members, but they approved Gwinn's ballot proposal by a 5–3 vote. Councilor Scott Peters, whose district included the Mt. Soledad park, noted the competing pressures. "There will be a lot of hard feelings if the cross is moved," he said, "but there will be harder feelings if people don't get to weigh in on that." The council added to its approval of what became Proposition K, a statement that if the measure failed, the city would honor the agreement between Jim McElroy and Charles Berwanger to remove and relocate the Easter Cross, setting the vote for the election on November 2, 2004.

Hardly anyone expected the measure to fail, but the latest effort to "save the cross" would be overshadowed on the November ballot by other campaigns, including the battle for the White House between President George W. Bush and Senator John Kerry. But as the election neared, the low-key debate over Proposition K suddenly hit the headlines. Charles LiMandri, a San Diego lawyer whose practice centered on personal injury and medical malpractice cases, announced that the Thomas More Law Center would lead the fight to save the Easter Cross. Founded in 2000 and lavishly funded by Thomas Monaghan, who owned the Domino's Pizza chain, the More Center was based in Ann Arbor, Michigan, and described itself as "the sword and shield for people of faith" and "dedicated to the defense and promotion of the religious freedom of Christians, time-honored family values, and the sanctity of human life." Led and staffed by Catholic lawyers, the More Center focused most of its efforts on issues such as abortion and same-sex marriage. Early in 2004, LiMandri became director of the center's West Coast office, located in his law firm, and jumped into the Mt. Soledad case shortly after the city council placed Proposition K on the ballot.

LiMandri was afraid that the divided city council vote on the ballot measure and the active opposition to its passage by Bill Kellogg of the Memorial Association might sway voters who were concerned about the prospect of further and costly litigation over the Easter Cross. Kellogg, in fact, along with the commander of the La Jolla American Legion post, had signed the ballot pamphlet argument against Proposition K, urging a "no" vote "to preserve the Mt. Soledad Cross and save our tax dollars!" LiMandri countered with a ballot argument, which he signed along with three retired navy officers, warning voters that the cross was "threatened by special interests trying to strip San Diego of its historical identity." He also wrote an op-ed article in the *San Diego Union-Tribune*, denouncing the "atheists and the current leadership of the Mt. Soledad Memorial Association" for its "shameless betrayal" of veterans who "sacrificed their lives" in the nation's wars.

LiMandri's denunciation of the Memorial Association and its American Legion supporters, in a city with many veterans, may have backfired. When the ballots were counted, 59 percent of San Diego's voters rejected Proposition K. They also elected a new city attorney to replace Casey Gwinn, who was barred by a term-limit law from a third term. His successor, Michael Aguirre, had lost four previous elections—for Congress, for city council, and as San Diego county attorney—and squeaked past one of Gwinn's deputies by a 1 percent margin. A Democrat and self-professed advocate for "underdogs," Aguirre had ducked questions about Proposition K during his campaign, but he now faced decisions about the city's position in the Mt. Soledad case, which had returned to Judge Thompson for approval of the settlement that Jim McElroy and Charles Berwanger had fashioned.

Even before the voters rejected Proposition K, however, Charles LiMandri had filed a brief with Thompson on behalf of Richard Steel, a former navy pilot who had signed LiMandri's ballot pamphlet argument against the proposition. LiMandri asked Thompson to rule that San Diego retained "title to the land" on which the Easter Cross sat and to "completely remove any power of the Association to remove the cross." In a press release, LiMandri also urged Thompson not to "surrender to the demands of a hypersensitive atheist who is set on destroying one of San Diego's most treasured landmarks." LiMandri sounded less optimistic after the defeat of Proposition K. "At this point, we do not anticipate bringing a legal challenge, but we're still reviewing that," he said. He faced another legal obstacle, because the Thomas More Law Center was not a party to the Mt. Soledad case, and Judge Thompson could simply ignore his brief.

Asking Congress to Save the Easter Cross

LiMandri had another card up his sleeve, however, which he pulled out shortly after voters rejected Proposition K. On November 10, 2004, he sent a letter to Congressman Duncan Hunter, who represented a suburban San Diego district and chaired the powerful House Armed Services Committee. LiMandri told Hunter that "our best hope to preserve the Mt. Soledad Cross is to have it declared a Federal National Memorial Park" and urged him to join "the fight to save the Cross." Along with Congressman Randy "Duke" Cunningham, whose district included the Mt. Soledad park and who served on the defense appropriations subcommittee, Hunter slipped an amendment into a $300 billion military appropriations bill. Adopted without any committee hearing or floor debate, the measure authorized the San Diego city council to transfer the cross site to the National Park Service as a veterans memorial. President Bush signed the bill on December 8, 2004, two days after Mike Aguirre took office as San Diego's city attorney.

One of Aguirre's first decisions was to abandon Casey Gwinn's fervent defense of the Easter Cross. With a council meeting set for March 8, 2005, Aguirre sent its members a legal opinion on February 24, stating flatly that the cross was unconstitutional and that transferring the site to the Park Service would simply invite further litigation. Aguirre noted that the Park Service might not even accept the transfer, because a federal judge had recently ruled against a cross in the Mojave National Preserve, a decision the Ninth Circuit had upheld in June 2004. Aguirre's memo now placed both the city attorney and Charles Berwanger on Jim McElroy's side, with no party in the Mt. Soledad case still defending the cross's continued presence in the park.

More than 350 people, dominated by cross supporters, crowded the city's municipal auditorium for the council meeting on March 8. During an emotional six-hour hearing, sixty speakers implored the council to "save the cross" by giving the site to the Park Service, while fifteen others, mainly veterans, argued for moving the cross to the nearby Presbyterian church. Bill Kellogg of the Memorial Association warned the council that Park Service officials might not allow his group to continue maintaining the site and selling plaques to veterans' families. "Moving the cross to private land will save the cross," he said, "and will allow the association to operate the memorial walls and honor veterans for posterity." The deciding vote on the issue was cast by councilor Scott Peters, who had supported Proposition K a year earlier and who predicted "a lot of hard feelings if the cross is moved." But he also voted to move the cross if that measure failed. "As a public official," Peters now told the audience, "I promised with my hand on the Bible, so help me God, to uphold the Constitution, and I can't ignore what the Ninth Circuit Court of Appeals is doing." When the council finally voted, the motion to transfer the Easter Cross to the Park Service lost by a 5–3 margin, and council members left the auditorium to a chorus of boos. Mayor Dick Murphy, one of the three council dissenters, vowed to continue the fight. "It's not over until it's over," he said.

Murphy was right; the cross fight was not over. Public reaction to the council's vote was immediate and emphatic, spearheaded by one of San Diego's former mayors, Roger Hedgecock, who had begun a new career as a radio talk-show host, billing himself as "Southern California's Radio Mayor." Shedding his previous image as a "moderate" Republican, he moved sharply to the right, lambasting "liberals" and skewering the "spineless" city officials who had voted to move the Mt. Soledad Cross. "We're done with judges and lawyers and lawmakers," he told his listeners. "The council folks may march up the hill with axes or drive a bulldozer up the mount intent upon destruction. There they will find the townsfolk. And this time the vote will be simple. Take down our cross after you take us down!"

Behind his fiery rhetoric, Hedgecock had a plan to block the council. He and Rick Roberts, a fellow right-wing radio voice, called together a group of cross supporters to plot their strategy. Roberts invited a long-time friend, Phil Thalheimer, to attend the meeting. Thalheimer, who owned a pilot-training school, had lost a council race against Scott Peters and was eager to punish him for voting to remove the Easter Cross. Before the meeting ended, Thalheimer agreed to chair a new organization, "San Diegans for the Mt. Soledad National War Memorial." On March 13, 2005, Thalheimer announced a petition drive to overturn the council decision through a ballot referendum in the July 26 primary election for mayoral and council candidates. The council vote to remove the cross, Thalheimer said, "means that this symbol, both an indelible part of San Diego's landscape and a salute to our veterans, will be torn down and carted off without a fight." Many observers found it odd that the latest drive to save the Easter Cross was headed by Thalheimer, who is Jewish. "I know that a lot of people have questioned why a practicing Jew would chair a committee to preserve a war memorial that includes a Christian cross," he later said. "But for me, it's a free speech issue. Once you start knocking off symbols, a cross or a Star of David, it's a very slippery slope."

Under the city's election rules, Thalheimer's group needed to collect thirty-four thousand signatures of registered voters to place their proposition on the ballot. This proved to be an easy task. Approached at shopping centers and Sunday church services, more than seventy-three thousand San Diego voters signed petitions to reverse the city council's vote to remove the Easter Cross, which filled thirteen boxes that Phil Thalheimer and Mayor Dick Murphy carried into the city clerk's office on the filing date of April 7, 2005. "It's a clear and absolute demand by the citizens of San Diego that they want this war memorial to stay where it is," Thalheimer said of the petition campaign. "It can't be clearer." It was not so clear, however, to Jim McElroy, who told reporters he would file a lawsuit to block a vote on the proposed referendum. But Thalheimer's group found an unlikely ally in city attorney Mike Aguirre. "The voters have a right to review all major decisions by their elected officials," he said. Aguirre repeated, however, his opinion that voter approval of the referendum would most likely fail to survive judicial scrutiny. "The court can still decide it is unconstitutional," he added, "especially if it is done to send a religious message."

Two months after their vote to remove the Easter Cross, San Diego's city councilors met once more in the municipal auditorium on May 17, 2005, for another emotional six-hour marathon at which nearly a hundred people spoke. Some cross supporters broke down in tears, and one called any effort to move the cross a "hate crime" against Christians. Phil Thalheimer urged the council to place a third proposition on the July ballot, authorizing transfer of the cross site to the National Park Service. "Please, transfer it today," he said. "Listen to the city of San Diego." The council listened, and six members—including two who had voted in March to remove the Easter Cross—placed Proposition A before the voters, directing the city to "donate to the federal government all of the city's rights, title, and interests in the Mt. Soledad Veterans Memorial property." The councilors left the meeting as cross supporters sang "Onward Christian Soldiers."

Phil Thalheimer headed the five citizens who signed the ballot pamphlet argument supporting Proposition A, along with Congressman "Duke" Cunningham, talk-show hosts Roger Hedgecock and Rick Roberts, and Jerry Coleman, the long-time radio voice of the San Diego Padres baseball team. They urged voters to "Honor our Veterans! Protect our Memorial! Transfer the Land!" The countering argument, signed by Jim McElroy and the minister of San Diego's Unitarian Universalist Church, warned that "the land transfer would be illegal and will cost taxpayers more money in lawsuits." Thalheimer's group had raised almost $150,000 to promote the proposition with radio and newspaper advertisements, but McElroy dismissed this effort as futile. "I think it would be like burning dollar bills to win a popularity contest," he said, vowing to challenge Proposition A in court.

Cross supporters did win the popularity contest on July 26, by the same margin of 76 percent that voters had given Proposition F in 1992, thirteen years earlier. "It still doesn't mean a damn thing," McElroy responded. "Voters should have never voted on it. And when the court tells them this is not going to work, what else have they got?" Charles LiMandri of the Thomas More Law Center, who stayed on the sidelines during the Proposition A campaign, strapped on his group's "sword and shield for people of faith" and vowed to fight McElroy for years to come. "This is going to be going on past our lifetimes," he said. "This culture war isn't going to end. We see this as a bigger battle. We're fighting for the minds, hearts, and souls of America."

The Cross Case Moves to State Court

LiMandri faced two problems, however, in challenging McElroy to more courtroom battles. McElroy had already beaten him to the punch before the July election, filing a lawsuit in San Diego Superior Court that sought to block the vote and declare Proposition A unconstitutional. McElroy took the unusual step of switching from federal to state court because Judge Thompson, after presiding over the case for sixteen years, had shown no inclination to enforce his 1991 order to remove the cross. Although Judge Patricia Yim Cowett allowed the vote to proceed, she gave McElroy a victory in round thirteen of the legal battle, handing down a thirty-four-page "tentative" opinion on September 2. She noted that Thalheimer's ballot argument for Proposition A had urged voters to "save" the cross and also quoted statements of council members who had voted to transfer the cross site to the National Park Service. Councilor Tony Young said that he voted to place Proposition A on the ballot to ensure that "the cross is going to stay up there," with Brian Maienshein agreeing that he wanted "to preserve the cross on Mt. Soledad." The "consistent, repeated, and numerous references to saving the cross," Cowett wrote, showed "an unconstitutional preference of the Christian religion to the exclusion of other religious and non-religious beliefs in violation of the No Preference Clause of the California Constitution." Before she issued her final ruling, Cowett said, she would hear arguments from the parties on October 3, making it clear that she would be unlikely to change her mind.

LiMandri's second problem was that he did not represent any party in the Mt. Soledad case and would be unable to argue before Judge Cowett at the October 3 hearing. All of the lawyers in the case—Mike Aguirre, Jim McElroy, and Charles Berwanger—agreed with Cowett's tentative ruling and would certainly not oppose her final decision. That lineup changed, however, with Aguirre's sudden and unexpected announcement, on September 7, that he was hiring LiMandri to represent the voters who had adopted Proposition A. "My job is to in a good-faith way try to vindicate their vote even though I disagree with it," Aguirre explained, adding that "voters deserve their day in court." LiMandri agreed that cross supporters deserved a lawyer "who passionately believes in them." On his part, Jim McElroy greeted the news with outrage and scorn. "This is like hiring the Ku Klux Klan to represent you in a desegregation case," he fumed.

LiMandri's presence at the hearing, in fact, gave Judge Cowett another reason to confirm her tentative ruling with a final decision on October 7, 2005. Quoting from the Thomas More Law Center's website, she noted its goal of "providing legal representation to defend and protect Christians and their religious beliefs." Hiring him to represent the city, Cowett wrote, "gives the clear appearance of fostering an excessive government entanglement with religion." She took pains to assure readers that her opinion "does not attempt to, nor does it actually, demonstrate hostility to religion."

Judge Cowett left one crucial question unanswered: In which courtroom would round fifteen in the case be fought? Her decision was limited to the constitutional issues raised by the Mt. Soledad Cross and had not included any order directing its removal from the park. "The city is the only party that can appeal," Jim McElroy noted. "I don't think the city is going to want to appeal. It's going to cost them a ton of money for their time and effort." Aguirre had until December 6, sixty days from Cowett's ruling, to file an appeal with the state appellate court, and he took a wait-and-see position, suggesting in the interim that cross supporters and opponents meet with a retired magistrate and settle the case through mediation. McElroy dismissed this idea, saying that the city council should honor the settlement agreement with the Memorial Association and prepare to move the cross. If the council balked, McElroy would ask Judge Thompson, who had postponed hearings in his courtroom to wait for Cowett's decision, to enforce his 1991 cross-removal order. Thompson had also, however, suggested that he might put off any further proceedings until the Ninth Circuit ruled on a pending appeal by the Memorial Association, which disputed the city's claim to ownership of the entire cross site, including the granite walls and the plaques the association had erected. McElroy and Berwanger had written a letter to Thompson, which Mike Aguirre also signed, noting that all parties had agreed to the cross's removal. Resolution of the land-ownership issue, they argued, should not delay Thompson's approval of the settlement agreement, which would not disturb the memorial walls. Obviously waiting for Aguirre's decision on appealing Cowett's ruling, Thompson did not respond and left the lawyers hanging.

Widely known as a quick-draw lawyer, Aguirre had a reason to keep his gun holstered while the sixty-day clock ran on filing an appeal of Cowett's decision. San Diego politics had been in an uproar ever since Mayor Dick Murphy, buffeted by charges of mismanaging the city's bil-lion-dollar pension fund, had abruptly resigned and left office on July 15, 2005. He was replaced in an election that November by former San Diego police chief Jerry Sanders, who had pledged to continue the legal battle to keep the Easter Cross on Mt. Soledad.

The morning after his victory celebration, Sanders called Roger Hedgecock, who had boosted his campaign, with a surprise announce-ment on the air. Mike Aguirre, Sanders told Hedgecock's listeners, had agreed to appeal Judge Cowett's ruling against the Easter Cross. Aguirre then called to confirm the news. "I'm not going to insist that every-thing I want goes through," he said. "I still think it's unconstitutional. But I'm going to try to work collaboratively with him," Aguirre said of the mayor-elect. Despite his personal opinion that efforts to overturn Judge Cowett's rulings would prove futile, Aguirre went ahead and filed an appeal with the state's Fourth Circuit Court of Appeals. Charles LiMandri of the Thomas More Law Center, whose participation in the case had irked Judge Cowett, predicted victory for cross supporters. "We need two out of three judges" on the appellate court, he said, "and I think it's unlikely we'll get three judges as liberal as she is."

Angered that Aguirre had bowed to Mayor Sanders in filing the appeal, Jim McElroy promptly went back to Judge Thompson in the fed-eral court, seeking a ruling to enforce the original injunction to remove the cross from Mt. Soledad. Although Thompson had indicated that he would defer any decision until the state judges ruled on the city's appeal, he changed his mind after a hearing in December 2005. On March 3, 2006, Thompson ended the fourteenth round in this judicial slug-fest. "It is now time, and perhaps long overdue," he said firmly, "for this Court to enforce its original permanent injunction forbidding the presence of the Mount Soledad Cross on City property." Thompson noted that he had spent years hearing arguments over the cross, as had the Ninth Circuit judges who had twice upheld his orders to remove it, in rulings the Supreme Court had twice declined to review. "Consistently, every court that has addressed the issue has ruled that the presence of the Latin cross on Mount Soledad" violated the "no preference" clause of the California constitution. He gave the city ninety days to remove the cross, a deadline of August 1, 2006, and threatened to impose a daily fine of $5,000 if the city did not comply with this final ruling. As far as Thompson was concerned, the fight was over.

Back to Congress with Another Plan to Save the Cross

But the cross did not come down. Rising from the judicial canvas, Mayor Sanders began swinging with an appeal to President Bush to seize the cross under the federal government's "eminent domain" powers. Sanders also pressed the city council to authorize an appeal to the Ninth Circuit, along with a request for a judicial stay of Thompson's order. On May 22, 2006, Sanders flew to Washington and met with White House officials and lawyers to seek Bush's intervention. He returned empty-handed to San Diego. "They indicated it's going to be tough to get this done," he told reporters. Most likely, the president's lawyers were wary of inheriting a lawsuit that might expose the federal government to heavy legal fees and the prospect of judicial defeat. Sanders also asked the San Diego city council to instruct Mike Aguirre to file a stay request with the Ninth Circuit. The council approved this measure by a 5–3 margin on May 23, disregarding Aguirre's warning that its chances of success were "remote." Four weeks later, on June 21, the Ninth Circuit denied—without comment—the stay request, although it also docketed the city's appeal for argument in October 2006. By that time, of course, the case might have been mooted, because denial of the stay request kept the clock running on Judge Thompson's August deadline for removing the cross from Mt. Soledad.

Reeling on the judicial ropes from the Ninth Circuit's blow, San Diego officials launched a final counterpunch. By another 5–3 vote, the city council directed Aguirre to seek a stay of Thompson's order from the Supreme Court. Under the Court's rules, this request would be decided by Justice Anthony Kennedy, who handled "emergency" appeals in Ninth Circuit cases. Although he dutifully complied with the council's order, Aguirre expressed his doubt that it would succeed. "It is unusual for the Supreme Court in a case this far advanced to issue a stay order," he told reporters. But he was wrong in this prediction. On June 3, 2006, Kennedy granted a "temporary" stay in the case, "pending further order" by himself or the full Court. Kennedy waited only five days before he issued his "further order" on June 8, extending the stay of Judge Thompson's order, at least until the California appellate judges and the Ninth Circuit ruled on the city's appeals from Judge Cowett's and the Ninth Circuit's rulings.

The city's legal reprieve gave cross supporters time to plot their next effort to circumvent Judge Thompson's removal order and its review by the Ninth Circuit. Coming to the city's aid, Representative Duncan Hunter wielded his clout as chairman of the House Armed Services Committee. In June 2006, he introduced a bill to exercise the federal government's eminent domain power and transfer the cross site to the Defense Department, conditioned on a "memorandum of understanding" with the Mount Soledad Memorial Association to maintain the site. On July 19, the House adopted Hunter's bill by a vote of 349 to 74, with all of his fellow Republicans behind him. Even a majority of House Democrats, perhaps wary of offending voters in an election year, cast "yea" votes for the bill. By a unanimous voice vote on July 31, the Senate followed suit, sending Hunter's bill to the White House for President Bush's signature. Flanked at his Oval Office desk by cross supporters, including Bill Kellogg, Phil Thalheimer, and Charles LiMandri, Bush signed the transfer bill on August 14. This ceremony symbolized the potency of the cross as a political issue.

Back to the Federal Courts with a New Lawsuit

Jim McElroy, however, stood in the way of this latest effort to "federalize" the Mount Soledad Cross. On August 22, he filed a new lawsuit, naming the Defense Department as the defendant, on behalf of the

Jewish War Veterans and three San Diego residents: Richard Smith, a navy veteran and a physician, who is Jewish; Mina Sagheb, who is Muslim; and Judith Copeland, a San Diego attorney. (Perhaps drained by years of unpaid pro bono work, McElroy later turned the case over to the San Diego affiliate of the American Civil Liberties Union.) The case was assigned to district judge Barry Ted Moskowitz, placed on the bench by President Bill Clinton in 1995. For the first time since 1989, Judge Thompson no longer presided over the Mt. Soledad case.

Although federal cases have long been randomly assigned to judges by computers, Charles LiMandri of the Thomas More Law Center nonetheless suggested that the Jewish War Veterans (JWV) had somehow arranged to bring their suit before a "practicing Jew" who would supposedly be prejudiced against the cross as a Christian symbol. Perhaps to avoid criticism that his religion might bias his rulings in the cases or because of ties to the Jewish War Veterans, Judge Moskowitz—without revealing his reasons—recused himself and transferred the cross cases to Judge Larry Alan Burns, who was named to the federal bench in 2003 by President George W. Bush. This move, from a judge considered liberal by most lawyers to one with a conservative reputation, most likely affected the later rulings in the Mt. Soledad case.

Before Judge Burns held any hearings in the consolidated cases, the California appellate court and the Ninth Circuit both dropped out of this judicial ménage à trois, dismissing the pending appeals as "moot" because, after the federal government's seizure of the Mt. Soledad Cross site, the city no longer held title to the property and had no legal "interest" in the case's outcome. Meanwhile, rulings in other Establishment Clause cases gave Judge Burns much-needed precedent for the order and the opinion he issued on July 29, 2008. The Supreme Court's 2005 decision in the *Van Orden* case, on which the Ninth Circuit based its *Card v. Everett* ruling, earlier in 2008, both dealt with displays of the Ten Commandments. Once again, as we have seen earlier, Justice Stephen Breyer's concurring opinion in *Van Orden* came to the rescue of a lower-court judge who was faced, as Judge Burns admitted, with a "hard case." Had Judge Moskowitz not recused himself from the Mt. Soledad case, we can only speculate whether he would have found it more like *McCreary County*, because both cases initially began with "stand-alone" displays of religious texts or symbols, with their installations accompanied by Christian prayers and with purportedly "secular" elements added only after they were challenged in court.

In his opinion, Judge Burns looked for a "secular purpose" behind the Mt. Soledad Cross that would satisfy the Supreme Court's *Lemon* test. He acknowledged that he "must be convinced the government's secular purpose is bona fide, and not merely a sham or secondary to a greater religious objective." Burns noted the plaintiffs' argument that Congress seized the cross site "not to preserve it as a veterans' memorial but because of political pressure inflamed by local religious and city leaders who didn't want the cross removed from the memorial" and the "selective evidence showing, unsurprisingly, that Christian leaders and groups spoke out vehemently against removing the cross, and urged the federal government to take the property instead." But he dismissed this argument and evidence. "For the United States to recognize the service and sacrifice of its war veterans by preserving a memorial in their honor is laudable and unquestionably secular," he wrote.

Judge Burns echoed Justice Breyer's "context" argument in *Van Orden*. "The Latin cross," he wrote, "is, to be sure, the preeminent symbol of Christianity, but it does not follow the cross has no other meaning or significance. Depending on the context in which it is displayed, the cross may evoke no particular religious impression at all." Burns concluded with his finding that "the memorial at Mt. Soledad, including its Latin cross, communicates the primarily non-religious messages of military service, death, and sacrifice. As such, despite its location on public land, the memorial is Constitutional."

Unsurprisingly, Judge Burns's ruling sent the Mt. Soledad case back to the Ninth Circuit, on an appeal by the Jewish War Veterans. The court's computer could not have selected a more receptive three-judge panel for the JWV. All three judges were considered members of the court's liberal bloc and had been placed on the bench by Democratic presidents: Harry Pregerson by Jimmy Carter in 1979, Margaret McKeown by Bill Clinton in 1998, and Richard Paez by Clinton in 2000. All three had also voted in earlier cases against cross displays. With the judicial deck stacked against her, Kathryn Kovacs, who argued for the Defense Department, urged the panel to consider the "very clear statement" in the legislative history that Congress had a "secular" purpose in seizing the cross site for the federal government. "There is no indication from the circumstances that Congress was acting for religious reasons," she said.

Matthew Jones, who now represented the Jewish War Veterans, faced a "devil's advocate" question from Judge McKeown. "If you are reluctant to say it's a sham," she asked, "shouldn't we be reluctant to invade the congressional purpose, and say what it wasn't?" Citing the *McCreary County* case, Jones replied that the "secular" elements around the cross had been added after the original suit was filed in 1989, and that the religious "purpose" of the cross's installation in 1954 still remained. After the arguments concluded, David Blair-Loy, the ACLU's staff attorney in San Diego, concealed his reaction in this understatement: "We think we got a very fair hearing." On the other side, Joe Infranco, a lawyer for the Alliance Defense Fund, one of the Religious Right amicus groups that supported the cross, found some encouragement in Judge McKeown's question to Matthew Jones. "The congressional intent is key here," Infranco said.

However, when the panel issued its unanimous decision on January 4, 2011, Infranco was proved wrong. Writing for her colleagues, Judge McKeown focused her opinion on a lengthy review of the Easter Cross's history. "For most of its life, the Memorial has consisted of the Cross alone," she wrote. There was no physical indication that the Cross was intended as a war memorial, however, until a plaque was added to the site in 1989, after litigation over the Cross had begun. At the same time, the Cross's religious nature has been widely recognized and promoted since it was first erected. . . . The use of such a distinctively Christian symbol to honor all veterans sends a strong message of endorsement and exclusion. It suggests that the government is so connected to a particular religion that it treats that religion's symbolism as its own, as universal. To many non-Christian veterans, this claim of universality is alienating."

The panel made clear that the forty-three-foot cross could no longer remain as the centerpiece of the memorial. Sending the case back to Judge Burns for "further proceedings," McKeown said the ruling "does not mean that the Memorial could not be modified to pass constitutional muster nor does it mean that no cross can be part of this veteran's memorial. We take no position on those issues." Presumably,

Burns could order Defense Department officials to fashion a more religiously inclusive design, perhaps with symbols of Judaism, Islam, Buddhism, Hinduism, and even atheism. Finding agreement on which religious—or nonreligious —symbols to include would seem difficult, to say the least. To avoid squabbling between contending religious and secular groups, perhaps something along the lines of the widely admired Vietnam memorial in Washington, D.C., might satisfy all but the die-hard Christians who fought for more than twenty years to keep the Easter Cross in the Mt. Soledad park. The Christian groups will undoubtedly pressure the Defense Department to appeal the panel's ruling to the Supreme Court, bypassing the "further proceedings" before Judge Burns, who most likely does not relish the task assigned to him by the panel.

Whatever course is taken, the Mt. Soledad case will certainly not end for at least two or three more years after the Ninth Circuit's ruling, setting new records for legal longevity and illustrating once again that religion, politics, nationalism, and law are a highly combustible mixture in our increasingly diverse and disputatious society. Justice Oliver Wendell Holmes, more than a century ago, was prescient in saying that "We live by symbols."

13

Religious Politics, Judicial Snarls, and the Mojave Desert Cross Case

We saw in the Mt. Soledad Cross case how political factors, on both the local and the national levels, have kept that conflict on federal court dockets for more than twenty years, with no final outcome to date. During a shorter time span, another cross case reached the Supreme Court and confronted the justices with complicated issues of jurisdiction and the limits of injunctive relief. Given my extended account of the Mt. Soledad case, I will briefly review the facts and the procedural history of the suit that challenged an eight-foot-tall cross in a remote section of the Mojave National Preserve, which covers some 1.6 million acres (about twenty-five hundred square miles) of San Bernardino County in southern California. The preserve is owned by the federal government and administered by the National Park Service, a branch of the U.S. Interior Department. About 90 percent of the land is federal property, with the remainder owned by ranchers and "desert rats" who have built homes within the preserve. Unlike the Mt. Soledad

Cross, which is located in a big city and visible to thousands of passing motorists and hundreds of park visitors every day, the Mojave Desert cross—bolted to a rock outcropping called "Sunrise Rock"—is ten miles from the nearest highway, accessible only from a two-lane road and a hiking trail. Erected in 1934 by members of the Death Valley Post of the Veterans of Foreign Wars, the cross—like its San Diego counterpart—was the site of annual Easter sunrise services.

The Mojave Desert cross stood unchallenged until 2000, when Frank Buono, a former assistant superintendent of the preserve, who had retired and moved to Oregon but who visited the preserve two or three times a year, filed suit in the Central District of California's federal courts, naming then interior secretary Gail Norton as a defendant. Buono was represented by lawyers from the Southern California affiliate of the ACLU. Buono, a Catholic, said he had no objections to crosses but simply to the presence of the "Sunrise Rock" cross on federal property. He sought an injunction and an order to remove the cross from the preserve. Buono's suit was assigned to district judge Robert J. Timlin, who had been placed on the bench by President Bill Clinton in 1994. In their reply to the suit, the Interior Department's lawyers argued that Buono had suffered no "personal" injury from the cross's presence in the preserve and thus lacked "standing" to bring the case.

Before Judge Timlin issued his initial ruling in the case, the VFW and other veterans' groups (who constitute a potent voting bloc) persuaded Congress to designate the cross and its adjoining land "as a national memorial commemorating United States participation in World War I and honoring the American veterans of that war." That congressional act did not dissuade Judge Timlin from ruling that Frank Buono had standing to bring his suit and from issuing a permanent injunction that forbade the government "from permitting the display of the Latin cross in the area of Sunrise Rock in the Mojave National Preserve." The government appealed that ruling to the Ninth Circuit, which stayed the order to remove the cross pending further proceedings. But the Court affirmed Judge Timlin's findings that Buono had standing to bring his suit and that the cross's presence on federal property violated the Establishment Clause. The Ninth Circuit Court further concluded that a "reasonable observer" of the cross would perceive it as governmental endorsement of religion.

From a procedural standpoint, it may seem puzzling (and, in retrospect, perhaps a mistake) that Interior Department lawyers—for reasons they did not disclose—failed to seek Supreme Court review of the Ninth Circuit's ruling. Under the judicial doctrine of **res judicata** (from the Latin for "the matter is settled"), the government could no longer dispute Buono's standing or Judge Timlin's finding of an Establishment Clause violation. The government later attempted to attack both findings, however, based on another congressional act in 2004, inserted as a "rider" into a Defense Department appropriations bill. This act directed the interior secretary to transfer the government's interest in the cross site to the VFW, as part of a "land-swap" with a nearby rancher, Henry Sandoz, who agreed to give five acres of his property to the Interior Department in exchange. After Buono asked Judge Timlin to block this land-swap deal, Timlin agreed and enjoined the government from implementing it. The Ninth Circuit again upheld this ruling, leaving intact the "res judicata" effects of Timlin's earlier rulings on Buono's standing and the Establishment Clause violation.

The Supreme Court Looks at the "Land Swap" Deal

If this account of the first four judicial rounds in Frank Buono's case seems convoluted to a layperson (not to mention a lawyer), it certainly is. The case appeared to be over with the Ninth Circuit's latest ruling, leaving no issue for the Supreme Court to review. However, the government sought and was granted in 2009 a certiorari petition, arguing that the "land-swap" deal approved by Congress represented a "changed circumstance" that allowed the justices to review Judge Timlin's earlier rulings, with oral arguments scheduled for October 7, 2009. By this time, Interior Secretary Norton had been replaced as the defendant by Ken Salazar, named to that post by President Obama. This change in administration, from a Republican to a Democratic president, however, did not change the government's decision to defend the "Sunrise Rock" cross, perhaps to avoid offending the VFW and other veterans' groups and their congressional supporters.

Reporters flocked to the Supreme Court's chamber for the oral arguments in *Salazar v. Buono*, drawn not only by the case's "hot-button" issue of crosses on public land (as they had for arguments in the Ten Commandments cases), but also to witness the debut as an advocate by Solicitor General (and now Justice) Elena Kagan. One might wonder why Kagan, who could have deferred to the Interior Department lawyers who handled the case in the lower courts, chose this case for her initial Supreme Court argument. Perhaps she had an ambitious eye on her possible elevation to the Court and wanted to impress President Obama with her hitherto-untested advocacy skills. If so, the headline-hunting reporters were disappointed, because the arguments steered quickly into a law-school seminar on the law of injunctions and congressional power to upset them, with Kagan sounding flustered in dealing with questions from the bench.

The only rhetorical sparks during the oral arguments were ignited by a colloquy between Justice Antonin Scalia (living up to his reputation as the Court's grand inquisitor) and Peter Eliasberg, the ACLU lawyer who represented Frank Buono, also making his first Supreme Court argument. This heated exchange followed an observation by Eliasberg that the "Sunrise Rock" cross honored only Christian veterans, rather than "all of the people who fought for America in World War I." These excerpts from the argument transcript are worth quoting here, to illustrate the verbal sparring that sometimes enlivens the Court's proceedings:

Scalia: The cross doesn't honor non-Christians who fought in the war?

Eliasberg: I believe that's actually correct.

Scalia: Where does it say that?

Eliasberg: It doesn't say that, but a cross is the predominant symbol of Christianity and it signifies that Jesus is the son of God and died to redeem mankind for our sins. . . .

Scalia: It's erected as a war memorial. I assume it is erected to honor all of the war dead. The cross is the most common symbol of the resting place of the dead, and it doesn't seem to me—what would you have them erect? Some conglomerate of a cross, a star of David, and you know, a Moslem half moon and star?

Eliasberg: Well, Justice Scalia, if I may go to your first point. The cross is the most common symbol of the resting place of Christians. I have been in Jewish cemeteries. There is never a cross on a tombstone of a Jew. (Laughter). . . .

Scalia: I don't think you can leap from that to the conclusion that the only war dead that the cross honors are the Christian war dead. I think that's an outrageous conclusion.

Eliasberg: Well, my point here is to say that there is a reason the Jewish War Veterans came in [as an amicus group] and said we don't feel honored by this cross. This cross can't honor us because it is a religious symbol of another religion.

The next day's headlines reflected the reporters' frustration at leaving the Supreme Court chamber with only the testy exchange between Peter Eliasberg and Justice Scalia to spice up an otherwise bland dish. The *Washington Post* headline read "Court Wades Shallowly into Church and State: Argument over Cross on Public Land, Deals Minimally with the Broader Issue." Reporters and court watchers waited for more than six months between the oral arguments and the Court's ruling on April 28, 2010, only to find another judicial fizzle. Justice Anthony Kennedy could persuade just one colleague, Chief Justice John Roberts, to fully join his announcement of the "judgment of the Court," joined "in part" by Justice Samuel Alito. This lengthy delay in deciding the case reflected the behind-the-scenes debates among the justices over the proper resolution of the "standing" and "injunctive relief" issues, which prompted a flurry of draft opinions between the judicial chambers on both sides and culminated in six separate and widely divergent opinions.

In his plurality opinion, Kennedy conceded that the government's failure to appeal the Ninth Circuit decision upholding Judge Timlin's rulings on Frank Buono's standing to bring his suit, and that the "Sunrise Rock" cross violated the Establishment Clause, became "res judicata to the parties" and barred the government from "ask[ing] this Court to reconsider the propriety of the 2002 injunction or the District Court's reasons for granting it." Addressing the issue of whether the congressional approval of the "land-swap" deal in 2004 represented any "changed circumstances" that might allow a new look at the injunctive relief Judge Timlin later granted to Buono, Kennedy wrote that because of "the highly fact-specific nature of the inquiry, it is best left to the District Court to undertake the analysis in the first instance." He concluded his opinion with these words: "The judgment of the Court of Appeals is reversed, and the case is remanded for further proceedings."

Justice Kennedy, however, could not resist expressing his personal feelings about the "Sunrise Rock" cross. "[A] Latin cross," he wrote, "is not merely a reaffirmation of Christian beliefs. It is a symbol often used to honor and respect those whose heroic acts, noble contributions, and patient striving help secure an honored place in history for this Nation and its people. Here, one Latin cross in the desert evokes far more than religion. It evokes thousands of small crosses in foreign fields marking the graves of Americans who fell in battles, battles whose tragedies are compounded if the fallen are forgotten."

Four of Justice Kennedy's colleagues joined his "judgment of the Court" with grudging but seemingly inconsistent agreement with the remand order. Chief Justice Roberts, in a three-sentence concurrence, noted that Peter Eliasberg had conceded during his oral argument that it "likely would be consistent with the injunction" for the government—as Roberts put it—"to tear down the cross, sell the land to the Veterans of Foreign Wars, and return the cross to them, with the VFW immediately raising the cross again. I do not see how it can make a difference for the Government to skip that empty ritual and do what Congress told it to do—sell the land with the cross on it." Such a move would seemingly obviate any need for a remand of the case to the lower courts. In his separate concurrence, Justice Alito wrote that "I would not remand this case for the lower courts to decide whether implementation of the land-transfer statute . . . would violate the District Court's injunction or the Establishment Clause."

Justice Scalia, writing for himself and Justice Clarence Thomas, argued that Frank Buono lacked standing in the first place to bring his suit. "In this case," he wrote, "Congress has determined that transferring the memorial to private hands best serves the public interest and complies with the Constitution, and the Executive defends that decision and seeks to carry it out. Federal courts have no warrant to revisit that decision—and to risk replacing the people's judgment with their own—unless and until a proper case has been brought before them. This is not it."

These concurrences, in effect, left the remand order with only one vote—that of Justice Kennedy—behind it. Given their implicit and explicit objections to the remand order, it made no logical sense for Roberts, Alito, Scalia, and Thomas to "concur" in a judgment with which they disagreed. But justices need not make sense in supporting an outcome they prefer—in this case, keeping the "Sunrise Rock" cross in place for at least another few years—while they wait for a "proper" case to decide the constitutionality of crosses on public land or the sale or "swap" of that land to achieve the same purpose. Justice Kennedy expressed his frustration at the muddled outcome of *Salazar v. Buono* in these words: "To date, this Court's jurisprudence in this area has refrained from making sweeping pronouncements, and this case is ill suited for announcing categorical rules." The same might have been said, in fact, about the muddled and divergent rulings in the Ten Commandments cases from Kentucky and Texas. The late Justice William J. Brennan was fond of saying (and once said to me) that "with five votes, you can do anything here." One can only speculate about the arm-twisting and cajolery it took for Justice Kennedy to line up the five votes he needed to issue a remand order that four of his colleagues obviously thought was unwarranted and unnecessary. But he prevailed in this effort, at the cost of logical and jurisprudential consistency.

The four dissenters in *Salazar v. Buono* were also divided on its disposition, although not nearly to the extent of the badly fractured majority. Justice John Paul Stevens, in his final Establishment Clause opinion, after thirty-five years on the bench, wrote for himself and Justices Ruth Bader Ginsburg and Sonia Sotomayor. Stevens agreed with Judge Timlin and the Ninth Circuit that congressional approval in 2004 of the "land-swap" deal "not only failed to cure the Establishment Clause violation [but] would perpetuate rather than cure that unambiguous endorsement of a sectarian message." Stevens also noted that the "land-swap" provision had been "tucked silently into an appropriations bill" and was passed "without any deliberation whatsoever" by Congress, an implied rebuke to the cross's supporters and their congressional allies.

Justice Stephen Breyer, in a separate dissent, chided his colleagues for even granting review in the first place. Citing the law of injunctions, Breyer wrote that "we cannot properly reach beyond that law to

consider the underlying Establishment Clause and standing questions."
He found "no federal question of general significance in this case.
I believe we should not have granted the petition for certiorari. Having
granted it, the Court should now dismiss the writ as improvidently granted.
Since the Court has not done so, however, I believe that we should simply
affirm the Ninth Circuit's judgment." The Court rarely dismisses cases
as **improvidently granted,** meaning in effect that the justices made a
mistake in agreeing to review them in the first place. Considering the
anomaly in this case (unprecedented, to my knowledge) of a "plurality" opinion that represented the views of only one justice, Anthony
Kennedy, and that all eight of his colleagues, for differing reasons,
opposed its remand to the lower courts, Justice Breyer's law-professor
lecture strikes me as perfectly warranted.

The Court's fractured opinions in the "Sunrise Rock" cross case
resulted in a remand to Judge Timlin, with an order to reconsider
whether the latest congressional action would negate his original injunction that ordered its removal. It's difficult to predict how long Timlin
will take to consider the issues and give another ruling, which most
likely would produce another appeal to the Ninth Circuit, by which-
ever side loses in that judicial round. Such an appeal would likely take
another year or more before an appellate decision, with another trip
to the Supreme Court for a final decision. Much like the Mt. Soledad
case, the "Sunrise Rock" case illustrates once again that the contest-
ing sides in these battles over religious symbols on public property are
determined, tenacious, and unwilling to give up until the Supreme
Court issues a definitive ruling. Yet so far, the justices have dodged giving definitive rulings in Establishment Clause cases, leaving this area of
law in a state of seemingly permanent disarray.

Between them, the Mt. Soledad and "Sunrise Rock" cross cases
illustrate the impact of political factors on the legal process. Whether
the issue is abortion, affirmative action, gay rights, campaign financing,
presidential powers, capital punishment, or religion, politics—on both
sides of the political spectrum—influences these cases from beginning
to end, however inconclusive the ending may be. As a result, judges at
all levels are challenged to resolve issues that often remain irresolvable
within the American political system. Readers of this book, I think,

would do well to consider the implications of this fact. In the end, to bend a famous statement by General Carl von Clausewitz, "law is a continuation of politics by other means."

An Evaluation of the Ten Commandments and Cross Cases

I chose the Ten Commandments and cross cases for this book as recent examples of the difficulties that have faced judges in applying the command of the First Amendment that prohibits any "establishment of religion." It has been five decades since that provision was first interpreted by the Supreme Court in 1947 in the *Everson* case. As we have seen, the Court's unanimous agreement in that case that governments at all levels must be "neutral" in conflicts between religious believers and nonbelievers, showing preference to neither side, did not settle the issue. In fact, judges in dozens of Establishment Clause cases, including justices of the Supreme Court, have remained divided—often by one-vote margins—over the proper and allowable role of religion in the public square. Cases that involved public funding of religious schools, school-sponsored prayer, the display of Nativity crèches and menorahs in public buildings and parks, and even bans on students' wearing of rosaries and Stars of David in schools have provoked lawsuits and controversies in hundreds of communities across the country. In this regard, the Ten Commandments and cross cases are not unique but rather are symptomatic of deeper conflicts within American society.

In my view, these religion cases are skirmishes in the "culture war" that has been waged in American politics during the last several decades, between supporters of so-called traditional values, who would impose their values on their fellow citizens through law and government, and those who oppose those efforts as coercive and intolerant. Almost twenty years have passed since Pat Buchanan—a conservative pundit and politician—first popularized that phrase in a fiery speech to the Republican National Convention in 1992: "There is a religious war going on in this country, a cultural war as critical to the kind of nation we shall be as the Cold War itself, for this war is for the soul of America."

The cultural war in which Buchanan cast himself as a warrior began, of course, several decades before his speech. In the legal realm, it was first sparked by the Supreme Court decisions in 1962 and 1963 that ruled that teacher-led prayers and Bible reading in public schools violated the Establishment Clause. This provoked an outcry from Christian preachers and politicians and even efforts to amend the Constitution to overturn the Court's decisions, which proved unsuccessful. The Court's ruling in 1973, in *Roe v. Wade*, that laws banning abortion violated the Due Process Clause of the Constitution also created a growing storm of opposition and equally unsuccessful efforts to overturn the decision through constitutional amendment. More recently, state and federal judicial rulings that same-sex marriage is protected by the Due Process and Equal Protection clauses against legislative abridgement and state constitution bans, approved by substantial majorities of lawmakers and voters, have begun journeys through the legal system that will most likely wind up in the Supreme Court. Each of these issues reflects the ongoing nature of the culture wars that divide Americans of sharply differing values.

I selected the Ten Commandments and cross cases for another purpose, to illustrate and explain for readers the step-by-step process by which conflicts that arise in America's towns and cities sometimes turn into lawsuits that progress from trial courts through appellate courts and then to the Supreme Court, often—as in these cases— returning to lower courts for a final resolution. This process is governed by judicial rules that may seem complicated to a layperson—and even to many lawyers—but these rules are essential to the functioning of the legal system. I hope I have explained them in terms that are understandable.

Given the long-standing and wide divisions between Americans on both sides of the metaphorical "wall of separation" between church and state, I think it is fitting to conclude this section with the words of Supreme Court justice Robert Jackson. In 1943, in a case that overturned a West Virginia law requiring the expulsion of public-school students who objected on religious grounds to reciting the Pledge of

Allegiance in their classrooms, Jackson wrote, "The very purpose of a Bill of Rights was to withdraw certain subjects from the vicissitudes of political controversy, to place them beyond the reach of majorities and officials." The "fundamental rights" of every American, he added, "may not be submitted to vote; they depend on the outcome of no elections." Jackson's words, I believe, are as profound and meaningful today as they were almost seventy years ago. Perhaps they should be posted on the walls of every courthouse and classroom across our Nation.

Conclusion

O ur guided tour of the American legal system has taken us into twenty courtrooms (some for multiple visits) in thirteen states and the District of Columbia, in cases that were heard and decided by more than one hundred judges and argued by more than thirty lawyers on both sides. Along the way, we spent time in courtrooms at every level of the state and federal judicial system, from a state court in Union County, Tennessee, to the chamber of the United States Supreme Court in Washington, D.C.

We have looked closely at only a tiny number of the 34 million cases that enter the system each year, both civil and criminal. I could easily have selected cases for this book that, in my opinion, show the system working at its very best, cases that most of us would agree resulted in justice being served to all parties. Or I could have picked cases that show the system at its worst (there are plenty of examples), in which people's constitutional rights were violated, with no redress available, even from the highest court in the land. In fact, the cases I chose have mixed outcomes.

It's obvious (at least, to me) that Paul House did not receive a fair trial in 1986 and spent twenty-two years on Death Row for a murder he almost certainly did not commit. This was largely the result of a stubborn and careless prosecutor, Paul Phillips; an incompetent (or barely competent) defense lawyer, Chuck Burks; and easily persuaded jurors. House did finally leave Death Row, though, with the murder charge dismissed, primarily due to the skilled work, during a fifteen-year period, of two determined lawyers, Steve Kissinger and Mike Pemberton; the equally determined efforts of a federal appellate judge, Gilbert Merritt, to demolish the weak prosecution case; and the willingness of five Supreme Court justices to give Paul House a new hearing on his claims against Phillips and Burks. But House will not get back those twenty-two years of wrongful imprisonment, nor will Phillips and Burks face any discipline for their roles in this miscarriage of justice.

The Ten Commandments cases from Kentucky and Texas also had mixed outcomes. There's an anomaly here that's worth noting. Law students are frequently reminded by their professors that "like cases should come out alike," but they are also trained in the skill of "distinguishing" cases that are very much alike, for the benefit of their clients. As we've seen, the consequences of Breyer's opinion in the *Van Orden* case have forced lower-court judges to "distinguish" the Ten Commandments cases on their dockets, thus creating the very "divisiveness" that Justice Breyer hoped—but failed—to avoid.

Despite my disavowal of any intention to impose "lessons" on this book's readers, there is one lesson that I think should be obvious to each reader. And that's the conjunction of three factors that affect our legal system, and which all of the cases in this book exemplify. The first is that the "system" itself is, in reality, an abstraction, much like the "legal fictions" of the hypothetical "reasonable person" in tort law or the Supreme Court's ruling, back in the 1870s, that corporations were "persons" under the Fourteenth Amendment and thus entitled to protections against their employees in personal injury cases. Any system or institution is made up of real people, who have separate functions and duties and who have their own values and interests, which often clash, as we have seen. Judges, in the end, are less like umpires and more like team managers, with plenty of rules that must be followed but with a stake in the outcome they have more than a modicum of control over.

The legal system, designed to resolve these clashes and conflicts, is governed by laws, rules, and regulations that require interpretation and application at each stage of the legal process. In many cases, this interpretation is relatively simple, and most cases are disposed of at an early stage, with a ruling that is based on precedent and generally accepted legal principles. It's the "hard" cases, particularly those that reach the appellate stage and produce divided opinions, where judges have the most leeway in making and justifying their decisions. The people who make these decisions and write opinions that are often sharply worded and diametrically opposed come to the bench with very different experiences, personal and political ideologies (although few judges would use that term), and opinions on issues that have long divided Americans and still do, issues such as abortion, affirmative action, and gay rights, to name just a few.

The Senate confirmation hearings during the last few decades, including those of Robert Bork, Clarence Thomas, Sonia Sotomayor, and Elena Kagan, have brought these divisions into the public spotlight, however much the potential justices (with the notable exception of Bork) have tried to fudge their real views and proclaim their devotion to "impartial" judging. The last thing any Supreme Court nominee wants is to be accused of putting his or her personal values first and of desiring to "legislate from the bench." But that's what both liberal and conservative judges do, whenever they vote to strike down a law (such as gun control or public display of the Ten Commandments) that a legislative majority, reflecting "the will of the people," has enacted. Conflicts between "majority rule" and "minority rights" have divided Americans—and judges—since the Constitution was ratified and will no doubt continue for decades to come, because they leave little room for compromise among the partisans on both sides. That's a lesson I hope readers of this book will recognize, think about, and discuss and debate with their fellow citizens.

Appendix of Supreme Court Opinions

This Appendix is designed to provide interested readers with access to the Supreme Court opinions in the cases discussed in this book's text: the Paul House murder case, and the Ten Commandments cases from Kentucky and Texas; *McCreary County* v. *ACLU of Kentucky*, and *Van Orden* v. *Perry*. I have (lightly) edited the opinions to remove citations to the case records, citations to some of the cases cited as precedent, and discussion of issues that were not central to the analysis in the various opinions. I have noted substantial excisions in this manner: [. . .]. I have retained, however, the case facts that the opinions' authors considered relevant, and discussion of the legal issues that were applied to these facts. I hope readers find this format useful. Those who wish to consult the full versions of the opinions can easily find them on such Internet search engines as Google, by typing in the case name, followed by "opinions."

I. OPINIONS IN *HOUSE V. BELL*

Justice Kennedy delivered the opinion of the Court.

Some 20 years ago in rural Tennessee, Carolyn Muncey was murdered. A jury convicted petitioner Paul Gregory House of the crime and sentenced him to death, but new revelations cast doubt on the jury's verdict. House, protesting his innocence, seeks access to federal court to pursue habeas corpus relief based on constitutional claims that are procedurally barred under state law. Out of respect for the finality of state-court judgments federal habeas courts, as a general rule, are closed to claims that state courts would consider defaulted. In certain exceptional cases involving a compelling claim of actual innocence, however, the state procedural default rule is not a bar to a federal habeas corpus petition. See *Schlup* v. *Delo* (1995). After careful review of the full record, we conclude that House has made the stringent showing required by this exception; and we hold that his federal habeas action may proceed.

I

We begin with the facts surrounding Mrs. Muncey's disappearance, the discovery of her body, and House's arrest. Around 3 P.M. on Sunday, July 14, 1985, two local residents found her body concealed amid brush and tree branches on an embankment roughly 100 yards up the road from her driveway. Mrs. Muncey had been seen last on the evening before, when, around 8 P.M., she and her two children—Lora Muncey age 10, and Matthew Muncey, age 8—visited their neighbor, Pam Luttrell. According to Luttrell, Mrs. Muncey mentioned her husband, William Hubert Muncey Jr., known in the community as "Little Hube" and to his family as "Bubbie." As Luttrell recounted Mrs. Muncey's comment, Mr. Muncey "had gone to dig a grave, and he hadn't come back, but that was all right, because [Mrs. Muncey] was going to make him take her fishing the next day." Mrs. Muncey returned home, and some time later, before 11:00 P.M. at the latest, Luttrell "heard a car rev its motor as it went down the road," something Mr. Muncey customarily did when he drove by on his way home. Luttrell then went to bed.

Around 1 A.M., Lora and Matthew returned to Luttrell's home, this time with their father, Mr. Muncey, who said his wife was missing. Muncey asked Luttrell to watch the children while he searched for his wife. After he left, Luttrell talked with Lora. According to Luttrell:

"[Lora] said she heard a horn blow, she thought she heard a horn blow, and somebody asked if Bubbie was home, and her mama, you know, told them—no. And then she said she didn't know if she went back to sleep or not, but then she heard her mama going down the steps crying and I am not sure if that is when she told me that she heard her mama say—oh God, no, not me, or if she told me that the next day, but I do know that she said she heard her mother going down the steps crying." [. . .]

Lora did not describe hearing any struggle. Some time later, Lora and her brother left the house to look for their mother, but no one answered when they knocked at the Luttrells' home, and another neighbor, Mike Clinton, said he had not seen her. After the children returned home, according to Lora, her father came home and "fixed him a bologna sandwich and he took a bit of it and he says—sissy, where is mommy at, and I said—she ain't been here for a little while." Lora recalled that Mr. Muncey went outside and, not seeing his wife, returned to take Lora and Matthew to the Luttrells' so that he could look further.

The next afternoon Billy Ray Hensley, the victim's first cousin, heard of Mrs. Muncey's disappearance and went to look for Mr. Muncey. As he approached the Munceys' street, Hensley allegedly "saw Mr. House come out from under a bank, wiping his hands on a black rag." Just when and where Hensley saw House, and how well he could have observed him, were disputed at House's trial. Hensley admitted on cross-examination that he could not have seen House "walking up or climbing up" the embankment; rather, he saw House, in "[j]ust a glance," "appear out of nowhere," "next to the embankment," On the Munceys' street, opposite the area where Hensley said he saw House, a white Plymouth was parked near a sawmill. Hensley, after turning onto the Munceys' street, continued down the road and turned into their driveway. "I pulled up in the driveway where I could see up toward Little Hube's house," Hensley testified, "and I seen Little Hube's car wasn't there, and I backed out in the road, and come back [the other way]." As he traveled up the road, Hensley saw House traveling in the opposite direction in the white Plymouth. House "flagged [Hensley] down" through his windshield, and the two cars met about 300 feet up the road from the Munceys' driveway. According to Hensley, House said he had heard Mrs. Muncey was missing and was looking for her husband. Though House had only recently moved to the area, he was acquainted with the Munceys, had attended a dance with them, and had visited their home. He later told law enforcement officials he considered both of the Munceys his friends. According to Hensley, House said he had heard that Mrs. Muncey's husband, who was an alcoholic, was elsewhere "getting drunk."

As Hensley drove off, he "got to thinking to [him]self—he's hunting Little Hube, and Little Hube drunk—what would he be doing off that bank . . . ." His suspicion aroused, Hensley later returned to the Munceys' street with a friend named Jack Adkins. The two checked different spots on the embankment, and though Hensley saw nothing where he looked, Adkins found Mrs. Muncey. Her body lay across from the sawmill near the corner where House's car had been parked, dumped in the woods a short way down the bank leading toward a creek.

Around midnight, Dr. Alex Carabia, a practicing pathologist and county medical examiner, performed an autopsy. Dr. Carabia put the time of death between 9 and 11 P.M. Mrs. Muncey had a black eye, both her hands were bloodstained up to the wrists, and she had bruises on her legs and neck. Dr. Carabia described the bruises as consistent with a "traumatic origin," *i.e.*, a fight or a fall on hard objects. Based on the neck bruises and other injuries, he concluded Mrs. Muncey had been choked, but he ruled this out as the cause of death. The cause of death, in Dr. Carabia's view, was a severe blow to the left forehead that inflicted both a laceration penetrating to the bone and, inside the skull, a severe right-side hemorrhage, likely caused by Mrs. Muncey's brain slamming into the skull opposite the impact. Dr. Carabia described this head injury as consistent either with receiving a blow from a fist or other instrument or with striking some object.

The county sheriff, informed about Hensley's earlier encounter with House, questioned House shortly after the body was found. That evening, House answered further questions during a voluntary interview at the local jail. Special Agent Ray Presnell of the Tennessee Bureau of Investigation (TBI) prepared a statement of House's answers, which House signed. Asked to describe his whereabouts on the previous evening, House claimed—falsely, as it turned out—that he spent the entire evening with his girlfriend, Donna Turner, at her trailer. Asked whether he was wearing the same pants he had worn the night before, House replied—again, falsely—that he was. House was on probation at the time, having recently been released on parole following a sentence of five years to life for aggravated sexual assault in Utah. [. . .] In fact House had not been at Turner's home. After initially supporting House's alibi, Turner informed authorities that House left her trailer around 10:30 or 10:45 P.M. to go for a walk. According to Turner's trial testimony, House returned later—she was not sure when—hot and panting, missing his shirt and his shoes. House, Turner testified, told her that while he was walking on the road near her home, a vehicle pulled up beside him, and somebody inside "called him some names and then they told him he didn't belong here anymore." House said he tried to ignore the taunts and keep walking, but the vehicle pulled in behind him, and "one of them got out and grabbed him by the shoulder . . . and [House] swung around with his right hand" and "hit something." According to Turner, House said "he took off down the bank and started running and he said that he—he said it seemed forever where he was running. And he said they fired two shots at him while he took off down the bank . . . ." House claimed the assailants "grabbed ahold of his shirt," which Turner remembered as "a blue tank top, trimmed in yellow," and "they tore it to where it wouldn't stay on him and he said—I just throwed it off when I was running." Turner, noticing House's bruised knuckle, asked how he hurt it, and House told her "that's where he hit." Turner testified that she "thought maybe my ex-husband had something to do with it." [. . .]

Law enforcement officers also questioned the victim's husband. Though Mrs. Muncey's comments to Luttrell gave no indication she knew this, Mr. Muncey had spent the evening at a weekly dance at a recreation center roughly a mile and a half from his home. In his statement to law

enforcement—a statement House's trial counsel claims he never saw—
Mr. Muncey admitted leaving the dance early, but said it was only for a brief
trip to the package store to buy beer. He also stated that he and his wife had
had sexual relations Saturday morning.

Late in the evening on Monday, July 15—two days after the murder—law
enforcement officers visited Turner's trailer. With Turner's consent, Agent
Scott seized the pants House was wearing the night Mrs. Muncey disappeared. The heavily soiled pants were sitting in a laundry hamper; years later,
Agent Scott recalled noticing "reddish brown stains" he "suspected" were
blood. Around 4 P.M. the next day, two local law enforcement officers set out
for the Federal Bureau of Investigation in Washington, D. C., with House's
pants, blood samples from the autopsy, and other evidence packed together in
a box. They arrived at 2:00 A.M. the next morning. On July 17, after initial FBI
testing revealed human blood on the pants, House was arrested.

II

The State of Tennessee charged House with capital murder. At House's trial,
the State presented testimony by Luttrell, Hensley, Adkins, Lora Muncey,
Dr. Carabia, the sheriff, and other law enforcement officials. Through
TBI Agents Presnell and Scott, the jury learned of House's false statements. Central to the State's case, however, was what the FBI testing
showed—that semen consistent (or so it seemed) with House's was present on
Mrs. Muncey's nightgown and panties, and that small bloodstains consistent
with Mrs. Muncey's blood but not House's appeared on the jeans belonging
to House. [Justice Kennedy then reviewed the scientific evidence presented
at the trial, which is discussed in the text.]

In the defense case House called Hankins, Clinton, and Turner, as well
as House's mother, who testified that House had talked to her by telephone
around 9:30 P.M. on the night of the murder and that he had not used her
car that evening. House also called the victim's brother, Ricky Green, as a
witness. Green testified that on July 2, roughly two weeks before the murder,
Mrs. Muncey called him and "said her and Little Hube had been into it and
she said she was wanting to leave Little Hube, she said she was wanting to get
out—out of it, and she was scared." Green recalled that at Christmastime in
1982 he had seen Mr. Muncey strike Mrs. Muncey after returning home drunk.

As Turner informed the jury, House's shoes were found several months
after the crime in a field near her home. Turner delivered them to authorities.
Though the jury did not learn of this fact (and House's counsel claims he did
not either), the State tested the shoes for blood and found none. House's shirt
was not found.

The State's closing argument suggested that on the night of her murder, Mrs. Muncey "was deceived . . . . She had been told [her husband] had had an accident." [. . .] In the State's rebuttal, after defense counsel questioned House's motive "to go over and kill a woman that he barely knew[,] [w]ho was still dressed, still clad in her clothes," the prosecutor [. . .] told the jury, "you may have an idea why he did it":

"The evidence at the scene which seemed to suggest that he was subjecting this lady to some kind of indignity, why would you get a lady out of her house, late at night, in her night clothes, under the trick that her husband has had a wreck down by the creek? . . . Well, it is because either you don't want her to tell what indignities you have subjected her to, or she is unwilling and fights against you, against being subjected to those indignities. In other words, it is either to keep her from telling what you have done to her, or it is that you are trying to get her to do something that she nor any mother on that road would want to do with Mr. House, under those conditions, and you kill her because of her resistance. That is what the evidence at the scene suggests about motive." [. . .]

In addition the government suggested the black rag Hensley said he saw in House's hands was in fact the missing blue tank top, retrieved by House from the crime scene. And the prosecution reiterated the importance of the blood. "[D]efense counsel," he said, "does not start out discussing the fact that his client had blood on his jeans on the night that Carolyn Muncey was killed. . . . He doesn't start with the fact that nothing that the defense has introduced in this case explains what blood is doing on his jeans, all over his jeans, that is scientifically, completely different from his blood." [. . .] The jury found House guilty of murder in the first degree.

The trial advanced to the sentencing phase. As aggravating factors to support a capital sentence, the State sought to prove: (1) that House had previously been convicted of a felony involving the use or threat of violence; (2) that the homicide was especially heinous, atrocious, or cruel in that it involved torture or depravity of mind; and (3) that the murder was committed while House was committing, attempting to commit, or fleeing from the commission of, rape or kidnaping. [. . .] In closing the State urged the jury to find all three aggravating factors and impose death. [. . .] The jury unanimously found all three aggravating factors and concluded "there are no mitigating circumstances sufficiently substantial to outweigh the statutory aggravating circumstance or circumstances." The jury recommended a death sentence, which the trial judge imposed.

III

[Justice Kennedy then reviewed the proceedings in the Tennessee state courts on House's appeal from his conviction and death sentence, and the subsequent appeal to the U.S. Court of Appeals for the Sixth Circuit, which are discussed in the text.]

We granted certiorari, and now reverse.

IV

As a general rule, claims forfeited under state law may support federal habeas relief only if the prisoner demonstrates cause for the default and prejudice from the asserted error. The rule is based on the comity and respect that must be accorded to state-court judgments. The bar is not, however, unqualified. In an effort to "balance the societal interests in finality, comity, and conservation of scarce judicial resources with the individual interest in justice that arises in the extraordinary case," the Court has recognized a miscarriage-of-justice exception. "'[I]n appropriate cases,'" the Court has said, "the principles of comity and finality that inform the concepts of cause and prejudice 'must yield to the imperative of correcting a fundamentally unjust incarceration.'"

In *Schlup*, the Court adopted a specific rule to implement this general principle. It held that prisoners asserting innocence as a gateway to defaulted claims must establish that, in light of new evidence, "it is more likely than not that no reasonable juror would have found petitioner guilty beyond a reasonable doubt." This formulation, *Schlup* explains, "ensures that petitioner's case is truly 'extraordinary,' while still providing petitioner a meaningful avenue by which to avoid a manifest injustice." In the usual case the presumed guilt of a prisoner convicted in state court counsels against federal review of defaulted claims. Yet a petition supported by a convincing *Schlup* gateway showing "raise[s] sufficient doubt about [the petitioner's] guilt to undermine confidence in the result of the trial without the assurance that that trial was untainted by constitutional error"; hence, "a review of the merits of the constitutional claims" is justified.

For purposes of this case several features of the *Schlup* standard bear emphasis. First, although "[t]o be credible" a gateway claim requires "new reliable evidence—whether it be exculpatory scientific evidence, trustworthy eyewitness accounts, or critical physical evidence—that was not presented at trial," the habeas court's analysis is not limited to such evidence. There is no dispute in this case that House has presented some new reliable evidence; the State has conceded as much. In addition, because the District Court held an evidentiary hearing in this case, and because the State does not challenge the court's decision to do so, we have no occasion to elaborate on *Schlup*'s observation that when considering an actual-innocence claim in the context of a request for an evidentiary hearing, the District Court need not "test the new evidence by a standard appropriate for deciding a motion for summary judgment," but rather may "consider how the timing of the submission and the likely credibility of the affiants bear on the probable reliability of that evidence." Our review in this case addresses the merits of the *Schlup* inquiry, based on a fully developed record, and with respect to that inquiry *Schlup* makes plain that the habeas court must consider "'all the evidence,'" old and new, incriminating and exculpatory, without regard to whether it would necessarily be admitted under "rules of admissibility that would govern at trial." Based on this total record, the court must make "a probabilistic determination about what reasonable, properly instructed jurors would do." The court's function is not to make an independent factual determination about what likely occurred, but rather to assess the likely impact of the evidence on reasonable jurors.

Second, it bears repeating that the *Schlup* standard is demanding and permits review only in the "'extraordinary'" case. At the same time, though, the *Schlup* standard does not require absolute certainty about the petitioner's guilt or innocence. A petitioner's burden at the gateway stage is to demonstrate that more likely than not, in light of the new evidence, no reasonable juror would find him guilty beyond a reasonable doubt—or, to remove the double negative, that more likely than not any reasonable juror would have reasonable doubt. [. . .]

When confronted with a challenge based on trial evidence, courts presume the jury resolved evidentiary disputes reasonably so long as sufficient evidence supports the verdict. Because a *Schlup* claim involves evidence the trial jury did not have before it, the inquiry requires the federal court to assess how reasonable jurors would react to the overall, newly supplemented record. If new evidence so requires, this may include consideration of "the credibility of the witnesses presented at trial." [. . .] The State . . . argues that the District Court's findings in this case tie our hands, precluding a ruling in House's favor absent a showing of clear error as to the District Court's specific determinations. This view overstates the effect of the District Court's ruling. Deference is given to a trial court's assessment of evidence presented to it in the first instance. Yet the *Schlup* inquiry, we repeat, requires a holistic judgment about "'all the evidence,'" and its likely effect on reasonable jurors applying the reasonable-doubt standard. As a general rule, the inquiry does not turn on discrete findings regarding disputed points of fact, and "[i]t is not the district court's independent judgment as to whether reasonable doubt exists that the standard addresses." Here, although the District Court attentively managed complex proceedings, carefully reviewed the extensive record, and drew certain conclusions about the evidence, the court did not clearly apply *Schlup*'s predictive standard regarding whether reasonable jurors would have reasonable doubt. As we shall explain, moreover, we are uncertain about the basis for some of the District Court's conclusions—a consideration that weakens our reliance on its determinations.

With this background in mind we turn to the evidence developed in House's federal habeas proceedings.

DNA Evidence

First, in direct contradiction of evidence presented at trial, DNA testing has established that the semen on Mrs. Muncey's nightgown and panties came from her husband, Mr. Muncey, not from House. The State, though conceding this point, insists this new evidence is immaterial. At the guilt phase at least, neither sexual contact nor motive were elements of the offense, so in the State's view the evidence, or lack of evidence, of sexual assault or sexual advance is of no consequence. We disagree. In fact we consider the new disclosure of central importance.

From beginning to end the case is about who committed the crime. When identity is in question, motive is key. The point, indeed, was not lost on the prosecution, for it introduced the evidence and relied on it in the final guilt-phase closing argument. Referring to "evidence at the scene," the prosecutor suggested that House committed, or attempted to commit, some "indignity" on Mrs. Muncey that neither she "nor any mother on that road would want to do with Mr. House." Particularly in a case like this where the proof was, as the State Supreme Court observed, circumstantial, we think a jury would have given this evidence great weight. Quite apart from providing proof of motive, it was the only forensic evidence at the scene that would link House to the murder.

Law and society, as they ought to do, demand accountability when a sexual offense has been committed, so not only did this evidence link House to the crime; it likely was a factor in persuading the jury not to let him go free. At sentencing, moreover, the jury came to the unanimous conclusion, beyond a reasonable doubt, that the murder was committed in the course of a rape or kidnapping. The alleged sexual motivation relates to both those determinations. This is particularly so given that, at the sentencing phase, the jury was advised that House had a previous conviction for sexual assault.

A jury informed that fluids on Mrs. Muncey's garments could have come from House might have found that House trekked the nearly two miles to the victim's home and lured her away in order to commit a sexual offense. By contrast, a jury acting without the assumption that the semen could have come from House would have found it necessary to establish some different motive, or, if the same motive, an intent far more speculative. When the only direct evidence of sexual assault drops out of the case, so, too, does a central theme in the State's narrative linking House to the crime. In that light, furthermore, House's odd evening walk and his false statements to authorities, while still potentially incriminating, might appear less suspicious.

Bloodstains

The other relevant forensic evidence is the blood on House's pants, which appears in small, even minute, stains in scattered places. As the prosecutor told the jury, they were stains that, due to their small size, "you or I might not detect[,] [m]ight not see, but which the FBI lab was able to find on [House's] jeans." [. . .] At trial, the government argued "nothing that the defense has introduced in this case explains what blood is doing on his jeans, all over [House's] jeans, that is scientifically, completely different from his blood." House, though not disputing at this point that the blood is Mrs. Muncey's, now presents an alternative explanation that, if credited, would undermine the probative value of the blood evidence.

During House's habeas proceedings, Dr. Cleland Blake, an Assistant Chief Medical Examiner for the State of Tennessee and a consultant in forensic pathology to the TBI for 22 years, testified that the blood on House's pants was chemically too degraded, and too similar to blood collected during the autopsy, to have come from Mrs. Muncey's body on the night of the crime. The blood samples collected during the autopsy were placed in test tubes without preservative. Under such conditions, according to Dr. Blake, "you will have enzyme degradation. You will have different blood group degradation, blood marker degradation." The problem of decay, moreover, would have been compounded by the body's long exposure to the elements, sitting outside for the better part of a summer day. In contrast, if blood is preserved on cloth, "it will stay there for years"; indeed, Dr. Blake said he deliberately places blood drops on gauze during autopsies to preserve it for later testing. The blood on House's pants, judging by Agent Bigbee's tests, showed "similar deterioration, breakdown of certain of the named numbered enzymes" as in the autopsy samples. "[I]f the victim's blood had spilled on the jeans while the victim was alive and this blood had dried," Dr. Blake stated, "the deterioration would not have occurred," and "you would expect [the blood on the jeans] to be different than what was in the tube." Dr. Blake thus concluded the blood on the jeans came from the autopsy samples, not from Mrs. Muncey's live (or recently killed) body.

Other evidence confirms that blood did in fact spill from the vials. It appears the vials passed from Dr. Carabia, who performed the autopsy, into the hands of two local law enforcement officers, who transported it to the FBI, where Agent Bigbee performed the enzyme tests. The blood was contained in four vials, evidently with neither preservative nor a proper seal. The vials, in turn, were stored in a styrofoam box, but nothing indicates the box was kept cool. Rather, in what an evidence protocol expert at the habeas hearing described as a violation of proper procedure, the styrofoam box was packed in the same cardboard box as other evidence including House's pants (apparently in a paper bag) and other clothing (in separate bags). The cardboard box was then carried in the officers' car while they made the 10-hour journey from Tennessee to the FBI lab. Dr. Blake stated that blood vials in hot conditions (such as a car trunk in the summer) could blow open; and in fact, by the time the blood reached the FBI it had hemolyzed, or spoiled, due to heat exposure. By the time the blood passed from the FBI to a defense expert, roughly a vial and a half were empty, though Agent Bigbee testified he used at most a quarter of one vial. Blood, moreover, had seeped onto one corner of the styrofoam box and onto packing gauze inside the box below the vials.

In addition, although the pants apparently were packaged initially in a paper bag and FBI records suggest they arrived at the FBI in one, the record does not contain the paper bag but does contain a plastic bag with a label listing the pants and Agent Scott's name—and the plastic bag has blood on it. The blood appears in a forked streak roughly five inches long and two inches wide running down the bag's outside front. Though testing by House's expert confirmed the stain was blood, the expert could not determine the blood's source. Speculations about when and how the blood got there add to the confusion regarding the origins of the stains on House's pants. [. . .]

In sum, considering "'all the evidence,'" on this issue, we think the evidentiary disarray surrounding the blood, taken together with Dr. Blake's testimony and the limited rebuttal of it in the present record, would prevent reasonable jurors from placing significant reliance on the blood evidence. [. . .] Thus, whereas the bloodstains, emphasized by the prosecution, seemed strong evidence of House's guilt at trial, the record now raises substantial questions about the blood's origin.

A Different Suspect

Were House's challenge to the State's case limited to the questions he has raised about the blood and semen, the other evidence favoring the prosecution might well suffice to bar relief. There is, however, more; for in the post-trial proceedings House presented troubling evidence that Mr. Muncey, the victim's husband, himself could have been the murderer.

At trial, as has been noted, the jury heard that roughly two weeks before the murder Mrs. Muncey's brother received a frightened phone call from his sister indicating that she and Mr. Muncey had been fighting, that she was scared, and that she wanted to leave him. The jury also learned that the brother once saw Mr. Muncey "smac[k]" the victim. House now has produced evidence from multiple sources suggesting that Mr. Muncey regularly abused his wife. For example, one witness—Kathy Parker, a lifelong area resident who denied any animosity towards Mr. Muncey—recalled that Mrs. Muncey "was constantly with black eyes and busted mouth." In addition Hazel Miller, who is Kathy Parker's mother and a lifelong acquaintance of Mr. Muncey, testified at the habeas hearing that two or three months before the victim's death Mr. Muncey came to Miller's home and "tried to get my daughter [Parker] to go out with him." According to Miller, Muncey said "[h]e was upset with his wife, that they had had an argument and he said he was going to get rid of that woman one way or the other."

Another witness—Mary Atkins, also an area native who "grew up" with Mr. Muncey and professed no hard feelings, claims she saw Mr. Muncey "backhan[d]" Mrs. Muncey on the very night of the murder. Atkins recalled that during a break in the recreation center dance, she saw Mr. Muncey and his wife arguing in the parking lot. Mr. Muncey "grabbed her and he just backhanded her." After that, Mrs. Muncey "left walking." There was also testimony from Atkins' mother, named Artie Lawson. A self-described "good friend" of Mr. Muncey, Lawson said Mr. Muncey visited her the morning after the murder, before the body was found. According to Lawson, Mr. Muncey asked her to tell anyone who inquired not only that she had been at the dance the evening before and had seen him, but also that he had breakfasted at her home at 6 o'clock that morning. Lawson had not in fact been at the dance, nor had Mr. Muncey been with her so early.

Of most importance is the testimony of Kathy Parker and her sister Penny Letner. They testified at the habeas hearing that, around the time of House's trial, Mr. Muncey had confessed to the crime. Parker recalled that she and "some family members and some friends [were] sitting around drinking" at Parker's trailer when Mr. Muncey "just walked in and sit down." Muncey, who had evidently been drinking heavily, began "rambling off . . . [t]alking about what happened to his wife and how it happened and he didn't mean to do it." According to Parker, Mr. Muncey "said they had been into [an] argument and he slapped her and she fell and hit her head and it killed her and he didn't mean for it to happen." Parker said she "freaked out and run him off."

Letner similarly recalled that at some point either "during [House's] trial or just before," Mr. Muncey intruded on a gathering at Parker's home. Appearing "pretty well blistered," Muncey "went to crying and was talking about his wife and her death and he was saying that he didn't mean to do it." "[D]idn't mean to do what[?]," Letner asked, at which point Mr. Muncey explained:

"[S]he was 'bitching him out' because he didn't take her fishing that night, that he went to the dance instead. He said when he come home that she was still on him pretty heavily 'bitching him out' again and that he smacked her and that she fell and hit her head. He said I didn't mean to do it, but I had to get rid of her, because I didn't want to be charged with murder."

Letner, who was then 19 years old with a small child, said Mr. Muncey's statement "scared [her] quite badly," so she "got out of there immediately."

Asked whether she reported the incident to the authorities, Letner stated, "I was frightened, you know. . . . I figured me being 19 year old they wouldn't listen to anything I had to say." Parker, on the other hand, claimed she (Parker) in fact went to the Sherriff's Department, but no one would listen:

"I tried to speak to the Sheriff but he was real busy. He sent me to a deputy. The deputy told me to go upstairs to the courtroom and talk to this guy, I can't remember his name. I never did really get to talk to anybody."

Parker said she did not discuss the matter further because "[t]hey had it all signed, sealed and delivered. We didn't know anything to do until we heard that they reopened [House's] trial." Parker's mother, Hazel Miller, confirmed she had driven Parker to the courthouse, where Parker "went to talk to some of the people about this case."

Other testimony suggests Mr. Muncey had the opportunity to commit the crime. According to Dennis Wallace, a local law enforcement official who provided security at the dance on the night of the murder, Mr. Muncey left the dance "around 10:00, 10:30, 9:30 to 10:30." Although Mr. Muncey told law enforcement officials just after the murder that he left the dance only briefly and returned, Wallace could not recall seeing him back there again. Later that evening, Wallace responded to Mr. Muncey's report that his wife was missing. Muncey denied he and his wife had been "a fussing or a fighting"; he claimed his wife had been "kidnapped." Wallace did not recall seeing any blood, disarray, or knocked-over furniture, although he admitted he "didn't pay too much attention" to whether the floor appeared especially clean. According to Wallace, Mr. Muncey said "let's search for her" and then led Wallace out to search "in the weeds" around the home and the driveway (not out on the road where the body was found).

In the habeas proceedings, then, two different witnesses (Parker and Letner) described a confession by Mr. Muncey; two more (Atkins and Lawson) described suspicious behavior (a fight and an attempt to construct a false alibi) around the time of the crime; and still other witnesses described a history of abuse.

As to Parker and Letner, the District Court noted that it was "not impressed with the allegations of individuals who wait over ten years to come forward with their evidence," especially considering that "there was no physical evidence in the Munceys' kitchen to corroborate [Mr. Muncey's] alleged confession that he killed [his wife] there." Parker and Letner, however, did attempt to explain their delay coming forward, and the record indicates no reason why these two women, both lifelong acquaintances of Mr. Muncey, would have wanted either to frame him or to help House. Furthermore, the record includes at least some independent support for the statements Parker and Letner attributed to Mr. Muncey. The supposed explanation for the fatal fight—that his wife was complaining about going fishing—fits with Mrs. Muncey's statement to Luttrell earlier that evening that her husband's absence was "all right, because she was going to make him take her fishing the next day." And Dr. Blake testified, in only partial contradiction of Dr. Carabia, that Mrs. Muncey's head injury resulted from "a surface with an edge" or "a hard surface with a corner," not from a fist. (Dr. Carabia had said either a fist or some other object could have been the cause.)

Mr. Muncey testified at the habeas hearing, and the District Court did not question his credibility. Though Mr. Muncey said he seemed to remember visiting Lawson the day after the murder, he denied either killing his wife or confessing to doing so. Yet Mr. Muncey also claimed, contrary to Constable Wallace's testimony and to his own prior statement, that he left the dance on the night of the crime only when it ended at midnight. Mr. Muncey, moreover, denied ever hitting Mrs. Muncey; the State itself had to impeach him with a prior statement on this point.

It bears emphasis, finally, that Parker's and Letner's testimony is not comparable to the sort of eleventh-hour affidavit vouching for a defendant and incriminating a conveniently absent suspect that Justice O'Connor described in her concurring opinion in *Herrera* as "unfortunate" and "not uncommon" in capital cases; nor was the confession Parker and Letner described induced under pressure of interrogation. The confession evidence here involves an alleged spontaneous statement recounted by two eyewitnesses with no evident motive to lie. For this reason it has more probative value than, for example, incriminating testimony from inmates, suspects, or friends or relations of the accused.

The evidence pointing to Mr. Muncey is by no means conclusive. If considered in isolation, a reasonable jury might well disregard it. In combination, however, with the challenges to the blood evidence and the lack of motive with respect to House, the evidence pointing to Mr. Muncey likely would reinforce other doubts as to House's guilt. [. . .]

Conclusion

This is not a case of conclusive exoneration. Some aspects of the State's evidence—Lora Muncey's memory of a deep voice, House's bizarre evening walk, his lie to law enforcement, his appearance near the body, and the blood on his pants—still support an inference of guilt. Yet the central forensic proof connecting House to the crime—the blood and the semen—has been called into question, and House has put forward substantial evidence pointing to a different suspect. Accordingly, and although the issue is close, we conclude that this is the rare case where—had the jury heard all the conflicting testimony—it is more likely than not that no reasonable juror viewing the record as a whole would lack reasonable doubt.

V

In addition to his gateway claim under *Schlup*, House argues that he has shown freestanding innocence and that as a result his imprisonment and planned execution are unconstitutional. In *Herrera*, decided three years before *Schlup*, the Court assumed without deciding that "in a capital case a truly persuasive demonstration of 'actual innocence' made after trial would render the execution of a defendant unconstitutional, and warrant federal habeas relief if there were no state avenue open to process such a claim." "[T]he threshold showing for such an assumed right would necessarily be extraordinarily high," the Court explained, and petitioner's evidence there fell "far short of that which would have to be made in order to trigger the sort of constitutional claim which we have assumed, *arguendo*, to exist." House urges the Court to answer the question left open in *Herrera* and hold not only that freestanding innocence claims are possible but also that he has established one.

We decline to resolve this issue. We conclude here, much as in *Herrera*, that whatever burden a hypothetical freestanding innocence claim would require, this petitioner has not satisfied it. To be sure, House has cast considerable doubt on his guilt—doubt sufficient to satisfy *Schlup*'s gateway standard for obtaining federal review despite a state procedural default. In *Herrera*, however, the Court described the threshold for any hypothetical freestanding innocence claim as "extraordinarily high." The sequence of the Court's decisions in *Herrera* and *Schlup*—first leaving unresolved the status of freestanding claims and then establishing the gateway standard—implies at the least that *Herrera* requires more convincing proof of innocence than *Schlup*. It follows, given the closeness of the *Schlup* question here, that House's showing falls short of the threshold implied in *Herrera*.

House has satisfied the gateway standard set forth in *Schlup* and may proceed on remand with procedurally defaulted constitutional claims. The judgment of the Court of Appeals is reversed, and the case is remanded for further proceedings consistent with this opinion.

It is so ordered.

Justice Alito took no part in the consideration or decision of this case.

Chief Justice Roberts, with whom Justice Scalia and Justice Thomas join, concurring in the judgment in part and dissenting in part.

To overcome the procedural hurdle that Paul House created by failing to properly present his constitutional claims to a Tennessee court, he must demonstrate that the constitutional violations he alleges "ha[ve] probably resulted in the conviction of one who is actually innocent," such that a federal court's refusal to hear the defaulted claims would be a "miscarriage of justice." *Schlup* v. *Delo* (1995). To make the requisite showing of actual innocence, House must produce "new *reliable* evidence" and "must show that it is more likely than not that no reasonable juror would have convicted him in the light of the new evidence." The question is not whether House was prejudiced at his trial because the jurors were not aware of the new evidence, but whether all the evidence, considered together, proves that House was actually innocent, so that no reasonable juror would vote to convict him. Considering all the evidence, and giving due regard to the District Court's findings on whether House's new evidence was reliable, I do not find it probable that no reasonable juror would vote to convict him, and accordingly I dissent.

Because I do not think that House has satisfied the actual innocence standard set forth in *Schlup*, I do not believe that he has met the higher threshold for a freestanding innocence claim, assuming such a claim exists. See *Herrera* v. *Collins* (1993). I therefore concur in the judgment with respect to the Court's disposition of that separate claim.

I

In *Schlup*, we stated that a habeas petitioner attempting to present a defaulted claim to a federal court must present "new *reliable* evidence—whether it be exculpatory scientific evidence, trustworthy eyewitness accounts, or critical physical evidence—that was not presented at trial." Implicit in the requirement that a habeas petitioner present reliable evidence is the expectation that a factfinder will assess reliability. The new evidence at issue in *Schlup* had not been subjected to such an assessment—the claim in *Schlup* was for an evidentiary hearing—and this Court specifically recognized that the "new statements may, of course, be unreliable." The Court stated that the District Court, as the "reviewing tribunal," was tasked with assessing the "probative force" of the petitioner's new evidence of innocence, and "may have to make some credibility assessments." Indeed, the Supreme Court took the unusual step of remanding the case to the Court of Appeals "with instructions to remand to the District Court," so that the District Court could consider how the "likely credibility of the affiants" bears upon the "probable reliability" of the new evidence. In short, the new evidence is not simply taken at face value; its reliability has to be tested.

Critical to the Court's conclusion here that House has sufficiently demonstrated his innocence are three pieces of new evidence presented to the

District Court: DNA evidence showing that the semen on Carolyn Muncey's clothing was from her husband, Hubert Muncey, not from House; testimony from new witnesses implicating Mr. Muncey in the murder; and evidence indicating that Mrs. Muncey's blood spilled from test tubes containing autopsy samples in an evidence container. To determine whether it should open its door to House's defaulted constitutional claims, the District Court considered this evidence in a comprehensive evidentiary hearing. As House presented his new evidence, and as the State rebutted it, the District Court observed the witnesses' demeanor, examined physical evidence, and made findings about whether House's new evidence was in fact reliable. This factfinding role is familiar to a district court. "The trial judge's major role is the determination of fact, and with experience in fulfilling that role comes expertise." The State did not contest House's new DNA evidence excluding him as the source of the semen on Mrs. Muncey's clothing, but it strongly contested the new testimony implicating Mr. Muncey, and it insisted that the blood spillage occurred *after* the FBI tested House's jeans and determined that they were stained with Mrs. Muncey's blood.

At the evidentiary hearing, sisters Kathy Parker and Penny Letner testified that 14 years earlier, either during or around the time of House's trial, they heard Mr. Muncey drunkenly confess to having accidentally killed his wife when he struck her in their home during an argument, causing her to fall and hit her head. *Schlup* provided guidance on how a district court should assess this type of new evidence: The court "may consider how the timing of the submission and the likely credibility of the affiants bear on the probable reliability of that evidence," and it "must assess the probative force of the newly presented evidence in connection with the evidence of guilt adduced at trial." Consistent with this guidance, the District Court concluded that the sisters' testimony was not credible. The court noted that it was "not impressed with the allegations of individuals who wait over ten years to come forward." It also considered how the new testimony fit within the larger web of evidence, observing that Mr. Muncey's alleged confession contradicted the testimony of the Munceys' "very credible" daughter, Lora Tharp, who consistently testified that she did not hear a fight in the house that night, but instead heard a man with a deep voice who lured her mother from the house by saying that Mr. Muncey had been in a wreck near the creek.

The District Court engaged in a similar reliability inquiry with regard to House's new evidence of blood spillage. At the evidentiary hearing, House conceded that FBI testing showed that his jeans were stained with Mrs. Muncey's blood, but he set out to prove that the blood spilled from test tubes containing autopsy samples, and that it did so before the jeans were tested by the FBI. The District Court summarized the testimony of the various witnesses who handled the evidence and their recollections about bloodstains and spillage; it acknowledged that House's expert, Dr. Cleland Blake, disagreed with FBI Agent Paul Bigbee about how to interpret the results of Agent Bigbee's genetic marker analysis summary. After reviewing all the evidence, the District Court stated: "Based upon the evidence introduced during the evidentiary hearing . . . the court concludes that the spillage occurred *after* the FBI crime laboratory received and tested the evidence."

Normally, an appellate court reviews a district court's factual findings only for clear error. See Fed. Rule Civ. Proc. 52(a) ("Findings of fact, whether based on oral or documentary evidence, shall not be set aside unless clearly errone-ous, and due regard shall be given to the opportunity of the trial court to judge of the credibility of the witnesses.") The Sixth Circuit deferred to the District Court's factual findings, and *Schlup* did not purport to alter—but instead reaffirmed and highlighted—the district court's critical role as factfinder. Yet the majority asserts that the clear error standard "overstates the effect of the District Court's ruling," and then dismisses the District Court's reliability find-ings because it is "uncertain about" them, while stopping short of identifying clear error. This is a sharp departure from the guidance in *Schlup*.

In *Schlup*, we contrasted a district court's role in assessing the reliabil-ity of new evidence of innocence with a district court's role in deciding a summary judgment motion. We explained that, in the latter situation, the district court does not assess credibility or weigh the evidence, but simply determines whether there is a genuine factual issue for trial. Assessing the reliability of new evidence, on the other hand, is a typical factfinding role, requiring credibility determinations and a weighing of the "probative force" of the new evidence in light of "the evidence of guilt adduced at trial." We found it "obviou[s]" that a habeas court conducting an actual innocence inquiry must do more than simply check whether there are genuine factual issues for trial. The point of the actual innocence inquiry is for the federal habeas court to satisfy itself that it should suspend the normal procedural default rule, disregard the important judicial interests of finality and comity, and allow a state prisoner to present his defaulted constitutional claims to a federal court.

The majority surprisingly states that this guidance is inapplicable here because this case involves a "fully developed record," while the district court in *Schlup* had declined to conduct an evidentiary hearing. But the guidance is clearly applicable: The point in *Schlup* was not simply that a hearing was required, but why—because the district court had to assess the probative force of the petitioner's newly presented evidence, by engaging in factfinding rather than performing a summary judgment-type inquiry. That is precisely what the District Court did here. In addition to a "fully developed record," we have the District Court's factual findings about the reliability of the new evidence in that record, factual findings which the majority disregards without finding clear error.

The majority essentially disregards the District Court's role in assessing the reliability of House's new evidence. With regard to the sisters' testimony, the majority casts aside the District Court's determination that their statements came too late and were too inconsistent with credible record evidence to be reliable, instead observing that the women had no obvious reason to lie, that a few aspects of their testimony have record support, and that they recounted an uncoerced confession. As for the District Court's express finding that the autopsy blood spilled after the FBI tested House's jeans, the majority points to Dr. Blake's testimony that blood enzymes "are generally better preserved on cloth." [. . .]

The majority's assessment of House's new evidence is precisely the summary judgment-type inquiry *Schlup* said was inappropriate. By casting aside the District Court's factual determinations made after a comprehensive evidentiary hearing, the majority has done little more than reiterate the factual disputes presented below. Witnesses do not testify in our courtroom, and it is not our role to make credibility findings and construct theories of the possible ways in which Mrs. Muncey's blood could have been spattered and wiped on House's jeans. The District Court did not painstakingly conduct an evidentiary hearing to compile a record for us to sort through transcript by transcript and photograph by photograph, assessing for ourselves the reliability of what we see. *Schlup* made abundantly clear that reliability determinations were essential, but were for the district court to make. We are to defer to the better situated District Court on reliability, unless we determine that its findings are clearly erroneous. We are not concerned with "the district court's independent judgment as to whether reasonable doubt exists," but the District Court here made basic factual findings about the reliability of House's new evidence; it did not offer its personal opinion about whether it doubted House's guilt. *Schlup* makes clear that those findings are controlling unless clearly erroneous.

I have found no clear error in the District Court's reliability findings. Not having observed Ms. Parker and Ms. Letner testify, I would defer to the District Court's determination that they are not credible, and the evidence in the record undermining the tale of an accidental killing during a fight in the Muncey home convinces me that this credibility finding is not clearly erroneous. Dr. Alex Carabia, who performed the autopsy, testified to injuries far more severe than a bump on the head: Mrs. Muncey had bruises on the front and back of her neck, on both thighs, on her lower right leg and left knee, and her hands were bloodstained up to the wrists; her injuries were consistent with a struggle and traumatic strangulation. And, of course, Lora [Muncey] has consistently recalled a deep-voiced visitor arriving late at night to tell Mrs. Muncey that her husband was in a wreck near the creek.

I also find abundant evidence in the record to support the District Court's finding that blood spilled within the evidence container after the FBI received and tested House's jeans. Agent Bigbee testified that there was no leakage in the items submitted to him for testing. The majority's entire analysis on this point assumes the agent flatly lied, though there was no attack on his credibility below. [. . .] I suppose it is theoretically possible that the jeans were contaminated by spillage before arriving at the FBI, that Agent Bigbee either failed to note or lied about such spillage, and that the FBI then transferred the jeans into a plastic bag and put them back inside the evidence container with the spilled blood still sloshing around sufficiently to contaminate the outside of the plastic bag as extensively as it did. This sort of unbridled speculation can theoretically defeat any inconvenient fact, but does not suffice to convince me that the District Court's factual finding—that the blood spilled *after* FBI testing—was clearly erroneous. [. . .]

The District Court attentively presided over a complex evidentiary hearing, often questioning witnesses extensively during the presentation of critical evidence. The court concisely summarized the evidence presented, then dutifully made findings about the reliability of the testimony it heard and the evidence it observed. We are poorly equipped to second-guess the District Court's reliability findings and should defer to them, consistent with the guidance we provided in *Schlup*.

II

With due regard to the District Court's reliability findings, this case invites a straightforward application of the legal standard adopted in *Schlup*. A petitioner does not pass through the *Schlup* gateway if it is "more likely than not that there is *any* juror who, acting reasonably, would have found the petitioner guilty beyond a reasonable doubt."

The majority states that if House had presented just one of his three key pieces of evidence—or even two of the three—he would not pass through the *Schlup* gateway. ("Were House's challenge to the State's case limited to the questions he has raised about the blood and semen, the other evidence favoring the prosecution might well suffice to bar relief [. . .] If considered in isolation, a reasonable jury might well disregard [the evidence pointing to Mr. Muncey]. In combination, however, with the challenges to the blood evidence and the lack of motive with respect to House, the evidence pointing to Mr. Muncey likely would reinforce other doubts as to House's guilt"). According to the majority, House has picked the trifecta of evidence that places conviction outside the realm of choices *any* juror, acting reasonably, would make. Because the case against House remains substantially unaltered from the case presented to the jury, I disagree.

At trial, the State presented its story about what happened on the night of Mrs. Muncey's murder. The Munceys' daughter heard a deep-voiced perpetrator arrive at the Muncey home late at night and tell Mrs. Muncey that her husband had been in a wreck near the creek. [Lora Muncey] relayed her testimony again at the evidentiary hearing, and the District Court determined that she was a "very credible witness."

When police questioned House after witnesses reported seeing him emerge from the embankment near Mrs. Muncey's body shortly before it was discovered, he told two different officers that he never left Donna Turner's trailer the previous evening, even recounting the series of television programs he watched before going to bed. He had worked to concoct an alibi we now know was a lie. [. . .] Ms. Turner initially confirmed House's alibi, but she changed her story when police warned her that covering up a homicide was a serious offense. Ms. Turner then told police that House had in fact left her house that night between 10:30 and 10:45 P.M. He came back some time later panting and sweating, shirtless and shoeless, and with various injuries.

Also on the day the body was found, Sheriff Earl Loy asked House if he was wearing the same clothes he wore the night before. House "hesitated," then stated that he had changed his shirt, *but not his jeans*. In other words, he specifically tried to conceal from the police that he had worn other jeans the night before, for reasons that were to become clear. Ms. Turner revealed that House's statement that he had not changed his jeans was a lie, and police retrieved House's dirty jeans from Ms. Turner's hamper. Of course, FBI testing revealed that House's jeans were stained with Mrs. Muncey's blood, and the District Court determined that House's new evidence of blood spillage did not undermine those test results. If in fact Mrs. Muncey's blood only got on House's jeans from later evidentiary spillage, House would have had no reason to lie to try to keep the existence of the concealed jeans from the police.

Through Ms. Turner's testimony at trial, the jury also heard House's story about what happened that night. He left Ms. Turner's trailer late at night to go for a walk. When he returned some time later—panting, sweating, and missing his shirt and shoes—he told her that some men in a truck tried to kill him. When Ms. Turner asked House about his injuries, he attributed them to fighting with his assailants. House retold this story to the District Court, saying that he initially lied to police because he was on parole and did not want to draw attention to himself. In other words, having nothing to hide and facing a murder charge, House lied—and when he was caught in the lie, he said he lied not to escape the murder charge, but solely to avoid unexplained difficulties with his parole officer. The jury rejected House's story about the night's events, and the District Court "considered Mr. House's demeanor and found that he was not a credible witness."

The jury also heard House's attempt to implicate Mr. Muncey in his wife's murder by calling Mrs. Muncey's brother, Ricky Green, as a witness. Mr. Green testified that two weeks before the murder, his sister called him to say that she and Mr. Muncey had been fighting, that she wanted to leave him, and that she was scared. Mr. Green also testified that the Munceys had marital problems, and that he had previously seen Mr. Muncey hit his wife. The jury rejected House's attempt to implicate Mr. Muncey, and the District Court was not persuaded by House's attempt to supplement this evidence at the evidentiary hearing, finding that his new witnesses were not credible.

Noticeably absent from the State's story about what happened to Mrs. Muncey on the night of her death was much mention of the semen found on Mrs. Muncey's clothing. House's single victory at the evidentiary hearing was new DNA evidence proving that the semen was deposited by Mr. Muncey. The majority identifies the semen evidence as "[c]entral to the State's case" against House, but House's jury would probably be quite surprised by this characterization. At trial, Agent Bigbee testified that from the semen stains on Mrs. Muncey's clothing, he could determine that the man who deposited the semen had type A blood, and was a secretor. Agent Bigbee also testified that House and Mr. Muncey both have type A blood, that House is a secretor, and that "[t]here is an *eighty (80%) percent* chance that [Mr. Muncey] is a secretor." Moreover, Agent Bigbee informed the jury that because 40 percent of people have type A blood, and 80 percent of those people are secretors, the semen on Mrs. Muncey's clothing could have been deposited by roughly one out of every three males. The jury was also informed several times by the defense that Mrs. Muncey's body was found fully clothed.

The majority describes House's sexual motive as "a central theme in the State's narrative linking House to the crime," and states that without the semen evidence, "a jury . . . would have found it necessary to establish some different motive, or, if the same motive, an intent far more specula-tive." The State, however, consistently directed the jury's attention *away* from motive, and sexual motive was far from a "central theme" of the State's case— presumably because of the highly ambiguous nature of the semen evidence recounted above. [. . .] The State did not mention the semen evidence in its opening statement to the jury, instead focusing on premeditation. The defense used its opening statement to expose lack of motive as a weakness in the State's case. After the State's equivocal presentation of the semen evi-dence through Agent Bigbee's testimony at trial, the State again made no reference to the semen evidence or to a motive in its closing argument, prompting the defense to again highlight this omission ("[W]hy was Carolyn

Muncey killed? We don't know. Is it important to have some motive? In your minds? What motive did Paul Gregory House have to go over and kill a woman that he barely knew? Who was still dressed, still clad in her clothes").

In rebuttal, the State disclaimed any responsibility to prove motive, again shifting the jury's focus to premeditation:

"The law says that if you take another person's life, you beat them, you strangle them, and then you don't succeed, and then you kill them by giving them multiple blows to the head, and one massive blow to the head, and that that causes their brains to crash against the other side of their skull, and caused such severe bleeding inside the skull itself, that you die—that it does not make any difference under God's heaven, what the motive was. That is what the law is. The law is that if motive is shown, it can be considered by the jury as evidence of guilt. But the law is that if you prove that a killing was done, beyond a reasonable doubt, by a person, and that he premeditated it, he planned it, it is not necessary for the jury to conclude why he did it."

As a follow-up to this explanation, when the trial was almost over and only in response to the defense's consistent prodding, the State made its first and only reference to a possible motive, followed immediately by another disclaimer:

"Now, you may have an idea why he did it. The evidence at the scene which seemed to suggest that he was subjecting this lady to some kind of indignity, why would you get a lady out of her house, late at night, in her night clothes, under the trick that her husband has had a wreck down by the creek? . . . Why is it that you choke her? Why is it that you repeatedly beat her? Why is it that she has scrapes all over her body? Well, it is because either you don't want her to tell what indignities you have subjected her to, or she is unwilling and fights against you, against being subjected to those indignities . . . . That is what the evidence at the scene suggests about motive. But motive is not an element of the crime. It is something that you can consider, or ignore. Whatever you prefer. The issue is not motive. The issue is premeditation."

It is on this "obliqu[e]" reference to the semen evidence during the State's closing argument that the majority bases its assertion that House's sexual motive was a "central theme in the State's narrative." Although it is possible that one or even some jurors might have entertained doubt about House's guilt absent the clearest evidence of motive, I do not find it more likely than not that *every* juror would have done so, and that is the legal standard under *Schlup*. The majority aphoristically states that "[w]hen identity is in question, motive is key." Not at all. Sometimes, when identity is in question, alibi is key. Here, House came up with one—and it fell apart, later admitted to be fabricated when his girlfriend would not lie to protect him. Scratches from a cat, indeed. Surely a reasonable juror would give the fact that an alibi had been made up and discredited significant weight. People facing a murder charge, who are innocent, do not make up a story out of concern that the truth might somehow disturb their parole officer. And people do not lie to the police about which jeans they were wearing the night of a murder, if they have no reason to believe the jeans would be stained with the blood shed by the victim in her last desperate struggle to live.

In *Schlup*, we made clear that the standard we adopted requires a "stronger showing than that needed to establish prejudice." In other words, House must show more than just a "reasonable probability that . . . the factfinder would have had a reasonable doubt respecting guilt." *Strickland* v. *Washington* (1984). House must present such compelling evidence of innocence that it becomes more likely than not that no single juror, acting reasonably, would vote to convict him. The majority's conclusion is that given the sisters' testimony (if believed), and Dr. Blake's rebutted testimony about how to interpret Agent Bigbee's enzyme marker analysis summary (if accepted), combined with the revelation that the semen on Mrs. Muncey's clothing was deposited by her husband (which the jurors knew was just as likely as the semen having been deposited by House), no reasonable juror would vote to convict House. Given the District Court's reliability findings about the first two pieces of evidence, the evidence before us now is not substantially different from that considered by House's jury. I therefore find it more likely than not that in light of this new evidence, at least one juror, acting reasonably, would vote to convict House. The evidence as a whole certainly does not establish that House is actually innocent of the crime of murdering Carolyn Muncey, and accordingly I dissent.

II. OPINIONS IN *MCCREARY COUNTY V. ACLU OF KENTUCKY*

Justice Souter delivered the opinion of the Court [joined by Justices Stevens, O'Connor, Breyer, and Ginsburg]

Executives of two counties posted a version of the Ten Commandments on the walls of their courthouses. After suits were filed charging violations of the Establishment Clause, the legislative body of each county adopted a resolution calling for a more extensive exhibit meant to show that the Commandments are Kentucky's "precedent legal code." The result in each instance was a modified display of the Commandments surrounded by texts containing religious references as their sole common element. After changing counsel, the counties revised the exhibits again by eliminating some documents, expanding the text set out in another, and adding some new ones.

The issues are whether a determination of the counties' purpose is a sound basis for ruling on the Establishment Clause complaints, and whether evaluation of the counties' claim of secular purpose for the ultimate displays may take their evolution into account. We hold that the counties' manifest objective may be dispositive of the constitutional enquiry, and that the development of the presentation should be considered when determining its purpose.

I

In the summer of 1999, petitioners McCreary County and Pulaski County, Kentucky (hereinafter Counties), put up in their respective courthouses large, gold-framed copies of an abridged text of the King James version of the Ten Commandments, including a citation to the Book of Exodus. In McCreary County, the placement of the Commandments responded to an order of the county legislative body requiring "the display [to] be posted in 'a very high traffic area' of the courthouse." In Pulaski County, amidst reported controversy over the propriety of the display, the Commandments were hung in a ceremony presided over by the county Judge-Executive, who called them "good rules to live by" and who recounted the story of an astronaut who became convinced "there must be a divine God" after viewing the Earth from the moon. The Judge-Executive was accompanied by the pastor of his church, who called the Commandments "a creed of ethics" and told the press after the ceremony that displaying the Commandments was "one of the greatest things the judge could have done to close out the millennium." [. . .]

In each county, the hallway display was "readily visible to . . . county citizens who use the courthouse to conduct their civic business, to obtain or renew driver's licenses and permits, to register cars, to pay local taxes, and to register to vote." In November 1999, respondents American Civil Liberties Union of Kentucky et al. sued the Counties in Federal District Court . . . and sought a preliminary injunction against maintaining the displays, which the ACLU charged were violations of the prohibition of religious establishment included in the First Amendment of the Constitution. Within a month, and before the District Court had responded to the request for injunction, the legislative body of each County authorized a second, expanded display, by nearly identical resolutions reciting that the Ten Commandments are "the precedent legal code upon which the civil and criminal codes of . . . Kentucky are founded." As directed by the resolutions, the Counties expanded the displays of the Ten Commandments in their locations, presumably along with copies of the resolution, which instructed that it, too, be posted. In addition to the first display's large framed copy of the edited King James version of the Commandments, the second included eight other documents in smaller frames, each either having a religious theme or excerpted to highlight a religious element.

After argument, the District Court entered a preliminary injunction on May 5, 2000, ordering that the "display . . . be removed from [each] County Courthouse IMMEDIATELY" and that no county official "erect or cause to be erected similar displays." The court's analysis of the situation followed the three-part formulation first stated in *Lemon* v. *Kurtzman* (1971). As to governmental purpose, it concluded that the original display "lack[ed] any secular purpose" because the Commandments "are a distinctly religious document, believed by many Christians and Jews to be the direct and revealed word of God." Although the Counties had maintained that the original display was meant to be educational, "[t]he narrow scope of the display—a single religious text unaccompanied by any interpretation explaining its role as a foundational document—can hardly be said to present meaningfully the story of this country's religious traditions." The court found that the second version also "clearly lack[ed] a secular purpose" because the "Count[ies] narrowly tailored [their] selection of foundational documents to incorporate only those with specific references to Christianity." The Counties filed a notice of appeal from the preliminary injunction but voluntarily dismissed it after hiring new lawyers. They then installed another display in each courthouse, the third within a year. No new resolution authorized this one, nor did the Counties repeal the resolutions that preceded the second. The posting consists of nine framed documents of equal size, one of them setting out the Ten Commandments explicitly identified as the "King James Version" at Exodus 20:3–17. [. . .]

Assembled with the Commandments are framed copies of the Magna Carta, the Declaration of Independence, the Bill of Rights, the lyrics of the Star Spangled Banner, the Mayflower Compact, the National Motto, the Preamble to the Kentucky Constitution, and a picture of Lady Justice. The collection is entitled "The Foundations of American Law and Government Display" and each document comes with a statement about its historical and legal significance. The comment on the Ten Commandments reads:

"The Ten Commandments have profoundly influenced the formation of Western legal thought and the formation of our country. That influence is clearly seen in the Declaration of Independence, which declared that 'We hold these truths to be self-evident, that all men are created equal, that they are endowed by their Creator with certain unalienable Rights, that among these are Life, Liberty, and the pursuit of Happiness.' The Ten Commandments provide the moral background of the Declaration of Independence and the foundation of our legal tradition."

The ACLU moved to supplement the preliminary injunction to enjoin the Counties' third display, and the Counties responded with several explanations for the new version, including desires "to demonstrate that the Ten Commandments were part of the foundation of American Law and Government" and "to educate the citizens of the county regarding some of the documents that played a significant role in the foundation of our system of law and government." The court, however, took the objective of proclaiming the Commandments' foundational value as "a religious, rather than secular, purpose" under *Stone* v. *Graham* (1980), and found that the assertion that the Counties' broader educational goals are secular "crumble[s] . . . upon an examination of the history of this litigation," In light of the Counties' decision to post the Commandments by themselves in the first instance, contrary to *Stone*, and later to "accentuat[e]" the religious objective by surrounding the Commandments with "specific references to Christianity," the District Court understood the Counties' "clear" purpose as being to post the Commandments, not to educate.

As requested, the trial court supplemented the injunction, and a divided panel of the Court of Appeals for the Sixth Circuit affirmed. The Circuit majority stressed that under *Stone*, displaying the Commandments bespeaks a religious object unless they are integrated with other material so as to carry "a secular message." The majority judges saw no integration here because of a "lack of a demonstrated analytical or historical connection [between the Commandments and] the other documents." They noted in particular that the Counties offered no support for their claim that the Ten Commandments "provide[d] the moral backdrop" to the Declaration of Independence or otherwise "profoundly influenced" it. The majority found that the Counties' purpose was religious, not educational, given the nature of the Commandments as "an active symbol of religion [stating] 'the religious duties of believers.'" The judges in the majority understood the identical displays to emphasize "a single religious influence, with no mention of any other religious or secular influences," and they took the very history of the litigation as evidence of the Counties' religious objective.

Judge Ryan dissented on the basis of wide recognition that religion, and the Ten Commandments in particular, have played a foundational part in the evolution of American law and government; he saw no reason to gainsay the Counties' claim of secular purposes. The dissent denied that the prior displays should have any bearing on the constitutionality of the current one: a "history of unconstitutional displays can[not] be used as a sword to strike down an otherwise constitutional display."

We granted certiorari, and now affirm.

II

Twenty-five years ago in a case [*Stone v. Graham,* 1980] prompted by posting the Ten Commandments in Kentucky's public schools, this Court recognized that the Commandments "are undeniably a sacred text in the Jewish and Christian faiths" and held that their display in public classrooms violated the First Amendment's bar against establishment of religion. *Stone* found a predominantly religious purpose in the government's posting of the Commandments, given their prominence as "'an instrument of religion.'" The Counties ask for a different approach here by arguing that official purpose is unknowable and the search for it inherently vain. In the alternative, the Counties would avoid the District Court's conclusion by having us limit the scope of the purpose enquiry so severely that any trivial rationalization would suffice, under a standard oblivious to the history of religious government action like the progression of exhibits in this case.

A

Ever since *Lemon* v. *Kurtzman* summarized the three familiar considerations for evaluating Establishment Clause claims, looking to whether government action has "a secular legislative purpose" has been a common, albeit seldom dispositive, element of our cases. Though we have found government action motivated by an illegitimate purpose only four times since *Lemon*, and "the secular purpose requirement alone may rarely be determinative . . . , it nevertheless serves an important function."

The touchstone for our analysis is the principle that the "First Amendment mandates governmental neutrality between religion and religion, and between religion and nonreligion." When the government acts with the ostensible and predominant purpose of advancing religion, it violates that central Establishment Clause value of official religious neutrality, there being no neutrality when the government's ostensible object is to take sides. Manifesting a purpose to favor one faith over another, or adherence to religion generally, clashes with the "understanding, reached . . . after decades of religious war, that liberty and social stability demand a religious tolerance that respects the religious views of all citizens . . . " By showing a purpose to favor religion, the government "sends the . . . message to . . . nonadherents 'that they are outsiders, not full members of the political community, and an accompanying message to adherents that they are insiders, favored members. . . .'" [. . .]

B

Despite the intuitive importance of official purpose to the realization of Establishment Clause values, the Counties ask us to abandon *Lemon*'s purpose test, or at least to truncate any enquiry into purpose here. Their first argument is that the very consideration of purpose is deceptive: according to them, true "purpose" is unknowable, and its search merely an excuse for courts to act selectively and unpredictably in picking out evidence of subjective intent. The assertions are as seismic as they are unconvincing.

Examination of purpose is a staple of statutory interpretation that makes up the daily fare of every appellate court in the country, and governmental purpose is a key element of a good deal of constitutional doctrine. [. . .] With enquiries into purpose this common, if they were nothing but hunts for mares' nests deflecting attention from bare judicial will, the whole notion of purpose in law would have dropped into disrepute long ago.

But scrutinizing purpose does make practical sense, as in Establishment Clause analysis, where an understanding of official objective emerges from readily discoverable fact, without any judicial psychoanalysis of a drafter's heart of hearts. The eyes that look to purpose belong to an "'objective observer,'" one who takes account of the traditional external signs that show up in the "'text, legislative history, and implementation of the statute,'" or comparable official act. [. . .] There is, then, nothing hinting at an unpredictable or disingenuous exercise when a court enquires into purpose after a claim is raised under the Establishment Clause. [. . .]

Nor is there any indication that the enquiry is rigged in practice to finding a religious purpose dominant every time a case is filed. In the past, the test has not been fatal very often, presumably because government does not generally act unconstitutionally, with the predominant purpose of advancing religion. That said, one consequence of the corollary that Establishment Clause analysis does not look to the veiled psyche of government officers could be that in some of the cases in which establishment complaints failed, savvy officials had disguised their religious intent so cleverly that the objective observer just missed it. But that is no reason for great constitutional concern. If someone in the government hides religious motive so well that the "'objective observer, acquainted with the text, legislative history, and implementation of the statute,'" cannot see it, then without something more the government does not make a divisive announcement that in itself amounts to taking religious sides. A secret motive stirs up no strife and does nothing to make outsiders of non-adherents, and it suffices to wait and see whether such government action turns out to have (as it may even be likely to have) the illegitimate effect of advancing religion.

C

After declining the invitation to abandon concern with purpose wholesale, we also have to avoid the Counties' alternative tack of trivializing the enquiry into it. The Counties would read the cases as if the purpose enquiry were so naive that any transparent claim to secularity would satisfy it, and they would cut context out of the enquiry, to the point of ignoring history, no matter what bearing it actually had on the significance of current circumstances. There is no precedent for the Counties' arguments, or reason supporting them.

1

Lemon said that government action must have "a secular . . . purpose," and after a host of cases it is fair to add that although a legislature's stated reasons will generally get deference, the secular purpose required has to be genuine, not a sham, and not merely secondary to a religious objective. [. . .] Even the Counties' own cited authority confirms that we have not made the purpose test a pushover for any secular claim.

The Counties' second proffered limitation can be dispatched quickly. They argue that purpose in a case like this one should be inferred, if at all, only from the latest news about the last in a series of governmental actions, however close they may all be in time and subject. But the world is not made brand new every morning, and the Counties are simply asking us to ignore perfectly probative evidence; they want an absentminded objective observer, not one presumed to be familiar with the history of the government's actions and competent to learn what history has to show. The Counties' position just bucks common sense: reasonable observers have reasonable memories, and our precedents sensibly forbid an observer "to turn a blind eye to the context in which [the] policy arose."

III

[. . .] We take *Stone* as the initial legal benchmark, our only case dealing with the constitutionality of displaying the Commandments. *Stone* recognized that the Commandments are an "instrument of religion" and that, at least on the facts before it, the display of their text could presumptively be understood as meant to advance religion: although state law specifically required their posting in public school classrooms, their isolated exhibition did not leave room even for an argument that secular education explained their being there. But *Stone* did not purport to decide the constitutionality of every possible way the Commandments might be set out by the government, and under the Establishment Clause detail is key. [. . .] Hence, we look to the record of evidence showing the progression leading up to the third display of the Commandments.

A

The display rejected in *Stone* had two obvious similarities to the first one in the sequence here: both set out a text of the Commandments as distinct from any traditionally symbolic representation, and each stood alone, not part of an arguably secular display. *Stone* stressed the significance of integrating the Commandments into a secular scheme to forestall the broadcast of an otherwise clearly religious message, and for good reason, the Commandments being a central point of reference in the religious and moral history of Jews and Christians. They proclaim the existence of a monotheistic god (no other gods). They regulate details of religious obligation (no graven images, no sabbath breaking, no vain oath swearing). And they unmistakably rest even the universally accepted prohibitions (as against murder, theft, and the like) on the sanction of the divinity proclaimed at the beginning of the text. Displaying that text is thus different from a symbolic depiction, like tablets with 10 roman numerals, which could be seen as alluding to a general notion of law, not a sectarian conception of faith. Where the text is set out, the insistence of the religious message is hard to avoid in the absence of a context plausibly suggesting a message going beyond an excuse to promote the religious point of view. The display in *Stone* had no context that might have indicated an object beyond the religious character of the text, and the Counties' solo exhibit here did nothing more to counter the sectarian implication than the postings at issue in *Stone*. Actually, the posting by the Counties lacked even the *Stone* display's implausible disclaimer that the Commandments were set out to show their effect on the civil law. What is more, at the ceremony for posting the framed Commandments in Pulaski County, the county executive was accompanied by his pastor, who testified to the certainty of the existence of God. The reasonable observer could only think that the Counties meant to emphasize and celebrate the Commandments' religious message.

This is not to deny that the Commandments have had influence on civil or secular law; a major text of a majority religion is bound to be felt. The point is simply that the original text viewed in its entirety is an unmistakably religious statement dealing with religious obligations and with morality subject to religious sanction. When the government initiates an effort to place this statement alone in public view, a religious object is unmistakable.

B

Once the Counties were sued, they modified the exhibits and invited additional insight into their purpose in a display that hung for about six months. This new one was the product of forthright and nearly identical Pulaski and McCreary County resolutions listing a series of American historical documents with theistic and Christian references, which were to be posted in order to furnish a setting for displaying the Ten Commandments and any "other Kentucky and American historical documen[t]" without raising concern about "any Christian or religious references" in them. [. . .] In this second display, unlike the first, the Commandments were not hung in isolation, merely leaving the Counties' purpose to emerge from the pervasively religious text of the Commandments themselves. Instead, the second version was required to include the statement of the government's purpose expressly set out in the county resolutions, and underscored it by juxtaposing the Commandments to other documents with highlighted references to God as their sole common element. The display's unstinting focus was on religious passages, showing that the Counties were posting the Commandments precisely because of their sectarian content. That demonstration of the government's objective was enhanced by serial religious references and the accompanying resolution's claim about the embodiment of ethics in Christ. Together, the display and resolution presented an indisputable, and undisputed, showing of an impermissible purpose.

Today, the Counties make no attempt to defend their undeniable objective, but instead hopefully describe version two as "dead and buried." Their refusal to defend the second display is understandable, but the reasonable observer could not forget it.

C

1

After the Counties changed lawyers, they mounted a third display, without a new resolution or repeal of the old one. The result was the "Foundations of American Law and Government" exhibit, which placed the Commandments in the company of other documents the Counties thought especially significant in the historical foundation of American government. In trying to persuade the District Court to lift the preliminary injunction, the Counties cited several new purposes for the third version, including a desire "to educate the citizens of the county regarding some of the documents that played a significant role in the foundation of our system of law and government." The Counties' claims did not, however, persuade the court, intimately familiar with the details of this litigation, or the Court of Appeals, neither of which found a legitimizing secular purpose in this third version of the display. The conclusions of the two courts preceding us in this case are well warranted.

These new statements of purpose were presented only as a litigating position, there being no further authorizing action by the Counties' governing boards. And although repeal of the earlier county authorizations would not have erased them from the record of evidence bearing on current purpose, the extraordinary resolutions for the second display passed just months earlier were not repealed or otherwise repudiated. Indeed, the sectarian spirit of the common resolution found enhanced expression in the third display, which quoted more of the purely religious language of the Commandments than the first two displays had done. Nor did the selection of posted material suggest a clear theme that might prevail over evidence of the continuing religious object. In a collection of documents said to be "foundational" to American government, it is at least odd to include a patriotic anthem, but to omit the Fourteenth Amendment, the most significant structural provision adopted since the original Framing. And it is no less baffling to leave out the original Constitution of 1787 while quoting the 1215 Magna Carta even to the point of its declaration that "fish-weirs shall be removed from the Thames." If an observer found these choices and omissions perplexing in isolation, he would be puzzled for a different reason when he read the Declaration of Independence seeking confirmation for the Counties' posted explanation that the "Ten Commandments' . . . influence is clearly seen in the Declaration,"; in fact the observer would find that the Commandments are sanctioned as divine imperatives, while the Declaration of Independence holds that the authority of government to enforce the law derives "from the consent of the governed." If the observer had not thrown up his hands, he would probably suspect that the Counties were simply reaching for any way to keep a religious document on the walls of courthouses constitutionally required to embody religious neutrality.

2

In holding the preliminary injunction adequately supported by evidence that the Counties' purpose had not changed at the third stage, we do not decide that the Counties' past actions forever taint any effort on their part to deal with the subject matter. We hold only that purpose needs to be taken seriously under the Establishment Clause and needs to be understood in light of context; an implausible claim that governmental purpose has changed should not carry the day in a court of law any more than in a head with common sense. It is enough to say here that district courts are fully capable of adjusting preliminary relief to take account of genuine changes in constitutionally significant conditions. Nor do we have occasion here to hold that a sacred text can never be integrated constitutionally into a governmental display on the subject of law, or American history. We do not forget, and in this litigation have frequently been reminded, that our own courtroom frieze was deliberately designed in the exercise of governmental authority so as to include the figure of Moses holding tablets exhibiting a portion of the Hebrew text of the later, secularly phrased Commandments; in the company of 17 other lawgivers, most of them secular figures, there is no risk that Moses would strike an observer as evidence that the National Government was violating neutrality in religion.

IV

The importance of neutrality as an interpretive guide is no less true now than it was when the Court broached the principle in *Everson* v. *Board of Ed. of Ewing* (1947), and a word needs to be said about the different view taken in today's dissent. We all agree, of course, on the need for some interpretative help.

The First Amendment contains no textual definition of "establishment," and the term is certainly not self-defining. [. . .] There is no simple answer, for more than one reason.

The prohibition on establishment covers a variety of issues from prayer in widely varying government settings, to financial aid for religious individuals and institutions, to comment on religious questions. In these varied settings, issues of about interpreting inexact Establishment Clause language, like difficult interpretative issues generally, arise from the tension of competing values, each constitutionally respectable, but none open to realization to the logical limit.

[. . .] Given the variety of interpretative problems, the principle of neutrality has provided a good sense of direction: the government may not favor one religion over another, or religion over irreligion, religious choice being the prerogative of individuals under the Free Exercise Clause. The principle has been helpful simply because it responds to one of the major concerns that prompted adoption of the Religion Clauses. The Framers and the citizens of their time intended not only to protect the integrity of individual conscience in religious matters, but to guard against the civic divisiveness that follows when the Government weighs in on one side of religious debate; nothing does a better job of roiling society, a point that needed no explanation to the descendants of English Puritans and Cavaliers (or Massachusetts Puritans and Baptists). A sense of the past thus points to governmental neutrality as an objective of the Establishment Clause, and a sensible standard for applying it. To be sure, given its generality as a principle, an appeal to neutrality alone cannot possibly lay every issue to rest, or tell us what issues on the margins are substantial enough for constitutional significance, a point that has been clear from the Founding era to modern times. [. . .] But invoking neutrality is a prudent way of keeping sight of something the Framers of the First Amendment thought important.

The dissent, however, puts forward a limitation on the application of the neutrality principle, with citations to historical evidence said to show that the Framers understood the ban on establishment of religion as sufficiently narrow to allow the government to espouse submission to the divine will. The dissent identifies God as the God of monotheism, all of whose three principal strains (Jewish, Christian, and Muslim) acknowledge the religious importance of the Ten Commandments. On the dissent's view, it apparently follows that even rigorous espousal of a common element of this common monotheism, is consistent with the establishment ban.

But the dissent's argument for the original understanding is flawed from the outset by its failure to consider the full range of evidence showing what the Framers believed. The dissent is certainly correct in putting forward evidence that some of the Framers thought some endorsement of religion was compatible with the establishment ban; the dissent quotes the first President as stating that "national morality [cannot] prevail in exclusion of religious principle," for example, and it cites his first Thanksgiving proclamation giving thanks to God. Surely if expressions like these from Washington and his contemporaries were all we had to go on, there would be a good case that the neutrality principle has the effect of broadening the ban on establishment beyond the Framers' understanding of it (although there would, of course, still be the question of whether the historical case could overcome some 60 years of precedent taking neutrality as its guiding principle).

But the fact is that we do have more to go on, for there is also evidence supporting the proposition that the Framers intended the Establishment Clause to require governmental neutrality in matters of religion, including neutrality in statements acknowledging religion. The very language of the Establishment Clause represented a significant departure from early drafts that merely prohibited a single national religion, and, the final language instead "extended [the] prohibition to state support for 'religion' in general." The historical record, moreover, is complicated beyond the dissent's account by the writings and practices of figures no less influential than Thomas Jefferson and James Madison. Jefferson, for example, refused to issue Thanksgiving Proclamations because he believed that they violated the Constitution. And Madison, whom the dissent claims as supporting its thesis, criticized Virginia's general assessment tax not just because it required people to donate "three pence" to religion, but because "it is itself a signal of persecution. It degrades from the equal rank of Citizens all those whose opinions in Religion do not bend to those of the Legislative authority." [. . .] The fair inference is that there was no common understanding about the limits of the establishment prohibition, and the dissent's conclusion that its narrower view was the original understanding, stretches the evidence beyond tensile capacity. What the evidence does show is a group of statesmen, like others before and after them, who proposed a guarantee with contours not wholly worked out, leaving the Establishment Clause with edges still to be determined. And none the worse for that. Indeterminate edges are the kind to have in a constitution meant to endure, and to meet "exigencies which, if foreseen at all, must have been seen dimly, and which can be best provided for as they occur." *McCulloch* v. *Maryland* (1819).

While the dissent fails to show a consistent original understanding from which to argue that the neutrality principle should be rejected, it does manage to deliver a surprise. As mentioned, the dissent says that the deity the Framers had in mind was the God of monotheism, with the consequence that government may espouse a tenet of traditional monotheism. This is truly a remarkable view. Other members of the Court have dissented on the ground that the Establishment Clause bars nothing more than governmental preference for one religion over another, but at least religion has previously been treated inclusively. Today's dissent, however, apparently means that government should be free to approve the core beliefs of a favored religion over the tenets of others, a view that should trouble anyone who prizes religious liberty. Certainly history cannot justify it; on the contrary, history shows that the religion of concern to the Framers was not that of the monotheistic faiths generally, but Christianity in particular, a fact that no member of this Court takes as a premise for construing the Religion Clauses. Justice Story probably reflected the thinking of the framing generation when he wrote in his Commentaries that the purpose of the Clause was "not to countenance, much less to advance, Mahometanism, or Judaism, or infidelity, by prostrating Christianity; but to exclude all rivalry among Christian sects." The Framers would, therefore, almost certainly object to the dissent's unstated reasoning that because Christianity was a monotheistic "religion," monotheism with Mosaic antecedents should be a touchstone of establishment interpretation. Even on originalist critiques of existing precedent there is, it seems, no escape from interpretative consequences that would surprise the Framers. Thus, it appears to be common ground in the interpretation of a Constitution "intended to endure for ages to come," *McCulloch* v. *Maryland,* that applications unanticipated by the Framers are inevitable.

Historical evidence thus supports no solid argument for changing course (whatever force the argument might have when directed at the existing precedent), whereas public discourse at the present time certainly raises no doubt about the value of the interpretative approach invoked for 60 years now. We are centuries away from the St. Bartholomew's Day massacre and the treatment of heretics in early Massachusetts, but the divisiveness of religion in current public life is inescapable. This is no time to deny the prudence of understanding the Establishment Clause to require the Government to stay neutral on religious belief, which is reserved for the conscience of the individual.

V

Given the ample support for the District Court's finding of a predominantly religious purpose behind the Counties' third display, we affirm the Sixth Circuit in upholding the preliminary injunction.

It is so ordered.

Justice O'Connor, concurring.

I join in the Court's opinion. The First Amendment expresses our Nation's fundamental commitment to religious liberty by means of two provisions—one protecting the free exercise of religion, the other barring establishment of religion. They were written by the descendents of people who had come to this land precisely so that they could practice their religion freely. Together with the other First Amendment guarantees—of free speech, a free press, and the rights to assemble and petition—the Religion Clauses were designed to safeguard the freedom of conscience and belief that those immigrants had sought. They embody an idea that was once considered radical: Free people are entitled to free and diverse thoughts, which government ought neither to constrain nor to direct.

Reasonable minds can disagree about how to apply the Religion Clauses in a given case. But the goal of the Clauses is clear: to carry out the Founders' plan of preserving religious liberty to the fullest extent possible in a pluralistic society. By enforcing the Clauses, we have kept religion a matter for the individual conscience, not for the prosecutor or bureaucrat. At a time when we see around the world the violent consequences of the assumption of religious authority by government, Americans may count themselves fortunate: Our regard for constitutional boundaries has protected us from similar travails, while allowing private religious exercise to flourish. The well-known statement that "[w]e are a religious people," *Zorach* v. *Clauson* (1952), has proved true. Americans attend their places of worship more often than do citizens of other developed nations, and describe religion as playing an especially important role in their lives. Those who would renegotiate the boundaries between church and state must therefore answer a difficult question: Why would we trade a system that has served us so well for one that has served others so poorly?

Our guiding principle has been James Madison's—that "[t]he Religion . . . of every man must be left to the conviction and conscience of every man." Memorial and Remonstrance Against Religious Assessments. To that end, we have held that the guarantees of religious freedom protect citizens from religious incursions by the States as well as by the Federal Government. *Everson* v. *Board of Ed. of Ewing* (1947). Government may not coerce a person into worshiping against her will, nor prohibit her from worshiping according to it. It may not prefer one religion over another or promote religion over nonbelief. It may not entangle itself with religion. And government may not, by "endorsing religion or a religious practice," "mak[e] adherence to religion relevant to a person's standing in the political community." *Wallace* v. *Jaffree* (1985) (O'Connor, J., concurring in judgment).

When we enforce these restrictions, we do so for the same reason that guided the Framers—respect for religion's special role in society. Our Founders conceived of a Republic receptive to voluntary religious expression, and provided for the possibility of judicial intervention when government action threatens or impedes such expression. Voluntary religious belief and expression may be as threatened when government takes the mantle of religion upon itself as when government directly interferes with private religious practices.

When the government associates one set of religious beliefs with the state and identifies nonadherents as outsiders, it encroaches upon the individual's decision about whether and how to worship. In the marketplace of ideas, the government has vast resources and special status. Government religious expression therefore risks crowding out private observance and distorting the natural interplay between competing beliefs. Allowing government to be a potential mouthpiece for competing religious ideas risks the sort of division that might easily spill over into suppression of rival beliefs. Tying secular and religious authority together poses risks to both.

Given the history of this particular display of the Ten Commandments, the Court correctly finds an Establishment Clause violation. The purpose behind the counties' display is relevant because it conveys an unmistakable message of endorsement to the reasonable observer.

It is true that many Americans find the Commandments in accord with their personal beliefs. But we do not count heads before enforcing the First Amendment. See *West Virginia Bd. of Ed.* v. *Barnette* (1943) ("The very purpose of a Bill of Rights was to withdraw certain subjects from the vicissitudes of political controversy, to place them beyond the reach of majorities and officials and to establish them as legal principles to be applied by the courts"). Nor can we accept the theory that Americans who do not accept the Commandments' validity are outside the First Amendment's protections. There is no list of approved and disapproved beliefs appended to the First Amendment—and the Amendment's broad terms ("free exercise," "establishment," "religion") do not admit of such a cramped reading. It is true that the Framers lived at a time when our national religious diversity was neither as robust nor as well recognized as it is now. They may not have foreseen the variety of religions for which this Nation would eventually provide a home. They surely could not have predicted new religions, some of them born in this country. But they did know that line-drawing between religions is an enterprise that, once begun, has no logical stopping point. They worried that "the same authority which can establish Christianity, in exclusion of all other Religions, may establish with the same ease any particular sect of Christians, in exclusion of all other Sects." [Madison] Memorial. The Religion Clauses, as a result, protect adherents of all religions, as well as those who believe in no religion at all.

We owe our First Amendment to a generation with a profound commitment to religion and a profound commitment to religious liberty—visionaries who held their faith "with enough confidence to believe that what should be rendered to God does not need to be decided and collected by Caesar." *Zorach,* (Jackson, J., dissenting). In my opinion, the display at issue was an establishment of religion in violation of our Constitution. For the reasons given above, I join in the Court's opinion.

Justice Scalia, with whom The Chief Justice and Justice Thomas join, and with whom Justice Kennedy joins as to Parts II and III, dissenting.

I would uphold McCreary County and Pulaski County, Kentucky's (hereinafter Counties) displays of the Ten Commandments. I shall discuss first, why the Court's oft repeated assertion that the government cannot favor religious practice is false; second, why today's opinion extends the scope of that falsehood even beyond prior cases; and third, why even on the basis of the Court's false assumptions the judgment here is wrong.

I

A

On September 11, 2001, I was attending in Rome, Italy, an international conference of judges and lawyers, principally from Europe and the United States. That night and the next morning virtually all of the participants watched, in their hotel rooms, the address to the Nation by the President of the United States concerning the murderous attacks upon the Twin Towers and the Pentagon, in which thousands of Americans had been killed. The address ended, as Presidential addresses often do, with the prayer "God bless America." The next afternoon I was approached by one of the judges from a European country, who, after extending his profound condolences for my country's loss, sadly observed "How I wish that the Head of State of my country, at a similar time of national tragedy and distress, could conclude his address 'God bless _____.' It is of course absolutely forbidden."

That is one model of the relationship between church and state—a model spread across Europe by the armies of Napoleon, and reflected in the Constitution of France, which begins "France is [a] . . . secular . . . Republic." Religion is to be strictly excluded from the public forum. This is not, and never was, the model adopted by America. George Washington added to the form of Presidential oath prescribed by Art. II, §1, cl. 8, of the Constitution, the concluding words "so help me God." The Supreme Court under John Marshall opened its sessions with the prayer, "God save the United States and this Honorable Court." The First Congress instituted the practice of beginning its legislative sessions with a prayer. The same week that Congress submitted the Establishment Clause as part of the Bill of Rights for ratification by the States, it enacted legislation providing for paid chaplains in the House and Senate. The day after the First Amendment was proposed, the same Congress that had proposed it requested the President to proclaim "a day of public thanksgiving and prayer, to be observed, by acknowledging, with grateful hearts, the many and signal favours of Almighty God." President Washington offered the first Thanksgiving Proclamation shortly thereafter, devoting November 26, 1789, on behalf of the American people "'to the service of that great and glorious

Being who is the beneficent author of all the good that is, that was, or that will be,'" thus beginning a tradition of offering gratitude to God that continues today. The same Congress also reenacted the Northwest Territory Ordinance of 1787, Article III of which provided: "Religion, morality, and knowledge, being necessary to good government and the happiness of mankind, schools and the means of education shall forever be encouraged." And of course the First Amendment itself accords religion (and no other manner of belief) special constitutional protection.

These actions of our First President and Congress and the Marshall Court were not idiosyncratic; they reflected the beliefs of the period. Those who wrote the Constitution believed that morality was essential to the well-being of society and that encouragement of religion was the best way to foster morality. The "fact that the Founding Fathers believed devotedly that there was a God and that the unalienable rights of man were rooted in Him is clearly evidenced in their writings, from the Mayflower Compact to the Constitution itself." President Washington opened his Presidency with a prayer, and reminded his fellow citizens at the conclusion of it that "reason and experience both forbid us to expect that National morality can prevail in exclusion of religious principle." President John Adams wrote to the Massachusetts Militia, "we have no government armed with power capable of contending with human passions unbridled by morality and religion. . . . Our Constitution was made only for a moral and religious people. It is wholly inadequate to the government of any other." Thomas Jefferson concluded his second inaugural address by inviting his audience to pray:

"I shall need, too, the favor of that Being in whose hands we are, who led our fathers, as Israel of old, from their native land and planted them in a country flowing with all the necessaries and comforts of life; who has covered our infancy with His providence and our riper years with His wisdom and power and to whose goodness I ask you to join in supplications with me that He will so enlighten the minds of your servants, guide their councils, and prosper their measures that whatsoever they do shall result in your good, and shall secure to you the peace, friendship, and approbation of all nations."

James Madison, in his first inaugural address, likewise placed his confidence "in the guardianship and guidance of that Almighty Being whose power regulates the destiny of nations, whose blessings have been so conspicuously dispensed to this rising Republic, and to whom we are bound to address our devout gratitude for the past, as well as our fervent supplications and best hopes for the future."

Nor have the views of our people on this matter significantly changed. Presidents continue to conclude the Presidential oath with the words "so help me God." Our legislatures, state and national, continue to open their sessions with prayer led by official chaplains. The sessions of this Court continue to open with the prayer "God save the United States and this Honorable Court." Invocation of the Almighty by our public figures, at all levels of government, remains commonplace. Our coinage bears the motto "IN GOD WE TRUST." And our Pledge of Allegiance contains the acknowledgment that we are a Nation "under God." As one of our Supreme Court opinions rightly observed, "We are a religious people whose institutions presuppose a Supreme Being."

With all of this reality (and much more) staring it in the face, how can the Court *possibly* assert that "'the First Amendment mandates governmental neutrality between . . . religion and nonreligion,'" and that "[m]anifesting a purpose to favor . . . adherence to religion generally," is unconstitutional? Who says so? Surely not the words of the Constitution. Surely not the history and traditions that reflect our society's constant understanding of those words. Surely not even the current sense of our society, recently reflected in an Act of Congress adopted *unanimously* by the Senate and with only 5 nays in the House of Representatives, criticizing a Court of Appeals opinion that had held "under God" in the Pledge of Allegiance unconstitutional. Nothing stands behind the Court's assertion that governmental affirmation of the society's belief in God is unconstitutional except the Court's own say-so, citing as support only the unsubstantiated say-so of earlier Courts going back no farther than the mid-20th century. And it is, moreover, a thoroughly discredited say-so. It is discredited, to begin with, because a majority of the Justices on the current Court (including at least one Member of today's majority) have, in separate opinions, repudiated the brain-spun "*Lemon* test" that embodies the supposed principle of neutrality between religion and irreligion. And it is discredited because the Court has not had the courage (or the foolhardiness) to apply the neutrality principle consistently.

What distinguishes the rule of law from the dictatorship of a shifting Supreme Court majority is the absolutely indispensable requirement that judicial opinions be grounded in consistently applied principle. That is what prevents judges from ruling now this way, now that—thumbs up or thumbs down—as their personal preferences dictate. Today's opinion forthrightly (or actually, somewhat less than forthrightly) admits that it does not rest upon consistently applied principle. In a revealing footnote, the Court acknowledges that the "Establishment Clause doctrine" it purports to be applying "lacks the comfort of categorical absolutes." What the Court means by this lovely euphemism is that sometimes the Court chooses to decide cases on the principle that government cannot favor religion, and sometimes it does not. The footnote goes on to say that "[i]n special instances we have found good reason" to dispense with the principle, but "[n]o such reasons present themselves here." It does not identify all of those "special instances," much less identify the "good reason" for their existence.

[. . .] Besides appealing to the demonstrably false principle that the government cannot favor religion over irreligion, today's opinion suggests that the posting of the Ten Commandments violates the principle that the government cannot favor one religion over another. That is indeed a valid principle where public aid or assistance to religion is concerned, or where the free exercise of religion is at issue, but it necessarily applies in a more limited sense to public acknowledgment of the Creator. If religion in the public forum had to be entirely nondenominational, there could be no religion in the public forum at all. One cannot say the word "God," or "the Almighty," one cannot offer public supplication or thanksgiving, without contradicting the beliefs of some people that there are many gods, or that God or the gods pay no attention to human affairs. With respect to public acknowledgment of religious belief, it is entirely clear from our Nation's historical practices that the Establishment Clause permits this disregard of polytheists and believers in unconcerned deities, just as it permits the disregard of devout atheists. The Thanksgiving Proclamation issued by George Washington at the instance of the First Congress was scrupulously nondenominational—but it was monotheistic.

[. . .] Historical practices thus demonstrate that there is a distance between the acknowledgment of a single Creator and the establishment of a religion. The former is, as *Marsh* v. *Chambers* put it, "a tolerable acknowledgment of beliefs widely held among the people of this country." The three most popular religions in the United States, Christianity, Judaism, and Islam—which combined account for 97.7% of all believers—are monotheistic. All of them, moreover (Islam included), believe that the Ten Commandments were given by God to Moses, and are divine prescriptions for a virtuous life. Publicly honoring the Ten Commandments is thus indistinguishable, insofar as discriminating against other religions is concerned, from publicly honoring God. Both practices are recognized across such a broad and diverse range of the population—from Christians to Muslims—that they cannot be reasonably understood as a government endorsement of a particular religious viewpoint.

B

A few remarks are necessary in response to the criticism of this dissent by the Court, as well as Justice Stevens' criticism in the related case of *Van Orden* v. *Perry*. *Justice Stevens'* writing is largely devoted to an attack upon a straw man. "[R]eliance on early religious proclamations and statements made by the Founders is . . . problematic," he says, "because those views were not espoused at the Constitutional Convention in 1787 nor enshrined in the Constitution's text." But I have not relied upon (as he and the Court in this case do) mere "proclamations and statements" of the Founders. I have relied primarily upon official acts and official proclamations of the United

States or of the component branches of its Government, including the First Congress's beginning of the tradition of legislative prayer to God, its appointment of congressional chaplains, its legislative proposal of a Thanksgiving Proclamation, and its reenactment of the Northwest Territory Ordinance; our first President's issuance of a Thanksgiving Proclamation; and invocation of God at the opening of sessions of the Supreme Court. The only mere "proclamations and statements" of the Founders I have relied upon were statements of Founders who occupied federal office, and spoke in at least a quasi-official capacity—Washington's prayer at the opening of his Presidency and his Farewell Address, President John Adams' letter to the Massachusetts Militia, and Jefferson's and Madison's inaugural addresses. The Court and Justice Stevens, by contrast, appeal to no official or even quasi-official action in support of their view of the Establishment Clause—only James Madison's Memorial and Remonstrance Against Religious Assessments, written before the federal Constitution had even been proposed, two letters written by Madison long after he was President, and the quasi-official *inaction* of Thomas Jefferson in refusing to issue a Thanksgiving Proclamation. The Madison Memorial and Remonstrance, dealing as it does with enforced contribution to religion rather than public acknowledgment of God, is irrelevant; one of the letters is utterly ambiguous as to the point at issue here, and should not be read to contradict Madison's statements in his first inaugural address, quoted earlier; even the other letter does not disapprove public acknowledgment of God, unless one posits (what Madison's own actions as President would contradict) that reference to God contradicts "the equality of *all* religious sects." And as to Jefferson: the notoriously self-contradicting Jefferson did not choose to have his nonauthorship of a Thanksgiving Proclamation inscribed on his tombstone. What he did have inscribed was his authorship of the Virginia Statute for Religious Freedom, a governmental act which begins "Whereas Almighty God hath created the mind free . . . ."

It is no answer for Justice Stevens to say that the understanding that these official and quasi-official actions reflect was not "enshrined in the Constitution's text." The Establishment Clause, upon which Justice Stevens would rely, *was* enshrined in the Constitution's text, and these official actions show *what it meant*. There were doubtless some who thought it should have a broader meaning, but those views were plainly rejected. Justice Stevens says that reliance on these actions is "bound to paint a misleading picture," but it is hard to see why. What is more probative of the meaning of the Establishment Clause than the actions of the very Congress that proposed it, and of the first President charged with observing it?

Justice Stevens also appeals to the undoubted fact that some in the founding generation thought that the Religion Clauses of the First Amendment should have a *narrower* meaning, protecting only the Christian religion or perhaps only Protestantism. I am at a loss to see how this helps his case, except by providing a cloud of obfuscating smoke. (Since most thought the Clause permitted government invocation of monotheism, and some others thought it permitted government invocation of Christianity, he proposes that it be construed not to permit any government invocation of religion at all.) At any rate, those narrower views of the Establishment Clause were as clearly rejected as the more expansive ones. Washington's First Thanksgiving Proclamation is merely an example. *All* of the actions of Washington and the First Congress upon which I have relied, virtually all Thanksgiving Proclamations throughout our history, and *all* the other examples of our Government's favoring religion that I have cited, have invoked God, but not Jesus Christ.

[. . .] Justice Stevens argues that original meaning should not be the touchstone anyway, but that we should rather "expoun[d] the meaning of constitutional provisions with one eye towards our Nation's history and the other fixed on its democratic aspirations." [. . .] Even assuming, however, that the meaning of the Constitution ought to change according to "democratic aspirations," why are those aspirations to be found in Justices' notions of what the Establishment Clause ought to mean, rather than in the democratically adopted dispositions of our current society? As I have observed above, numerous provisions of our laws and numerous continuing practices of our people demonstrate that the government's invocation of God (and hence the government's invocation of the Ten Commandments) is unobjectionable—including a statute enacted by Congress almost unanimously less than three years ago, stating that "under God" in the Pledge of Allegiance is constitutional. To ignore all this is not to give effect to "democratic aspirations" but to frustrate them.

Finally, I must respond to Justice Stevens' assertion that I would "marginaliz[e] the belief systems of more than 7 million Americans" who adhere to religions that are not monotheistic. Surely that is a gross exaggeration. The beliefs of those citizens are entirely protected by the Free Exercise Clause, and by those aspects of the Establishment Clause that do not relate to government acknowledgment of the Creator. Invocation of God despite their beliefs is permitted not because nonmonotheistic religions cease to be religions recognized by the religion clauses of the First Amendment, but because governmental invocation of God is not an establishment. Justice Stevens fails to recognize that in the context of public acknowledgments of God there are legitimate *competing* interests: On the one hand, the interest of that minority in not feeling "excluded"; but on the other, the interest of the overwhelming majority of religious believers in being able to give God thanks and supplication *as a people,* and with respect to our national endeavors. Our national tradition has resolved that conflict in favor of the majority. It is not for this Court to change a disposition that accounts, many Americans think, for the phenomenon remarked upon in a quotation attributed to various authors, including Bismarck, but which I prefer to associate with Charles de Gaulle: "God watches over little children, drunkards, and the United States of America."

II

As bad as the *Lemon* test is, it is worse for the fact that, since its inception, its seemingly simple mandates have been manipulated to fit whatever result the Court aimed to achieve. Today's opinion is no different. In two respects it modifies *Lemon* to ratchet up the Court's hostility to religion. First, the Court justifies inquiry into legislative purpose, not as an end itself, but as a means to ascertain the appearance of the government action to an "'objective observer.'" Because in the Court's view the true danger to be guarded against is that the objective observer would feel like an "outside[r]" or "not [a] full membe[r] of the political community," its inquiry focuses not on the *actual purpose* of government action, but the "purpose apparent from government action." Under this approach, even if a government could show that its actual purpose was not to advance religion, it would presumably violate the Constitution as long as the Court's objective observer would think otherwise.

I have remarked before that it is an odd jurisprudence that bases the unconstitutionality of a government practice that does not *actually* advance religion on the hopes of the government that it *would* do so. But that oddity pales in comparison to the one invited by today's analysis: the legitimacy of a government action with a wholly secular effect would turn on the *misperception* of an imaginary observer that the government officials behind the action had the intent to advance religion.

Second, the Court replaces *Lemon*'s requirement that the government have "*a* secular . . . purpose," with the heightened requirement that the secular purpose "predominate" over any purpose to advance religion. The Court treats this extension as a natural outgrowth of the longstanding requirement that the government's secular purpose not be a sham, but simple logic shows the two to be unrelated. If the government's proffered secular purpose is not genuine, then the government has no secular purpose at all. The new demand that secular purpose predominate contradicts *Lemon*'s more limited requirement, and finds no support in our cases. [. . .] I have urged that *Lemon*'s purpose prong be abandoned, because (as I have discussed in Part I) even an *exclusive* purpose to foster or assist religious practice is not necessarily invalidating. But today's extension makes things even worse. By shifting the focus of *Lemon*'s purpose prong from the search for a genuine, secular motivation to the hunt for a predominantly religious purpose, the Court converts what has in the past been a fairly limited inquiry into a rigorous review of the full record. Those responsible for the adoption of the Religion Clauses would surely regard it as a bitter irony that the religious values they designed those Clauses to *protect* have now become so distasteful to this Court that if they constitute anything more than a subordinate motive for government action they will invalidate it.

III

Even accepting the Court's *Lemon*-based premises, the displays at issue here were constitutional.

A

To any person who happened to walk down the hallway of the McCreary or Pulaski County Courthouse during the roughly nine months when the Foundations Displays were exhibited, the displays must have seemed unremarkable—if indeed they were noticed at all. The walls of both courthouses were already lined with historical documents and other assorted portraits; each Foundations Display was exhibited in the same format as these other displays and nothing in the record suggests that either County took steps to give it greater prominence. [. . .]

B

On its face, the Foundations Displays manifested the purely secular purpose that the Counties asserted before the District Court: "to display documents that played a significant role in the foundation of our system of law and government." That the Displays included the Ten Commandments did not transform their apparent secular purpose into one of impermissible advocacy for Judeo-Christian beliefs. Even an isolated display of the Decalogue conveys, at worst, "an equivocal message, perhaps of respect for Judaism, for religion in general, or for law." But when the Ten Commandments appear alongside other documents of secular significance in a display devoted to the foundations of American law and government, the context communicates that the Ten Commandments are included, not to teach their binding nature as a religious text, but to show their unique contribution to the development of the legal system. This is doubly true when the display is introduced by a document that informs passersby that it "contains documents that played a significant role in the foundation of our system of law and government."

[. . .] Acknowledgment of the contribution that religion has made to our Nation's legal and governmental heritage partakes of a centuries-old tradition. Members of this Court have themselves often detailed the degree to which religious belief pervaded the National Government during the founding era. Display of the Ten Commandments is well within the mainstream of this practice of acknowledgment. Federal, State, and local governments across the Nation have engaged in such display. The Supreme Court Building itself includes depictions of Moses with the Ten Commandments in the Courtroom and on the east pediment of the building, and symbols of the Ten Commandments "adorn the metal gates lining the north and south sides of the Courtroom as well as the doors leading into the Courtroom." Similar depictions of the Decalogue appear on public buildings and monuments throughout our Nation's Capital. *Ibid.* The frequency of these displays testifies to the popular understanding that the Ten Commandments are a foundation of the rule of law, and a symbol of the role that religion played, and continues to play, in our system of government.

Perhaps in recognition of the centrality of the Ten Commandments as a widely recognized symbol of religion in public life, the Court is at pains to dispel the impression that its decision will require governments across the country to sandblast the Ten Commandments from the public square. The constitutional problem, the Court says, is with the Counties' *purpose* in erecting the Foundations Displays, not the displays themselves. The Court adds in a footnote: "One consequence of taking account of the purpose underlying past actions is that the same government action may be constitutional if taken in the first instance and unconstitutional if it has a sectarian heritage."

This inconsistency may be explicable in theory, but I suspect that the "objective observer" with whom the Court is so concerned will recognize its absurdity in practice. By virtue of details familiar only to the parties to litigation and their lawyers, McCreary and Pulaski Counties, Kentucky, and Rutherford County, Tennessee, have been ordered to remove the same display that appears in courthouses from Mercer County, Kentucky to Elkhart County, Indiana. Displays erected in silence (and under the direction of good legal advice) are permissible, while those hung after discussion and debate are deemed unconstitutional. Reduction of the Establishment Clause to such minutiae trivializes the Clause's protection against religious establishment; indeed, it may inflame religious passions by making the passing comments of every government official the subject of endless litigation.

C

In any event, the Court's conclusion that the Counties exhibited the Foundations Displays with the purpose of promoting religion is doubtful. In the Court's view, the impermissible motive was apparent from the initial displays of the Ten Commandments all by themselves: When that occurs, the Court says, "a religious object is unmistakable." Surely that cannot be. If, as discussed above, the Commandments have a proper place in our civic history, even placing them by themselves can be civically motivated—especially when they are placed, not in a school (as they were in the *Stone* case upon which the Court places such reliance), but in a courthouse. The Court has in the past prohibited government actions that "proselytize or advance any one, or . . . disparage any other, faith or belief," or that apply some level of coercion (though I and others have disagreed about the form that coercion must take). The passive display of the Ten Commandments, even standing alone, does not begin to do either.

Nor is it the case that a solo display of the Ten Commandments advances any one faith. They are assuredly a religious symbol, but they are not so closely associated with a single religious belief that their display can reasonably be understood as preferring one religious sect over another. The Ten Commandments are recognized by Judaism, Christianity, and Islam alike as divinely given. The Court also points to the Counties' second displays, which featured a number of statements in historical documents reflecting a religious influence, and the resolutions that accompanied their erection, as evidence of an impermissible religious purpose. In the Court's view, "[t]he [second] display's unstinting focus . . . on religious passages, show[s] that the Counties were posting the Commandments precisely because of their sectarian content." No, all it necessarily shows is that the exhibit was meant to focus upon the historic role of religious belief in our national life—which is entirely permissible. And the same can be said of the resolution. To forbid any government focus upon this aspect of our history is to display what Justice Goldberg called "untutored devotion to the concept of neutrality," that would commit the Court (and the Nation) to a revisionist agenda of secularization.

Turning at last to the displays actually at issue in this case, the Court faults the Counties for not *repealing* the resolution expressing what the Court believes to be an impermissible intent. Under these circumstances, the Court says, "no reasonable observer could swallow the claim that the Counties had cast off the objective so unmistakable in the earlier displays." Even were I to accept all that the Court has said before, I would not agree with that assessment. To begin with, of course, it is unlikely that a reasonable observer *would even have been aware* of the resolutions, so there would be nothing to "cast off." The Court implies that the Counties may have been able to remedy the "taint" from the old resolutions by enacting a new one. But that action would have been wholly unnecessary in light of the explanation that the Counties included *with the displays themselves*: A plaque next to the documents informed all who passed by that each display "contains documents that played a significant role in the foundation of our system of law and government." Additionally, there was no reason for the Counties to repeal or repudiate the resolutions adopted with the hanging of the second displays, since they related *only to the second displays*. After complying with the District Court's order to remove the second displays "immediately," and erecting new displays that in

content and by express assertion reflected a *different* purpose from that identified in the resolutions, the Counties had no reason to believe that their previous resolutions would be deemed to be the basis for their actions. After the
Counties discovered that the sentiments expressed in the resolutions could be
attributed to their most recent displays (in oral argument before this Court),
they repudiated them immediately.

In sum: The first displays did not necessarily evidence an intent to further
religious practice; nor did the second displays, or the resolutions authorizing them; and there is in any event no basis for attributing whatever intent
motivated the first and second displays to the third. Given the presumption
of regularity that always accompanies our review of official action, the Court
has identified no evidence of a purpose to advance religion in a way that is
inconsistent with our cases. The Court may well be correct in identifying the
third displays as the fruit of a desire to display the Ten Commandments, but
neither our cases nor our history support its assertion that such a desire ren-
ders the fruit poisonous.

For the foregoing reasons, I would reverse the judgment of the Court of
Appeals.

III. OPINIONS IN *VAN ORDEN* V. *PERRY*

**Chief Justice Rehnquist announced the judgment of the Court and deliv-
ered an opinion, in which Justice Scalia, Justice Kennedy, and Justice
Thomas join.**

The question here is whether the Establishment Clause of the First
Amendment allows the display of a monument inscribed with the Ten
Commandments on the Texas State Capitol grounds. We hold that it does.

The 22 acres surrounding the Texas State Capitol contain 17 monuments
and 21 historical markers commemorating the "people, ideals, and events that
compose Texan identity." The monolith challenged here stands 6-feet high
and 3-feet wide. It is located to the north of the Capitol building, between the
Capitol and the Supreme Court building. Its primary content is the text of
the Ten Commandments. An eagle grasping the American flag, an eye inside
of a pyramid, and two small tablets with what appears to be an ancient script are
carved above the text of the Ten Commandments. Below the text are two Stars
of David and the superimposed Greek letters Chi and Rho, which represent
Christ. The bottom of the monument bears the inscription "PRESENTED TO

THE PEOPLE AND YOUTH OF TEXAS BY THE FRATERNAL ORDER OF
EAGLES OF TEXAS 1961."

The legislative record surrounding the State's acceptance of the monument from the Eagles—a national social, civic, and patriotic organization—
is limited to legislative journal entries. After the monument was accepted,
the State selected a site for the monument based on the recommendation
of the state organization responsible for maintaining the Capitol grounds. The
Eagles paid the cost of erecting the monument, the dedication of which was
presided over by two state legislators.

Petitioner Thomas Van Orden is a native Texan and a resident of Austin. At
one time he was a licensed lawyer, having graduated from Southern Methodist
Law School. Van Orden testified that, since 1995, he has encountered the Ten
Commandments monument during his frequent visits to the Capitol grounds.
His visits are typically for the purpose of using the law library in the Supreme
Court building, which is located just northwest of the Capitol building.

Forty years after the monument's erection and six years after Van Orden
began to encounter the monument frequently, he sued numerous state officials in their official capacities under [42 U.S. Code Sec. 1983] seeking both a
declaration that the monument's placement violates the Establishment Clause
and an injunction requiring its removal. After a bench trial, the District
Court held that the monument did not contravene the Establishment Clause.
It found that the State had a valid secular purpose in recognizing and commending the Eagles for their efforts to reduce juvenile delinquency. The
District Court also determined that a reasonable observer, mindful of
the history, purpose, and context, would not conclude that this passive monument conveyed the message that the State was seeking to endorse religion.
The Court of Appeals affirmed the District Court's holdings with respect
to the monument's purpose and effect. We granted certiorari, and now affirm.

Our cases, Januslike, point in two directions in applying the Establishment
Clause. One face looks toward the strong role played by religion and religious
traditions throughout our Nation's history. As we observed in *School Dist. of
Abington Township* v. *Schempp* (1963):

"It is true that religion has been closely identified with our history and
government. . . . The fact that the Founding Fathers believed devotedly that
there was a God and that the unalienable rights of man were rooted in Him
is clearly evidenced in their writings, from the Mayflower Compact to the
Constitution itself. . . . It can be truly said, therefore, that today, as in
the beginning, our national life reflects a religious people who, in the words
of Madison, are 'earnestly praying, as . . . in duty bound, that the Supreme
Lawgiver of the Universe . . . guide them into every measure which may be
worthy of his [blessing . . . .]'" The other face looks toward the principle that

governmental intervention in religious matters can itself endanger religious freedom.

This case, like all Establishment Clause challenges, presents us with the difficulty of respecting both faces. Our institutions presuppose a Supreme Being, yet these institutions must not press religious observances upon their citizens. One face looks to the past in acknowledgment of our Nation's heritage, while the other looks to the present in demanding a separation between church and state. Reconciling these two faces requires that we neither abdicate our responsibility to maintain a division between church and state nor evince a hostility to religion by disabling the government from in some ways recognizing our religious heritage:

"When the state encourages religious instruction or cooperates with religious authorities by adjusting the schedule of public events to sectarian needs, it follows the best of our traditions. For it then respects the religious nature of our people and accommodates the public service to their spiritual needs. To hold that it may not would be to find in the Constitution a requirement that the government show a callous indifference to religious groups. . . . [W]e find no constitutional requirement which makes it necessary for government to be hostile to religion and to throw its weight against efforts to widen the effective scope of religious influence." *Zorach* v. *Clauson* (1952). [. . .]

These two faces are evident in representative cases both upholding and invalidating laws under the Establishment Clause. Over the last 25 years, we have sometimes pointed to *Lemon* v. *Kurtzman* (1971), as providing the governing test in Establishment Clause challenges. Yet, just two years after *Lemon* was decided, we noted that the factors identified in *Lemon* serve as "no more than helpful signposts." Many of our recent cases simply have not applied the *Lemon* test. Others have applied it only after concluding that the challenged practice was invalid under a different Establishment Clause test.

Whatever may be the fate of the *Lemon* test in the larger scheme of Establishment Clause jurisprudence, we think it not useful in dealing with the sort of passive monument that Texas has erected on its Capitol grounds. Instead, our analysis is driven both by the nature of the monument and by our Nation's history.

As we explained in *Lynch* v. *Donnelly* (1984): "There is an unbroken history of official acknowledgment by all three branches of government of the role of religion in American life from at least 1789." For example, both Houses passed resolutions in 1789 asking President George Washington to issue a Thanksgiving Day Proclamation to "recommend to the people of the United States a day of public thanksgiving and prayer, to be observed by acknowledging, with grateful hearts, the many and signal favors of Almighty God." [. . .]

Recognition of the role of God in our Nation's heritage has also been reflected in our decisions. We have acknowledged, for example, that "religion has been closely identified with our history and government," *School Dist. of Abington Township* v. *Schempp,* and that "[t]he history of man is inseparable from the history of religion," *Engel* v. *Vitale* (1962). This recognition has led us to hold that the Establishment Clause permits a state legislature to open its daily sessions with a prayer by a chaplain paid by the State. [. . .] With similar reasoning, we have upheld laws, which originated from one of the Ten Commandments, that prohibited the sale of merchandise on Sunday.

In this case we are faced with a display of the Ten Commandments on government property outside the Texas State Capitol. Such acknowledgments of the role played by the Ten Commandments in our Nation's heritage are common throughout America. We need only look within our own Courtroom. Since 1935, Moses has stood, holding two tablets that reveal portions of the Ten Commandments written in Hebrew, among other lawgivers in the south frieze. Representations of the Ten Commandments adorn the metal gates lining the north and south sides of the Courtroom as well as the doors leading into the Courtroom. Moses also sits on the exterior east facade of the building holding the Ten Commandments tablets.

Similar acknowledgments can be seen throughout a visitor's tour of our Nation's Capital. For example, a large statue of Moses holding the Ten Commandments, alongside a statue of the Apostle Paul, has overlooked the rotunda of the Library of Congress' Jefferson Building since 1897. And the Jefferson Building's Great Reading Room contains a sculpture of a woman beside the Ten Commandments with a quote above her from the Old Testament (Micah 6:8). A medallion with two tablets depicting the Ten Commandments decorates the floor of the National Archives. Inside the Department of Justice, a statue entitled "The Spirit of Law" has two tablets representing the Ten Commandments lying at its feet. In front of the Ronald Reagan Building is another sculpture that includes a depiction of the Ten Commandments. So too a 24-foot-tall sculpture, depicting, among other things, the Ten Commandments and a cross, stands outside the federal courthouse that houses both the Court of Appeals and the District Court for the District of Columbia. Moses is also prominently featured in the Chamber of the United States House of Representatives.

[. . .] Of course, the Ten Commandments are religious—they were so viewed at their inception and so remain. The monument, therefore, has religious significance. According to Judeo-Christian belief, the Ten Commandments were given to Moses by God on Mt. Sinai. But Moses was a lawgiver as well as a religious leader. And the Ten Commandments have an undeniable historical meaning, as the foregoing examples demonstrate. Simply having religious content or promoting a message consistent with a religious doctrine does not run afoul of the Establishment Clause.

There are, of course, limits to the display of religious messages or symbols. For example, we held unconstitutional a Kentucky statute requiring the posting of the Ten Commandments in every public schoolroom. *Stone* v. *Graham* (1980). In the classroom context, we found that the Kentucky statute had an improper and plainly religious purpose. [*Stone*] stands as an example of the fact that we have "been particularly vigilant in monitoring compliance with the Establishment Clause in elementary and secondary schools." Neither *Stone* itself nor subsequent opinions have indicated that *Stone*'s holding would extend to a legislative chamber . . . or to capitol grounds.

The placement of the Ten Commandments monument on the Texas State Capitol grounds is a far more passive use of those texts than was the case in *Stone,* where the text confronted elementary school students every day. Indeed, Van Orden, the petitioner here, apparently walked by the monument for a number of years before bringing this lawsuit. [. . .] Texas has treated her Capitol grounds monuments as representing the several strands in the State's political and legal history. The inclusion of the Ten Commandments monument in this group has a dual significance, partaking of both religion and government. We cannot say that Texas' display of this monument violates the Establishment Clause of the First Amendment.

The judgment of the Court of Appeals is affirmed.

It is so ordered.

Justice Breyer, concurring in the judgment.

In *School Dist. of Abington Township* v. *Schempp* (1963), Justice Goldberg, joined by Justice Harlan, wrote, in respect to the First Amendment's Religion Clauses, that there is "no simple and clear measure which by precise application can readily and invariably demark the permissible from the impermissible." One must refer instead to the basic purposes of those Clauses. They seek to "assure the fullest possible scope of religious liberty and tolerance for all." They seek to avoid that divisiveness based upon religion that promotes social conflict, sapping the strength of government and religion alike. They seek to maintain that "separation of church and state" that has long been critical to the "peaceful dominion that religion exercises in [this] country," where the "spirit of religion" and the "spirit of freedom" are productively "united," "reign[ing] together" but in separate spheres "on the same soil." A. de Tocqueville, Democracy in America (1835) [. . .]

The Court has made clear, as Justices Goldberg and Harlan noted, that the realization of these goals means that government must "neither engage in nor compel religious practices," that it must "effect no favoritism among sects or between religion and nonreligion," and that it must "work deterrence of no religious belief." The government must avoid excessive interference with, or promotion of, religion. But the Establishment Clause does not compel the government to purge from the public sphere all that in any way partakes of the religious. Such absolutism is not only inconsistent with our national traditions, but would also tend to promote the kind of social conflict the Establishment Clause seeks to avoid.

Thus, as Justices Goldberg and Harlan pointed out, the Court has found no single mechanical formula that can accurately draw the constitutional line in every case. Where the Establishment Clause is at issue, tests designed to measure "neutrality" alone are insufficient, both because it is sometimes difficult to determine when a legal rule is "neutral," and because

"untutored devotion to the concept of neutrality can lead to invocation or approval of results which partake not simply of that noninterference and noninvolvement with the religious which the Constitution commands, but of a brooding and pervasive devotion to the secular and a passive, or even active, hostility to the religious."

Neither can this Court's other tests readily explain the Establishment Clause's tolerance, for example, of the prayers that open legislative meetings; certain references to, and invocations of, the Deity in the public words of public officials; the public references to God on coins, decrees, and buildings; or the attention paid to the religious objectives of certain holidays, including Thanksgiving. [. . .] If the relation between government and religion is one of separation, but not of mutual hostility and suspicion, one will inevitably find difficult borderline cases. And in such cases, I see no test-related substitute for the exercise of legal judgment. That judgment is not a personal judgment. Rather, as in all constitutional cases, it must reflect and remain faithful to the underlying purposes of the Clauses, and it must take account of context and consequences measured in light of those purposes. While the Court's prior tests provide useful guideposts—and might well lead to the same result the Court reaches today—no exact formula can dictate a resolution to such fact-intensive cases.

The case before us is a borderline case. It concerns a large granite monument bearing the text of the Ten Commandments located on the grounds of the Texas State Capitol. On the one hand, the Commandments' text undeniably has a religious message, invoking, indeed emphasizing, the Diety. On the other hand, focusing on the text of the Commandments alone cannot conclusively resolve this case. Rather, to determine the message that the text here conveys, we must examine how the text is *used*. And that inquiry requires us to consider the context of the display.

In certain contexts, a display of the tablets of the Ten Commandments can convey not simply a religious message but also a secular moral message (about proper standards of social conduct). And in certain contexts, a display of the tablets can also convey a historical message (about a historic relation between those standards and the law)—a fact that helps to explain the display of those tablets in dozens of courthouses throughout the Nation, including the Supreme Court of the United States. [. . .] Here the tablets have been used as part of a display that communicates not simply a religious message, but a secular message as well. The circumstances surrounding the display's placement on the capitol grounds and its physical setting suggest that the State itself intended the latter, nonreligious aspects of the tablets' message to predominate. And the monument's 40-year history on the Texas state grounds indicates that that has been its effect.

The group that donated the monument, the Fraternal Order of Eagles, a private civic (and primarily secular) organization, while interested in the religious aspect of the Ten Commandments, sought to highlight the Commandments' role in shaping civic morality as part of that organization's efforts to combat juvenile delinquency. The Eagles' consultation with a committee composed of members of several faiths in order to find a nonsectarian text underscores the group's ethics-based motives. The tablets, as displayed on the monument, prominently acknowledge that the Eagles donated the display, a factor which, though not sufficient, thereby further distances the State itself from the religious aspect of the Commandments' message.

The physical setting of the monument, moreover, suggests little or nothing of the sacred. The monument sits in a large park containing 17 monuments and 21 historical markers, all designed to illustrate the "ideals" of those who settled in Texas and of those who have lived there since that time. The setting does not readily lend itself to meditation or any other religious activity. But it does provide a context of history and moral ideals. It (together with the display's inscription about its origin) communicates to visitors that the State sought to reflect moral principles, illustrating a relation between ethics and law that the State's citizens, historically speaking, have endorsed. That is to say, the context suggests that the State intended the display's moral message—an illustrative message reflecting the historical "ideals" of Texans—to predominate.

If these factors provide a strong, but not conclusive, indication that the Commandments' text on this monument conveys a predominantly secular message, a further factor is determinative here. As far as I can tell, 40 years passed in which the presence of this monument, legally speaking, went unchallenged (until the single legal objection raised by petitioner). And I am not aware of any evidence suggesting that this was due to a climate of intimidation. Hence, those 40 years suggest more strongly than can any set of formulaic tests that few individuals, whatever their system of beliefs, are likely to have understood the monument as amounting, in any significantly detrimental way, to a government effort to favor a particular religious sect, [or] primarily to promote religion over nonreligion. Those 40 years suggest that the public visiting the capitol grounds has considered the religious aspect of the tablets' message as part of what is a broader moral and historical message reflective of a cultural heritage.

This case, moreover, is distinguishable from instances where the Court has found Ten Commandments displays impermissible. The display is not on the grounds of a public school, where, given the impressionability of the young, government must exercise particular care in separating church and state. This case also differs from *McCreary County*, where the short (and stormy) history of the courthouse Commandments' displays demonstrates the substantially religious objectives of those who mounted them, and the effect of this readily apparent objective upon those who view them. That history there indicates a governmental effort substantially to promote religion, not simply an effort primarily to reflect, historically, the secular impact of a religiously inspired document. And, in today's world, in a Nation of so many different religious and comparable nonreligious fundamental beliefs, a more contemporary state effort to focus attention upon a religious text is certainly likely to prove divisive in a way that this longstanding, pre-existing monument has not.

For these reasons, I believe that the Texas display—serving a mixed but primarily nonreligious purpose, not primarily "advanc[ing]" or "inhibit[ing] religion," and not creating an "excessive government entanglement with religion,"—might satisfy this Court's more formal Establishment Clause tests. But, as I have said, in reaching the conclusion that the Texas display falls on the permissible side of the constitutional line, I rely less upon a literal application of any particular test than upon consideration of the basic purposes of the First Amendment's Religion Clauses themselves. This display has stood apparently uncontested for nearly two generations. That experience helps us understand that as a practical matter of *degree* this display is unlikely to prove divisive. And this matter of degree is, I believe, critical in a borderline case such as this one.

At the same time, to reach a contrary conclusion here, based primarily upon on the religious nature of the tablets' text would, I fear, lead the law to exhibit a hostility toward religion that has no place in our Establishment Clause traditions. Such a holding might well encourage disputes concerning the removal of longstanding depictions of the Ten Commandments from public buildings across the Nation. And it could thereby create the very kind of religiously based divisiveness that the Establishment Clause seeks to avoid. Justices Goldberg and Harlan concluded in *Schempp* that "[t]he First Amendment does not prohibit practices which by any realistic measure create none of the dangers which it is designed to prevent and which do not so directly or substantially involve the state in religious exercise or in the favoring of religion as to have meaningful and practical impact."

That kind of practice is what we have here. I recognize the danger of the slippery slope. Still, where the Establishment Clause is at issue, we must "distinguish between real threat and mere shadow." Here, we have only the shadow.

In light of these considerations, I cannot agree with today's plurality's analysis. Nor can I agree with Justice Scalia's dissent in *McCreary County*. [. . .]

I concur in the judgment of the Court.

Justice Souter, with whom Justice Stevens and Justice Ginsburg join, dissenting.

Although the First Amendment's Religion Clauses have not been read to mandate absolute governmental neutrality toward religion, the Establishment Clause requires neutrality as a general rule, *e.g.*, *Everson* v. *Board of Ed. of Ewing* (1947), and thus expresses Madison's condemnation of "employ[ing] Religion as an engine of Civil policy." A governmental display of an obviously religious text cannot be squared with neutrality, except in a setting that plausibly indicates that the statement is not placed in view with a predominant purpose on the part of government either to adopt the religious message or to urge its acceptance by others.

Until today, only one of our cases addressed the constitutionality of posting the Ten Commandments, *Stone* v. *Graham* (1980). A Kentucky statute required posting the Commandments on the walls of public school classrooms, and the Court described the State's purpose (relevant under the tripartite test laid out in *Lemon* v. *Kurtzman* (1971) as being at odds with the obligation of religious neutrality.

"The pre-eminent purpose for posting the Ten Commandments on schoolroom walls is plainly religious in nature. The Ten Commandments are undeniably a sacred text in the Jewish and Christian faiths, and no legislative recitation of a supposed secular purpose can blind us to that fact. The Commandments do not confine themselves to arguably secular matters, such as honoring one's parents, killing or murder, adultery, stealing, false witness, and covetousness. Rather, the first part of the Commandments concerns the religious duties of believers: worshipping the Lord God alone, avoiding idolatry, not using the Lord's name in vain, and observing the Sabbath Day." What these observations underscore are the simple realities that the Ten Commandments constitute a religious statement, that their message is inherently religious, and that the purpose of singling them out in a display is clearly the same.

Thus, a pedestrian happening upon the monument at issue here needs no training in religious doctrine to realize that the statement of the Commandments, quoting God himself, proclaims that the will of the divine being is the source of obligation to obey the rules, including the facially secular ones. In this case, moreover, the text is presented to give particular prominence to the Commandments' first sectarian reference, "I am the Lord thy God." That proclamation is centered on the stone and written in slightly larger letters than the subsequent recitation. To ensure that the religious nature of the monument is clear to even the most casual passerby, the word "Lord" appears in all capital letters (as does the word "am"), so that the most eye-catching segment of the quotation is the declaration "I AM the Lord thy God." What follows, of course, are the rules against other gods, graven images, vain swearing, and Sabbath breaking. And the full text of the fifth Commandment puts forward filial respect as a condition of long life in the land "which the Lord they God giveth thee."

To drive the religious point home, and identify the message as religious to any viewer who failed to read the text, the engraved quotation is framed by religious symbols: two tablets with what appears to be ancient script on them, two Stars of David, and the superimposed Greek letters Chi and Rho as the familiar monogram of Christ. Nothing on the monument, in fact, detracts from its religious nature, and the plurality does not suggest otherwise. It would therefore be difficult to miss the point that the government of Texas is telling everyone who sees the monument to live up to a moral code because God requires it, with both code and conception of God being rightly understood as the inheritances specifically of Jews and Christians. And it is likewise unsurprising that the District Court expressly rejected Texas's argument that the State's purpose in placing the monument on the capitol grounds was related to the Commandments' role as "part of the foundation of modern secular law in Texas and elsewhere."

The monument's presentation of the Commandments with religious text emphasized and enhanced stands in contrast to any number of perfectly constitutional depictions of them, the frieze of our own Courtroom providing a good example, where the figure of Moses stands among history's great lawgivers. While Moses holds the tablets of the Commandments showing some Hebrew text, no one looking at the lines of figures in marble relief is likely to see a religious purpose behind the assemblage or take away a religious message from it. Only one other depiction represents a religious leader, and the historical personages are mixed with symbols of moral and intellectual abstractions like Equity and Authority. Since Moses enjoys no especial prominence on the frieze, viewers can readily take him to be there as a lawgiver in the company of other lawgivers; and the viewers may just as naturally see the tablets of the Commandments (showing the later ones, forbidding things like killing and theft, but without the divine preface) as background from which the concept of law emerged, ultimately having a secular influence in the history of the Nation. Government may, of course, constitutionally call attention to this influence, and may post displays or erect monuments recounting this aspect of our history no less than any other, so long as there is a context and that context is historical. Hence, a display of the Commandments accompanied by an exposition of how they have influenced modern law would most likely be constitutionally unobjectionable. And the Decalogue could, as *Stone* suggested, be integrated constitutionally into a course of study in public schools.

Texas seeks to take advantage of the recognition that visual symbol and written text can manifest a secular purpose in secular company, when it argues that its monument (like Moses in the frieze) is not alone and ought to be viewed as only 1 among 17 placed on the 22 acres surrounding the state capitol. Texas, indeed, says that the Capitol grounds are like a museum for a collection of exhibits, the kind of setting that several Members of the Court have said can render the exhibition of religious artifacts permissible, even though in other circumstances their display would be seen as meant to convey a religious message forbidden to the State. So, for example, the Government of the United States does not violate the Establishment Clause by hanging Giotto's Madonna on the wall of the National Gallery.

But 17 monuments with no common appearance, history, or esthetic role scattered over 22 acres is not a museum, and anyone strolling around the lawn would surely take each memorial on its own terms without any dawning sense that some purpose held the miscellany together more coherently than fortuity and the edge of the grass. One monument expresses admiration for pioneer women. One pays respect to the fighters of World War II. And one quotes the God of Abraham whose command is the sanction for moral law. The themes are individual grit, patriotic courage, and God as the source of Jewish and Christian morality; there is no common denominator. [. . .]

If the State's museum argument does nothing to blunt the religious message and manifestly religious purpose behind it, neither does the plurality's reliance on generalities culled from cases factually different from this one. In fact, it is not until the end of its opinion that the plurality turns to the relevant precedent of *Stone*, a case actually dealing with a display of the Decalogue.

When the plurality finally does confront *Stone,* it tries to avoid the case's obvious applicability by limiting its holding to the classroom setting. The plurality claims to find authority for limiting *Stone*'s reach this way in the opinion's citations of two school-prayer cases, *School Dist. of Abington Township* v.

Schempp (1963), and *Engel* v. *Vitale* (1962). But *Stone* relied on those cases for widely applicable notions, not for any concept specific to schools. [. . .] Thus, the schoolroom was beside the point of the citations, and that is presumably why the *Stone* Court failed to discuss the educational setting, as other opinions had done when school was significant. *Stone* did not, for example, speak of children's impressionability or their captivity as an audience in a school class. In fact, *Stone*'s reasoning reached the classroom only in noting the lack of support for the claim that the State had brought the Commandments into schools in order to "integrat[e] [them] into the school curriculum." Accordingly, our numerous prior discussions of *Stone* have never treated its holding as restricted to the classroom.

Nor can the plurality deflect *Stone* by calling the Texas monument "a far more passive use of [the Decalogue] than was the case in *Stone,* where the text confronted elementary school students every day." Placing a monument on the ground is not more "passive" than hanging a sheet of paper on a wall when both contain the same text to be read by anyone who looks at it. The problem in *Stone* was simply that the State was putting the Commandments there to be seen, just as the monument's inscription is there for those who walk by it.

To be sure, Kentucky's compulsory-education law meant that the schoolchildren were forced to see the display every day, whereas many see the monument by choice, and those who customarily walk the Capitol grounds can presumably avoid it if they choose. But in my judgment (and under our often inexact Establishment Clause jurisprudence), such matters often boil down to judgment, this distinction should make no difference. The monument in this case sits on the grounds of the Texas State Capitol. There is something significant in the common term "statehouse" to refer to a state capitol building: it is the civic home of every one of the State's citizens. If neutrality in religion means something, any citizen should be able to visit that civic home without having to confront religious expressions clearly meant to convey an official religious position that may be at odds with his own religion, or with rejection of religion.

Finally, though this too is a point on which judgment will vary, I do not see a persuasive argument for constitutionality in the plurality's observation that Van Orden's lawsuit comes "[f]orty years after the monument's erection . . . ," an observation that echoes the State's contention that one fact cutting in its favor is that "the monument stood . . . in Austin . . . for some forty years without generating any controversy or litigation." It is not that I think the passage of time is necessarily irrelevant in Establishment Clause analysis. We have approved framing-era practices because they must originally have been understood as constitutionally permissible, and we have recognized that Sunday laws have grown recognizably secular over time. There is also an analogous argument, not yet evaluated, that ritualistic religious expression can become so numbing over time that its initial Establishment Clause violation becomes at some point too diminished for notice. But I do not understand any of these to be the State's argument, which rather seems to be that 40 years without a challenge shows that as a factual matter the religious expression is too tepid to provoke a serious reaction and constitute a violation. Perhaps, but the writer of Exodus chapter 20 was not lukewarm, and other explanations may do better in accounting for the late resort to the courts. Suing a State over religion puts nothing in a plaintiff's pocket and can take a great deal out, and even with volunteer litigators to supply time and energy, the risk of social ostracism can be powerfully deterrent. I doubt that a slow walk to the courthouse, even one that took 40 years, is much evidentiary help in applying the Establishment Clause.

I would reverse the judgment of the Court of Appeals.

Justice Stevens, with whom Justice Ginsburg joins, dissenting.

The sole function of the monument on the grounds of Texas' State Capitol is to display the full text of one version of the Ten Commandments. The monument is not a work of art and does not refer to any event in the history of the State. It is significant because, and only because, it communicates the following message:

"I AM the LORD thy God.

"Thou shalt have no other gods before me.

"Thou shalt not make to thyself any graven images.

"Thou shalt not take the Name of the Lord thy God in vain.

"Remember the Sabbath day, to keep it holy.

"Honor thy father and thy mother, that thy days may be long upon the land which the Lord thy God giveth thee.

"Thou shalt not kill.

"Thou shalt not commit adultery.

"Thou shalt not steal.

"Thou shalt not bear false witness against thy neighbor.

"Thou shalt not covet thy neighbor's house.

"Thou shalt not covet thy neighbor's wife, nor his manservant, nor his maidservant, nor his cattle, nor anything that is thy neighbor's."

Viewed on its face, Texas' display has no purported connection to God's role in the formation of Texas or the founding of our Nation; nor does it provide the reasonable observer with any basis to guess that it was erected to honor any individual or organization. The message transmitted by Texas' chosen display is quite plain: This State endorses the divine code of the "Judeo-Christian" God.

For those of us who learned to recite the King James version of the text long before we understood the meaning of some of its words, God's Commandments may seem like wise counsel. The question before this Court, however, is whether it is counsel that the State of Texas may proclaim without violating the Establishment Clause of the Constitution. If any fragment of Jefferson's metaphorical "wall of separation between church and State" is to be preserved–if there remains any meaning to the "wholesome 'neutrality' of which this Court's [Establishment Clause] cases speak,"–a negative answer to that question is mandatory.

I

In my judgment, at the very least, the Establishment Clause has created a strong presumption against the display of religious symbols on public property. The adornment of our public spaces with displays of religious symbols and messages undoubtedly provides comfort, even inspiration, to many individuals who subscribe to particular faiths. Unfortunately, the practice also runs the risk of "offend[ing] nonmembers of the faith being advertised as well as adherents who consider the particular advertisement disrespectful."

Government's obligation to avoid divisiveness and exclusion in the religious sphere is compelled by the Establishment and Free Exercise Clauses, which together erect a wall of separation between church and state. This metaphorical wall protects principles long recognized and often recited in this Court's cases. The first and most fundamental of these principles, one that a majority of this Court today affirms, is that the Establishment Clause demands religious neutrality–government may not exercise a preference for one religious faith over another. This essential command, however, is not merely a prohibition against the government's differentiation among religious sects. We have repeatedly reaffirmed that neither a State nor the Federal Government "can constitutionally pass laws or impose requirements which aid all religions as against non-believers, and neither can aid those religions based on a belief in the existence of God as against those religions founded on different beliefs." *Torcaso* v. *Watkins* (1961) This principle is based on the straightforward notion that governmental promotion of orthodoxy is not saved by the aggregation of several orthodoxies under the State's banner.

Acknowledgments of this broad understanding of the neutrality principle are legion in our cases. Strong arguments to the contrary have been raised from time to time, perhaps the strongest in then-Justice Rehnquist's scholarly dissent in *Wallace* v. *Jaffree* (1985). Powerful as his argument was, we squarely rejected it and thereby reaffirmed the principle that the Establishment Clause requires the same respect for the atheist as it does for the adherent of a Christian faith. As we wrote, "the Court has unambiguously concluded that the individual freedom of conscience protected by the First Amendment embodies the right to select any religious faith or none at all."

In restating this principle, I do not discount the importance of avoiding an overly strict interpretation of the metaphor so often used to define the reach of the Establishment Clause. The plurality is correct to note that "religion and religious traditions" have played a "strong role . . . throughout our nation's history." This Court has often recognized "an unbroken history of official acknowledgment . . . of the role of religion in American life." Given this history, it is unsurprising that a religious symbol may at times become an important feature of a familiar landscape or a reminder of an important event in the history of a community. The wall that separates the church from the State does not prohibit the government from acknowledging the religious beliefs and practices of the American people, nor does it require governments to hide works of art or historic memorabilia from public view just because they also have religious significance.

This case, however, is not about historic preservation or the mere recognition of religion. The issue is obfuscated rather than clarified by simplistic commentary on the various ways in which religion has played a role in American life, and by the recitation of the many extant governmental "acknowledgments" of the role the Ten Commandments played in our Nation's heritage. Surely, the mere compilation of religious symbols, none of which includes the full text of the Commandments and all of which are exhibited in different settings, has only marginal relevance to the question presented in this case.

The monolith displayed on Texas Capitol grounds cannot be discounted as a passive acknowledgment of religion, nor can the State's refusal to remove it upon objection be explained as a simple desire to preserve a historic relic. This Nation's resolute commitment to neutrality with respect to religion is flatly inconsistent with the plurality's wholehearted validation of an official state endorsement of the message that there is one, and only one, God.

II

When the Ten Commandments monument was donated to the State of Texas in 1961, it was not for the purpose of commemorating a noteworthy event in Texas history, signifying the Commandments' influence on the development of secular law, or even denoting the religious beliefs of Texans at that time. To the contrary, the donation was only one of over a hundred largely identical monoliths, and of over a thousand paper replicas, distributed to state and local governments throughout the Nation over the course of several decades. This ambitious project was the work of the Fraternal Order of Eagles, a well-respected benevolent organization whose good works have earned the praise of several Presidents.

As the story goes, the program was initiated by the late Judge E. J. Ruegemer, a Minnesota juvenile court judge and then-Chairman of the Eagles National Commission on Youth Guidance. Inspired by a juvenile offender who had never heard of the Ten Commandments, the judge approached the Minnesota Eagles with the idea of distributing paper copies of the Commandments to be posted in courthouses nationwide. The State's Aerie undertook this project and its popularity spread. When Cecil B. DeMille, who at that time was filming the movie The Ten Commandments, heard of the judge's endeavor, he teamed up with the Eagles to produce the type of granite monolith now displayed in front of the Texas Capitol and at courthouse squares, city halls, and public parks throughout the Nation. Granite was reportedly chosen over DeMille's original suggestion of bronze plaques to better replicate the original Ten Commandments.

The donors were motivated by a desire to "inspire the youth" and curb juvenile delinquency by providing children with a "code of conduct or standards by which to govern their actions." It is the Eagles' belief that disseminating the message conveyed by the Ten Commandments will help to persuade young men and women to observe civilized standards of behavior, and will lead to more productive lives. Significantly, although the Eagles' organization is nonsectarian, eligibility for membership is premised on a belief in the existence of a "Supreme Being." As described by the Eagles themselves:

"'in searching for a youth guidance program, [we] recognized that there can be no better, no more defined program of Youth Guidance, and adult guidance as well, than the laws handed down by God Himself to Moses more than 3000 years ago, which laws have stood unchanged through the years. They are a fundamental part of our lives, the basis of all our laws for living, the foundation of our relationship with our Creator, with our families and with our fellow men. All the concepts we live by—freedom, democracy, justice, honor—are rooted in the Ten Commandments.

The desire to combat juvenile delinquency by providing guidance to youths is both admirable and unquestionably secular. But achieving that goal through biblical teachings injects a religious purpose into an otherwise secular endeavor. By spreading the word of God and converting heathens to Christianity, missionaries expect to enlighten their converts, enhance their satisfaction with life, and improve their behavior. Similarly, by disseminating the "law of God"—directing fidelity to God and proscribing murder, theft, and adultery—the Eagles hope that this divine guidance will help wayward youths conform their behavior and improve their lives. In my judgment, the significant secular by-products that are intended consequences of religious instruction–indeed, of the establishment of most religions–are not the type of "secular" purposes that justify government promulgation of sacred religious messages.

Though the State of Texas may genuinely wish to combat juvenile delinquency, and may rightly want to honor the Eagles for their efforts, it cannot effectuate these admirable purposes through an explicitly religious medium. The State may admonish its citizens not to lie, cheat or steal, to honor their parents and to respect their neighbors' property; and it may do so by printed words, in television commercials, or on granite monuments in front of its public buildings. Moreover, the State may provide its schoolchildren and adult citizens with educational materials that explain the important role that our forebears' faith in God played in their decisions to select America as a refuge from religious persecution, to declare their independence from the British Crown, and to conceive a new Nation. The message at issue in this case, however, is fundamentally different from either a bland admonition to observe generally accepted rules of behavior or a general history lesson.

The reason this message stands apart is that the Decalogue is a venerable religious text. As we held 25 years ago, it is beyond dispute that "[t]he Ten Commandments are undeniably a sacred text in the Jewish and Christian faiths." *Stone* v. *Graham* (1980). For many followers, the Commandments represent the literal word of God as spoken to Moses and repeated to his followers after descending from Mount Sinai. The message conveyed by the Ten Commandments thus cannot be analogized to an appendage to a common article of commerce ("In God we Trust") or an incidental part of a familiar recital ("God save the United States and this honorable Court"). Thankfully, the plurality does not attempt to minimize the religious significance of the Ten Commandments. Attempts to secularize what is unquestionably a sacred text defy credibility and disserve people of faith. [. . .]

Even if, however, the message of the monument, despite the inscribed text, fairly could be said to represent the belief system of all Judeo-Christians, it would still run afoul of the Establishment Clause by prescribing a compelled code of conduct from one God, namely a Judeo-Christian God, that is rejected by prominent polytheistic sects, such as Hinduism, as well as nontheistic religions, such as Buddhism. And, at the very least, the text of the Ten Commandments impermissibly commands a preference for religion over irreligion. Any of those bases, in my judgment, would be sufficient to conclude that the message should not be proclaimed by the State of Texas on a permanent monument at the seat of its government.

I do not doubt that some Texans, including those elected to the Texas Legislature, may believe that the statues displayed on the Texas Capitol grounds, including the Ten Commandments monument, reflect the "ideals . . .

that compose Texan identity." But Texas, like our entire country, is now a much more diversified community than it was when it became a part of the United States or even when the monument was erected. Today there are many Texans who do not believe in the God whose Commandments are displayed at their seat of government. Many of them worship a different god or no god at all. Some may believe that the account of the creation in the Book of Genesis is less reliable than the views of men like Darwin and Einstein.

[. . .] Critical examination of the Decalogue's prominent display at the seat of Texas government, rather than generic citation to the role of religion in American life, unmistakably reveals on which side of the "slippery slope," this display must fall. God, as the author of its message, the Eagles, as the donor of the monument, and the State of Texas, as its proud owner, speak with one voice for a common purpose—to encourage Texans to abide by the divine code of a "Judeo-Christian" God. If this message is permissible, then the shining principle of neutrality to which we have long adhered is nothing more than mere shadow.

III

The plurality relies heavily on the fact that our Republic was founded, and has been governed since its nascence, by leaders who spoke then (and speak still) in plainly religious rhetoric. The Chief Justice cites, for instance, George Washington's 1789 Thanksgiving Proclamation in support of the proposition that the Establishment Clause does not proscribe official recognition of God's role in our Nation's heritage. Further, the plurality emphatically endorses the seemingly timeless recognition that our "institutions presuppose a Supreme Being." Many of the submissions made to this Court by the parties and *amici*, in accord with the plurality's opinion, have relied on the ubiquity of references to God throughout our history.

The speeches and rhetoric characteristic of the founding era, however, do not answer the question before us. I have already explained why Texas' display of the full text of the Ten Commandments, given the content of the actual display and the context in which it is situated, sets this case apart from the countless examples of benign government recognitions of religion. But there is another crucial difference. Our leaders, when delivering public addresses, often express their blessings simultaneously in the service of God and their constituents. Thus, when public officials deliver public speeches, we recognize that their words are not exclusively a transmission from *the* government because those oratories have embedded within them the inherently personal views of the speaker as an individual member of the polity. The permanent placement of a textual religious display on state property is different in kind; it amalgamates otherwise discordant individual views into a collective statement of government approval. Moreover, the message never ceases to transmit itself to objecting viewers whose only choices are to accept the message or to ignore the offense by averting their gaze. In this sense, although Thanksgiving Day proclamations and inaugural speeches undoubtedly seem official, in most circumstances they will not constitute the sort of governmental endorsement of religion at which the separation of church and state is aimed.

The plurality's reliance on early religious statements and proclamations made by the Founders is also problematic because those views were not espoused at the Constitutional Convention in 1787 nor enshrined in the Constitution's text. Thus, the presentation of these religious statements as a unified historical narrative is bound to paint a misleading picture. It does so here. In according deference to the statements of George Washington and John Adams, The Chief Justice and Justice Scalia fail to account for the acts and publicly espoused views of other influential leaders of that time. Notably absent from their historical snapshot is the fact that Thomas Jefferson refused to issue the Thanksgiving proclamations that Washington had so readily embraced based on the argument that to do so would violate the Establishment Clause. The Chief Justice and Justice Scalia disregard the substantial debates that took place regarding the constitutionality of the early proclamations and acts they cite, and paper over the fact that Madison more than once repudiated the views attributed to him by many, stating unequivocally that with respect to government's involvement with religion, the "'tendency to a usurpation on one side, or the other, or to a corrupting coalition or alliance between them, will be best guarded against by an entire abstinence of the Government from interference, in any way whatever, beyond the necessity of preserving public order, & protecting each sect against trespasses on its legal rights by others.'" [. . .]

To reason from the broad principles contained in the Constitution does not, as Justice Scalia suggests, require us to abandon our heritage in favor of unprincipled expressions of personal preference. The task of applying the broad principles that the Framers wrote into the text of the First Amendment is, in any event, no more a matter of personal preference than is one's selection between two (or more) sides in a heated historical debate. We serve our constitutional mandate by expounding the meaning of constitutional provisions with one eye towards our Nation's history and the other fixed on its democratic aspirations.

The principle that guides my analysis is neutrality. The basis for that principle is firmly rooted in our Nation's history and our Constitution's text. I recognize that the requirement that government must remain neutral between religion and irreligion would have seemed foreign to some of the Framers; so too would a requirement of neutrality between Jews and Christians.

Fortunately, we are not bound by the Framers' expectations–we are bound by the legal principles they enshrined in our Constitution. Story's vision that States should not discriminate between Christian sects has as its foundation the principle that government must remain neutral between valid systems of belief. As religious pluralism has expanded, so has our acceptance of what constitutes valid belief systems. The evil of discriminating today against atheists, "polytheists[,] and believers in unconcerned deities," *McCreary County* (Scalia, J., dissenting), is in my view a direct descendent of the evil of discriminating among Christian sects. The Establishment Clause thus forbids it and, in turn, forbids Texas from displaying the Ten Commandments monument the plurality so casually affirms.

IV

The Eagles may donate as many monuments as they choose to be displayed in front of Protestant churches, benevolent organizations' meeting places, or on the front lawns of private citizens. The expurgated text of the King James version of the Ten Commandments that they have crafted is unlikely to be accepted by Catholic parishes, Jewish synagogues, or even some Protestant denominations, but the message they seek to convey is surely more compatible with church property than with property that is located on the government side of the metaphorical wall.

The judgment of the Court in this case stands for the proposition that the Constitution permits governmental displays of sacred religious texts. This makes a mockery of the constitutional ideal that government must remain neutral between religion and irreligion. If a State may endorse a particular deity's command to "have no other gods before me," it is difficult to conceive of any textual display that would run afoul of the Establishment Clause.

The disconnect between this Court's approval of Texas' monument and the constitutional prohibition against preferring religion to irreligion cannot be reduced to the exercise of plotting two adjacent locations on a slippery slope. Rather, it is the difference between the shelter of a fortress and exposure to "the winds that would blow" if the wall were allowed to crumble. That wall, however imperfect, remains worth preserving.

I respectfully dissent.

Sources and Suggestions
for Further Reading

This is the first book I've written that didn't require a single trip to a law library. With the Internet now at my fingertips, virtually every source I needed for this book—including judicial opinions, legal documents, and newspaper articles—was easily available. Thanks to Google and other search engines, entering a few keywords could locate what I needed, generally within one second or less.

For example, to find the full text of the Supreme Court opinions in the Ten Commandments case of *McCreary County v. ACLU of Kentucky*, go to Google and type in "mccreary county" and "supreme court opinions." I just did this, and Google responded in .25 seconds with several links to the opinions, which you can easily gain access to and print out. The *McCreary County* opinions begin at 545 U.S. 844, which means volume 545 of the *United States Reports*, at page 844. This is the official report of Supreme Court opinions, which are also available on several other websites. My point is that finding (or checking) the sources I used in this book has become vastly easier and quicker with the Internet at our disposal. If you want to read (and copy) newspaper articles and commentary on the *McCreary County* case, use the keywords "mccreary county" and "washington post" or "new york times" (or other papers), and you'll get them in a flash. This recent and rapid advance in electronic technology is the main reason I have dispensed with footnotes and end notes (which hardly anyone reads or checks anyway) in this book. Should any reader have trouble locating a source, however, I'd be glad to provide one by return e-mail at pirons@dssmail .ucsd.edu.

Two other advances in technology have made it easier to gain access to judicial records. One is the PACER system, an acronym for Public Access to Electronic Court Records. This online system allows users to find and copy records of all federal courts; registration is free, and records may be copied (the current fee is eight cents a page), with monthly billing to a credit card. Just go to pacer.gov to begin the registration process and get log-in and password numbers. Another way of finding court records is through the websites of all federal and most state courts; the Supreme Court's website is supremecourtus.gov, which provides links to docket entries and opinions.

There is still a place, fortunately, for books in the Internet Age, and I'll offer a few suggestions on issues raised in this book. Of course, with the advent of Amazon.com and tools such as Amazon's Kindle, you don't need to visit a library to find books. They can be purchased and uploaded on Kindle in less than a minute (or books that aren't available on Kindle can be shipped in a day or two). The following list of books is highly selective and far from comprehensive. Not surprisingly, it's weighted toward works on the Supreme Court and constitutional law, because those are fields that attract the most readers. There are very few books on the lower courts and the steps through which cases reach the Supreme Court (a gap this book attempts to close). This listing is in no particular order and gives only a thumbnail sketch of each book. Readers who want a fuller description of any book can easily find one on websites such as Amazon.com or in reviews in newspapers, magazines, and journals. There's a helpful compendium of reviews in an annual issue of the *Michigan Law Review*.

I'll begin with books on jurisprudence and judging. A classic in the field is Benjamin Cardozo, *The Nature of the Judicial Process* (1921), by a highly respected former New York state judge and Supreme Court justice; Cardozo was one of the first to look at the impact of psychology on judicial decision making. More recent approaches to jurisprudence include the work of Ronald Dworkin in three books: *Taking*

Rights Seriously (1977); *Freedom's Law* (1996); and *Justice in Robes* (2008). Another prolific scholar is John Rawls, whose seminal work *A Theory of Justice* (1971) set forth a "morality-based" foundation for a just society.

Some books in this field are more polemical than analytical. The most prominent critic of "liberal" jurisprudence is Robert Bork, a former federal appellate judge (and failed Supreme Court nominee), in *The Tempting of America* (1990), and *Slouching toward Gomorrah* (1996). Bork's main counterweight on the left is Mark Tushnet, whose twenty books include *Red, White, and Blue: A Critical Analysis of Constitutional Law* (1988). There are several books by former and current federal judges and Supreme Court justices that offer differing perspectives on the judicial role. Frank M. Coffin, who served on the First Circuit Court of Appeals, wrote two good "from the inside" accounts of the appellate function: *The Ways of a Judge: Views from the Federal Appellate Bench* (1980), and *On Appeal: Courts, Lawyering, and Judging* (1994). Richard Posner, currently a member of the Seventh Circuit bench and a leading advocate of the "law and economics" school of jurisprudence, expressed this approach in *How Judges Think* (2008). Two current Supreme Court justices have taken opposite positions: Antonin Scalia in *A Matter of Interpretation* (1997) and Stephen Breyer in *Active Liberty* (2005).

There is a whole library of books about Supreme Court cases, although few devote much attention to the processes by which these cases reach the Court. I won't list them here, because they are easy to find by case name, but I do want to recommend a very useful series (currently fifty-one titles) called Landmark Law Cases and American Society, published by the University Press of Kansas; these are relatively short and quite readable books. The books in this series include works on such well-known cases as *Regents v. Bakke*; *Brown v. Board of Education*; *Bush v. Gore*; *Dred Scott v. Sandford*; *Marbury v. Madison*; and *Roe v. Wade*. I also want to single out three books about cases that did not reach the Supreme Court but that provide good accounts of the legal process: *A Civil Action*, by Jonathan Harr (1996; which became a movie starring John Travolta); *Class Action*, by Clara Bingham and Laura Leedy Gansler (2002; which also became a movie called *North Country*, whose cast included Sissy Spacek); and *Battleground: One*

Mother's Crusade, the Religious Right, and the Struggle for Control of Our Classrooms (1993), by Stephen Bates, which should have become a movie.

As I said, this is a short and very selective list of books on law and the legal process, but I hope readers of this book will find it useful in pursuing their interests.

Index